D1709666

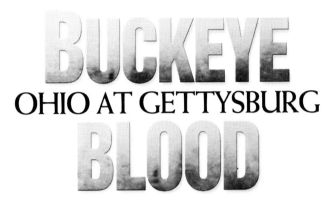

BUCKEYE
OHIO AT GETTYSBURG
BLOOD

BOOKS WRITTEN OR CO-WRITTEN BY RICHARD A. BAUMGARTNER

Kennesaw Mountain June 1864

Blue Lightning: Wilder's Mounted Infantry Brigade in the Battle of Chickamauga
1999 Alexander C. McClurg Award recipient

Echoes of Battle: The Struggle for Chattanooga

Echoes of Battle: The Atlanta Campaign
1994 Richard B. Harwell Award recipient

Richard A. Baumgartner

BUCKEYE
OHIO AT GETTYSBURG
BLOOD

BLUE ACORN PRESS
Huntington, West Virginia

Published by

BLUE ACORN PRESS
P.O. Box 2684
Huntington, West Virginia 25726

ISBN 1-885033-29-X

Baumgartner, Richard A., 1953—

BUCKEYE BLOOD: OHIO AT GETTYSBURG

Illustrated. Includes bibliographical references and index.

History — American Civil War

First Edition: January 2003
Manufactured in the United States of America

CONTENTS

	Acknowledgments	7
	Preface	9
One	PRELUDE	
	'No rest or quiet till we find the foe and bring him to term'	13
Two	JULY 1	
	'The position was one which no troops in the world could have held'	37
Three	JULY 2	
	'They came on us yelling like demons with bayonets'	77
Four	JULY 3	
	'A ghastly sight to see men slaughtered so'	125
Five	AFTERMATH	
	'So fearful was the spectacle, it was too much for tears'	167
Six	EPILOGUE	
	'Gettysburg, by-and-by, will become an American Mecca'	205
	Appendix A	214
	Appendix B	215
	Notes	217
	Bibliography	233
	Index	239

ACKNOWLEDGMENTS

A significant amount of assistance and cooperation was required to complete an undertaking of this sort, and I am deeply grateful to many individuals and institutions that were indispensable providing research materials, photographs, suggestions and periodic doses of encouragement.

I am especially indebted to a number of good friends who contributed images from their Civil War photography collections — particularly Larry Strayer of Dayton, Ohio; Brad L. Pruden of Marietta, Georgia; Karl Sundstrom of North Riverside, Illinois; and Dennis Keesee of New Albany, Ohio. I have been a frequent, welcome guest in all their homes, where uncounted hours during the past decade were spent perusing hundreds of cartes de visite and cased "hard" images, or bent over camera and copy stand.

Others of instrumental help include Ohioans Matt Burr of Bellevue, Tony Lemut of Parma, and Dr. Ken Lawrence of Orwell. Jacqueline Ann Lane of Warren County was most gracious allowing me full access to Lieutenant Colonel Benjamin Morgan's sizeable collection of 75th Ohio papers in her possession. From the Hardin County seat of Kenton, Richard W. Fink unselfishly loaned Gettysburg-related material from his extensive 82nd Ohio files, which eventually will be transformed into a book-length history of this under-appreciated regiment.

On the production side, Michael Stretch of Mason, Ohio, expertly assisted with graphics and designed the book's attractive dust jacket.

Sincere appreciation for additional valuable contributions, large and small, also is extended to the following people and institutions, listed alphabetically by state:

In Arizona: Anne L. Foster, Sharlot Hall Museum, Prescott.

In Arkansas: Joyce Roper, Bald Knob.

In California: John Halliday, Benecia; Barbara Linderholm, Davis; Susan Naulty, The Richard Nixon Library & Birthplace, Yorba Linda.

In Connecticut: Edward C. Browne Jr., Pomfret; John P. Burnham Jr., Chaplin.

In Florida: Dorrit Morgan, Tampa.

In Illinois: Angelo D. Juarez, Crete; Jeffrey J. Kowalis, Orland Park; Marshall D. Krolick, Chicago.

In Indiana: Leigh Darbee, Indiana Historical Society, Indianapolis; Terry Laird, Valparaiso; Bob Willey, New Haven.

In Maryland: Gil Barrett, Laurel; Roger D. Hunt, Rockville.

In Michigan: Jerry Everts, Lambertville; Michael Waskul, Ypsilanti.

In Minnesota: David G. Thomson, Edina.

In New York: Scott Hilts, Arcade.

In Ohio: Bob Albertini, N. Olmsted; Dr. Stephen

Altic, Columbus; Marian Andre, Portsmouth; Gary Arnold and the library reference staff, Ohio Historical Society, Columbus; Peter J. Bahra & Anne B. Shepherd, Cincinnati Historical Society Library; Norman Beiser, Cincinnati; Timothy R. Brookes, East Liverpool; Dr. Kenneth R. Callahan, Maple Heights; Richard F. Carlile, Dayton; Barry L. Cornell, Rittman; Ron Chojnacki, Medina; Gary Delscamp, Dayton; Robert Everhart, New Paris; Firelands Historical Society, Norwalk; James C. Frasca, Croton; Jeff Geist, Johnstown; Joseph H. Gillis, Youngstown; John Gurnish, Mogadore; Hardin County Historical Museum, Kenton; Charles "Chip" Horr, Portsmouth; Gary L. Knepp, Batavia; Jane Lightner & Anna Carlson, Preble County Historical Society, Eaton; Mary Kate Liming, Felicity; Donald Lingafelter, Mentor; David McCullough, Leipsic; Thomas Molocea, Boardman; David Neuhardt, Yellow Springs; John Sanford, Dunbar Library, Wright State University, Dayton; Mac Schumm, Circleville; Nelson Schwab Jr., Cincinnati; Maureen Shepard, Cardington; Russ Sherhag, Massillon; Robert Van Dorn, Findlay; David A. Vermilion, The Dawes Arboretum, Newark; Steven H. Ward, Dayton; Dr. Todd E. Williams, Wyoming; Eric J. Wittenberg, Columbus; Brian Zimmerman, Canton.

In Oklahoma: Stanley R. Burleson, Yukon; Jean Jolly, Tulsa.

In Pennsylvania: Gregory A. Coco, Bendersville; D. Scott Hartwig & John Heiser of the Gettysburg National Military Park staff; Mary Holt, Carnegie Library of Pittsburgh; Dr. Richard J. Sommers & Randy Hackenburg, U.S. Army Military History Institute, Carlisle Barracks; Ken Turner, Ellwood City; Michael J. Winey, Mechanicsburg.

In Virginia: Dr. Thomas P. & Beverly Lowry, Woodbridge.

In Washington, D.C: Dr. Lenore Barbian, National Museum of Health and Medicine.

Richard A. Baumgartner

PREFACE

During an early phase of research for this story I was asked why yet another book about the battle of Gettysburg needed to be written. I pondered the question before answering. In recent years, after all, a spate of books and magazine articles has appeared in print, covering the 1863 battle from one end of the field to the other. Some of these have been broad in scope, while others have minutely dissected the actions of single regiments or 15 minutes of fighting along just one farm fence. With such a flood of detail, what more could be said?

I replied that even for casual students of the titanic struggle at Gettysburg, or any other Civil War battle, there probably could never be enough good material published. Academic and amateur research doubtless will continue for decades to come, occasionally unearthing and presenting fresh, new information, perspective and analysis. In the near future, at least, the final word about Gettysburg will not be written.

By explanation, I pointed out that my own subject — the participation of Ohio troops in the battle — never before had been covered in depth. For more than 10 years I felt the paucity of detail pertaining to Ohio in Gettysburg literature was odd, especially considering that of 18 Northern states represented, only Pennsylvania, New York and Massachusetts had more soldiers engaged.

Some 4,400 Buckeyes were present for duty when the battle opened, and of these 1,271 were killed, wounded, captured or missing.

Nineteen Ohio infantry, artillery and cavalry organizations fought at Gettysburg, or were involved in the battle's immediate aftermath. Nine of them belonged to the Army of the Potomac's much-maligned 11th Corps, which was roughly handled north of town in the first day's fight. In addition, Ohio was represented in the 2nd, 5th and 12th corps, the Artillery Reserve and the Cavalry Corps. Native or resident Buckeyes, ranging in rank from private to brigadier general and serving in other organizations, also were sprinkled throughout the army at Gettysburg: men like Volney Ball and Jacob Shenkel of the 62nd Pennsylvania; George P. Metcalf of the 136th New York; Patrick Tucker of the 11th U.S. Infantry; John C. Tidball of the Horse Artillery; Rufus R. Dawes of the Iron Brigade's 6th Wisconsin; and George Armstrong Custer, commander of a Michigan cavalry brigade.

Originally part of the Northwest Territory, Ohio was considered a "western" state militarily and politically when the war began. A majority of the 313,180 soldiers and sailors it furnished to the Union cause served in western theaters of operation, and consequently much of its citizens' attention focused on those arenas during the conflict.

This readily was apparent when surveying the state's daily and weekly newspapers for soldier correspondence published in Gettysburg's wake. July 1863 was not a slow news month for Ohio's editors. Four other major events affecting the state occurred almost simultaneously. Foremost was the fall of Vicksburg, Mississippi, to the western army led by native Buckeye Ulysses S. Grant. Among his victorious troops were 37 Ohio regiments and batteries. Another 65 belonging to Ohioan William S. Rosecrans' Army of the Cumberland had just helped maneuver an opposing Rebel army out of middle Tennessee in the so-called Tullahoma campaign. Closer to home, Confederate John Hunt Morgan's cavalry raid through 29 southern and eastern Ohio counties electrified the entire state. So, too, did Ohio's gubernatorial race between Unionist candidate John Brough and Peace Democrat Clement L. Vallandigham, an outspoken critic of the Lincoln Administration who campaigned from exile in Canada. All these stories vied with the struggle at Gettysburg for limited editorial space.

In Ohio communities and counties having sizeable numbers of participants at Gettysburg their newspapers, especially Republican organs, generally published citizen-soldier accounts of the battle during July and August 1863. Such correspondence, more often than not, was supplied to editors by family members and friends who first received it. Some newspapers, like those in Akron, Cleveland, Delaware, Toledo and Washington Court House, possessed regularly contributing correspondents serving among the soldiers in the field.

While letters submitted to newspapers were a primary source for this work, just as much reliance was placed on contemporary correspondence, diaries, journals and courts-martial testimony found in private or public collections, and in after-action reports published in the multi-volume *Official Records* of the War of the Rebellion. Liberal use of accounts culled from these documents (retaining original spelling) creates a tangible sense of immediacy, although postwar memoirs, reminiscences, veteran periodicals and regimental histories were consulted as well. It was discovered during six years of research that several Ohio units left only meager written evidence of their presence and contributions at Gettysburg. This is lamentable, but it is hoped more valuable material will surface as a result of *Buckeye Blood's* publication.

A common thread shared with my previous books is the body of photographs and illustrations complementing the text. In tandem with accumulation of first-person narratives, considerable effort was expended to gather a visual record of a portion of those Ohioans present in the battle. A few portraits were taken in postwar years. Most, however, are wartime. To my knowledge, the images reproduced here represent the largest compilation of Ohio soldiers at Gettysburg ever assembled.

All ranks listed in the text and captions were those held by individuals at the specific time, and were verified through regimental rosters, adjutant general reports, and compiled service and pension records. In some cases ages were determined by census or cemetery records.

Two decades after the war a former Ohio artilleryman whose battery assisted repulsing what popularly became known as Pickett's Charge on the last day of the battle, wrote that "The men who stood at Gettysburg know the magic of that word to conjure up a picture that it is impossible to paint in all its terrible grandeur or to properly describe."

If I have succeeded portraying a small part of Ohio's participation in this great Civil War battle and campaign, it is for the reader to decide. Hopefully, the following pages will help fill a long overlooked niche in Gettysburg's compelling story.

Richard A. Baumgartner
Huntington, West Virginia

"The battle of Gettysburg was the supreme crisis of the war. Everything was staked upon its issue."

Captain Alfred E. Lee
82nd Ohio

ONE

'No rest or quiet till we find the foe and bring him to term'

PRELUDE

It was a macabre sight, one Lieutenant Elijah Hayden had never witnessed before. The skeletal remains of soldiers — Union or Confederate, he could not tell — littered the ground in a desolate, weed-choked field outside Centerville, Virginia. Fleshless bones poked skyward from eroded, shallow graves. Skulls were strewn indiscriminately amid decaying battlefield effluvia, their begrimed, sun-baked jaws locked in obscene grins. "It was horid to look upon," the 34-year-old officer admitted the next day in a letter to his daughter, Ella, back in Elyria, Ohio. A number of graves "had one hand Sticking out and Some of them one foot or head. There was one place in Some woods that we passed through that there was about 2 dozen that had never been buried at all." [1]

Hayden's melancholic description quickly shifted to more cheerful topics. He advised Ella to

Major General Joseph Hooker (opposite page, standing at center with members of his staff) received command of the Army of the Potomac in late January 1863. After his death in 1879 Hooker was buried in Cincinnati, his wife's hometown.

Karl Sundstrom Collection

procure an album for all the photographs he was planning to send her. "I will write everyday if I can while this excitement lasts," he promised. "Be a good Girl and try to please your mother. Excuse bad writing fo[r] I have no place to write but on the ground." [2]

Less than two weeks later Ella's father was dead, the victim of a Rebel bullet fired during the third day of battle at Gettysburg. On Independence Day 1863 his body, wrapped in a blanket, was deposited in a shallow battlefield grave not unlike those he had so recently seen. [3]

Hayden's journey to Gettysburg began two months earlier, as it had for most Ohioans belonging to the Army of the Potomac. Following Major General Joseph Hooker's stinging defeat May 2-4 at Chancellorsville, the Federal army withdrew to its old camps north of the Rappahannock River near Falmouth, Virginia. Hooker's adversary, General Robert E. Lee, reoccupied the Rappahannock's south bank with his Army of Northern Virginia. Both sides rested, refitted, reorganized and resumed watching each other across the river as they had done for the first four months of 1863.

But a notable difference was plainly evident in the wake of Lee's spectacular Chancellorsville victory. In spite of proportionately higher casualties, the Army of Northern Virginia was flushed by suc-

13

cess. An air of invincibility permeated its ranks. Even the shocking news of Lieutenant General Thomas J. "Stonewall" Jackson's death on May 10 from pneumonia attendant to an arm wound inflicted by friendly fire at Chancellorsville failed to subvert the spirited ardor of most Rebel combatants. Brigadier General Henry J. Hunt, the Army of the Potomac's artillery chief, insightfully observed that Lee's victory "confirmed the exultant Confederates in their conviction — which now became an article of faith — that both in combat and in generalship the superiority of the Southerner was fully established." After Chancellorsville, Hunt noted, "morale of the Confederate army was ... much higher." Lee's troops "were by this time nearly all veterans, led by officers having the confidence of their Government, which took pains to inspire its soldiers with the same feeling. Their successes were extolled and magnified, their reverses palliated or ignored." [4]

In sharp contrast, the mood in the North bordered on despondency. The Chancellorsville campaign, according to historian Edwin B. Coddington, was for Unionists "one of the most frustrating experiences of the war. It started out with the assurance of a quick and decisive victory and ended in ignominious defeat." [5]

Coupled with heavy losses, the Army of the Potomac also was staggered psychologically. Officers and enlisted men alike were discouraged by the poor performance of the army and its leading commanders. Finger-pointing began immediately around Federal campfires and in editorial offices as blame was heaped upon those who appeared to be most culpable. The press helped fuel the divisive debate, though the common soldier and at least one Union division commander dismissed newspaper accounts of the Chancellorsville operations as "pure fiction, not to be found even in this fertile age of romancers." [6]

General Hooker earned his share of blue-coated critics, many Buckeyes among them. William E. Parmelee, a 19-year-old bookkeeper from Fulton County serving as a private in Battery H, 1st Ohio Light Artillery (OVLA), observed that in none of the battles he had experienced were the army's commanding officers more confused than at Chancellorsville. [7] Parmelee's battery commander reflected: "I think (if we can imagine Grant allowing his army to be placed where Hooker's was [May 3] at noon)

that he would have made his soldiers fry their boots, if there was nothing else to eat, before he would have recrossed the river." [8] Sergeant Luther B. Mesnard, a Fairfield farmer in Company D, 55th Ohio, thought "Hooker evidently showed an incapacity for commanding a great army. Though he was 'fighting' Joe Hooker he seemed to hesitate and shrink from contact or combat with the enemy. While the rebel army suffered quite as heavy losses as our army at Chancellorsville yet the moral effect [on us] was that of defeat. A loss of about one third

Major General Oliver Otis Howard lost his right arm in the 1862 battle of Fair Oaks, Virginia. In March 1863 he succeeded Franz Sigel as commander of the 11th Corps, an assignment that angered many Germans in its ranks. Ill feeling was aggravated further when Howard accepted no personal responsibility for the corps' collapse at Chancellorsville.

of our regiment in killed and wounded left many vacancies in our ranks and much sadness as we settled down to camp life again. ..." [9]

By far the most vituperative recrimination was hurled at Major General Oliver O. Howard's 11th Corps, which occupied the Army of the Potomac's vulnerable right flank at Chancellorsville. Howard's troops had the misfortune of laying precisely in the path of Stonewall Jackson's crushing assault early on the evening of May 2. Largely unprepared to receive the Confederate onslaught (many of the front-line Federals had stacked arms and were cooking meals), the bulk of the 11th Corps was sent reeling rearward. A few regiments retreated after firing only two or three volleys. Frantic efforts by others temporarily slowed the Rebel advance, but those offering resistance soon found themselves exposed to withering fire from front, flank and rear. In the midst of what the one-armed Howard later called "a terrible gale," his corps fragmented and gave way in disorder. [10] A frenzy of self-preservation gripped hundreds of men, many of them literally sprinting toward safety. "They saved their lives," wrote E.B.

"Stampede of the Eleventh Corps" at Chancellorsville. Thomas Evans, a member of the 25th Ohio, wrote: "Old Stonewall Jackson had flanked us with his whole corps and now rained grape and cannister and minnie balls in our ranks like hail. In 15 minutes we were all cut to pieces. There was no place left us but to flee for our lives which we did with a right good grace. We soon became scattered to the four winds, every one for themselves." Like 30 others in his regiment, Evans was captured.

Coddington, "but in so doing they lost their reputations and became the scapegoats of the Northern army." [11]

Two weeks after the battle Colonel James S. Robinson, whose 82nd Ohio lost 81 officers and men in the rout, penned a darkly humorous account to a friend in Hardin County. "Your letter of May 2 duly received," it began. "While you was writing that letter we were enjoying the luxury [of] cannon balls and musketry. And late in the evening treated ourselves to a foot-race on a grand scale, in which about all the officers and men of the 11th Corps retired for the prize. Our Brig. General won the stakes. He imitated the example of the militia captain, and started early in the race. But being a favorite at headquarters and that kind of fleetness not in the bills, the papers have failed to inform the public of the exact time it required to get from the front to the river, *under the fire of the enemy.*

"It is us poor devils who are branded as cowards who stood at our posts and tried to stem the torrent, until it was reduced to a certainty that one of two things had to be done, either run or be all killed or gobbled up. I remembered just at that time that favorite and familiar stanza,

'That he who fights and runs away
May live to fight another day.'

"And so I gave the order to 'march in retreat.' This movement under fire is easily executed. It simply amounts to an about face and then the run comes in. This is a movement in which the field officers are supposed to be in advance." [12]

One of Robinson's company commanders, Captain William D.W. Mitchell, lost his first lieutenant killed in the May 2 melee. "Some of the fighting was Splendidly Terific," he related, "exceeding anything I ever heard or saw before. The rebs put a ball through my blouse on the top of my left shoulder but it did not hit the flesh. A miss is as good as a mile and I believe no man goes until his time comes." Mitchell little knew when writing these lines to his sister on May 10 that his own "time" was measured in scant weeks. [13]

Not all of Howard's troops panicked and ran, although those who performed creditably still attracted disparaging remarks simply by 11th Corps' association. With a single gun supported by two companies from the 61st Ohio, Captain Hubert Dilger of Battery I, 1st OVLA, covered an entire brigade's withdrawal while keeping a vital road free from Confederate pursuit. His exploit later earned him a Medal of Honor but, as early Chancellorsville chronicler Augustus C. Hamlin wrote, for more than three decades Dilger's heroism did not receive "the least notice whatever." [14]

Blanket condemnation of the corps rankled many Ohioans, including Private Isaac W. Gardner, a member of Dilger's battery. "Some of the Regiments in our Corps did some excellent fighting that night," he informed his parents, "although you do not hear much said about it. Those that ran that night you hear mentioned in every paper but those that did well they seem to forget about and so it conveys the idea that all were alike. That some did run I do not dispute, because there is black sheep in every fold, and it would be hard for such a large body of men to be got together without some cowards in it." [15]

For 10 minutes early in the fight the 75th Ohio, numbering about 400 officers and men with a few rallied New Yorkers and Pennsylvanians, stoutly confronted two entire Rebel brigades and two artil-

Richard W. Fink Collection

Sergeant Jefferson P. Davis of Company H, 82nd Ohio, was wounded at Chancellorsville but recovered to be promoted lieutenant in October 1863. Carte de visite by E.S. Walker, Columbus.

Courtesy of Dorrit Morgan

By the time he turned 30, Robert Reily, born in 1820 at Hamilton, Ohio, had amassed a small fortune working in a Cincinnati silk importing business. He helped raise the 75th Ohio during the fall of 1861 and was promoted its colonel in January 1863. His regiment, although losing heavily, was among a few 11th Corps units not surprised by the Confederate flank attack at Chancellorsville. Reily's prior warnings to superior officers were dismissed or ignored. Once the assault began the 75th fought valiantly, but within 10 minutes was overwhelmed. Reily was shot in the left leg, captured and suffered amputation of the limb while a prisoner. He died a short time later. Less than three weeks earlier his brother, James Reily, was killed leading a charge of the 4th Texas Cavalry at Bayou Teche, Louisiana.

lery pieces spewing deadly canister into its ranks. A fatal leg wound dropped the 75th's commander, Colonel Robert Reily, from his horse. "Ball and shell were coming as thick as hail," wrote First Lieutenant Oscar D. Ladley of Company G. "Our col. was shot, horses, mules, straglers and every thing else came tearing past us and we had to leave also."[16] Led by Captain Benjamin Morgan of Company F, the regiment fell back in good order to a new line formed by the rest of its brigade. This position, too, was soon enveloped by three enemy brigades and the 75th was forced "to skedaddle through the wilderness to escape capture."[17]

Morgan seethed in the battle's aftermath, writing to his wife that "there is great dissatisfaction in our Corp[s], as Officers and men are suffering the stigma of retreating when the fault lies entirely with those in Command, either Hooker or Howard for placing us in such a position to get flanked and surprised by overwhelming numbers. Our losses will tell that we were obliged to fall back but not one man of the 75th retreated until ordered which is all that can be expected or wished of men."[18]

As quickly as the press and the balance of Hooker's army affixed blame for the Chancellorsville disaster on Howard's men, it singled out the 11th Corps' large ethnic component for the worst abuse. As much as three-fifths of the command was foreign-born, 50 percent being native Germans or first generation German-Americans. Prejudice against various ethnic groups was nothing new in America by the time of the Civil War, but an influx of thousands of immigrants and refugees following the German revolution of 1848 had inspired a fresh wave of chauvinistic resentment. Much negative feeling toward Germans resulted from the liberal politics, anti-clerical and radical, anti-slavery views espoused by some of the so-called "Forty-Eighters." In Ohio, where sizeable numbers of foreigners congregated in Franklin, Hamilton, Cuyahoga, Stark and Tuscarawas counties, two Cleveland newspapers in the mid-1850s referred to Germans as "reds" and "hairlipped Dutch." Another paper, conversely, saw Germans as being saviors of the slaves. After the war began, *Die Deutsche Organisation,* with its central office located in Cleveland, advocated severe reparations against the South and deeding of confiscated farms to soldiers and former slaves.[19]

Such extreme stances easily engendered outright hatred in Confederate states, leading to bigoted vitriol that found its way into more than one Southern newspaper. An anti-German editorial published June 12, 1863 in the *Knoxville Register* was among the most caustic:

Of late, in all battles and in all recent incursions made by Federal cavalry, we have found the great mass of Northern soldiers to consist of Dutchmen. The plundering thieves captured by Forrest, who stole half the jewelry and watches in a dozen counties of Alabama, were immaculate Dutchmen. The national odor of Dutchmen, as distinctive of the race as that which, constantly ascending to heaven, has distended the nostrils of the negro, is as unmistakable as that peculiar to a pole-cat, an old pipe, or a lager-bier saloon. Crimes, thefts, and insults to the women of the South, invariably mark the course of these stinking bodies of animated *sour-krout*. Rosecrans himself is an unmixed Dutchman, an accursed race which has overrun the vast districts of the country Northwest.

It happens that we entertain a greater degree of respect for an Ethiopian in the ranks of the Northern armies than for an odoriferous Dutchman, who can have no possible interest in this revolution. *Why not hang every Dutchman captured?* This is not too harsh. No human being will assert the contrary. Why should we not hang a Dutchman, who deserves infinitely less of our sympathy than Sambo.[20]

Despite the fact that an overwhelming majority of Germans in the North supported Union war efforts, their countrymen in the 11th Corps suffered from the vocal, if unjust, abuse. Until February 1863 they had been commanded by Major General Franz Sigel, an immensely popular "Forty-Eighter" from Baden. But a week after Chancellorsville, wrote a 3rd Corps officer, " 'I fights mit Sigel' is played out. Tell S. that his Dutchmen can't begin to stand up against the fury and rush of Americans, even if they are Rebels!"[21]

Reproach also came from within. "The 11th Corps is composed principally of New York dutch ... and they never have stood fire and I sup[p]ose never will," complained Lieutenant Ladley of the 75th Ohio. "The d——d dutch has disgraced us long enough," hissed the 82nd Ohio's lieutenant colonel, David Thomson. "I will leave this corps if I have to leave the army. I will not stand all this."[22]

Thomson's disdain apparently was shared by a

Ethnic prejudice in Ohio

In 1850, Ohio's German population — more than 27 percent living in Cincinnati — had risen to 111,257. Although overt manifestations of negative nativist feeling largely dissolved in 1861 with the patriotic response of Ohio's foreign-born residents in defense of the Union, the previous decade witnessed some ugly incidents across the state.

Members of a Columbus German singing society were attacked twice in 1855, the second time after a July 4 picnic. A barrage of stones was met by revolver fire, inflicting casualties on both sides. Local police searched Columbus' German neighborhood without proper warrants, and a howling mob shouted "Kill the damn Dutch." That same year a band of Cincinnati nativists marched to attack one of the city's German enclaves, but was met by gunfire and barricades thrown up in the streets. Election day riots were common in Ohio during the 1850s. On several occasions German saloons were raided and ballot boxes destroyed.

There were even a few among the state's radical Germans whose words helped promote stereotyping and prejudice. Christian Esselen, a university-trained idealist who briefly published the *Atlantis* in Cleveland, referred to Cincinnati's German inhabitants as being devoid of all interests except freedom to drink beer, and believed they had sunk to a lower social scale in the United States than in their homeland. Another educated German emigré described the majority of his fellow countrymen as "shabbily dressed, rude sauerkraut eaters whose lives revolved almost wholly around beer, pipes, and skat playing."

majority of surviving members of Brigadier General Nathaniel C. McLean's "Ohio Brigade," composed of the 25th, 55th, 75th and 107th Ohio regiments, and the 17th Connecticut. McLean's command incurred nearly 700 casualties at Chancellorsville, by far the largest loss in any 11th Corps' brigade. Stunned by the 25th Ohio's 152 killed, wounded and missing, Captain Nathaniel J. Manning of Company K lashed out: "It is melancholy to think of — to have as good a Regiment as this sacrificed for the cowardice of a lot of poltroons, for such are the troops of some of the Divisions in this corps." According to Captain Benjamin Morgan of the 75th, once McLean's troops returned to their old camps at Brooke's Station, Virginia, they sought to sever ties with the organization. "The Officers of the Line sent a petition to the Secretary of War," Morgan wrote, "asking that the brigade be sent to the Western Army. This, of course, had to be sent through Corps Headquarters. Howard failed in his duty to forward it, but returned it with endorsement that if every Officer did not erase his name from that document they would be immediately dismissed upon the field."[23]

Two names not attached to the petition belonged to the 107th Ohio, the only "German" infantry organization from the Buckeye State serving in the Army of the Potomac. The regiment's 47-year-old commander, Colonel Seraphim Meyer, had been shot in the right wrist and captured May 2. His youngest son Edward, captain of Company C, received severe lung and neck wounds, and also was taken prisoner. Both were paroled by month's end, but not before the elder officer spent eight days with scant medical attention in Richmond's Libby Prison.[24]

Though raised in August 1862 as a German regiment, one-third of the 107th's officers and men were native-born Americans, many unable to speak German at all. Stark and Cuyahoga counties furnished the largest number of volunteers, with the remainder recruited from Wayne, Tuscarawas, Richland, Crawford, Columbiana, Lorain, Huron, Seneca, Summit and Defiance counties. Company C, perhaps, contained the highest percentage of native Germans. On the eve of Gettysburg it mustered 42 enlisted men, only seven of whom were born in Ohio or Pennsylvania. Thirty-five had emigrated from Europe, their places of nativity being listed as Baden (six), Bavaria (five), Württemberg (five), Hesse (four), Prussia (three), Germany (two), Alsace (two), Hannover (one) and Saxony (one). Another six were from Switzerland.[25]

Colonel Meyer, a linguist fluent in German, French and English, was himself an emigré. Born November 27, 1815 in Bourbach le Bas, Alsace, he settled in Stark County in 1828 with his parents, who helped establish Canton's first Catholic church. A decade later he was admitted to the bar, partner-

ing in three different Canton law firms before becoming Stark County prosecuting attorney. With war's outbreak in 1861, his three sons enlisted in Ohio regiments, two of them eventually reaching officer grade. Following President Abraham Lincoln's summer of 1862 appeal for 300,000 additional volunteers, Meyer, with no previous military experience, was granted authority to raise and organize the 107th. This was accomplished in relatively little time, and the prosecutor resigned his position to accept the regiment's colonelcy.[26]

A Mexican War veteran and former Monroe County prosecuting attorney, Colonel William Pitt Richardson of Woodsfield was seriously wounded at Chancellorsville while commanding the 25th Ohio. The regiment lost 152 of 349 officers and men engaged. Ten days later Second Lieutenant Joseph H. Hollis of Company F related to his brother that the battle was beyond description. "How little people at Home know about war. Our camp [at Brooke's Station] is more gloomy than it ever yet was known to be. Our Col was wounded in the brest and passing into his [right] arm .... many a man [was] left killed or wounded upon the battle field. Our ranks are thined by this wicked Rebellion, everything looks so very dull. One more fight and we are all gone."

A brief training period was spent at Camp Cleveland, where the 107th was drilled by commands given in both German and English. Almost immediately the men discovered their colonel possessed some peculiarities. It required "great exertion or effort" for Meyer to enunciate commands. He literally screamed. One observer noted "that in intonation of voice and manner he differed from other officers. It was such as to attract attention and sometimes caused laughter." The colonel's other noticeable trait was the way he rode his horse — leaning so far forward from the saddle that he appeared to be hugging the animal's neck. Both unusual habits later would contribute inadvertently to Meyer's arrest and court-martial for misbehavior and cowardice at Gettysburg.[27]

Chancellorsville was a bloody, sobering introduction to combat for Meyer and the 107th, which suffered 133 casualties, including its surgeon. "Although the result of the first engagement of this regiment has not been what one would desire it to be," wrote Lieutenant Colonel Charles Mueller on May 9, "yet I cannot refrain from stating that the regiment behaved well. Officers and men stood like veterans, *i.e.,* as long as a stand could be made against the overwhelming numbers and the deadly fire pouring in upon the flank and front of the regiment."[28]

In a fair fight Mueller believed he could count on his men, even if those outside the 11th Corps did not.

During the rest of May the Army of the Potomac began restoring itself. "For a few weeks we seemed to wait for something to turn up," reflected Major Samuel H. Hurst of the 73rd Ohio. "We had a month of very pleasant spring life in our camp among the pine hills of Stafford [County]." Nineteen-year-old Private John Kratz of Company C, 107th Ohio, also enjoyed the vernal idyll. "The weather is very warm here now," he told his parents on May 29. "The sun burns through our tents that some of our lazy boys, such as henry kinkler[,] John Dunne[,] Jake Starck and others cannot hardly stand it." Kratz assured his homefolk that, unlike many of his comrades, he did not want for anything, except writing paper. "I suppose you thought i lost my knappsack in the [Chancellorsville] fight, i did not, i had mine on my back all the time in the engagement. Some of the boys had them lying in their rear, and when we began to retreat they did not

Karl Sundstrom Collection

An unidentified private belonging to Company I, 107th Ohio. Carte de visite by J.G. Price Photographer, New Philadelphia.

stop to pick them up."[29]

Equipment and supplies lost in the recent battle were replaced by quartermaster and commissary departments while the ranks gradually recovered their spirit. At the same time, a good deal of internal restructuring occurred as the army mended. In addition to his loss of 17, 287 killed, wounded and captured at Chancellorsville, General Hooker was confronted in May and June with demobilizing thousands of troops whose enlistments were expiring. None of the Ohio regiments or batteries fell in this category, but reorganization directly affected

Brigadier General
Francis C. Barlow.

USAMHI

Brigadier General
Adelbert Ames.

Mass. MOLLUS, USAMHI

those Buckeyes in the 11th Corps and all the state's Potomac artillerymen.

First, there were changes in commanders. Although Brigadier General Adolph von Steinwehr and Major General Carl Schurz retained the corps' 2nd and 3rd divisions, respectively, command of the 1st Division was given to Brigadier General Francis C. Barlow, a Harvard graduate from New York who formerly led von Steinwehr's 2nd Brigade. Orland Smith, a Chillicothe resident, railroad executive and colonel of the 73rd Ohio, replaced Barlow. General McLean was removed from command of the 1st Division's 2nd (Ohio) Brigade and replaced by newly promoted Brigadier General Adelbert Ames — at 27, one of the youngest general officers in the army. A native of Maine, Ames had graduated fifth in the U.S. Military Academy's May 1861 class, and as colonel led the 20th Maine at Fredericksburg. In recommending Ames for promotion, Brigadier General Charles Griffin (a Granville, Ohio, native) characterized him as "able and ambitious." He and Barlow owned proven military records (Ames later received a Medal of Honor for gallantry at First Bull Run), and both were strict disciplinarians. Barlow, however, was openly distrustful of the corps' foreign element. "You know how I have always been down on the 'Dutch' & I do not abate my contempt now," he wrote home on May 8.[30]

Regimental reshuffling accompanied command changes. When the 134th New York was transferred out of Orland Smith's brigade, it was replaced by the 55th Ohio from Ames' command, reducing the latter officer's brigade to four regiments. The 82nd Ohio, having fought at Chancellorsville as an unattached regiment, was added to Colonel Wladimir Krzyzanowski's 2nd Brigade of Schurz's division.[31]

A completely new arrangement was adopted for the artillery. Batteries were grouped into brigades, with each of the seven infantry corps assigned one brigade and the Cavalry Corps two. Five other brigades constituted the Artillery Reserve — nearly double its size from Chancellorsville. Through centralized control the artillery's "punch" was greatly increased. Guns could be rushed to critical areas in battle as they were needed to give Federal forces much better concentration of firepower. As for the Ohio artillerymen in the Potomac army, Battery L, 1st OVLA, belonged to the 5th Corps' artillery brigade, Batteries I and K remained with the 11th Corps, and Battery H, on June 19, became part of the 3rd Volunteer Brigade, Artillery Reserve.[32]

Vacancies in Buckeye units created by attrition and other causes were filled throughout the month of May. Lieutenant Colonel Charles B. Gambee was promoted colonel of the 55th, replacing John C. Lee who resigned May 8. Woodsfield newspaperman Jeremiah Williams, major of the 25th Ohio, was commissioned lieutenant colonel and assumed regimental command from his seriously wounded predecessor, William P. Richardson. In the 75th, Major Andrew L. Harris, a Butler Countian and 1860 graduate of Miami University, received his eagles when it was confirmed Colonel Reily had died of his Chancellorsville leg wound, and the regiment's lieutenant colonel, Charles W. Friend, resigned. Company F's captain, Benjamin Morgan, was the likeliest candidate to fill Friend's position. "As I expect my promotion every mail," Morgan explained to his wife, "I have not sent you any [money], as I will have to buy a horse and accouterments, besides new uniform. ... It will cost me considerable for an outfit. Suppose you will like to be a Major or Lieut. Colonel's wife. I am recommended for the latter. Colonel Riley's [sic] horse is here with us for sale, and I can do no better than buy him at $200.00. A fine animal. I fancy I see you smile at me being mounted but the boys think I do well." [33]

In the Ohio artillery, Cincinnatian William L. DeBeck's resignation as commander of Battery K paved the way for 43-year-old Lewis Heckman's promotion to captain. Battery H's new commander was First Lieutenant George W. Norton of Toledo. One of his artillerists remembered him as being "an entirely different type of man who would forget the regulation commands, often giving orders in terms of the farm, so it was easy for the boys to tag him the 'Bold Farmer.' " Norton took control of the battery when Captain James F. Huntington was elevated to command the Artillery Reserve's 3rd Brigade. Born in Massachusetts, the 36-year-old Huntington was operating a Marietta hardware store when war broke out. He particularly distinguished himself at Hazel Grove on the Chancellorsville battlefield, where Battery H lost four of its six guns May 3 in fierce, close-order fighting. Small in stature and prone to fiery bouts of temper, Huntington was nicknamed "Jack of Clubs." He and Norton possessed completely different personalities, but their men believed "the two made [a] strong team, working smoothly together." [34]

Captain Frank C. Gibbs' Battery L badly needed two lieutenants. Senior First Lieutenant Frederick Dorries had been killed by an enemy shell at Chancellorsville, and another officer was forced to resign because of physical disability. Dorries was succeeded by Herbert F. Guthrie, an acquaintance of Ohio congressman Samuel S. Cox. A year earlier, when the 22-year-old former book-

keeper was the battery's first sergeant, Cox urged Governor David Tod for Guthrie's promotion, describing him as "one of those 'ragged & greasy Ohioans' — sneered at by stylish N.Y. & N.E. troops. ..." The present first sergeant, Irishman James Gildea, received a second lieutenant's commission, but his papers were misplaced at 5th Corps' headquarters during the army's ensuing movements north. He was not mustered officially until three weeks after the battle of Gettysburg. [35]

The Cavalry Corps also underwent its own evolutionary phase. Hard campaigning had reduced considerably the corps' numerical strength in men and horses, weakening its effectiveness. A new chief, Brigadier General Alfred Pleasanton, took command on May 22,* while other changes occurred at division, brigade and regimental levels. In the 2nd Division, the 6th Ohio Cavalry was moved to the 2nd Brigade from the 1st, with Major Benjamin C. Stanhope in charge. He soon was replaced by Licking County native Major William Stedman, after Stanhope was mortally wounded in a skirmish June 17 at Aldie, Virginia. [36]

The only other Ohio troopers serving in the East at the time were Companies A and C, 1st Ohio Cavalry — roughly 85 officers and men from Fayette and Hamilton counties — assigned as headquarters guards for Major General Julius Stahel's division of the Department of Washington. The rest of the 1st Ohio belonged to the Army of the Cumberland, then in middle Tennessee. Near the end of June, Companies A and C were formed into the "First Ohio Squadron" commanded by Captain Noah Jones, and reassigned as escort to the Cavalry Corps' 3rd Division headquarters. [37]

Thus transformed, the Army of the Potomac stood poised along the Rappahannock as May's warm weather gave way to even hotter days in June. The Buckeye contingent, all veterans, watched and waited to see whether General Hooker or General Lee would make the next move. Lee grabbed the initiative first.

Believing that victory on Union soil would promote European intervention, as well as further discourage war-weary Northerners, Lee and Confederate authorities in Richmond decided to take the

---

* On the same day in the infantry, Major General Winfield S. Hancock assumed command of the 2nd Corps.

Major William Stedman, 6th Ohio Cavalry. Born in Granville, he lived most of his adult life in Portage County. Carte de visite by Stein's Photographic Gallery, Ravenna.

strategic offensive, the second time in nine months. An invasion of the rich, crop-abundant Cumberland Valley in Pennsylvania would shift operations away from ravaged northern Virginia. Harrisburg, Philadelphia, Baltimore and even Washington would be menaced. It also was hoped that invasion would relieve Northern pressure in middle Tennessee and at the besieged Mississippi city of Vicksburg, compelling Federal withdrawal of strength in those areas to counter the threat. The moment was propitious. Having just been reorganized and increased to 85,000 men, Lee's Army of Northern Virginia

might never have a better opportunity for success.[38]

Accordingly, on June 3 Lee began extricating his army from its positions near Fredericksburg. The First and Second corps under Lieutenant Generals James Longstreet and Richard S. Ewell, respectively, started first. Lieutenant General Ambrose P. Hill's Third Corps remained in its Rappahannock camps to deceive the Federals and did not begin leaving until June 14. Lee planned to reach the Shenandoah Valley, disperse or destroy several Federal garrisons stationed there, and march north, using the Blue Ridge as a natural barrier to screen observation and attack from the east. At Winchester and Stephenson's Depot, Virginia, on June 15, two of Ewell's divisions crushed an 8,800-man Union force commanded by Major General Robert H. Milroy. That same day Ewell's third division and a cavalry brigade crossed the Potomac River into Maryland near Williamsport.[39]

In the meantime, Hooker had been trying to divine Lee's intentions. Intelligence sources provided conflicting reports, many of them unreliable or fragmentary, and the general opted against moving the entire army hastily. Not until June 10 was he fully aroused to unfolding developments. In a message to President Lincoln, Hooker wrote that now was the time for a "rapid advance" on the Confederate capital, a possibility that worried the Rebel commander. But Lincoln replied: "I think Lee's army, and not Richmond, is your sure objective point. If he comes toward the Upper Potomac, follow on his flank and on his inside track, shortening your lines while he lengthens his. Fight him, too, when opportunity offers. If he stays where he is, fret him and fret him."[40]

Hooker shifted several of his corps northwest along the Rappahannock to protect his right flank. During this process he placed the 1st Corps' Major General John F. Reynolds in charge of the army's right wing. On the 13th the Federal commander finally obtained definite information concerning Lee's whereabouts, and issued orders for an orderly but speedy withdrawal from the river. Hooker wired Washington that operations of the Army of the Potomac's two wings now would "be governed by the movements of the enemy."[41]

Pursuing Lee over the next two and a half weeks tested the mettle of Hooker's men, who dismantled their camps and pressed northward by different roads, keeping Washington protected on the

Courtesy of Dr. Kenneth R. Callahan

soldiers who participated in the Gettysburg campaign frequently mention June's weather extremes, and how they affected the march. Roadways alternated between dust-choked trails and slimy mud sloughs as blazingly hot days were interspersed by ones of drenching thunderstorms. High temperatures and humidity caused widespread straggling and dozens of men dropped from the ranks with sunstroke. First Lieutenant James K. O'Reilly, 8th Ohio, was among those stricken. Leading Company E toward Dumfries, Virginia, on June 15, O'Reilly crumpled to the ground, vomited and fell unconscious. He was treated by Surgeon Joseph L. Brenton, who compelled the lieutenant to ride in an ambulance nearly all the way to Pennsylvania.[43]

O'Reilly's regiment belonged to the 2nd Corps, but similar episodes occurred throughout the army. "Hard dusty traveling – many boys give out – our Amb[ulance] loaded down," wrote Sergeant Martin L. Buchwalter, a 73rd Ohio diarist commanding a squad of 11th Corps' ambulances. One of Buchwalter's comrades, Private Anthony W. Ross of Company G, described to his wife several "excessively warm and dusty" forced marches between Stafford Court House and Goose Creek. "A great manny gave out but the most of us got through. ... oh, but the loads we have to carry — gun[,] cartridge box and 60 rounds of cartridges[,] 3 days Rashions[,] Blankets and knapsack which no boddy but a soldier that has got youst to carrying such loads could carry. [I] carried a chopping ax in addition to this load as I am one of the Regimental Pioneers." Ross' company commander, First Lieutenant Samuel Fellers, observed that "We marched

right. Their lines of march roughly paralleled the Confederate course, though no one seemed to know just where the "Johnnies" were headed. "I guess the rebels are making a move some where or we would not be moving in this direction," conjectured Lieutenant Ladley of the 75th Ohio. Musician Henry C. Henney of the 55th Ohio admitted in his diary on June 15, "We have no idea where we are going." Adjutant Stowel L. Burnham, 82nd Ohio, ventured a guess by telling his father: "The report here is, that the rebs are on a pleasure trip up north [to burn] Harrisburg, &c. I can hardly believe it. Think Hooker has been fooled most gloriously if it is so. As yet can hardly form an opinion, as we know nothing, and can not believe any thing we hear. Think there will be a big fight somewhere ... before long. They have concluded to lose Vicksburg, and will try to make it up here. Look out for stirring times is my motto."[42]

Letters, journals and memoirs written by Ohio

as far as thirty-eight miles in twenty-four hours, the men carrying knapsacks, guns, rations &c., and sixty rounds of ammunition. These things may seem to be impossible, but the patriotic soldiers stood it, with a hope (as many of them told me) to redeem the 11th corps."[44]

The 29th Ohio's journey from Dumfries to Fairfax Court House was "one of the hardest marches we ever had on account of the heat, according to Corporal Nathan L. Parmater. "Many a poor soldier boy fell dead while doing his duty trying to keep up with his Regt." This leg of the 12th Corps' trek was "long, hot and exhaustive," wrote First Sergeant Lawrence Wilson of Company D, 7th Ohio, "as was shown by the death of fifteen men of [Brigadier General John W.] Geary's division alone, having died along the road from fatigue and sunstroke."[45]

Mounted men fared better. Newly commissioned Lieutenant Colonel Benjamin Morgan of the 75th Ohio informed his wife: "We have marched at the rate of 30 miles a day under a burning sun, so you can fancy a little of the hardships of a soldiers life. It was not so hard on me this time as I now go a Horse-back, which I find makes a considerable difference. However, I can feel for them who walk from experience."[46]

A nighttime rainstorm pelted the guns, limbers and horses of Battery H, its "thoroughly soaked" artillerists reaching Hartwood Church by illuminating flashes of lightning. Mud along the battery's path to Manassas Junction via Catlett's Station on the Orange & Alexandria Railroad quickly dried with the return of sunshine. "For the distance," wrote Captain Huntington, "[that march] was the severest I have ever known. The heat was intense, the road ankle-deep in dust which filled the air with a dense and suffocating cloud, and worst yet, there was scarcely a drop of water to be found. The march was forced, with but brief halts. The infantry, borne down by their heavy loads, literally obstructed the roads." Huntington recalled that Major General George Sykes' division of the 5th Corps, "though renowned marchers, came in with but fifteen to twenty men to a company in ranks. Eleven men died outright from heat and exhaustion, and the 3rd [Corps] lost even more. Our cannoneers, having nothing to carry, and a chance to ride occasionally, were comparatively fresh, so we had no stragglers. ..."[47]

Nine miles to the north near Centerville, the 75th Ohio encountered several regiments of "greenhorn" troops recently arrived from the capital's de-

Detached service in pioneer units during the Gettysburg campaign was undertaken by the two soldiers at right. A teamster originally from Pennsylvania, Laughlin performed duty with the 1st Brigade pioneers, 2nd Division, 12th Corps. Geist was detailed June 9, 1863 to the 11th Corps' pioneers. The Hessian-born father of six was a Cleveland carpenter when he enlisted in August 1862.

Corporal Hiram Laughlin, Company C, 29th Ohio.

Sergeant Philip Geist, Company E, 107th Ohio.

fenses. They were met, quipped Oscar Ladley of Company G, with a bit of derision. "We had been marching for three days in the sun and dust and looked rather hard as you may imagine. They had been laying in camp around Washington ever since they came out and presented rather a neater appearance than we. One of the boys heard one of them say 'Your officers don't dress very nice.' He answered him, you march through rain[,] mud or dust and lay out every night without tents or blankets half the time and you wont dress very fine either. We looked very nice once too, but that time has past."[48]

Four evenings later in a heavy rain, the 4th and 8th Ohio reached Centerville with Colonel Samuel S. Carroll's brigade of the 2nd Corps. Born in 1832 just outside Washington, D.C., Carroll was a West Point graduate and Regular Army officer, appointed to command the 8th Ohio in December 1861. He possessed a booming voice that some claimed could be heard plainly above the din of battle. With bulging red side whiskers and prematurely balding head, the ambitious colonel was dubbed "Old Bricktop" by his men.[49]

Carroll's brigade, temporarily commanded by Colonel John Coons of the 14th Indiana, halted on the heights outside Centerville where everything, it seemed to First Lieutenant Thomas F. Galwey of the 8th, was "swimming in water. We could not pitch tents ... so, covering ourselves with our gum blankets, our arms reversed and bayonets driven down into the earth, we slept squatting, the rain pouring down upon us unceasingly. It was a most uncomfortable night." Galwey, just 15 years old when he enlisted in Company B at Cleveland in April 1861, passed over the nearby plains of Manassas toward Gainesville the following day. Like fellow officer Elijah Hayden of his regiment, Galwey was struck by the visible evidence of earlier fighting in the surrounding fields and woods. "The rains of two years have uncovered many of the shallow graves. ... In one place I saw a man's boot protruding from the grave; the stitches had rotted and the sole of the shoe warped downwards while the upper had curled upward, leaving the skeleton toes pointing to a land where there is no war."[50]

There were "lots of unburied skeletons, bones, and human skulls scattered about," noted 4th Ohio First Lieutenant Lemuel Jeffries, a former editor for the Wayne County *Democrat* in Wooster. "On some skeletons clung part of the tattered blue uniform." Captain George F. Laird, commanding the 4th's Company K, counted scores of unexploded shells and accouterments strewn over the ground, as well as the remains of abandoned artillery carriages. He thought the rain-washed graves with "grinning skulls staring at us from among the bleaching bones and old clothing" had been disturbed by cattle or wild hogs. "It was a sad sight."[51]

During the brief interlude at Gainesville some men of Carroll's brigade were greeted by acquaintances in the 1st Ohio Cavalry's escort companies, returning to Fairfax after reconnoitering with their division west of Warrenton. Bugler Samuel L. Gil-

Colonel Samuel Sprigg Carroll, 8th Ohio. A subordinate described him as being "a fine-looking officer, a bold rider, a skillful tactician, and one of the bravest and most brilliant brigade commanders in the Army."

lespie of Company A visited "some few old companions in the 4th and 8th Ohio," relating to them personal experiences of the Warrenton excursion. No Southern forces had been observed, but Gillespie thought "The rebel ladies were more insulting than ever, in the expressions of contempt for the invading Yankees, and were confident that we would soon be driven back."[52]

Gillespie's comrades in the Cavalry Corps' 2nd Division, meanwhile, had seen plenty of the enemy. On June 17, Brigadier General David M. Gregg's three brigades were ordered to the small town of Aldie, located on the western side of a gap in Bull Run Mountain. From the village Gregg's troopers were instructed to search for Rebels in Loudoun Valley between Aldie and Ashby's and Snicker's gaps in the Blue Ridge. The Federals encountered some of Confederate Major General "Jeb" Stuart's cavalry command almost immediately. Over the next four days a series of spirited clashes occurred at Aldie, Middleburg and Upperville between Gregg and Stuart, who had been screening Lee's movement north.[53] The 6th Ohio Cavalry was among those engaged in this fighting, its action at Aldie described by Captain Norman A. Barret of Company D:

We reached that place about three o'clock in the afternoon, and found the rebels in full possession. In fact, as we afterwards learned, they were just coming through the town to make a raid on us. After a brief skirmish, we drove them through the town, but they planted their batteries and drew up on the hills beyond, determined to check our passage. The 6th was ordered to the front, and we dashed through the town in columns of fours. As we reached the further edge the rebs opened on us with four guns. On we went at a gallop — shells bursting to the right, the left, before and behind us, but strangely enough none struck our line. We formed in a hollow out of range of their guns.

There was a body of rebel [dismounted cavalry] in a ravine beyond us which the Harris Light Cavalry [2nd New York] had vainly tried to dislodge. We were ordered to charge them and with a wild yell the regiment went in. Crack, smash, came the rebel shells as we rose the crest of the hill, but we heeded them not. Just at the foot of the hill was a gully from three to six feet deep and from four to twelve feet wide. This was filled with rebels, and a line of fire burst from it as we came on. We stopped not, nor faltered, most of our horses clearing it at a bound though a few went down. Once over, woe to the rebels. We made sixty prisoners on the spot, and left several stiffening on

Captain Norman A. Barret, Company D, 6th Ohio Cavalry, was promoted to major and lieutenant colonel before mustering out in October 1864. During his service he was a regular contributor to Warren's *Western Reserve Chronicle*.

Ken Lawrence Collection

the field. Three of our brave fellows were killed and twelve wounded, including Major Stanhope, who has since died of his wounds. At dark the rebels withdrew, and we camped for the night on the battlefield.[54]

At Upperville on the 21st, "a lovely Sabbath morning," Barret's regiment sparred again with Stuart's cavalry.

Just as we reached town we found them in line behind a stone wall, impassable for our horses. It was well for both parties that the wall intervened. Well for the rebels, else our sabres would have cut deep into their column, and well for us, otherwise not a man would have escaped.

Before their tremendous fire we recoiled, sheathed our sabres, unslung our carbines and went at them. Other troops came to our aid, and the rebels fled. Through the town they fled and we followed, fighting from house to house, and from wall to wall. Individual instances of bravery were not wanting. Captain [Delos R.] Northway, of Company A, with [20] of his men dashed on a body of rebels [many] times their own number, but not receiving proper support, was forced to retire, bringing out his men and receiving a severe sabre cut on his face, which for a time was no addition to his personal beauty.[55]

Northway downplayed his injury as "slight," writing two days later that Company A's fight outside Upperville was "the sharpest work it has ever been my fortune to know. Finding that we were not supported and knowing that the whole of my little

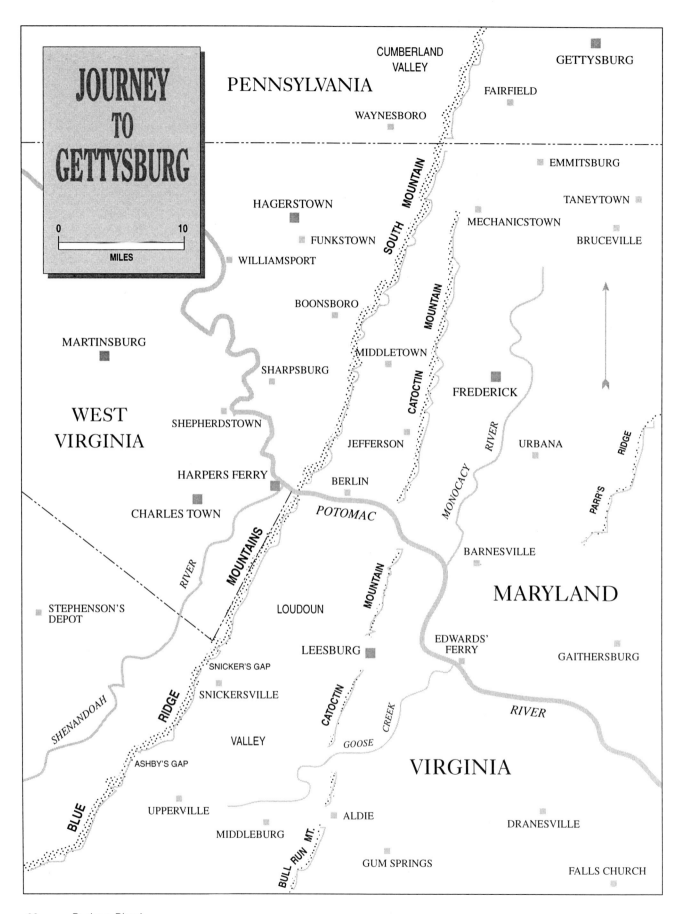

JOURNEY
TO
GETTYSBURG

0   10
MILES

CUMBERLAND
VALLEY

GETTYSBURG

PENNSYLVANIA

FAIRFIELD

WAYNESBORO

EMMITSBURG

TANEYTOWN

HAGERSTOWN

MECHANICSTOWN

BRUCEVILLE

FUNKSTOWN

WILLIAMSPORT

SOUTH MOUNTAIN

MOUNTAIN

BOONSBORO

MARTINSBURG

MIDDLETOWN

CATOCTIN

SHARPSBURG

FREDERICK

WEST
VIRGINIA

SHEPHERDSTOWN

JEFFERSON

MONOCACY RIVER

URBANA

PARR'S RIDGE

HARPERS FERRY

BERLIN

CHARLES TOWN

POTOMAC

RIVER

MOUNTAINS

BARNESVILLE

MOUNTAIN

MARYLAND

STEPHENSON'S
DEPOT

LOUDOUN

EDWARDS'
FERRY

GAITHERSBURG

LEESBURG

SNICKER'S GAP

CATOCTIN

RIVER

RIDGE

SNICKERSVILLE

GOOSE CREEK

SHENANDOAH

VALLEY

ASHBY'S GAP

BLUE

UPPERVILLE

MIDDLEBURG

BULL RUN MT.

ALDIE

VIRGINIA

DRANESVILLE

GUM SPRINGS

FALLS CHURCH

At Upperville, Virginia, on June 21, "each foot of ground was gained by hard fighting," wrote Sergeant Albert W. Stiles of Company A, 6th Ohio Cavalry. Stiles, pictured at left as commander of Company E in an 1865 photograph, was among 20 troopers led by Captain Delos Northway in a forlorn assault. Stiles recalled: "The order came to 'draw sabres' and then another to 'charge.' At the first sight of our company the enemy commenced to retire, but soon realizing that we were few in number, they rallied to meet us. I drew my revolver, fired six shots in quick succession into their ranks, threw the revolver at them and had just gotten my sabre well in hand when we were on to them. Just before meeting them Captain Northway's horse made a fearful lunge ahead, evidently having been given the spur freely and was nearly a half of its length ahead of mine. He raised in his stirrups, made a right cut against cavalry, his sabre fairly sissing as it cut the 'Johnny' in my front out of the way. His arm came back for a left cut, nearly striking me in the face. That was the last I saw of the captain for some time." A saber cut in the head knocked Stiles unconscious. He was taken prisoner and spent several months in Libby Prison before being exchanged.

Ken Lawrence Collection

force would either be killed or captured, unless we got out of it, I ordered the boys to fall back and we went out on double quick and in not very good order, you can bet. As it was, five of our men were captured, and four of us wounded." Among the latter was Sergeant Mortimer Baker, shot through an arm while in the act of sabering the Rebel trooper who wounded Northway.[56]

Another Ohio "casualty" of these events was Major William R. Sterling, one of Hooker's general staff officers and former captain of Company I, 7th Ohio. Sterling, accompanied by a signal officer and an orderly, was carrying dispatches from Hooker to General Pleasanton at Aldie on June 17 when the trio stopped for dinner at a private residence east of town. Before they could leave, all three were taken prisoner by Confederate partisan leader John S. Mosby and a small group of his rangers. The incredulous Sterling reportedly told his captors, "We have laughed so much at our men for being gobbled up by Mosby, that we cannot help laughing at being caught ourselves." The dispatches were in Stuart's hands before daylight of June 18, and much of their content about Federal troop locations was verified by Mosby's scouting reports. Conversely, the Union foray into Loudoun Valley also provided some reasonably good intelligence about Lee, and kept Stuart distanced from Bull Run Mountain's slopes.[57]

By this time the Army of the Potomac was stretched out in the form of a huge V — from Fair-

fax west to Gainesville and Thoroughfare Gap, then north to Goose Creek and Leesburg. For a full week between June 19 and 25 much of the army remained stationary, men and animals resting from the previous week's exertions. The respite was spent in a variety of ways. Near Fairfax, site of Hooker's headquarters, Battery H, 1st OVLA, occupied several days drilling with its 3-inch ordnance rifles. "Everything went off very nicely," mused an Ohio artillerist, though one of the lieutenants "made quite a number of blunders." Lieutenant Galwey of the 8th Ohio, outside Gainesville, was astonished to see "a twenty-acre field black with Chuck-Luck parties squatting on the grass. The rattle of dice in tin boxes, which had been pepper and mustard boxes, was almost ear-splitting." At Leesburg, where the 29th Ohio bivouacked in a pasture, the arrival of mail after an eight-day lapse especially cheered Nathan Parmater of Company E. "Also received [news]papers which are very anxiously looked for in times like these."[58]

On June 19 Parmater, a Conneaut schoolteacher, witnessed the execution of several 12th Corps' deserters not far from the 29th's camp. "The first and a part of the second Division was formed in a hollow square except one end being left opened, at which there were dug three graves, and soon came a team with three rough coffins, followed by an ambulance containing the three criminals. They were placed on their coffins, eyes bandaged and hands tied behind them, and a file of men placed in front of them with loaded guns. After a few words from the General and a prayer from a chaplain the command ready aim fire was given and the three fell backwards across their coffins, dead, pierced with some five or six balls each. Such a sight I hope I shall never be called to witness again." Military justice, it seemed to Parmater, was far swifter than the army's pursuit of the enemy. That soon changed.[59]

Signs of Confederate movement into Maryland and Pennsylvania suddenly grew more visible at Army of the Potomac headquarters on June 23 and 24. As historian E.B. Coddington phrased it, "the alarm bells rang loudly enough for even Hooker to hear, and he began to consider countermeasures." By the 25th, almost all of Lee's forces were over the Potomac River, some of them having penetrated as far as Chambersburg, Pennsylvania. Early that morning Hooker finally issued marching orders for his troops to begin their own passage into Maryland at Edwards' Ferry. Leading the way was General Reynolds' advance wing composed of the 1st, 3rd and 11th corps, and Stahel's cavalry.[60] Nine Ohio regiments and batteries of Howard's 11th Corps, followed by Stahel's Ohio headquarters' escort, were among the vanguard. Within 40 hours every Buckeye unit in the army was across the swollen, 200-yard-wide river. Those near the tail end cursed their "high commanders" for the pain endured getting them there.

For William Kepler and the 4th Ohio in the 2nd Corps, Edwards' Ferry was reached at 5 p.m. on the

L. M. Strayer Collection

Author's Photo

Battery H, 1st OVLA, was equipped with six extremely accurate 3-inch ordnance rifles, like the one above. *Left:* Private Philip N. Simmons of Battery H posed for Toledo photographer John Cadwallader wearing an enlisted man's mounted overcoat. Simmons was promoted to sergeant in June 1865.

26th after a long, muddy trek "at a rapid gait" from Gainesville via Gum Springs. For the past two weeks the regiment formed part of the army's rearguard. At the ferry, Kepler related, "we took supper, fixed ourselves down for the night, just got into a sound sleep when we were routed out, fell into line, waited awhile for orders to march, marched half a mile, halted about an hour, stood for some ten minutes — some of us getting out of sorts, some kept quiet, others blessed somebody, whilst everybody wondered, 'Why don't the Army of the Potomac move?' It didn't move for an hour; that is, our part did not until most of us got comfortably fixed, when we marched slowly across the pontoons, then halted, and stood or squatted down into the mud for about 'an age' (two hours); then moved a few steps, fumbled around in a wheat field; some swore until things 'seemed to get blue,' some yelled and all soon stacked arms, lay down, repented and went to sleep. Some of the boys called it 'a h—l of a time.' Such 'briggling about' was almost unpardonable. Who was to blame? No one knew." Spirits rebounded the next morning when the 4th realized "we are again in God's country." [61]

Their fellow Ohioans in the 11th Corps already had tramped to Middletown, nestled in the valley separating South and Catoctin mountains. Maryland, to Captain Leonidas M. Jewett of Company K, 61st Ohio, was "a land of milk and honey, to say nothing of many other good things to drink that went into the old canteen as we marched along." Fertile fields of wheat, oats, corn and grazing cattle amazed Jewett's Wyandot County men, so used to the "barren, worn-out lands of old Virginia." [62]

At one farm near Jefferson, 75th Ohio private William Southerton and his messmates of Company B were preparing to eat a soggy breakfast from their haversacks when a pleasant surprise materialized. "Here came the farm women," Southerton recalled, "bringing fresh bread and good sweet butter. Of all things! The loaves were a foot square and a foot thick, made of hop yeast — the finest bread I ever ate. We paid a nickel a loaf for the bread, and a few pennies for the butter. The women didn't want to take any money at all, but we insisted." The Buckeyes were told before leaving to remove as much milk as they desired from the springhouse, for which their generous hosts adamantly refused renumeration.[63]

Such magnanimity impressed Henry Henney, a

Brad L. Pruden Collection

Among the mudspattered 4th Ohio ranks crossing the Potomac River at Edwards' Ferry were Privates Joseph M. Harnit, *above,* Company K, a farmer from Marion, and Wesley H. Roloson, Company C, a Delaware County mason. Roloson, *below,* wore the distinctive 2nd Corps trefoil badge affixed to his jacket when photographed at the McAdams studio in Alexandria, Virginia.

Scott Hilts Collection

member of the 55th Ohio's field music, who "got lots of good things to eat" along the route to Middletown. Henney, though, observed several instances of misbehavior. "I was some demoralized to see some of the soldiers destroy property and pillage everything that they coveted. Surely where there is Union sentiment we should respect private property." On the other hand, a number of the valley's inhabitants, wrote Major Hurst of the 73rd Ohio, professed sympathies which "ran like the Kittocktin [sic] — Southward. Our boys did not have any extra respect for these Maryland rebels, who treated the 'Lincolnites' with sullen insolence, and charged double price for every thing they sold to our men; and from this cause, doubtless, arose the rumor that their chickens rested poorly of nights and their early potatoes were not likely to take the second growth."[64]

Another Ohioan in Hurst's brigade, George P.

Metcalf, related that "Stricter orders were now given to molest no property of any kind. It was said we were now in a loyal state and must keep our hands off every chicken, pan of milk, or jar of butter." Metcalf, a 19-year-old Medina County farmboy serving as a private in the 136th New York, remembered one special exception to the rules:

When in camp, we might make fires but [could] only take the top rail of a fence. These rail-fences were usually seven or eight rails high, and generally not more than enough rails in them to give us one apiece. We did, however, religiously observe the order: We always took the top rail; and the next in order took the top rail that was left; and so on until the top rail was the one that lay on top of the ground. It was a sight worth seeing to simply be a looker-on and see how quickly a fence a mile long would disappear when ten thousand soldiers were each after just one rail apiece for wood. The field looks like a moving piece of woods as every soldier, with a rail on his shoulder, is hurrying along to his tent; and many a farm covered thickly with rail fences was stripped of every rail in less than three minutes after the order to "Break ranks" was given. So eager and anxious were they to get something to start a fire with that, long before the campground for the night was reached, they would fall out of ranks, grab a rail and carry it on their shoulders to camp. Or perhaps one would hand his gun to his comrade and fall out of ranks and bring up the rear with a rail on each shoulder.

This was finally put a stop to; and then in order to get an undue advantage over the rails or get up a corner on a rail-fence, a fellow would fall out and stack up a pile and set guard over it, until the members of his company came back from stacking their guns and helped carry the pile to camp. This was unfair to those who stayed in the ranks. The Dutch regiments were the worst on this kind of practice, until finally they carried it so far that this kind of squatter sovereignty was not recognized, and one Dutchman on a pile of rails could not protect them

From Middletown on June 27, Captain Luther M. Buchwalter of Company A, 73rd Ohio, led a small reconnaissance party from the 11th Corps' 2nd Division to South Mountain. Little military activity could be seen from its crest, he reported, except a body of Union cavalry riding toward Hagerstown. Four months later the Ross County native was fatally wounded in battle at Wauhatchie, Tennessee. Buchwalter G.A.R. Post 460, organized in 1884 at Adelphi, Ohio, was named for him.

Major General George Gordon Meade's accession to army command elicited thoughts of guarded optimiism from at least one Buckeye. A member of the 55th Ohio wrote on June 30: "We have got a new Commander of the army of the Potomac[.] it is Gen Mead. Gen Hooker has been removed[.] this was done to blindfold the enemy while they are on the move. I hope and think that they will accomplish something good and that the Army of the Potomac can have the name of gaining one victory, which they have not done Since we belonged to it." An Ohio journalist commented that "altogether [Meade is] a man who impresses you rather as a thoughtful student than a dashing soldier."

Karl Sundstrom Collection

against a dozen who would make a rush for them, and him, too, if he did not give them up willingly.[65]

As wooden fencing went up in smoke between South Mountain and Middletown on June 27, General Hooker rode to Harpers Ferry, West Virginia. For two previous days he had been quarreling with Army general-in-chief Henry W. Halleck via telegraph over use of the town's 10,000-man garrison in his countermeasures against Lee. Hooker strongly urged abandoning Maryland Heights, the key to holding Harpers Ferry, and traveled there to investigate the situation personally. Halleck refused to approve his subordinate's advice. In a pique Hooker, stating he could not cover both Washington and Harpers Ferry with the forces at his disposal, asked to be relieved of command — his request making its way to President Lincoln's hands by late afternoon. Early the next morning at his Frederick, Maryland, headquarters, Hooker learned his resignation had been accepted. Major General George G. Meade, commander of the 5th Corps, was named his successor.[66]

The sudden change in Army of the Potomac leadership in the midst of an active campaign evoked mixed reaction from Ohio's soldiers. Thomas Galwey cynically exclaimed, "Thus the authorities are *not* carrying out President Lincoln's policy of not 'swapping horses when crossing a stream.' However, many of our senior officers are said to have lost confidence in Hooker after his failure at Chancellorsville, so maybe the change is good." Although he was a Hooker admirer, Captain Jewett of the 61st Ohio thought the occurrence was "as important

to the Union cause as the great battle of a few days afterwards. ... It was a critical time in the history of the war." The 8th Ohio's lieutenant colonel, Franklin Sawyer, believed the command transfer to be "very important," but recalled it "scarcely excited a comment" from his men. "We were intent upon the coming fray." As for Meade, wrote Captain Huntington of the artillery, "little was known outside his own Corps. But the army of the Potomac had become so case-hardened, that its fighting and staying qualities were but little affected by the signature attached to the orders that directed its movements."[67]

Another change on June 28 that *did* affect some of Ohio's cavalrymen was the replacement of General Stahel with Brigadier General H. Judson Kilpatrick. The First Ohio Squadron was retained as headquarters' escort for the Cavalry Corps' redesignated 3rd Division, composed of two brigades commanded by just-promoted Brigadier Generals Elon J. Farnsworth and George Armstrong Custer. Only hours before, the 23-year-old Custer, a Harrison County native born in the hamlet of New Rumley, had been a captain and aide-de-camp on General Pleasanton's staff. The Ohio troopers were allowed little time to size up Custer or Kilpatrick, who ordered them saddled and trotting off to Littlestown, Pennsylvania, by noon on the 29th. Three Confederate cavalry brigades under Stuart were reported close by, having traveled around the Federal rear and crossed the Potomac River scant miles from Washington. The two forces met in a sharp skirmish at Hanover, Pennsylvania, on June 30. Riding into town after the fight, Bugler Sam Gillespie of Kilpatrick's escort found "dead horses lying along the streets and upon the sidewalks where the battle had raged, with here and there a gray coat and then a blue, sleeping their last sleep together in the dust."[68]

Back in Maryland, Meade took firm control of the army, which was concentrating in the vicinity of Frederick. By nightfall of June 29 it was advanced almost to the Pennsylvania border on a 20-mile line extending from Emmitsburg to Westminster. Arriving there so quickly, however, proved no easy task.[69]

A torturous trip of some 35 miles between Monocacy Bridge and Uniontown was endured by the 2nd Corps' Buckeyes. "This was by far the most fatiguing march ever made by the [8th Ohio]," stated its commander, Franklin Sawyer. "Numerous little creeks and streams, swollen by recent rains, had to be forded, sometimes deep, but the men said 'the bath cooled them off,' and besides, as the march 'slows up' at a ford, it rested them somewhat. Towards the close of the march the men had become so weary they would even fall asleep as they rested on their muskets a moment at the ford." Lieutenant Galwey of Company B estimated more than two-thirds of the regiment (himself included) straggled during the night. The 8th's hospital steward, Charles H. Merrick, told his wife that when Carroll's brigade arrived outside Uniontown, "it was composed almost solely of those who rode. In our Regiment there was only nineteen men by actual count. Some companies not represented *at all*. But the Generals I suppose will see that the papers make a great blow about the wonderful march so that *they*

get a big name. ..." The brigade, boasted Captain Laird of the 4th Ohio, "marched *30 miles* in less than *14 hours*. That for distance we call a *very good* march. It certainly was a hard one, and if I was in the habit of using 'violent expletives' think I could with a clear conscience qualify the phrase. I said 'our Brigade' made the march but there was in reality only a few of us who did it. When the Brigade halted there was not over 150 men left. Our regiment had about 40, & I started with 1 Lieut. and 27 men and when I stopped had *3 men* left." Wrapping himself in a rubber blanket and using his haversack for a pillow, Laird instantly fell asleep.[70]

In the 12th Corps' 2nd Division, Nathan Parmater of the 29th Ohio was irritated by a chilling drizzle that accompanied his regiment's journey to Bruceville, south of Taneytown. In spite of the discomfort he was impressed by the cultivated fields between Frederick and Taneytown, acres of them covered with ripening wheat. But the pastoral scenery simply rolled by for the 29th's chaplain, Lyman D. Ames. The 50-year-old Conneaut minister bumped along the road sick in an ambulance. "Tired and nearly exhausted," Ames penned in his diary. "Need rest and quiet, find no chance either. Could I lie by for a few weeks, would be invaluable to me. No rest or quiet till we find the foe and bring him to term."[71]

Likewise, Sergeant Luther Mesnard of the 55th Ohio rode part of the way to Emmitsburg on June 29. He was suffering from diarrhea and tried to keep up with Company D, but was "compelled to stop often along [the] side of the road or any where I could get a chance. A soldier out of the ranks had no rights in the vast marching army." Finally he collapsed, unconscious. When he revived a half hour later, regimental Assistant Surgeon Henry K. Spooner administered a restorative and ordered Mesnard to finish the trip in an 11th Corps ambulance.[72]

Henry Henney of the 55th delighted in the "fine country" surrounding Catoctin Mountain's northern slopes. "But the girls are not so handsome," he decided. Jacob Smith of the 107th Ohio disagreed. Near the mountain's base, recalled the Company D private, "stood a small log house and the only inmates visible were a woman of about forty years of age in company with a girl or young woman of sixteen or seventeen years of age, the latter being as beautiful a type of young womanhood as I ever saw.

"Foot sore and stiff," Canton native George Faber Laird spent most of June 30 resting with the 4th Ohio near Uniontown, Maryland. The Company K captain judged "the country through which we are now passing is splendid and the inhabitants are kind and hospitable. They are glad to see us and supply the boys with many little delicacies, such as bread, butter &c, and as we pass along the ladies old and young stand waving by the road side, and hand us water and that is as kind an act as they can perform toward a tired soldier."

There alone in the mountain fastnesses ... she seemed like a fragrant rose blooming in the wilderness."[73]

There were "quite a number of ladies in camp to see our guns," wrote Corporal John H. Merrell from Battery H's bivouac near Bruceville. "They seem to be quite a curiosity to them." That night he also marveled at the manifestation of a rare nocturnal phenomenon. Moonshine refracting in a light sprinkle of rain produced a rainbow at 1 a.m. Merrell proclaimed it "one of the most singular things that I ever saw in my life."[74]

Rain continued falling intermittently on June 30 — another day of marching, though not as frantic, for much of the army. Its position covered Baltimore and Washington, while northern progress was directed generally toward the town of Gettysburg,

seat of Adams County, Pennsylvania. Meade learned from the latest intelligence reports that all of Lee's forces were in the Keystone State, two corps at or near Chambersburg, another at Carlisle and York, and Stuart's cavalry close to Hanover. Their movements, the Union general concluded, indicated a possible advance to Gettysburg. Although he drew up defensive contingency plans for a battle site along Pipe Creek in Maryland, Meade, on the 30th, placed four of his seven corps within 15 miles of Gettysburg. Two cavalry brigades under Brigadier General John Buford spent the night there, scouting and watching the road network leading west and north of the town.[75]

Southwest of Gettysburg the 11th Corps' three divisions camped just outside Emmitsburg. The men mustered and late in the afternoon mail was distributed. "There was considerable crowding around of the boys, all anxious to hear from home and loved ones," wrote the 107th Ohio's Jacob Smith. Dozens of men searched for shoes to replace those worn to a frazzle during the past two weeks of footslogging. Musician Henney was fortunate to buy a "stubby" pair for $2.50. Others were bereft of shirts or underwear, projecting a "neglected" appearance in stark contrast to the stereotype of Army of the Potomac soldiers being "cleanly, well-dressed men." But, as one 11th Corps private phrased it, "their pulses are regular, and their powder is dry."[76]

In the 75th Ohio's camp, William Southerton gleefully finished eating the last of some cherries he had foraged the previous day and stuffed in his haversack and pockets. Closer to Emmitsburg, Captain Jewett of the 61st Ohio pensively contemplated the immediate future. "That night," he recollected, "is to me as sacred as holy writ. The excitement, the knowledge of a great battle soon to be fought; the killing and wounding of many of the brave boys of Ohio and other loyal States of the Union; the wonder what fate awaited us — were all thoughts that flew through [my] mind."[77]

The evening's dinner for Jewett's men was drawn from three day's rations issued that morning. Coffee boiled while hardtack and salt-pork fried over crackling campfires. In the 82nd Ohio, tentmates Lieutenant Colonel David Thomson and Adjutant Stowel Burnham ate together at a makeshift table, blissfully unaware it was the last meal they would share. At dark, remembered another officer in the regiment, "the soldiers sought the refuge of their shelter-tents, and silence fell upon the camp, broken only by the tramp of sentinels and the heavy breathing of the sleepers."[78]

TWO

'The position was one which no troops in the world could have held'

JULY 1

The first gray tinge of daybreak painted the eastern horizon when Alfred E. Lee of the 82nd Ohio heard hoofbeats resonate through the regiment's camp. Lee, captain of Company E, had been unable to sleep and was writing to friends in Delaware County by the light of a flickering candle. He noticed a mounted orderly draw rein in front of Colonel James Robinson's quarters, then deliver a message. He deduced from the rider's haste that something important was in the offing, so was not surprised a short while later to hear Sergeant Major Jasper S. Snow notify him and the other company commanders to awaken their men and get ready for an early departure.[1]

By dawn the scene was repeated in 30 other 11th Corps' regimental and battery bivouacs. Striking tents and preparing breakfast were routine affairs, but this morning unmistakable tension hung in the air, made more palpable by the dampness and a common realization that today might bring heavy fighting. After all, Bobby Lee and his "Johnnies" were not supposed to be very far away.

The previous night 11th Corps leader Oliver O. Howard had visited General Reynolds, now the army's left wing commander, whose 1st Corps was camped along Marsh Creek five miles north of Howard's men at Emmitsburg. The two exchanged information, Reynolds producing a dispatch from ar-

my headquarters indicating Meade believed a general engagement was imminent. Howard returned to Emmitsburg about 1 a.m. At 3:30 he received orders from Meade to move within supporting distance of the 1st Corps, which in turn was to march six miles further to Gettysburg. At 8 o'clock, with his troops already waiting, Howard was directed by Reynolds to march to Gettysburg as well.[2]

Prior to leaving Emmitsburg, Howard, sharing Reynolds' concern of a possible enemy threat to the wing's left flank, ordered reconnaissances to the west and south. The duty fell to portions of four regiments, two of them from Ohio. Lieutenant Colonel William Henry Harrison Bown was sent to Mechanicstown [present-day Thurmont], Maryland, with four officers and 100 enlisted men from the 61st Ohio. The 75th Ohio furnished 103 officers and men for a scout toward Greencastle, Pennsylvania. This detachment was led by Captain George Benson "Ben" Fox of Company A, the 75th's acting major. In both regiments, 10 men were selected from each company for the respective missions. None returned to their commands until late in the day.[3]

By 8:30 the 11th Corps was on the move. Barlow's 1st Division took the direct, 11-mile route to Gettysburg along the Emmitsburg Road. The 3rd and 2nd divisions under Schurz and von Steinwehr, respectively, followed by marching along a slightly

The bravery of Captain Hubert Dilger, Battery I, 1st OVLA, was recognized in 1893 with a Medal of Honor for his actions at Chancellorsville. One of Dilger's superior officers commented: "The recollection of this noble soldier, with his manly bearing and graceful form, will never be effaced from my memory. He bore a large red scar upon his cheek. I know not how or when it was received, but I venture the assertion that it blushed from no dishonor."

Major General Carl Schurz, *above,* was an 1852 German emigré possessing remarkable oratorical talent and strong anti-slavery sentiments. German-American soldiers in the army regarded him second only to Franz Sigel, and those in the 11th Corps considered him their spiritual leader.

longer route via Chapel Road to Horner's Mills on the Taneytown Road. "Many of the men were nearly barefoot," recalled an Ohio officer, "but all were cheerful." At the Pennsylvania line that state's regiments "greeted the 'Old Keystone' with enthusiastic cheers, their drums and colors saluting and bands playing."[4]

Nearing Marsh Creek, Barlow's column was slowed by deep ruts carved in the mud by Reynolds' artillery and wagon train. A few laggard 1st Corps teamsters still partially clogged the pike with their vehicles. Howard and his staff took to adjoining fields, spurring their horses toward Gettysburg. Without obstructions, Schurz's division made better

time, passing Horner's Mills about 10:30. There, the bespectacled German received an order to hurry his command forward as quickly as possible.[5]

According to Captain Lee, 30 minutes passed before "the distant and ominous booming of artillery gave us our first intimation that we were in the vicinity of the enemy. The dull and occasional thunder sounded directly in advance, and told us [more] plainly than words of what we were approaching." What the captain did not yet know was that a battle had started three and a half hours earlier. West of Gettysburg, part of Buford's cavalry disputed the advance of a Confederate division from A.P. Hill's command long enough for the 1st Corps to arrive and replace the outnumbered, outgunned troopers. The fighting intensified. Hard pressed, Reynolds called for Howard to move up at once. Not long afterward he was shot in the head and killed. Howard learned the news at 11:30 while viewing the unfolding conflict from a Gettysburg balcony. With Reynolds gone, the one-armed general found himself the field's ranking Federal officer. He instructed Schurz to take control of the 11th Corps, while 3rd Division command devolved upon Brigadier General Alexander Schimmelfennig, a former Prussian engineer.[6]

Five miles back on the Taneytown Road, Captain Dilger of Battery I also heard the distant rumbling. He was riding near the head of Schimmelfennig's column with Schurz's assistant adjutant general, when a passing aide told them firing could be seen plainly from a hill a mile to the left. Dilger and his companion sauntered off for a look, soon noticing the noise completely abated. They decided to return to the road, but not before taking time to gorge themselves on ripe cherries discovered hanging in a clump of heavily laden trees.[7]

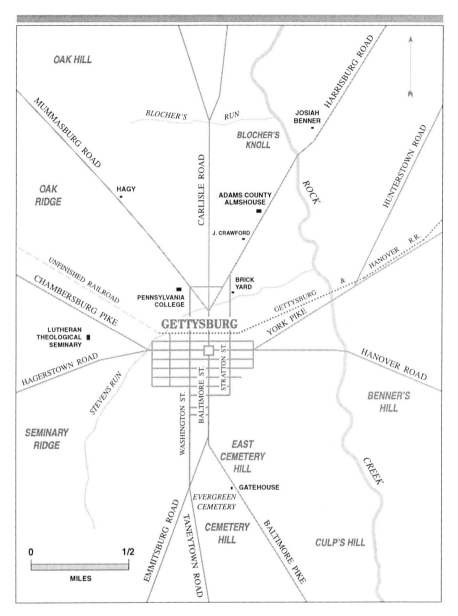

There were no such diversions allowed the rank and file once word spread to close up and double the pace. The 3rd Division pressed on "with alacrity and without stopping," wrote Captain Lee. "Those inclined to straggle were shamed out of it" or forced back into line by provost guards with fixed bayonets. Here and there "Pale and anxious looking women ... stood by the roadside giving drinks and food to the hurrying soldiers who could snatch them and go on."[8]

Ohioan George Metcalf, near the rear of von Steinwehr's 2nd Division, managed to grab a few grapes from a trellised vine. Wherever a house stood along the road "the occupants busied themselves by pumping water and turning it into tubs for the soldiers to drink. Few, compared with the great throng, could be accommodated. I could not get a drop and suffered the whole distance from thirst."[9]

About 12:30 the 3rd Division's van hustled past Cemetery Hill, a commanding point of ground just beyond Gettysburg's southern outskirts that Howard espied earlier and believed was his only tenable position. Unfortunately, by midday the embattled 1st Corps' right flank was under serious threat northwest of town. It needed to be prolonged or faced being turned. Oak Hill, situated off the endangered flank, offered promise as a platform to secure the Union line — provided its partially wooded slopes could be seized before the enemy occupied them. The task was assigned to Schimmelfennig's and Barlow's men, the closest troops available. Von Steinwehr's division, once arrived, would be held in reserve on Cemetery Hill.[10]

A cloudburst further drenched the sweat-soaked 3rd Division infantrymen double-quicking the last mile toward town. The leading regiment, the 45th New York, entered Gettysburg by Washington Street and moved north, emerging on the Mummasburg Road. As part of the regiment deployed as skirmishers, sudden cannon fire emanating near Oak Hill's base startled the New Yorkers. The first shells exploded harmlessly, but it was clearly apparent the shots came from Rebel guns. Confederates of Major General Robert E. Rodes' division, Ewell's corps, already covered Oak Hill in force and gained a decided advantage in position. The 11th Corps would be forced to fight in the gently undulating, exposed plain below.[11]

The morning's rapid marching had created large intervals between regiments, so the 3rd Division did not arrive in a compact body. Dilger's Ohio artillerymen were the first to follow the 45th New York through town, drivers cracking whips to hurry along the rain-matted horses pulling limbers, caissons and the battery's six bronze Napoleon smoothbores. Schimmelfennig instructed Dilger to take position wherever he thought best between the Mummasburg and Carlisle roads. Panting behind the caissons came the rest of the division's 1st Brigade, with Colonel Krzyzanowski's 2nd Brigade bringing up the rear.[12]

After a brief survey of the fields ahead of him, Dilger advanced Second Lieutenant Z. Clark Scripture's two-gun section to the "highest point" in view between an apple orchard on the Hagy farm and the Carlisle Road. Scripture, a resident of Ravenna, Ohio, unlimbered and began firing at enemy guns on Oak Hill. This immediately caught the attention of Captain R.C.M. Page, whose Virginia battery was harassing the 45th New York from Oak Hill's lower slope. Page turned his four smoothbores on Scripture, compelling Dilger to reinforce him with Battery I's other two sections. A sharp duel ensued at a range of 1,400 yards, which must have been rather unnerving to 11 Cincinnati recruits the battery received only nine days earlier.[13]

But its commander was no ordinary cannoneer. Trained at a German military academy with pre-war service in Baden, Dilger was considered one of the best artillery officers in the Army of the Potomac. The reputation was confirmed as he directed Battery I's intensifying fight with Page's guns. According to one account, "The first shot from the Ohio Battery flew over the Confederate Battery. At this the rebels yelled in derision. Capt. Dilger now sighted the gun himself and fired it. The shot dismounted a rebel gun and killed the horses. Capt. Dilger tried it a second time, sighting and firing the gun." For a few moments nothing could be seen through the white, sulphurous smoke. Standing just to the battery's rear, Colonel Philip P. Brown Jr. of the 157th New York asked, "What effect, Capt. Dilger?" Removing field glasses from his eyes the captain replied, "I have spiked a gun for them plugging it at the muzzle."

This extraordinary feat was grossly exaggerated, however. It is unlikely Dilger could have viewed the result of so lucky a shot through the smoke, and neither he nor the Confederates reported such an occurrence. Still, Page was pounded, losing 30 men and 17 horses — the worst damage suffered by any Rebel battery during the battle. It soon withdrew and another battery supporting it also fell silent.[14]

Colonel Philip P. Brown Jr.'s 157th New York supported Dilger early in his battery's action north of Gettysburg.

Karl Sundstrom Collection

While Dilger's guns roared, the 61st Ohio under Colonel Stephen J. McGroarty came up on Battery I's left and was ordered forward as skirmishers. McGroarty, a Cincinnati attorney born in Ireland, brought to the field only 143 effectives, two-fifths of the regiment remaining back in Maryland with Lieutenant Colonel Bown. At least 11 different Ohio counties were represented in the 61st, which took position on the 3rd Division skirmish line between the 45th New York and 74th Pennsylvania. Spaced two to three yards apart, McGroarty's men at once began firing their Enfield and .69 caliber rifle-muskets at an oncoming enemy skirmish line.[15]

Krzyzanowski's small 2nd Brigade made its appearance about this time, having jogged through Gettysburg "in a tumult of excitement." Captain Lee of the 82nd Ohio was certain he would never forget "the clanging of sabres, the clatter of horses' hoofs, the gleaming of arms, the sweaty, excited countenances of the troops, the shouts of command, and the booming of the deep-throated guns. Groups of men and women, terror stricken ... stood showering upon us their benedictions. The prattling child joined the young maiden and the trembling matron in waving 'God bless you' to the soldiers." Lee heard that General Reynolds was dead from some passing cavalrymen, who "spread various other rumors, less truthful but no less exciting, as to what was going on at the front."[16]

The brigade at first formed in double column of companies in an orchard northeast of Pennsylvania College, the 82nd on the extreme left within supporting distance of Dilger. During the maneuver the regiment's field musicians put their instruments to work. "We played the tune called 'The Yankees Are Coming'," explained Company I fifer Joseph Gillis. "It is a very quick piece and pretty. The Rebs let go

Colonel Stephen J. McGroarty, 61st Ohio.

Major David C. Beckett, 61st Ohio.

The 61st Ohio was led into the fields north of Pennsylvania College by the two officers at right. Reportedly wounded 23 times during the war, McGroarty lost his left arm in July 1864 at the battle of Peachtree Creek outside Atlanta. A younger brother, William H. McGroarty, was killed in Tennessee four months after Gettysburg while commanding Company G. Beckett, shown here as captain of Company F, was shot dead near Georgia's Kennesaw Mountain in June 1864.

Courtesy of Joseph H. Gillis

Musician Joseph Gillis, Company I, 82nd Ohio, was a 19-year-old shoemaker from Delaware, Ohio. After the battle he spent three weeks caring for Confederate wounded at the 11th Corps hospital.

Mass. MOLLUS, USAMHI

Colonel James S. Robinson, 82nd Ohio, began the war as a private and finished it a brevet major general. Born near Mansfield in 1827, Robinson was described by venerable 19th century Ohio historian Henry Howe: "He was bred a printer and editor, looks like the typical John Bull, but is every inch an American. He is a tall, somewhat huge man, with clear, weighty voice, one with strong convictions and frank in their expression."

solid shot. The first went about three feet from the back drummer, and you ought to have seen him juke. Several came very close before we got to the [orchard]. Then the Regt. was formed. The Col[onel] said 'Musicians to the Hospital, March.' I bid good-bye to the boys and left, and we had just got about five or six rods to the rear when the 82d went in on their nerve. ..."[17]

Rebel cannon fire was responsible for two casualties in the regiment as it formed. Corporal Isaiah Mahan of Company E was killed by a ricocheting solid shot and another man was wounded. To maintain calm, Colonel Robinson slightly shifted the 82nd's position. "Then," wrote Captain Lee, "the rolls were called, and the men quietly responded to their names amid the boom of cannon and the screech of exploding shells."[18]

Lee, a Delaware County lawyer who obtained a master's degree from Ohio Wesleyan University on the eve of his 1862 enlistment, watched intently as part of one of Rodes' brigades — three Alabama regiments commanded by Colonel Edward A. O'Neal — debouched from Oak Hill and assaulted the 1st Corps' far right flank. Federal musketry, aided by shrapnel fired from Dilger's six guns, blunted O'Neal's attack. Lee related: "As the combatants neared each other, random shots cracked spitefully, and were quickly followed by crashing volleys. In a few minutes the rebels, who had yielded at the first onset, were seen scampering to

the rear like frightened sheep. A loud cheer followed this success, and officers who had watched the movement through their glasses declared that we were 'getting along splendidly.' "[19]

General Schurz did not share such optimism. From Hagy's farm he, too, witnessed O'Neal's repulse, but also observed other Confederates maneuvering beyond the 3rd Division's center and right. These were Brigadier General George Doles' four Georgia regiments of Rodes' division and a battalion of Alabama sharpshooters commanded by Major

Adopted by the Federal Army in 1857, the smoothbore Napoleon field gun could throw a solid 12-pound iron ball 1,750 yards. It was much more lethal firing canister — a cylinder containing 27 half-inch balls — at massed infantry within 400 yards. Of the four Ohio batteries engaged at Gettysburg, three were equipped with Napoleons.

Author's Photo

Eugene Blackford. Most of Blackford's men already were engaged on the skirmish line, trading shots with the 61st Ohio and 45th New York. Because the 3rd Division contained fewer than 3,000 infantrymen it was thinly spread. A quarter-mile gap still existed between the 11th Corps' left flank at the Mummasburg Road and the 1st Corps' right. To compound matters, a message from Howard informed Schurz that a large Confederate force was reported approaching from the northeast. Howard cautioned him to prevent his own right flank from being turned. For the moment, however, the fight to the front was of more concern.[20]

Resumption of artillery fire from Oak Hill momentarily worried Captain Dilger, as shells directed his way were coming now from rifled pieces having better accuracy and range than his own 12-pounder Napoleons. He appealed to 11th Corps artillery chief Major Thomas W. Osborn, back on Cemetery Hill, for assistance. Osborn dispatched First Lieutenant William Wheeler's 13th New York Battery of four 3-inch rifles, which were unlimbered to Battery I's right. Wheeler's effective counterbattery fire delighted Dilger, providing him with an opportunity to redeploy his own guns. He boldly sent First Lieutenant Christian Weidman's section forward some 600 yards near the Carlisle Road. The advance brought Weidman's two Napoleons almost to the

skirmish line, a tactic Dilger relished. He left the lieutenant to bang away at the Confederates on Oak Hill and returned to reposition the battery's other four guns with Wheeler's rifles providing cover.[21]

The Buckeyes unexpectedly encountered a four-foot-deep ditch, which the 12-pounders and limbers could not traverse. Since there appeared no way to detour, Dilger shouted for his cannoneers to fill enough of the declivity with fence rails to enable the guns to pass over one at a time in column. In

First Lieutenant William Wheeler, 13th New York Battery. As a captain he was killed in 1864 while working his guns at Kolb's Farm near Kennesaw Mountain, Georgia.

Karl Sundstrom Collection

Private Friedrich Beiser, *left,* and Sergeant Joseph Brüggemeyer were German immigrants living in Cincinnati when they enlisted in September 1861. Both served in Battery I, 1st OVLA. A miller from Magdeburg, Beiser posed with his M1840 light artillery saber. Brüggemeyer, a native Prussian, was wounded in the right foot at Kennesaw Mountain in 1864.

spite of galling enemy fire, once this was accomplished he advanced Scripture's and First Lieutenant William Dammert's sections 400 yards to a wheatfield, then ordered the New Yorkers to join him. Wheeler first had to hack through a stout fence blocking his path with axes procured from the caissons. "While waiting here," he wrote, "I saw an infantry man's leg taken off by a shot, and whirled like a stone through the air, until it came against a caisson with a loud whack." When again in battery the rifles resumed shelling their counterparts on Oak Hill. Dilger's gun crews worked so feverishly that three caissons continuously were shuttled forward with ammunition. Even so, the supply nearly ran out twice. Surprisingly, casualties in both batteries so far were minimal. Only three of Dilger's men had been wounded, one of them mortally.[22]

With attention riveted toward Oak Hill, few of the Ohio artillerists likely noticed the head of General Barlow's 1st Division emerge from Gettysburg. His two brigades numbering less than 2,200 men were panting, having double-quicked the final two miles up the Emmitsburg Road and Baltimore Street. "Oh, that double-quick!" remembered the 75th Ohio's William Southerton. "Like a dog trot. Exhausting in the heat of mid-day. Some dropped with exhaustion. An ambulance drove along with the column and picked up all it could. [It] was only

a jolty wagon, but little better than nothing." [23]

Barlow's orders instructed him to form on the right of Schimmelfennig's 3rd Division. Without stopping, his jaded troops passed the rear of Krzyzanowski's massed brigade, skirted the north edge of town and continued along the Harrisburg Road to a swale near the Adams County Almshouse, where the column halted. The 1st Division's two brigades formed astride the road — Colonel Leopold von Gilsa's on the left and Adelbert Ames' to the right. There was little anyone could see offering good defensive ground. A few patches of trees dotted the surrounding open fields. Trees likewise lined the banks of Rock Creek just off Ames' right flank. Some 400 yards north of the Almshouse complex a rise in the ground known as Blocher's Knoll overlooked the creek. The knoll's northern slope was wooded, the summit cleared. It was not a dominating position, but did command the slight ridge on which the Almshouse buildings sat. Barlow decided to seize it using von Gilsa's tiny brigade, unaware that Confederate skirmishers already occupied Blocher's woods. He did not send word to Schurz of his intentions.[24]

The 2nd Brigade, under Ames, was massed east of the Harrisburg Road; from left to right the 107th Ohio, 25th Ohio and 17th Connecticut, with the 75th Ohio in support. Excluding stragglers and detached men, 1,269 were present for duty equipped. Lieutenant Colonel Jeremiah Williams' 25th Ohio was the brigade's smallest regiment at 220. Colonel Andrew Harris of the 75th, however, brought just 205 to the battlefield as 100 others were detailed that morning at Emmitsburg for a scouting mission. By far the largest regiment with 458 officers and men was the "German" 107th, whose colonel, Seraphim Meyer, had reassumed command June 27 at Middletown, Maryland. Wounded and captured at Chancellorsville, Meyer was paroled May 15 after eight days' confinement in Libby Prison. He reported to Camp Parole, Maryland, on May 25, and presumably was exchanged sometime in June.[25]

The ride to Gettysburg had been an uncomfortable one for Meyer, physically and mentally. Still bothered by his wrist injury, he also suffered from impaired vision and hearing, a kidney ailment and lingering pneumonia contracted five months earlier during cold-weather exposure in Virginia. Returning to the regiment was anything but joyous. In Ames and Barlow he discovered unknown brigade and division commanders, neither of whom were acquainted with the Ohio colonel. Given little time to formulate opinions of his immediate superiors, he was told of their reputation for strictness by the 107th's interim commander, Lieutenant Colonel Charles Mueller. Barlow, certainly, was no ally of the German element in his division, and Ames seemed to share similar prejudicial propensities. The 107th was the lone predominantly foreign regiment in the 2nd Brigade. Combined with renewed anti-German sentiment after Chancellorsville, and in light of subsequent events, Ames probably harbored a certain measure of distrust.

In Meyer's words, there was "great discontent & complaints ... on the part of officers and men, by reason of what they alledged [sic] to be harsh & severe treatment from these new commanders. I was informed that the commander of the Regiment [Mueller] was frequently & for most trivial reasons placed in arrest, & that the Regiment was treated with disfavor in every possible way. They cautioned me to look out, that now my turn would come. To avoid difficulty I redoubled my caution & zeal, & hoped thereby to gain the good will & favor of my commanders."[26]

One of Meyer's officers arrived on the field under arrest. Second Lieutenant John F. Tescher was charged with disobeying orders and neglect of duty

Timothy R. Brookes Collection

Born in Bern, Switzerland, Second Lieutenant John F. Tescher of Company G, 107th Ohio, resided in Wooster where he was employed as a clerk.

for having allowed a picket detail from Company G to straggle in "a shameful manner" at Goose Creek, Virginia, on June 19. Before his case could be tried, the Swiss-born Tescher was seriously wounded in the right thigh by a shell fragment near Blocher's Knoll.[27]

While Meyer watched von Gilsa's bluecoats head for the knoll, Ames ordered four companies from the 17th Connecticut to cover his own brigade's right front as skirmishers. Led by Major Allen G. Brady, the Connecticut men formed two lines and crossed Rock Creek with the intention of reaching the nearby farmyard of Josiah Benner. Before they could get there, Confederate artillery stationed several hundred yards to the northeast suddenly opened on Brady. The guns belonged to Major General Jubal Early's division, Ewell's corps, which was arriving from Heidlersburg, Pennsylvania. This was the enemy force Schurz was warned about earlier. The Confederates east of Rock Creek could see von Gilsa's movement as well as Dilger's and Wheeler's cannoneers shooting at Oak Hill. Early began deploying his infantry and at the same time ordered his artillery chief, Lieutenant Colonel Hilary Jones, to commence firing at visible Union targets.[28]

Von Gilsa wrested Blocher's knoll and woods from their Confederate occupants, but his sparse numbers were woefully inadequate to defend the spot long. There was no connection with Schimmelfennig's troops to the west, the main body of Doles' brigade menaced his left flank, and Ames' brigade was 300 or more yards to his right rear. At that moment Barlow may have been close by. An Ohio aide on his staff, First Lieutenant Edward C. Culp, wrote four days later that the boy-faced general "rode forward immediately, to the line of skirmishers, sending his orders back, instead of forward." One of these called for First Lieutenant Bayard Wilkeson to bring four of his 12-pounders from Battery G, 4th U.S. Artillery, to the knoll to answer Jones' fire. Lieutenant Colonel Williams' 25th Ohio was detached from Ames to follow the 19-year-old battery commander and support him.[29]

Unlimbering at the knoll's summit Wilkeson opened on Jones, who retaliated with "most trying" counterfire from two of his batteries. Wilkeson was cut down early in the duel, struck by a shell that almost severed his right leg. Other projectiles

Private John Henry Goddard was a well seasoned veteran of Battery I, 1st OVLA, by the time he sat for this quarter-plate tintype portrait. A fellow battery member wrote home just after the battle: "The hardships we haft to endure now would kill about half of those pale faces or conscripts, before they would get used to it."

screamed overhead, feeling for Dilger's position. The accuracy of Jones' artillerists proved far better than those shooting at the Ohioans from Oak Hill. Hot iron shards sliced through several Battery I horses, killing them. Corporal Charles R. Munroe was hit on his side at the waist, a wound from which he succumbed a year later at his home in Rootstown, Ohio. Munroe's best friend, Isaac Gardner, was thumbing his Napoleon's vent when a solid shot, barely missing his legs, smashed the gun's trail. A large piece of flying wood flattened Gunner James S. Austin, temporarily laming him. Another shot landed in front of Private James P. Sutliff, whose boot sole was completely ripped away and foot severely bruised. "Quite a number of the men were badly bruised, but not enough to call them wounded," wrote Private Charles J. Gillis, like Sutliff, a native of Portage County.[30]

General Early's infantry on the east side of Rock Creek fanned out to a three-brigade front with a fourth held in reserve. From left to right Colonel Isaac Avery's North Carolinians, Brigadier General Harry T. Hays' Louisianans and five of Brigadier General John B. Gordon's six Georgia regiments prepared for assault. Gordon, facing Blocher's Knoll, stepped off first, his advance coinciding with a forward movement by Doles' fellow Georgians across the creek from the north. Their combined strength of 2,821 outnumbered the knoll's Federal defenders more than two to one.[31]

Barlow aide Edward Culp had just delivered an order and was returning to the general on the knoll when "I caught a glimpse through an opening in the woods of moving troops. I rode back to get a fresh look from a little eminence, and became satisfied they were rebel reinforcements." Culp informed Barlow of what he had seen and both officers spurred their horses to von Gilsa's skirmish line. "One glance," the lieutenant recalled, "showed that I was correct. Thousands of fresh troops were hurled against our weakened lines."[32]

Barlow sent Culp dashing off to find General Howard with a plea for more artillery support. Another aide, possibly First Lieutenant John T. Wood of Company E, 25th Ohio, was dispatched to Ames to bring up the balance of the 2nd Brigade. The 25th Ohio, supporting Wilkeson's battery, was shifted to the extreme left of von Gilsa's position, fronting Doles along a small stream flowing east to Rock Creek. Companies A and F were thrown out as skirmishers. The regiment's left flank, however, was in the air.[33]

Looking rearward, Barlow could see Ames' men double-quicking forward, their Enfields carried at right shoulder shift. Colonel Meyer's 107th Ohio, the brigade's largest regiment, arrived first. Meyer was ordered to maneuver his 10 companies to a wheatfield left of the 25th Ohio — and immediately drew the ire of his brigade commander. Two or three times, according to Ames, he instructed the colonel through staff aides where the regiment should be placed. "He executed the order very imperfectly," Ames claimed. "Part of the regiment was faced to the left & moved off, part of it remained in its position, and in portions of the regiment there was the greatest confusion." Meyer's equestrian and vocal peculiarities, which had provoked laughter during earlier days on the drill field, especially attracted the West Pointer's displeased attention. "I noticed," Ames related, "that at the whistling of shells and bullets he would crouch down upon his horse, his breast nearly touching the neck of his horse. ... I reproved him at the time for his apparently cowardly conduct and unnecessary dodging at the sound, & even while reproving him for such conduct he repeated the same. He ... appeared beside himself & not at all cool. His commands were not the proper ones and not given in an intelligible manner." Disgusted, Ames rode off to attend to the rest of the brigade's reserve deployment, leaving Captain John M. Brown, brigade adjutant, and an aide to supervise the 107th's placement. Brown, who had served under Ames as adjutant of the 20th Maine, later said Meyer's commands to his men sounded like "screaming — the words could not be distinguished."[34]

Captain John M. Lutz of Company E, the 107th's ranking line officer, refuted the general's and Brown's statements, assuring that "all commands that Col. Meyer rec'd & gave to the Regt were carried out promptly & were understood distinctly." Lutz allowed that a slight delay in the 107th's move to the wheatfield was caused by an obstructing rail fence that had to be knocked down. He avowed Meyer's distinctive, high-pitched shouting and unusual style of horsemanship were long-standing habits and did not demoralize the men. There was nothing in his battlefield behavior different from that displayed on the parade ground.[35]

Never having seen Meyer drill troops, Ames

Ohio Bar Association

Pictured here about 1880, Colonel Seraphim Meyer returned from brief confinement in Libby Prison to command the 107th Ohio on the eve of battle at Gettysburg. For the previous six months he had been a very sick man. His son Edward described him being "greatly reduced in flesh" and "quite feeble and ill." When Meyer attempted to resign his commission in late July 1863, he admitted, "The hardships & exposures of the late campaigns ... combined with the depressing circumstances lately surrounding me, have ruined my health & physical constitution, to an extent to incapacitate me physically for the position I have occupied."

was completely unfamiliar with the colonel's personal quirks. He instantly interpreted them as manifestations of cowardice, which marked the Alsatian-born Ohioan for "severe treatment" and "disfavor" he sought to avoid. For the time being, though, both officers were confronted with a far worse situation boiling up in front of them.

Barlow's entire division was now at the knoll,

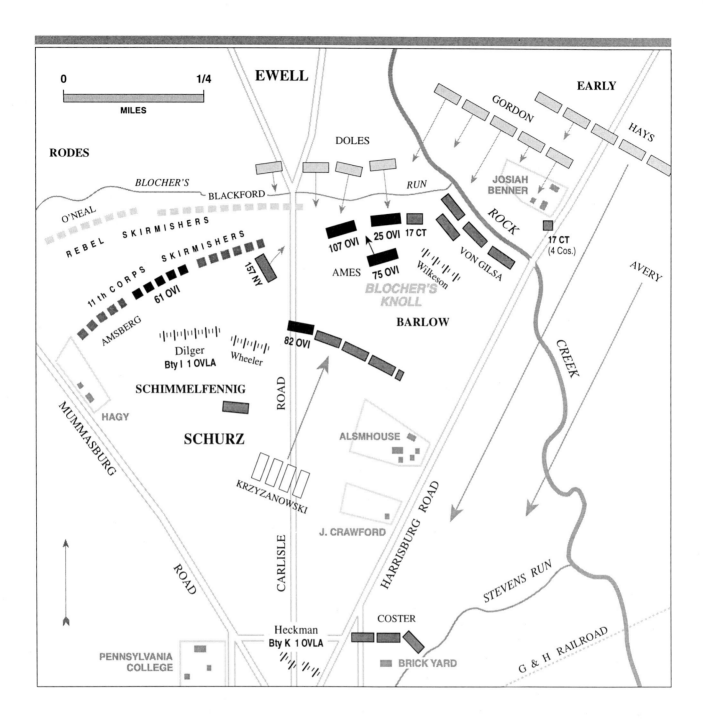

in the woods or along the creek bank, pushed forward so that it formed a projecting angle unconnected to Schimmelfennig's 3rd Division of the 11th Corps. Off to the west General Schurz was dismayed upon seeing Barlow's precarious position. He later conjectured the 1st Division commander had misunderstood orders, or "was carried away by the ardor of the conflict." Schurz urgently appealed to Howard for a reserve brigade on Cemetery Hill to support Barlow's unprotected right flank, and or-

dered Krzyzanowski up to bolster the 1st Division's left. Both moves came too late.[36]

Gordon's Georgians splashed across Rock Creek and crashed into von Gilsa's thin line, bellowing the Rebel yell. The assault's fury overwhelmed the German colonel's New Yorkers and Pennsylvanians, though many retired to the crest of Blocher's Knoll firing in stubborn defiance. Attempting to rally the broken ranks on the knoll's northeast slope, Barlow was hit by a bullet in the left side. Dismounting, he

Major General Jubal A. Early, CSA.

Brigadier General John B. Gordon, CSA.

Five regiments of Gordon's Georgia brigade, Early's division, struck Barlow's 11th Corps troops "with a resolution and spirit rarely excelled." Gordon, who finished the war as a Confederate corps commander even though he possessed no pre-war military training, reported that "The enemy made a most obstinate resistance until the colors on portions of the two lines were separated by a space of less than 50 paces, when his line was broken and driven back ... with immense loss in killed, wounded, and prisoners."

tried to walk. Two soldiers came up to assist him, but one was shot and Barlow was struck in the back by a spent ball. In a faint he lay down. Fleeing troops streamed past and soon the grievously injured general fell into Confederate hands.[37]

Von Gilsa's collapse forced Wilkeson's battery, under command of First Lieutenant Eugene Bancroft, to limber hurriedly and clatter off. It also exposed the right flank of Ames, who simultaneously was absorbing heavy fire from Doles' Georgians on the left. Colonel Harris, seeing von Gilsa's German regiments disintegrate from his vantage point with the 75th Ohio, was non-plussed. "True to their natural instinct, being hard pressed by superior numbers, [they] gave way, and thus left our Brigade, now equally engaged with an enemy in front and flank, to an enfilading fire of the most terrible kind." Jones' artillery east of the creek continued pumping shells Ames' way, adding to the din. "The ground shook," recalled one of Harris' Buckeyes. It was "a deafening and furious bombardment." To the 75th's right a member of "our Nut Meg brethren," as the 17th Connecticut was affectionately known by some of its Ohio comrades, wrote that much of the enemy ordnance passed harmlessly overhead. "Most of us threw off our knapsacks and in ranks stretched ourselves on the ground to ... escape the shells which were continually flying over us."[38]

Under increasing pressure the 25th and 107th Ohio also began to waver. The Rebels were "yelling like Indians in making a savage charge," reflected a corporal in the 107th. According to First Lieutenant

Charles Harrison of Company E, shortly after being attacked "the 2d company from the left gave way, whereupon [Colonel Meyer] rode up & asked 'What in the devil they meant by breaking.' [Then] we were ordered to face to the right & advance up to a piece of woods on the right. The order was obeyed. The Col. rode at the time opposite the 3d company of which I had command. While we were advancing another [company] gave way & Col. Meyer endeavored to rally them. The only proof of excitement I saw about the Col. that day was that he swore — which was not customary with him. He stood there until we were overpowered. ..."[39]

Doles' musketry ripped through the 107th's ranks. Within a few minutes seven officers went

Captain Augustus Vignos of Company H, 107th Ohio, hailed from the Stark County village of Louisville. A gunshot wound to his right arm necessitated amputation by 25th Ohio assistant surgeon Eli Wilson. In spite of the disability, Vignos was promoted to major.

Brad L. Pruden Collection

Captain Barnet T. Steiner of Company D, 107th Ohio, wrote a week after the battle that "I was Shot in the left Shoulder blade[,] the ball lodging in my breast where it still is and will likely remain." By month's end the 24-year-old teacher was back home in Canton, where he died August 15. After the war G.A.R. Post 511 at Pierce, Ohio, was given his name.

down, two with shell wounds and five shot in the arms or shoulders. Four were company commanders. Captain Augustus Vignos of Company H, a Stark County hotelkeeper, lost his right arm. Company D's captain, Barnet T. Steiner of Canton, took a minié ball in the left shoulder that stopped in his chest. Steiner's first sergeant, a corporal and six privates received wounds, two were killed and five taken prisoner. Captain Anton Peterson of Company G was captured, but in the confusion managed to escape. Lieutenant Colonel Mueller and Adjutant Peter F. Young had their horses killed beneath them. While waving his sword to encourage the 107th's left wing, Mueller's right forearm was shattered by a bullet. Thirty others in the regiment were killed or mortally wounded. One of these was John Kratz, the Company C private from Wooster who never seemed to have enough paper to write letters home. He was shot dead in the middle of the 107th's crumbling line.[40]

An even larger percentage of the 25th Ohio was being whittled away. Converging fire from Doles' left and Gordon's right carved large swaths in the Buckeyes' battle line, killing a dozen men outright and wounding Lieutenant Colonel Williams. The regiment's Sandusky County company, E, was hit especially hard. Ten privates were wounded and two killed. Three sergeants — Alexander Pemberton, Vincent Carroll and Charles Ladd — sustained limb wounds, which cost Carroll his left arm. Ladd suffered amputation of his right leg, from which he subsequently died. First Sergeant Elisha Biggerstaff was captured during a few moments of hand-to-hand fighting. Gordon's Georgians, wrote the 25th's commander, "were in such close conflict with the regiment ... that the flag-bearers struck each other with their flag-staffs." Unable to escape the frenzied melee, Williams, too, was compelled to sur-

Private John Kratz, Company C, 107th Ohio, was killed July 1.

Ron Chojnacki Collection

The 25th Ohio's wounded casualties included Corporals Michael Murray, Company A, and Zachariah Dailey, Company I, a Monroe County carpenter. The Irish-born Murray farmed in Belmont County and ended the war as captain of Company E.

Below: First Sergeant Joseph B. Alter, Company A, 75th Ohio, was felled by a bullet to the left thigh. A resident of Springdale in Hamilton County, he was a Mississippi native. Alter was promoted Company F's captain in 1864 and that summer was captured near Gainesville, Florida. He endured seven months' confinement at Camp Asylum in South Carolina. Carte de visite by Winder's Sky-Light Gallery, Cincinnati.

Gary Delscamp Collection

Corporal Michael Murray.

Dennis Keesee Collection

Corporal Zachariah Dailey.

Tony Lemut Collection

render. Captain Nathaniel Manning of Company K took over, but within minutes the Monroe County attorney was shot in the right thigh. He relinquished command of the regiment to Company H's second lieutenant, William Maloney.[41]

The 25th and Meyer's 107th teetered on the verge of complete breakdown. Seeing this, General Ames ordered the 17th Connecticut and 75th Ohio to move up from their reserve positions and check the Rebel onrush. Six companies of the 17th (the other four had retired from their skirmishing east of Rock Creek) under Lieutenant Colonel Douglas Fowler charged over the knoll's slope to the right of the 25th Ohio. They instantly met fleeing refugees from von Gilsa's brigade, followed by a sheet of withering Rebel musket fire, and recoiled. Among the first killed was Fowler, his head partially blown off by an exploding shell.[42]

"Fix bayonets!" shouted Colonel Harris to the 75th, whose slim numbers were intended to plug an interval between the 25th and 107th Ohio. "We passed to the front as ordered ... into the thin woods in front," he explained. "It was a fearful advance and made at a dreadful cost of life. We could go no farther, halted and opened fire. The enemy was close and still advancing. We checked them in our immediate front, but they continued to press on around both flanks. Our situation was perilous in the extreme." Twenty-year-old William Southerton, Company B, likened his falling comrades to cornstalks being scythed on his Athens County farm. "How frantically we gnawed paper from cartridges and loaded rifles," he wrote. "Confederates were closing in on all sides, and fast. What a horrible roar of battle! Smoke and fumes thick and acrid. One could scarcely see the [man] beside him. Casualties were terrible. Oh, so many were killed or wounded. ..." His good friend Sergeant Charles H. Deshler was shot below the knee. A few yards away Second Lieutenant George A. Russell grimaced with a smashed shin.[43]

When Company G's second lieutenant, Alonzo Ford, also went down with a ball in his left leg, First Sergeant Emanuel M. Shultz assumed command. Shultz, 30, had been born in Adams County, Pennsylvania, just a few miles from the conflict raging at Blocher's Knoll. Prior to the war he moved to Ohio, and was employed as a millwright in Dayton upon enlistment there in October 1861. His tenure as company commander was short-lived. Pierced through the body by a minié, Shultz collapsed lifeless at the feet of his men. He later was buried in St. John's Lutheran Church cemetery at Fairfield, Pennsylvania.[44]

Colonel Harris was appalled by the heavy losses his regiment was sustaining. "Without orders, I hesitated to fall back but it was soon evident that we could not stay in our exposed condition." Half his officers were dead or wounded, as was a third of the non-commissioned officers and privates. No longer content to wait for Ames' approval, he ordered the 75th to fall back.[45]

"We were overpowered by numbers," Company G sergeant Alphonso C. Davis flatly stated. "Since the battle of Chancellorsville a great many of our boys had sworn never to run again, and the consequence was that nearly all that were not killed or wounded were taken prisoners." Davis, a Preble County native from West Alexandria, ducked behind a tree, deciding "to hold it as long as possible, thinking I would have plenty of time to get away. After firing three or four shots, I looked around for the regiment and found it was 30 or 40 yards in the rear of me. I determined to have one more shot and then skedaddle, but before I got my rifle loaded a Reb halloed to me, 'lay down that gun you Yankee ———, or I will shoot you.' He was so close that I could not get my gun loaded before he would have

Lieutenant Colonel Benjamin Morgan, 75th Ohio, as he appeared early in 1862 while captain of Company F. At Blocher's Knoll, he recalled, "the boys went in with a cheer but were met by overwhelming numbers [and] suffered considerable loss."

been on to me, or I should have learned him to use better language; but as it was, I had to surrender to the thief."[46]

The 75th only held its new position momentarily. The regiment's left wing, wrote Lieutenant Colonel Benjamin Morgan, "began to waver when I went to the front to rally once again. I there received a shot in the left shoulder, penetrating through the left breast, but I still continued on my feet and endeavored to rally without hope. The Regiment gave way and I faltered until from loss of blood I was obliged to halt and lay down. I was soon surrounded by the enemy. ..."[47]

Born December 16, 1823 in Sussex, England,

Morgan had gone to sea as a 12-year-old cabin boy. He sailed aboard various vessels for 13 years, receiving an honorable discharge in 1849 as chief mate of the U.S. cutter *Duane*. For two years he traveled through the Mississippi, Ohio and Miami river valleys, eventually settling in Franklin, Ohio, where he married and became an American citizen. After the war began he recruited 76 men from Warren County for the "Franklin Grays," later designated Company F, 75th Ohio. Morgan was elected captain. He commanded the company in 1862's Shenandoah Valley campaign, at Second Bull Run and at Chancellorsville. He was commissioned lieutenant colonel just two weeks before the regiment's fruitless charge at Gettysburg.[48]

Morgan was passed by the whooping Southern battle line. "I now suffered excruciating agony, being in a very exposed position, shot and shell tearing and cutting all around. I managed to get to my feet and staggered back about ten paces. Still feeling my position very exposed, after resting awhile I got to my feet again and contrived to reach a safer place behind a large Oak tree. On my first move I was accosted by a Rebel who asked me for my pistol. I told him to take it; he thanked me and went on. My sword was knocked out of my hand by [a piece of] shell or ball previous to my being wounded. I was now accosted by a very fine young man whom I asked for water. He said he would get me some but hinted something about my belt and scabbard.

I told him to get me a canteen of water and he could have them. He soon returned and we made the exchange. Suffering considerably with thirst I thought *just then* I had made a good trade. By and by our men taken prisoners by the Rebs were marched to the rear." Among the captives were two members of Morgan's old Company F, who shook the lieutenant colonel's hands in farewell, convinced he could not survive. Private Joseph I. Gustin revealed Morgan's identity to a Confederate officer, and was told to remain behind to care for him. At sundown, four gray-clad soldiers conveyed Morgan by stretcher across Rock Creek to Josiah Benner's farmhouse, where General Barlow lay grievously wounded.[49]

Reduced drastically in numbers the 75th Ohio fell back obstinately toward the Almshouse, covering its brigade's retreat in extended skirmish order. Although heavy Rebel fire still was directed his way, Harris reported casualties were "slight" during the withdrawal.[50]

By this time Ames knew Barlow was wounded and assumed command of the 1st Division. He may have received the news from Captain Charles P. Wickham, a staff officer detailed from the 55th Ohio, as aides Lieutenant John Wood had suffered an arm wound and Captain William L. Hubbell, 17th Connecticut, was a prisoner. Acting Ames' aide Captain Nathaniel Haughton of Company A, 25th Ohio, was wounded as well, a ball gouging flesh from his right arm. Bandaged at the Almshouse,

Captain Charles P. Wickham, Company I, 55th Ohio, *far left,* and Captain Nathaniel Haughton, Company A, 25th Ohio, served respectively on Barlow's and Ames' staffs at Gettysburg. Both men later were promoted field grade officers, as illustrated here. Haughton, of Toledo, was wounded July 1 in the right arm. As a teenager, Wickham worked in the printing room of the *Norwalk Reflector.* He graduated from the Cincinnati Law School in 1858.

Haughton continued at his post through the next day.[51]

By seniority, Colonel Meyer was next in line on the field for 2nd Brigade command. But Ames instead told Harris to take over, later claiming "he was the only regimental commander I saw there doing his duty properly." It could have been a move made from expediency, for Ames reported that the "whole division was falling back with little or no regularity, regimental organizations having become destroyed." On the other hand, the general's initial impression of Meyer at Blocher's Knoll was bad. Perceiving the Ohio colonel's stooping in the saddle and shrill, "improper" manner of vocalizing commands to be "cowardly," the new division commander simply did not like him. Any confidence Ames may have had in Meyer evaporated near the Almshouse. The 107th's adjutant, Peter Young, "attracted my attention by his coolness and bravery" while rallying a squad of men with the regiment's marker flags along the Harrisburg Road. Meyer, however, was nowhere to be seen, and Ames mistakenly assumed the colonel was among the routed troops running toward Gettysburg. In reality, Meyer was on the far side of the Almshouse barn collecting some 50 to 75 members of his regiment in an attempt to form a line. Unaware of the effort, Ames transferred the brigade to Harris. He would deal with Meyer later.[52]

The 1st Division's disintegration seriously jeopardized the right of Schimmelfennig's 3rd Division. Before the defense of Blocher's Knoll wilted, General Schurz dispatched Krzyzanowski's brigade to support Barlow's (Ames') left flank. Moving in column of divisions, the Polish colonel's four regiments had just thrown down a fence on the east side of the Carlisle Road when the 1st Division broke. Confederate cannons shifted their fire to Krzyzanowski's solid formation, tearing out large gaps. "The enemy's batteries completely swept the plain from two or three directions," related Captain Alfred Lee of the 82nd Ohio. "The shells and shot howled, shrieked and plunged through the air like infuriated demons. There was no shelter, not even a stump or tree. Now a huge iron nugget plowed its way through the living mass, leaving in its track eight poor fellows torn and bleeding. The deadly 'thug,' and a submissive groan or two is all that is heard. Again and again the jagged fragments of iron sweep destructively through the ranks, but there is no wavering. ..."[53]

Colonel Wladimir Krzyzanowski commanded the 2nd Brigade of the 11th Corps' 3rd Division. Nicknamed "Kriz" by many Ohioans who had trouble pronouncing his name, the Polish officer observed that his troops, once engaged north of Gettysburg, "were sweaty, blackened by the gunpowder, and ... looked more like animals than human beings." A hard fall from his horse temporarily incapacitated Krzyzanowski, though he refused to leave the field for treatment.

Lieutenant Colonel David Thomson informed his daughter that "Several of our boys were torn to tatters, their blood and flesh scattered over their comrades. My boots have two holes and my coat torn by a shell. Our sergeant major [Jasper Snow] of Patterson had the most miraculous escape. About one half of a large shell struck his cheek just scratching it from the temple to the chin, cutting his ear and the side of his neck. That side swelled up immediately as though he had the mumps. ..."[54]

Captain Lee estimated three or four minutes passed when Gordon's Georgians appeared from the Rock Creek ravine. Doles' troops, from the Ohioan's viewpoint, approached further to the left. "As they came up out of the willows their serried muskets dazzled ... and their banners seemed to

These two unidentified 82nd Ohioans epitomized what a majority of Buckeye soldiers looked like upon entering the battle. Private Daniel Zachman of the 82nd's Company D succinctly condensed the regiment's July 1 action in his diary: "We reached Gettisburg and hat a hart fight. We lost about half our Regt."

out waiting for a response, Layton leveled his Enfield and discharged it. "By common impulse," Lee continued, "the whole line immediately delivered its fire, and the reverberations of the cannon were drowned by the volleys of musketry, which roared across the meadow. The enemy's musketry responded instantly to our own, and the combatants, standing like duelists, scarcely more than seventy-five yards apart, blazed away into each other's faces. Not many minutes elapsed before the ground was strewn with arms and accoutrements, with the bodies of the wounded and the dead." Sergeant Layton was among the former, his right thigh ripped open by a musket ball.[56]

During the brigade's deployment, Colonel Robinson discovered he had advanced the 82nd into a cornfield some distance beyond the left flank of the 75th Pennsylvania. Just as he noticed the error, his horse was killed beneath him. "I gave the command to fall back slowly, loading and firing at will. As I reached the line of battle on my right Colonel Francis Mahler, commanding the Seventy-fifth Pennsylvania Regiment, fell by my side, mortally wounded. Colonel Krzyzanowski, the brigade commander, had been disabled by being thrown from his horse in the early part of the engagement. By these two casualties I became the senior officer of the brigade and [temporarily assumed] its command."[57]

The 35-year-old Robinson had been in the ser-

flaunt an audacious challenge. On they came, one line after another in beautiful array, while our own line with equal steadiness advanced from the opposite direction. Soon the combatants were close enough almost to read the names on each other's battle-flags." Krzyzanowski's brigade transformed into battle line. The massed column unfolded, from left to right: 82nd Ohio, 75th Pennsylvania, 119th New York, 26th Wisconsin and two companies of the 58th New York.[55]

No order had yet been given to fire, claimed Lee. His first sergeant, William C. Layton, implored the captain, "Let me shoot that color-bearer." With-

vice since April 1861, enlisting as a private in the 4th Ohio Infantry's three-month organization. That fall he helped recruit the 82nd Ohio and was appointed its major. Following the battles of McDowell, Cross Keys and Cedar Mountain, he was promoted regimental commander after the death of Colonel James Cantwell at Groveton, Virginia, on August 29, 1862. Robinson was a native of Richland County, but had made Kenton, Ohio, his home since December 1847. By war's outbreak he was owner/ editor of *The Hardin County Republican,* and brought to the 82nd a principled sense of the newspaper's motto, "Be just, and fear not."[58]

Like Robinson, all of the 82nd's field officers were unhorsed. Thomson's mount "Charly" was shot three times before it collapsed, momentarily pinning one of the lieutenant colonel's legs. Adjutant Stowel Burnham received a hand wound, but insisted on remaining when told by Thomson to go to the rear. Then a ball drilled through one of his thighs, knocking Burnham from the saddle. His frightened horse was killed as it galloped away. The lieutenant regained his feet and attempted to leave the field, only to be struck in the arm and finally in the lower back. He sank to the ground.[59]

Surviving enlisted men of the 82nd Ohio were so impressed by Lieutenant Colonel David Thomson's "coolness and courage" at Gettysburg that, two months later, four resolutions extolling his conduct were drafted for newspaper publication. They also pooled money to buy him an engraved sword with solid silver scabbard. Following its presentation on September 5, Thomson wrote his children: "The whole thing is truly elegant & ... was a great surprise. I will send it home soon. It is too costly & fine for the field. It is regarded here by officers of the army a perfect beauty."

Hardin County Historical Museum

Major James S. Crall, 82nd Ohio.

Thomson, now commanding the regiment, observed that the 82nd's left wing was bent at an angle much closer to the enemy than the right. Wishing to correct alignment, he noticed Major James S. Crall standing by his unwounded horse behind the regiment's center. Thomson sprinted over, ordering the major "to mount and look to the line." Crall replied that he could not control the animal. Without argument, Thomson grabbed the reins, heaved himself into Crall's saddle and rode forward to straighten his fast-dissolving ranks. While doing so he heard Robinson bellow commands for the embattled brigade to fall back.[60]

Major August Ledig, who succeeded Mahler in command of the 75th Pennsylvania, claimed in his after-action report that the 82nd Ohio, to his left, "was flanked, and gave way." Years later, Thomson firmly denied Ledig's assertion. "I was constantly on horseback along the line. I was not dismounted more than a minute hence I did not loose [*sic*] sight of the line. By the time I arrived at the left with orders to retire as stated the enemy was very near, and in repassing a fence we lost heavily in killed, wounded & prisoners. Yet our regiment did not fall back except upon the order to do so." Captain Lee, understandably, echoed Thomson's defense. "I remember distinctly seeing the troops upon our right going back before the 82d began to withdraw. This is, of course, at variance with Major Ledig's statement. ... We might, with more propriety say the 75th Pa., on our right was flanked and gave way. The truth is the whole line, Division, was 'flanked and gave way,' and the position was one which no troops in the world, of equal numbers, could have held."[61]

Robinson recalled, "From this point we were gradually being pressed back by the power of overwhelming numbers. The men stubbornly contested every inch of ground. Our position was in every respect untenable. We were not permitted even to build a temporary barricade out of the numerous fence rails that incumbered our movements." The 44th and 4th Georgia regiments of Doles' brigade were closest to the 82nd, and their well-aimed volleys blasted the Buckeyes from northcentral Ohio. Seventy percent of the 258 officers and men present were killed, wounded or captured. The regiment's officer cadre was decimated, losing 19 of 22 — a third of them dead or mortally wounded. One of these was Captain William Mitchell of Company H, whose credo "No man goes until his time comes" proved painfully true. Badly wounded in the chest, the 42-year-old Union Countian lingered three weeks at the Henry Comfort house on Gettysburg's Baltimore Street before succumbing, his wife at his side. A volunteer nurse rooming across the street related that "the Captain's wife [was] in spasms all day. It was pitiful to witness the efforts at consolation made by her son, a little fellow in uniform. ..."[62]

Six men from Captain Lee's Company E were dead or dying, six were wounded and another seven soon found themselves prisoners.[63]   In a vivid account published on the battle's 20th anniversary, Lee wrote:

The enemy did not venture to charge, but maintained a severe fire, to which our response in the act of falling back was necessarily feeble. Forgetful that I had in my belt a good revolver, with five good loads in it, I picked up

a musket and asked a soldier for a cartridge. He gave me one, remarking as he did so that he did not think it would "go," as his ammunition had been dampened by the [morning] rain.

My next impulse was to load the musket and get at least one parting shot at the enemy. While I was thus engaged, a stalwart young fellow dropped at my side, and cried, "Oh, help me!" Having taken my hand, he struggled to rise, but could not, and, finding his efforts unavailing, murmured, "Oh, I'm gone! just leave me here." A moment or two later I too felt the sting of a bullet, and fell benumbed with pain. It was an instantaneous metamorphosis from strength and vigor to utter helplessness. The man nearest me, being called to for assistance, replied by a convulsive grasp at the spot where a bullet that instant

Courtesy of Jean Jolly

Captain William D.W. Mitchell, Company H, 82nd Ohio, died in the presence of his wife and son on July 22. Amidst a large gathering of mourners and music provided by the Marysville Band, he was buried August 3 in the cemetery at Summersville, Ohio. Early in the war Mitchell served four months as a lieutenant in the 13th Ohio Infantry.

Of the three 82nd Ohio enlisted men at right, two were July 1 casualties. Company G corporal Mathew G. Miller of New Bloomington, Ohio, was shot in the upper right hip. Private Philip Winslow, a Hardin County farmer belonging to Company G, was taken prisoner but paroled within eight weeks of the battle. He later was wounded at Resaca, Georgia, in May 1864. The third soldier, Private J.M. Harmon of Company F, escaped unharmed.

Left: Following amputation of his right leg above the knee, First Sergeant Henry Seas of Company D, 82nd Ohio, died July 17. The Stark County native had been a teacher prior to his November 1861 enlistment at Marion.

struck him. He passed on, limping as he went, and in a few minutes more the last blue blouse had disappeared, and the field swarmed with gray Confederates.

The musketry-firing having slackened, the enemy's line of battle now came forward in fine style, preceded by skirmishers. The crimson flags were flaunted more impudently than ever, and the entire Confederate force breathed exultation and defiance. Some of the victors seemed disposed to be even savage. A wounded man lying near me, who had raised himself on his elbow, probably to get an easier posture, was assailed with a volley of curses by a stalwart soldier in gray, who ordered him to lie down instantly, on pain of being shot dead. The soldier held his musket at a ready, evidently intending to execute his threat if not summarily obeyed.

The rebel skirmish-line now passed me, and one of the skirmishers, a gentle-faced young man, came near. He had obtained the sword of a Union officer, and carried it

swinging to the belt which was thrown over his neck. To the inquiry whether the Union wounded were going to be molested, he replied, "No, you need not be afraid. Ten minutes ago I would have shot you in a minute; but now that you are a prisoner you shall not be disturbed. Have you any arms?"

"Yes, a revolver."

"Well, I must take that." And, so saying, he stripped the weapon from [my] belt, and went on.[64]

Three-fourths of the 11th Corps' infantry north of Gettysburg were withdrawing toward town, leaving the 3rd Division's 1st Brigade practically alone to resist the onslaught. Most of these troops still were on the skirmish line or supporting the batteries of Dilger and Wheeler. In an attempt to thwart Doles, Schimmelfennig ordered forward his last re-

Corporal Ephraim Shellenberger.

Second Lieutenant James H. Bell.

Second Lieutenant James H. Bell, Corporal Ephraim Shellenberger and Private George Ackerman served in the 61st Ohio's Company D, which was recruited primarily from Cuyahoga County. Bell, a resident of Columbiana, Ohio, was slightly wounded July 1. He lost his left leg a year later at Peachtree Creek, Georgia. Ackerman was photographed in the Warren studio of C.C. Taylor.

Private George Ackerman.

serve, Colonel Philip Brown's 157th New York, to attack the Georgian's exposed right flank. Brown's men started from the rear of Dilger's guns, recalled a member of Company G, when someone yelled "Battalion, halt!" The artillerists "were shouting and Co. G were wondering why they were being taken through a battery while it was firing. 'About face!' [We] returned and moved to the left of the battery and then forward down the slope, the boys of Battery I firing over [our] heads." Two hundred yards beyond Dilger the New Yorkers wheeled in a right oblique, advancing at the command "Charge bayonets!" until they were 300 feet from their opponents. "Then the fighting began. It was murderous while it lasted — only about twenty minutes." In that short span Brown's regiment was shattered, losing 307 of 409 officers and men. He ordered a retreat, his staggered survivors mixing with portions of the rest of Colonel George von Amsberg's brigade.[65]

A hopeless situation faced Schimmelfennig's Federals remaining in the fields between the Mummasburg and Carlisle roads. Those to their right had been crushed and now, approaching 4 p.m., the 1st Corps line to the left along Oak and Seminary ridges also began unraveling. Common sense and survival instinct dictated it was time to leave.

Colonel McGroarty's 61st Ohio skirmishers, still in the vicinity of Dilger, disengaged and withdrew at first in relatively good order. Amazingly, only one man, Corporal Aristarches H. Williams of

Company D, had been killed on the skirmish line. But as the retreat progressed, enfilading fire from the right dropped a number of men with wounds, and a dozen were forced to surrender. A bullet hit Company D's first lieutenant Edmund V. Brent in the left wrist, passing up the Mount Vernon native's arm and exiting at the bicep. Second Lieutenant James H. Bell of the same company also was wounded, though slightly. Captain Henry R. Bending of Company I and Second Lieutenant Joseph R. Mell, Company F, were made prisoners. A pre-war machinist from Circleville, Bending spent the next 18 months in captivity. Mell, an artist born in Milton, Ohio, endured imprisonment at Richmond, Danville and Macon until March 1865, part of the time afflicted with dysentery.[66]

Dilger and Wheeler stuck to their guns, facing envelopment. According to Wheeler, "We held our position until the rebs had got almost in our rear,

when we withdrew … to another position on the road, where we fired a few more canisters and then retired. …" Using the same tactics he employed at Chancellorsville, Dilger covered Schimmelfennig's retreat by retiring two sections from each battery in leapfrog fashion. Peppering their pursuers with loads of canister, the artillerymen brought their pieces back by prolonge [ropes], stopped, fired and repeated the process several times before reaching a stone bridge spanning Stevens' Run near Pennsylvania College. A last dose of canister was unleashed, then the guns crossed the bridge and re-entered Gettysburg via Washington Street. Leonidas Jewett of the 61st commented, "The gallant Captain Dilger, with his Ohio Battery, won the admiration of all of us."[67]

To the northeast, Ames' final resistance at the Almshouse was snuffed by Gordon's Georgians, who triumphantly bagged scores of prisoners. Some of

Brad L. Pruden Collection

Above: Second Lieutenant Joseph R. Mell, Company F, 61st Ohio, wore a 20th Corps badge on his frock coat when this portrait was made in late spring or summer 1865, probably in Columbus. *Right:* Captain Henry R. Bending, Company I. Carte de visite by M.K. Marshall Photographer, Circleville.

Karl Sundstrom Collection

these were wounded men and their medical attendants, including Surgeon Charles L. Wilson and Assistant Surgeon Daniel B. Wren of the 75th Ohio. Wren's decision to stay behind with the injured cost him four months' confinement in Libby Prison.[68]

By General Early's directive, the Georgians halted. A fresh Federal battle line had made its appearance in Gettysburg's northeastern outskirts, threatening Gordon's left. The Yankees belonged to Colonel Charles R. Coster's brigade of von Steinwehr's 2nd Division, which occupied Howard's reserve position on Cemetery Hill. Coster's arrival represented the belated reinforcements Schurz anxiously requested earlier, but they proved to be too little too late. Bearing down on Coster's New Yorkers and Pennsylvanians were the Louisianans and North Carolinians of Harry Hays' and Avery's brigades, ordered forward by Early.[69]

Three of Coster's four regiments were arrayed in a brickyard east of Stratton Street. To their left between the Carlisle and Harrisburg roads, Captain Lewis Heckman unlimbered the four Napoleon smoothbores belonging to Battery K, 1st OVLA. His 12-pounders, presumably, were rushed through town from Cemetery Hill in response to Barlow's previous plea for additional cannon support. The 11th Corps' artillery chief, Major Osborn, avowed that Heckman "was not ordered in until the corps had begun to fall back. He was then put into position, with a view of holding the enemy in check until the corps had time to retire through the town to [Cemetery] hill beyond. ..." As the crews loaded their gun tubes, Heckman discovered Hays and Avery already were in easy range of Second Lieutenant Charles M. Schiely's right section. Angled slightly to Schiely's left rear were Second Lieutenant Columbus Rodamour's two guns. The Ohioans immediately opened fire.[70]

"We commenced giving them our best wishes in the shape of shell and canister, which mowed them down like wheat," wrote battery quartermaster sergeant Cecil C. Reed, a 20-year-old Clevelander. "But on they came, closing up their ranks wherever they were torn asunder by our shots, and they were not idle all the time either; they were pouring in their volleys with telling effect. Our men were falling fast and they were coming so close that some of their skirmishers were literally blown to pieces from the muzzles of our guns." These unfortunate Confederates doubtless belonged to Hays' brigade,

Detached from Company H, 55th Ohio, in January 1863, Private Marion G. Cross of Seneca County served at Gettysburg with Battery K, 1st OVLA.

approaching on a five-regiment front down and to either side of the Harrisburg Road. Hays reported the artillery fire his men endured was "unusually galling."[71]

Half the Louisianans and all of Avery's brigade smashed into Coster, buckling his flanks in brief but savage combat at the brickyard. Coster's losses totaled more than 575 with a high percentage taken prisoner. Those forced to flee headed for refuge in town, adding to the confusion building in Gettysburg's streets. While two of Avery's regiments dealt with their captives and regrouped, the 6th North Carolina pressed on in company with some of Hays' men, attracted by the tempting prize of Heckman's Napoleons. They had gotten "very close," the Ohio artillery captain reported, when he ordered both sections to limber and depart.[72] Sergeant Reed continued:

We found it would not be very healthy for us to remain, and we commenced making preparations for a retrograde movement; but when we came to move off the battery we found that one section [Schiely's] had lost nearly all their horses, so we had to abandon it, not however until the guns were well spiked and rendered unserviceable to the enemy. We finally came off with two guns and all [their] horses. Had it not been for Captain Heckman and his long experience as an artilleryman and an officer[,] I am afraid we might have lost some of the latter, but he had them far enough in the rear and so they

Second Lieutenant Charles M. Schiely, Battery K, 1st OVLA.

had time enough to get out. He said that he would rather give the rebels all his guns than to give them his ammunition at the present time.

I think there was quite an oversight in not sending us a support; if we had had one regiment there I think we could have got all our guns off. But we had to support ourselves the best we could. The boys used their revolvers with telling effect on the rebels. All of our officers' horses were shot from under them. Captain Heckman ran a very narrow escape; he had just dismounted when his favorite horse fell, pierced by two balls, but it was not long until he had the saddle off and was again mounted on a fresh horse. After he had got the battery off he rode back through the fire of the enemy to see if any of the boys were left on the field. We cannot compliment our Captain too highly for the interest he took in our welfare, and the daring deeds he performed that day will be long remembered by us.

The boys all stood to their posts like brave men, and not a man left his post until he was ordered to do so. We were under fire about one half hour. It was the warmest we ever experienced. The rebels fought desperately, and seemed very well pleased when they closed around our guns.[73]

With Lieutenant Rodamour's two guns extricated the Ohioans hastened back to Cemetery Hill, where Major Osborn complimented them. The battered Buckeyes then were ordered to the rear for rest. Out of action the remainder of the battle, Heckman tallied his casualties. Privates Lewis Opert of Cleveland and Charles Zeische of Cincinnati were dead. Of 10 wounded, Private Isaac Johnson and Lieutenant Schiely were injured worst. Johnson underwent amputation of his left leg at the thigh but died October 19. Schiely returned home to Cleveland July 13 with a gunshot wound in his left shoulder. He was discharged from service three months later. Private William H. Cobbledick, an Englishman by birth, sustained a hand wound but remained on duty. During Gettysburg's 50th battle anniversary reunion in 1913 he claimed, at age 90, to be the oldest Ohio veteran in attendance.[74]

Just south of where Heckman's two pieces were lost, the remnants of Krzyzanowski's brigade, partially under Colonel Robinson's acting command, filtered into Gettysburg. Lieutenant Colonel Thomson had just been told to move what was left of the 82nd Ohio through town, when a bullet plowed into Robinson's upper chest near the left shoulder. He was carried to the residence of two "maiden ladies" named McPherson, sisters of Edward McPherson,

U.S. deputy commissioner of internal revenue, whose farm west of Gettysburg was the scene of vicious 1st Corps' fighting on July 1. Robinson spent the night without medical attention lying on a kitchen floor.[75]

Outside, the streets, sidewalks, alleys and yard-lots were crammed with 11th Corps soldiers trying to elude pursuit. Although Captain Jewett of the 61st Ohio maintained for years that he never saw a more orderly retreat, many if not most regiments of the corps' 1st and 3rd divisions were fragmented and disorganized. Frightened animals hitched to army and civilian vehicles, their drivers swearing, compounded the confusion by creating traffic jams. Dead-end streets became traps for some. Others struggled along wounded, slowing able-bodied comrades. "If a man straggled he was certain to be captured," wrote Colonel Harris of the 75th Ohio, "and this was the case with many who were attempting to get off their wounded friends, and chose to die with them rather than leave them to the foe."[76]

Fifer Joseph Gillis and the 82nd Ohio's field musicians were assisting medical personnel at a Gettysburg dressing station. Gillis explained to his sister: "We the band, went to town to help with the wounded, and had not been there long till here comes the Yankees with the Rebs after them. My self and [Sylvanus] Young, a drummer, stepped out onto the pavement, and the Rebs said 'Halt, halt, you damn yankees.' Then I thought if they could catch me, why all right. Young and I jumped a little fence and into another street. Them after us full tilt. They got Young, but they could not get this chap. I dug out, skipping every other street till I was almost out of town." Gillis and two other 82nd soldiers he chanced to meet sprinted to safety. Drummer Young of Company K was not so fortun-

ate. The 23-year-old Ashland County farmer spent 12 weeks imprisoned at Richmond's Belle Isle, and died October 9 of pneumonia in the Confederate capital's General Hospital No. 21.[77]

Jacob Smith, 107th Ohio, drove an 11th Corps ambulance on July 1. From a "collecting point" at the southern edge of Gettysburg he had watched a portion of the 1st Corps' fight to the west, and noticed General Howard on Cemetery Hill scanning the surrounding terrain with field glasses. Near 4 p.m. Smith's squad was ordered to retrieve a load of wounded men. "Just as we reached the heart of the town on our way to the front, we encountered our forces falling back in confusion and disorder, filling the street so that it was an utter impossibility to make further progress forward, or to turn our teams about again. The enemy were close behind in

Private Joseph Chadwick, Company I, 82nd Ohio. Only one man from his company, Private Sidney Skinner of Delaware County, was killed July 1. Ten others were wounded, including brothers Lewis and Jacob Edelblute, who were shot in the face and left arm, respectively. Both were discharged as a result of their severe injuries.

hot pursuit." Smith recalled that "At this juncture the only way left for us to escape was to tear away a couple of panels of fence between two houses alongside of the street, and pass between the buildings, and then the other way up the back street. The fence was quickly removed, the wagons turned in and we passed through. The enemy were so near that in turning the corner back of the building more than half of the Ambulance men in our squad were captured. The enemy halted us, but I thought it my duty to get along as rapidly as possible, and by considerable effort and fast running I succeeded in getting out of their reach and inside our lines on Cemetery Hill."[78]

Lieutenant Culp, the 25th Ohio officer serving as an aide on Barlow's staff, made a hair-breadth escape of his own. Prior to Barlow's wounding he carried the general's request for additional artillery support to Howard. Culp was returning to the battlefield when he ran headlong into the retreat. "There was no organization, so far as I could see, and I sat upon my horse and saw thousands of soldiers pass." In the disorder he glimpsed a wounded captain of his regiment, probably Nathaniel Manning of Company K, clinging to a lamppost. "In caring for him, I discovered that I was liable to become a prisoner. I dashed up a street to find it absolutely blockaded with ambulances and abandoned wagons and caissons. I was still riding my horse, and too valuable a one to lose; besides, he had stood my friend in several hot places, and was reliable as steel. As a last resort, I rode up the steps of a veranda, opened the hall door and rode through the hall into a large sitting room in which the frightened family were gathered. I asked if there was a lane back of the lot I could get out through, and a young lady of perhaps 16 quickly opened the door, and requesting me to follow her tripped lightly through the house and to the back of the lot, where she commenced to let down some bars. Telling her not to mind [them], but get back and to the cellar as quickly as possible, I jumped my horse over the bars and just saved myself from a trip to Libby prison."[79]

Detached for division staff service at Gettysburg, Edward C. Culp was first lieutenant of Company F, 25th Ohio. By war's end he advanced to lieutenant colonel, but never mustered at that rank. He wrote a history of the 25th Ohio Veteran Volunteer Infantry, published in 1885.

Firelands Historical Society

William Southerton's salvation was owed to following implicitly his commander's orders. The 75th Ohio private recalled: "Giving the word to retreat, Colonel Harris led the way back through town. Confusion everywhere, and the Johnnies were right at our heels. Some of our boys took refuge in cellars when they were overtaken. Colonel Harris … was as anxious to get away as any of us. We were much like a parcel of schoolboys turned loose. The order was to follow Colonel Harris, stick close to him. Those who did made it through the town safely. And I was one of them. I was right at the colonel's heels."[80]

In Gettysburg's square, Colonel Meyer assembled about 100 officers and men of the 107th Ohio, apparently unaware that Harris had been placed in charge of Ames' brigade. Several members of the 107th later testified they heard various officers in the square say Meyer had command. According to Sergeant Major John Henry Brinker, the 17th Connecticut's adjutant "came up and said 'Col., you are the senior officer of the brigade' & asked if he should bring his men, and the Col. said he should." Meyer's own version was expressed two weeks later in a letter to the 11th Corps' chief of staff, Lieutenant Colonel Theodore A. Meysenburg. Meyer explained: "When we were ordered to fall back on the city I did so, without much confusion, although the first and second Brigades were considerably mixed up, & entered the streets together, closely followed by the ennemy [sic]. In the streets I collected my men together ready to take such position as might be directed, when some aid[e] came & directed me to take the command of the Brigade as Senior Officer, Genl. Ames having assumed command of the division. I was about doing so, when immediately another aid[e] came & directed me to turn over the command of my Regt. to the oldest Captain, & not to take the command of the Brigade, without assigning any reason for this extraordinary order."[81]

Perplexed and angry, Meyer sheathed his sword. Yet another messenger arrived and told him his men should be moved toward the town's southern edge. The colonel said Ames had ordered the 107th to the square, but the aide adamantly replied that *he* was ordering him to move. Meyer retorted icily, "If *you* have command, there is Capt. Weber. Let him take the men out." Without further comment, Captain Otto Weber of Company A shepherded those of the regiment in the square down Baltimore Street. Minutes later he was captured, the second time in two months. Colonel Meyer, accompanied by the 107th's bugler, Conrad F. Hornung, slipped away unmolested.[82]

The former prosecutor's problems had only begun. A "rabble of men" numbering in the hundreds milled about in the fields east of Cemetery Hill. On his own initiative, Meyer rode into the throng, revolver in hand, and attempted to restore order. Among others, he was assisted by Meysenburg and

Major Charles H. Howard, the general's younger brother and aide. Major Howard suggested to Meysenburg that the Ohio colonel be placed in command of the stragglers, and see to their return to the new 11th Corps positions then being organized and occupied. Meysenburg assented. When Meyer completed the task he sought out General Ames, asking him why he had been relieved. Ames answered that he would leave things as they were. His aide, Lieutenant Culp, claimed the general's response was far more emphatic. "I heard [Ames] say: 'Mr. Meyer, so long as I have a Sergeant left to command the Second Brigade your services will not be required. Your place is in the rear.'" Stunned, the hapless colonel took no further part in the battle, although he was allowed to "run loose," as Ames phrased it. On July 5 Meyer was arrested, charged by Ames with misbehavior in the presence of the enemy and cowardice. For two weeks he was "dragged along in the rear … like a culprit, to the scandal & mortification of my Regiment." After a week-long trial that ended August 2, Meyer was found not guilty of all charges and specifications. He resumed his sword and was ordered back to duty. The victory, however, proved hollow. Granted sick leave on August 11, his health was broken from the rigors of three exhausting campaigns. Then, in November, an examining board determined he did not possess sufficient knowledge of tactics and military administrative duties to qualify as a regimental commander. Faced with dismissal, Meyer resigned his commission February 8, 1864.[83]

Ron Chojnacki Collection

Second Lieutenant Samuel Miller.

Karl Sundstrom Collection

Captain William E. Scofield.

Second Lieutenant Samuel Miller, Company A, 107th Ohio, agreed with every surviving officer in the regiment that Colonel Meyer's conduct July 1 "was the same as on drill. There was nothing in his manner to discourage the men," as alleged by General Ames.

Captain William E. Scofield, Company A, 82nd Ohio, was the 11th Corps' assistant provost marshal at Gettysburg. The Marion native had this portrait made at Griswold & Howard's gallery in Columbus.

Karl Sundstrom Collection

Colonel Orland Smith, 73rd Ohio, commanded the 2nd Brigade, 2nd Division, 11th Corps. Born in Maine, he had resided in Ross County since 1852 and was an executive with the Marietta & Cincinnati Railroad. Carte de visite by F.A. Simonds, Chillicothe.

Anticipating a continuation of Confederate assaults, Federal commanders on Cemetery Hill rallied their men and established new defensive lines for the 11th and 1st corps' survivors. Corporal Frederick Nussbaum of the 107th Ohio recalled: "In the retreat General Howard did all he could to get the boys to rally again. He stopped near me while I was unloading a part of the contents of my knapsack ... and sabre in his only hand, he entreated the boys by yelling at the top of his voice, 'Rally Boys! Rally Boys! let us regain the name we lost at Chancellorsville.' " Howard and Schurz were joined by Major General Abner Doubleday, 1st Corps, and Major General Winfield S. Hancock, 2nd Corps, who was deputized by Meade to succeed Reynolds and Howard as left-wing commander, and represent him in his absence. Hancock reached the hill at the height of the retreat through town. In contrast to this disorder he noticed four regiments drawn up in battle line in Evergreen Cemetery, facing the enemy. It was Colonel Orland Smith's 2nd Brigade, von Stein-

wehr's division, composed of the 55th and 73rd Ohio, 136th New York and 33rd Massachusetts. Smith's troops that morning brought up the 11th Corps' rear and with Coster's brigade, prior to its mauling at the brickyard, had occupied Cemetery Hill as a reserve. Before meeting with General Howard to discuss the situation, Hancock paid the 2nd Brigade a short visit. Smith related: "He immediately rode along my lines and complimented the men and the dispositions. He saw Captain [John D.] Madeira and inquired who commanded [the] brigade. On being told, he desired to see me. I was called and introduced. Said he: 'My corps is on the way, but will not be here in time. This position should be held at all hazards. Now, Colonel, can you hold it?' Said I, 'I think I can.' 'Will you hold it?' 'I will.' " Private Andrew F. Sweetland of the 55th Ohio watched the interview from 20 feet away and remembered that "Hancock turned to the regiment, threw up one arm full length, and said in a strong, firm voice: 'Gentlemen, I want you to hold this line if all hell comes.' We threw up our caps and shouted: 'We will, General.' " [84]

Schurz, who spoke with Hancock shortly afterward, thought his timely arrival was especially inspirational to the defeated troops. "They all knew him by fame, and his stalwart figure, his proud mien, and his superb soldierly bearing seemed to verify all the things that fame had told about him. His mere presence was a reinforcement, and everybody on the field felt stronger for his being there." [85]

Orland Smith's men, wrote Major Samuel Hurst of the 73rd Ohio, "rested for a little while in the quiet cemetery on the hill, where the villagers of Gettysburg had buried their dead, and adorned their resting places with tasteful memorials. It was a solemn place to rest and reflect before going into battle." George Metcalf, the Medina County private serving in the 136th New York, had no previous

The Evergreen Cemetery brick gatehouse, surrounded by Union artillery pieces, horses, limbers and caissons. Based on a sketch by wartime artist Edwin Forbes, the view looks northeast.

battle experience. With his comrades he loaded and capped his rifle, "and one man out of every twelve was sent with the canteens of the others for water. We stood here amid the tombs of the dead awaiting orders. The dullest could see that danger was on every hand." Musician Henry Henney of the 55th Ohio noted in his journal that the artillery being emplaced on the hill "drove into the burial ground, crushing over tombstones and graves regardless of everything but the supreme necessity of getting their guns into position to open fire upon the Rebel renegades. ..." Dilger's was one of these batteries. His Buckeyes dropped their Napoleons' trails just west of the Baltimore Pike near Evergreen Cemetery's brick gatehouse.[86]

In general terms, the 11th Corps' infantry was disposed in an arc curving around Cemetery Hill from the northwest to the northeast. Smith's brigade eventually took position near the Taneytown Road and a section of the Emmitsburg Road northwest of the hill's crest. There were numerous rail and low stone fences in the area, and an apple orchard, which provided a modicum of cover. The 55th

Ohio was stationed on the brigade's right, its center facing the two roads' intersection. The right-wing companies had a partial view up Washington Street past scattered buildings, including the old Dobbin house and a barn on the south edge of town. To the 55th's left was the 73rd Ohio along the Taneytown Road, then the 136th New York and 33rd Massachusetts. During the forenoon of July 2 the latter regiment was detached and shifted to the east side of the Baltimore Pike, where it stayed for the battle's duration. Excluding the 33rd, Smith's line, resting under the cannon muzzles atop the hill's summit to its rear, numbered 1,147 officers and men. The 55th Ohio, 327 strong, was commanded by Colonel Charles Gambee of Bellevue and represented Huron, Erie, Seneca and Wyandot counties. The 73rd was led by Lieutenant Colonel Richard Long. A majority of its 338 effectives were Ross County farmers, but it also contained volunteers from Pike, Pickaway, Fayette, Highland, Hocking, Vinton, Jackson and Athens counties.[87]

Both regiments, as well as the 136th New York, threw out skirmishers. Bullets began zipping by and the Ohioans quickly discovered the shots emanated from fields to the front and buildings in Gettysburg to their right. Sporadic at first, this skirmish fire escalated seriously over the next two days. Several in the 73rd Ohio were wounded on July 1, recorded Sergeant George W. Gephart of Company E. "We were exposed to the fire of the enemy's sharp-shooters from the town 'till after dark, when we were moved a short distance to the rear."[88]

Ames' division stretched out east of the Baltimore Pike, some of its thinned ranks on or near East Cemetery Hill's slope fronting a narrow, stone-walled road called Brickyard Lane [adjacent to present-day Wainwright Avenue]. Ames' far left, occupied by the 107th and 25th Ohio of Harris' brigade, bent back perpendicular to the lane along another stone fence running upslope to the pike. Skirmishers, mostly from the 17th Connecticut, ensconced themselves in vacant lots between Harris' main line and more fences to the north. From its low but protective barrier the 107th faced Gettysburg, observed Frederick Nussbaum. "My company, C, was ordered by Sergeant Major Brinker to go into the open field as pickets; as I was the only officer present (a Corporal) with eight men, and within easy stone's throw of the Rebels who were stationed in the houses, I positively refused to obey the order and remained behind the stone wall. We would all have been shot down had we obeyed the orders of the excited Sergeant Major." Adjutant Peter Young's calmer head prevailed. The regiment was under his temporary command since Young's "coolness and bravery" near the Almshouse had caught Ames' eye earlier. Prussian-born, the 23-year-old lieutenant was a Cleveland dry goods salesman prior to enlistment in August 1862. He reported eight officers and 171 enlisted men available to hold the 107th's section of wall, a sad reduction from its noontime strength of 458.[89]

Angled to the 25th Ohio's right the 75th Ohio prolonged Harris' brigade front near Brickyard

Lieutenant Colonel Richard Long, 73rd Ohio. Carte de visite by F.A. Simonds, Chillicothe.

Lane, facing northeast. Combined, his three Ohio regiments numbered 300 or fewer men. The 75th, however, received some welcome reinforcements between 5 and 6 p.m. when Captain Ben Fox of Company A arrived with part of the 103-man detachment sent reconnoitering toward Greencastle that morning. Fox's scouts were recalled within a few miles of Monterey Springs, Pennsylvania, backtracked to Emmitsburg and hurried on to Gettysburg. "Some of the men with me could not keep up as twas so hot and Rainy," he wrote a few days later.

Fox was stunned to see how badly the regiment was chewed up. He learned his company's first lieutenant, Thomas Wheeler, was dead. Lieutenant Colonel Morgan was missing. With no other field officers present Fox, 21, was placed in command of the 75th by Colonel Harris. The Hamilton County officer also was briefed by his division commander. "Genl Ames told us to hold the position at all hazards," Fox related. "Our boys said *they would.*"[90]

Behind Harris' Buckeyes on East Cemetery Hill's summit sat six 3-inch ordnance rifles belonging to Captain Michael Wiedrich's Battery I, 1st New York Light Artillery, composed of German-Americans principally from Buffalo. Wiedrich's cannoneers fortified their position by constructing earthen lunettes for each piece as protection from sharpshooter fire. Before nightfall the left section was shifted west across the Baltimore Pike, leaving Wiedrich with four guns on the hill. To his right front, connecting with the right flank of Harris' command, was the weakened brigade of von Gilsa.[91]

As occasional shells whirled overhead and Confederate sharpshooters began searching for targets, Ohioans on the hill contemplated the future. William Southerton was overjoyed to see the return of

Captain Fox's detachment. "It was good to have the old crowd back together. We felt more secure." At the same time he chided himself for having discarded his blouse, thrown away during the sultry morning somewhere along the Emmitsburg Road. "My clothing was damp with perspiration and dew. I was cold."[92]

Southerton's discomfort paled compared to that of comrades lying injured, most in enemy hands, on the battlefield north of town. From his own regiment Privates John Davis, Benjamin Hartley, Jonathan Laraba, Thomas O'Garra, Perry Taylor, Corporal John Allison, Sergeant Philip Shiplin and Captain Mahlon B. Briggs suffered from grievous wounds. All eventually died. Carried bleeding to Josiah Benner's farmhouse, the 75th's Benjamin Morgan was grateful to receive "every attention and kindness from the family." Still, he believed his shoulder and chest wound was mortal. Colonel Robinson of the 82nd Ohio refused to contemplate his own chest injury might kill him. Lacking any doctor's assistance he poured water into the wound, "which ran through [my] body like through a sieve." In later years Robinson was convinced this rudimentary self-treatment saved his life.[93]

The unidentified artilleryman at far left belonged to either Dilger's Ohio or Wiedrich's New York battery. Note brass "I" and numeral "1" with crossed-cannon artillery insignia affixed to the man's cap, as well as a large 11th Corps badge pinned to his vest. With reference to the corps' retreats at Chancellorsville and Gettysburg, the disparaging term "Running Half-Moons" was derived from the badge's distinctive crescent shape.

Alfred Lee laid almost six hours near the Carlisle Road, shot in the right hip. Fortunately, the ball missed hitting bone and the captain retained the limb. Surviving members of his company witnessing him fall supposed him killed, and his death erroneously was reported in the *Delaware Gazette*. Lee, using the pen name "A.T. Sechand," was a regular contributor to the newspaper, which eulogized him July 10 as a "young man of decided ability, a good soldier, and his whole heart enlisted in the cause for which he gave up his life." The *Gazette's* editor was astounded when, that same evening, Lee hobbled into Delaware's American Hotel. With pleasure a retraction was published in the next issue, a description of Lee's wound concluding with the sentence, "We congratulate the gallant Captain upon his escape from death and safe arrival among his friends." [94]

Several other 82nd Ohio officers were not so lucky. From where Lee had propped himself to watch Early's and Rodes' Confederates sweep by, "the whole field was strewn with the prostrate bodies of men in blue." Among them were the lifeless forms of Lieutenants Philander C. Meredith and Henry Jacoby. Meredith, the son of a Richland County judge, had been shot through the head. Like Lee, Captain John Costin of Company F took a ball in the hip, but died 10 days later in spite of regimental Surgeon Jacob Cantwell's care. [95]

A slight wound suffered July 1 by Captain William J. Dickson of Company B, 82nd Ohio, kept him from duty for three and a half weeks. He was killed the following May at Resaca, Georgia.

Bob Albertini Collection

Lee was deeply affected by the suffering of First Lieutenant Stowel Burnham, who was hit four times in the 82nd's fight with Doles' Georgians. Burnham, born December 13, 1837 in North Windham, Connecticut, had been visiting a married sister at Kenton, Ohio, when he enlisted as a private in November 1861. Promotions quickly followed, and in mid-May 1863 he was appointed the regiment's adjutant. As such, he and Lieutenant Colonel Thomson became tentmates. They also were, in Thomson's words, "confidants, counselling together, having congenial tastes and common interests. His was a happy spirit. ... Uninfluenced by personal danger, he was actuated by the desire alone to perform his duties with fidelity. At the battle of Gettysburg his acts were characterized by the highest de-

First Lieutenant Stowel Lincoln Burnham, adjutant of the 82nd Ohio. "In battle he quailed not at danger, and never shirked it," wrote close friend Alfred Lee in a letter to Burnham's brother-in-law, Lester T. Hunt, of Kenton. "Even while in the midst of his suffering, when the rebels were commiserating [with] him, and expressing their sorrow that he had been wounded in such a 'bad cause,' he mildly reproached them, and gave them to understand that all his sufferings and even death could not abate his love for his country, or his willingness to sacrifice all in her behalf. Adjutant Burnham died a hero whom all his comrades in arms might well envy, and whom we all delight to honor."

Richard W. Fink Collection

gree of heroism."[96] A month afterward Lee mournfully described his friend's last few hours of life:

I raised myself a little, and looking around saw Adjutant Burnham lying a few yards from me in the direction of the lane. I did not see him fall, but my impression is that he was struck near the corn-field, and that he was carried back by our men to where I now saw him. He too raised on his elbow. I spoke to him, and he gave me a look of recognition. After the rebel infantry moved off a rebel battery came trotting up towards where the adjutant and I were lying. They stopped close by us and unlimbered their guns, so that one of their caissons stood close by me. I asked the artillerymen to help me out of the way, as I supposed they were going to commence firing. They took hold of me and carried me over to the fence separating [a] clover-field from the wheat-field east of it. They took me through a gap in the fence into the wheat-field, and laid me close by the fence under a little bush. I then asked them to bring the adjutant and put him too in a place of safety. They were already doing so. They laid him close by me in the same fence-corner.

The adjutant was suffering intense agony. I asked him where he was wounded. He said "in the bowels." This was his mortal wound. He also had a severe wound in the thick part of one of his thumbs. I think he also had a wound in one of his legs, but I am not positive. The rebels were very kind to us. They gave us water and whiskey from their canteens, but the adjutant could not get any thing to stay in his stomach. As often as he drank any thing he vomited. My impression at this time was that he was not mortally wounded, or at least that he would live a few days. I tried to encourage him in this hope, but he insisted that he would die. He constantly groaned with agony, and kept exclaiming, "O, this is terrible, captain,

Captain Alfred E. Lee of Company E, 82nd Ohio, was shot in the right hip while attempting to load a musket he picked up near the Carlisle Road. On July 25 an attending physician in his adopted hometown of Delaware described Lee's wound in medical terms: "The ball entered over the middle of the dorsum of the ilium, and emerged in front a little below the anterior superior spinous process, passing in close proximity to the hip joint." The doctor thought Lee might be totally disabled, but the captain recovered to serve during the war's last 18 months as a brigade-level staff officer in the 11th and 20th corps, Army of the Cumberland. A Belmont County native and graduate of Ohio Wesleyan University, he later was appointed consul general to Frankfurt-am-Main and edited the *Ohio State Journal.*

this is terrible." Sometimes he seemed a little easier for a few minutes, yet he suffered so that I felt I ought not to disturb him by talking to him much. My own wound was also very painful, and I was much weakened by loss of blood.

A rebel cavalryman came to us [Private James O. Marks of Lynchburg, Virginia, a courier on General Early's staff]. He offered to do any thing for us he could. He helped me conceal my [field] glass so that it might not be stolen. He offered to get us a surgeon or an ambulance if he could. He told the adjutant that if he had any word or any valuables that he wished to send to his friends he would attend to it if he possibly could. The adjutant then gave him his watch, telling him he wished it sent to you, and giving him your name and address. ...

It was now sunset, and a glorious sunset it was. The adjutant saw the golden clouds, and manifested a desire to be raised up so that he could look at it "once more." Some one attempted to raise him, but he could not endure the pain. I now fell into a kind of dozing or stupor. I do not know how long I was in this condition. I was aroused by the cavalryman, who told me he had brought one of our own surgeons to see me. This surgeon looked at the adjutant, who was now quite still, and pronounced him dead. The announcement startled me. I had not expected him to die so soon. Yet he was dead — poor fellow. I think he died shortly after sundown.[97]

At the same time this pathetic incident was enacted north of town, to the south and southeast the rest of the Army of the Potomac moved toward Gettysburg. Portions of Major General Henry W. Slocum's 12th Corps and Major General Daniel E. Sickles' 3rd Corps, having the shortest distances to march, arrived about 7 p.m. The 12th Corps' 2nd Division, under Brigadier General John W. Geary, contained four seasoned Ohio regiments — the 5th, 7th, 29th and 66th — all in Colonel Charles Candy's 1st Brigade. Candy, a native Kentuckian born in 1832, was a 12-year army veteran with pre-war service as a non-commissioned officer in the 1st Dragoons and 1st U.S. Infantry. Residing in Columbus in 1861, he assisted organization of the state's earliest military units before accepting staff positions with Generals George B. McClellan and Frederick W. Lander. In November of that year he received the 66th Ohio's colonelcy, and was elevated to brigade command in August 1862. Following Chancellorsville he submitted his resignation, but for unknown reasons withdrew it a day or two later. Candy rode to Gettysburg suffering from lumbago and a sore left arm injured in a horse fall. His old

regiment, composed of men from Champaign, Delaware, Clark, Logan, Union and Marion counties, was led by Lieutenant Colonel Eugene Powell.[98]

Cincinnati was home to the 5th Ohio commanded by Colonel John Halliday Patrick, a 43-year-old Scottish tailor from Edinburgh who had resided in the Queen City since 1848. The 5th's previous battle honors included Port Republic, Cedar Mountain, Antietam and Chancellorsville. In its first major engagement March 23, 1862 at Kernstown, Virginia, the regiment lost five color bearers shot down in succession, their banners perforated with 58 bullet holes. The 7th Ohio, too, suffered heavily at Kernstown and again at Cedar Mountain, sustaining 180

Gary Delscamp Collection

Colonel Charles Candy, 66th Ohio, led a 12th Corps' brigade to Gettysburg. Officers and men of the 66th knew Candy as a strict disciplinarian well versed in drill. "With him there was no commanding by proxy," a subordinate remembered.

dead and wounded out of 307 engaged. Colonel William R. Creighton was hit twice, but recuperated to retake command prior to Chancellorsville. Known to many in the army as the "Roosters," Creighton's men hailed from Cuyahoga (three companies out of Cleveland), Erie, Lake, Lorain, Mahoning, Portage and Trumbull counties. One 12th Corps field officer, a New Yorker, regarded the 7th as "one of the finest regiments in the service ... and was composed of exceptionally good material. Its ranks included men of culture and good social position, clergymen, students, teachers, bankers, farmers and mechanics." The 29th Ohio, likewise, was recruited from the northeast part of the state, primarily representing Ashtabula, Summit, Lake and Geauga counties. Having no field officers available on July 1, the regiment was led to Gettysburg by Captain Wilbur F. Stevens of Company B.[99]

Candy's brigade, which also contained the 28th and 147th Pennsylvania, began the morning bivouacked a mile east of Littlestown. Its overnight stay was enlivened by town citizens, remembered an Ohio non-commissioned officer, who "met us with buckets of cool delicious water, and [were] exceedingly glad to see us there. They had been visited [June 30] by a Regiment of Confederate cavalry, that was soon driven away by our cavalry advance." The respite was much appreciated, he affirmed, "because we were among our friends and out of Rebeldom."[100]

The 12th Corps started leaving Littlestown at sunup, although William H.H. Tallman of the 66th Ohio stated his regiment did not move until 9 a.m. The route was along the Baltimore Pike via the tiny hamlet of Two Taverns, situated roughly halfway between Littlestown and Gettysburg. Tallman, a Delaware native and first sergeant of Company E,

Sergeant Major Lyman H. McAdams, *top,* and Corporal Charles G. Tallcott, Company D, 29th Ohio, were Summit County farmers. Once word reached the regiment near Two Taverns that heavy fighting was in progress at Gettysburg, Private Samuel W. Hart of Company H recalled: "Immediately the bugles sounded, and we knew what that meant. 'Fall in! Fall in!' came the sharp commands. We unstacked our guns and swiftly fell into line, and down the pike we 'double-quicked it,' all the way, about five miles, to the battle field."

Colonel John H. Patrick, 5th Ohio. In May 1864 at New Hope Church, Georgia, he was fatally wounded in the bowels while the regiment charged a masked Confederate battery.

noted that marching was leisurely and punctuated by frequent halts. At one roadside farmhouse "we squandered our shinplasters for soft bread, butter, apple butter, and a cheese the like of which I never smelled before. This cheese was made up in round balls … and broken open perfumed the air for rods around us. Then commenced a lively pelting of each other with the cheese balls and the odor in and around our company was dense enough to cut with a knife." Another diversion was witnessed by Private Henry J. Knapp when the 29th Ohio stopped near a stream. "Many of our boys stripped off their clothes and went swimming," he claimed.[101]

This probably occurred close to Two Taverns, where the Ohioans rested at midday for almost four hours. Tallman continued:

Up to this time we had heard no sound of battle in our front, but on this little stream the sound of the cannonading could be distinctly heard, and from the frequency of the reports we knew a big fight was on. Between three and four p.m. the order was given to *Fall in*. From the sound of the bugle at the head of the division we knew it meant *hurry up*. Knapsacks and cartridge boxes were soon in place and in almost the time required to write this sentence our Brig. was on the move. …

The men panted like dogs on the chase and sweltered through clouds of dust that came back from [a battery] in our front. The order was quick march and no halts, but once or twice a stop was made [so] that the horses of the artillery might not give out entirely. In about an hour we began to meet men[,] women & children on foot[,] on horseback[,] in buggies and wagons, all fleeing from the vicinity of the cemetery, and places this side. As usual the boys would have their joke at the expense of the able bodied citizens, and would say to them, "Oh come back; we are going to have lots of fun." "What are you going away from the picnic for." "Come go back and we'll show you how to cock a cannon," and like expressions. But in a few minutes we began to meet wounded men who were able to walk and were hastening to the rear where … they could have their hurts looked after. Then silence fell upon the ranks, except to inquire what troops were engaged

and which side had the best of the fight so far. We were on the Baltimore Pike, marching toward the cemetery, and we could see troops moving into position and batteries taking their places along the line. We turned off of the roads into the fields on our left and moved over near the base of Little Round Top, leaving quite a gap between us and the Corps on our right.[102]

Candy's men and Brigadier General George S. Greene's New York brigade ended their march on Cemetery Ridge north of Little Round Top at the direction of General Hancock, who told their division commander, Geary, that an imperative need existed just then for troops to hold the Federal left. Candy and Greene formed lines facing west with skirmishers pushed well forward. Near sundown, Candy was ordered by Geary to occupy Little Round Top with two regiments. He sent the 147th Pennsylvania and 5th Ohio, both under command of Colonel Patrick, to the boulder-covered hill to watch for any Confederate advance. None came. With darkness approaching everyone's spirits lifted when more reinforcements arrived — a 1st Corps brigade and the 3rd Corps' 1st Division — marching in along the Emmitsburg Road. Although relieved by Sickles' men, Candy and Greene bivouacked in place for the night.[103]

More substantial reinforcements were not far off. The 5th Corps, inherited by Major General George Sykes after Meade's elevation to army command, was east of Gettysburg between the villages of Bonnaughtown and McSherrystown. Sykes began the day at Union Mills, Maryland, with a 10-mile march to Hanover as his itinerary. There, with his men already in camp, he received orders from Meade summoning the corps toward Gettysburg. "We pushed on as rapidly as men could in a blazing July sun," wrote James Gildea of Gibbs' Battery L, 1st OVLA, "and marched all night with only one hour rest."[104]

The 2nd Corps was even closer. Starting from Uniontown, Maryland, at 7 a.m., it reached Taney-

town, site of Meade's headquarters, by 10 and was afforded several hours of rest. Early in the afternoon, as Hancock rode ahead to ascertain affairs at Gettysburg, the corps resumed its march, taking the narrow Taneytown Road north. After a few miles, recalled Private William Kepler of the 4th Ohio, an ambulance carrying General Reynolds' body rolled past. "None were disposed to ask questions; but little could be learned, save that he had been killed early in the action, and that nearly the entire of Lee's force was at Gettysburg. There was profounder silence than ever; no more jokes, and as usual before a battle, hundreds of playing cards were strewn along the road." The 8th Ohio's Thomas Galwey picked up what scraps of news he could from passing couriers. "Nearly all report desperate fighting at Gettysburg but they are not agreed as to its results. But at dusk comes the report that the Eleventh Corps, mainly Germans, have skedaddled from the field, leaving the First Corps to extricate itself as best it could. Next we meet runaways from the Eleventh Corps itself, who in their broken English tell stories of the day's fight, of their own valor, of the enemy's overpowering numbers, of his terrible artillery, and so forth *ad nauseum*. ... We could see them as night came on, gathered in little crowds about their fires, boiling coffee and babbling German. All talking at once; without officers, without organization of any sort; a mere herd of stragglers." Two hours after sundown Kepler's and Galwey's regiments halted at the east base of Big Round Top,

David Neuhardt Collection

Cincinnati *Daily Gazette* correspondent Whitelaw Reid, a Xenia native, arrived on the battlefield too late July 1 to witness personally the 1st and 11th corps' collapse. To compensate, his published account of the first day's fighting was based secondhand on interviews mostly conducted that night with Federal officers. Using the pen name "Agate," Reid was 25 years old at Gettysburg, close to the time Cincinnati photographer Leon Van Loo made the portrait at left. His reporting of the 1862 battle of Shiloh already stamped Reid as a first-class newspaper correspondent, and his Gettysburg dispatches solidified a distinguished reputation. After the war he became editor and principal owner of the New York *Tribune*. He also was author of the monumental, two-volume work *Ohio In The War*.

then moved farther north to bivouac in a meadow near Powers Hill.[105]

General Meade arrived on Cemetery Hill from Taneytown shortly before midnight. After an exchange of greetings and a brief discussion with several of his generals at the cemetery gatehouse, the Army of the Potomac's new commander quickly inspected defenses east of the Baltimore Pike, then picked his way south in hazy moonlight along Cemetery Ridge to examine the terrain. While some of his soldiers slept, others remained awake and busy. In the 29th Ohio, Henry Knapp tended a little fire on the ridge, his messmates of Company H roasting pieces of fresh beef on sharpened sticks and bayonets.[106]

Jacob Smith, the 107th Ohio ambulance driver, spent the evening hauling blood-smeared men to the 11th Corps field hospital, established on the George Spangler farm just south of Granite School House Road. His attention was attracted to one severely wounded soldier in particular. "He had been shot through the mouth, the ball entering one side of his cheek and out the other; in its passage through it had broken out four or five teeth and cut his tongue pretty near off. He was also shot through one of his arms, and a musket ball had struck a small Bible which he carried in a pocket over his left breast, with sufficient force to go entirely through it, lodging and fastening a bunch of eight or ten letters which were in the pocket between the Bible and his body; his escape was truly miraculous as the ball came with sufficient force to have gone entirely through his body. The Bible in that case proved an effective shield." In spite of the day's rigors, Smith was detailed at midnight for attendant duty at the makeshift hospital. "Some [of the wounded] were murmuring and complaining continually, while others seemed perfectly resigned and cheerful though as badly wounded as the former. One or two of the wounded under [my] care died during the night."[107]

For a sizeable number of Buckeyes July 1 ended wrapped in a blanket on the grounds of Evergreen Cemetery. "We slept among the tombs," wrote a 73rd Ohio officer. Before settling down in the graveyard, Musician Henry Henney listened to the sounds of the Union army concentrating around him. "All night could be heard the rumble of cannons and artillery, moving into position along Cemetery Ridge. We could hear the shouting of men as they rode their horses over the soft ground. Fences were being levelled and every thing gotten into shape for the struggle which seemed imminent on the following day."[108]

THREE

'They came on us yelling like demons with bayonets'

JULY 2

Reveille at 4 a.m. coaxed awake the soundest sleepers in Colonel Sprigg Carroll's brigade. It was still dark, but waning moonlight provided enough illumination for the groggy men of the 4th and 8th Ohio to see that a great deal of activity already was going on around them. Coffee, the soldiers' ubiquitous elixir, warmed in cups or little tin boilers, and breakfast of "hard-tack and flitch" was procured from haversacks and hastily consumed. The men gathered up their traps, buckling and slinging accouterments over wool blouses before strapping knapsacks to their backs and retrieving weapons stacked along company lines. Some of the officers, having servants, received assistance with their personal equipment. In the 8th, Captain Azor H. Nickerson relied upon a former slave named Jerry to tote his haversack and a rubber coat on the march. Jerry, the captain mused, "was a mite of a fellow whom it would be base slander to mention as a 'colored' boy, for he was the blackest negro I ever saw. He was very young, too, and about as broad as he was tall."[1]

Corporal Thaddeus S. Potter of Company H was among the last aroused from sleep. Being dilatory afforded him nothing to eat, for "Old Bricktop" Carroll's loud voice commanded the brigade to fall in. Potter, with barely time to snatch his gear, took his place in the 8th's ranks of 209 officers and men. The 4th Ohio numbered 95 more, jotted Adjutant William Wallace in his diary, but with five men reporting sick the regiment was reduced to 299 effectives. At daybreak Carroll's column, followed by the balance of the 2nd Corps' 3rd Division, shuffled off toward Cemetery Hill.[2]

The Buckeyes of Candy's 12th Corps' brigade also were in motion. Having spent the night in the vicinity of Little Round Top, Candy and General Greene were ordered about 5:30 to move their commands to the army's right at Culp's Hill. It was a twin-peaked eminence located southeast of Cemetery Hill, overlooking Rock Creek to the east and the Baltimore Pike on the southwest. The hill's upper and lower summits were joined by a narrow ridge or saddle. The northern and eastern slopes of the upper hill were steep, thickly wooded and studded with large rocks. Greene's brigade formed facing east on the upper hill between 1st Corps troops to its left and the 2nd Brigade of Geary's division to its right. The 12th Corps' 1st Division extended the line in a southeast direction to Rock Creek. Candy's six regiments massed in a ravine behind Greene's right, also facing east. The 62-year-old Greene, with nearly four decades of engineering experience, immediately began entrenching.[3] Details from Candy's brigade assisted with the work.

"Culp's hill was covered with woods," wrote Ser-

77

geant Joseph L. Gaul of Company C, 5th Ohio. "Right and left the trees were felled and piled up, together with piles of cordwood which was conveniently near, and then strengthened with earth thrown up in every conceivable manner. Tin cups, plates, bayonets and hands were brought into requisition and used freely." Except for one 7th Ohio company sent to bolster Geary's skirmish line on Rock Creek's west bank, the Buckeyes in Candy's command spent a relatively uneventful day in their support position. Sergeant William Tallman of the 66th Ohio recalled, "All morning and well along in the afternoon nothing occurred to create any great excitement except an occasional shell would explode in front of or above our heads among the tree tops."[4]

Such was not the case for Tallman's Ohio comrades elsewhere. Those infantrymen in proximity to Gettysburg's southern outskirts, as well as the cannoneers on Cemetery Hill, became particular targets for keen-eyed Rebel sharpshooters posted in rifle pits or town buildings. Rank provided no immunity from the bullets. Lieutenant Edward Culp, one of five unwounded members of General Ames' and Colonel Harris' staffs, rotated carrying messages and orders. "When we returned," Culp wrote, "we reported to each other how many times we had been shot at. Perhaps you can't see anything amusing in that. *I couldn't.*" Harris told his assistant adjutant general, Captain John M. Brown, the enemy fire originated "from behind the fences and a brick kiln on the right, and from the houses on the left" of that portion of their brigade facing north. Eventually he became a victim himself, as Captain Ben Fox informed his father two days later. "Col Harris was shot in the back but the *hide* was *too tough* to let it enter. I don't want you to understand that he was shot square in the back but grazed along it — being a flank shot by a sharp shooter. The Reb sharp shooters played havock with many of us. ..." Harris, who suffered a wound in his right arm at McDowell, Virginia, in May 1862, provided a personal version of the close call: "I came near getting another one on [July] 2d — I was sitting on my horse ... and while there the sharpshooters commenced on me, and one ball struck me on the left side, making a very sore place, but not enough to make me quit my saddle."[5]

Colonel Orland Smith's three regiments stationed near the intersection of the Taneytown-Em-

Captain Samuel M. McClelland commanded Company H, 7th Ohio, on General Geary's Rock Creek skirmish line. A resident of Youngstown, McClelland was considered "an exceptionally brave man." He was promoted to lieutenant colonel in December 1863.

"Itinerary of the Seventh Ohio Volunteer Infantry, 1861-1864"

mitsburg roads were exposed to constant sharpshooter fire beginning at daylight. To retaliate, Smith's skirmishers were sent some 150 yards to the fields in front while others found places of concealment in nearby buildings on the brigade's right. A deadly game of cat-and-mouse sniping began, which continued through the day and into the next.

One party of 55th Ohio skirmishers entered a barn (probably belonging to John Ziegler, just behind the Dobbin house), finding it occupied by several 1st Corps soldiers who had failed to reach Cemetery Hill during the previous afternoon's retreat. Among the stragglers was Corporal Simon Hubler of the 143rd Pennsylvania. He recollected the Ohioans began shooting from apertures along the barn's heavy beams, and kept at it for an hour or more. In the meantime "the minie-balls were striking the barn at frequent intervals." According to Hubler, a lieutenant in charge of the 12-man detail "wanted someone to take a note up to his commanding officer, who was located with the regiment behind a stone wall about [200] yards distant from the barn where we were sheltered. The men who were under the Lieutenant hesitated about taking the note, and I volunteered to take it. I took the note and ran in a zig zag fashion toward the wall where the 55th Ohio was stationed. When I reached the wall I walked along in front of it for some distance, when someone shouted, 'Say, you Pennsylvanian, you had better jump over here or you'll get plugged.' During my run the bullets had sung un-

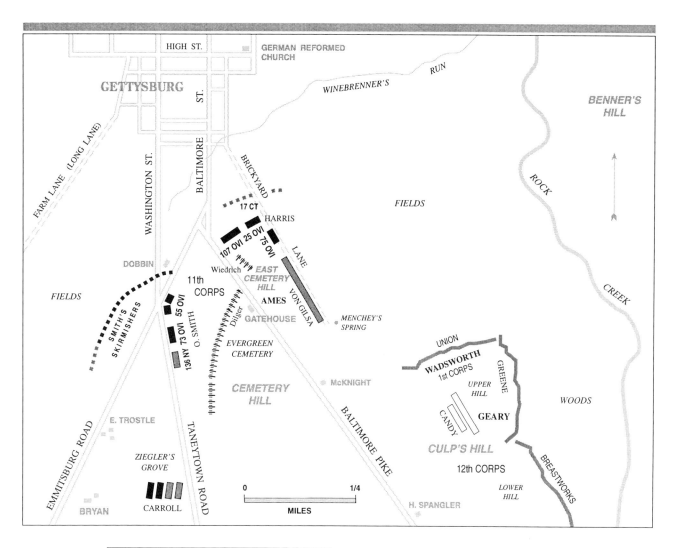

Colonel Charles B. Gambee, 55th Ohio, entered the dry goods business at Bellevue, Ohio, seven years before the war. He was killed in May 1864 at Resaca, Georgia, when a bullet struck him just above the heart.

Trials and Triumphs

comfortably near, so I hastily followed the advice which was given me and jumped over behind the wall."[6]

Hubler handed the message to the 55th's commander, Colonel Gambee. "Evidently the note contained a request for more men because [he] immediately detailed a squad of twelve more men, and inquired of me how they would find their way to the proper place. I told him that I was going to the barn because I had a wounded comrade there. I told the detail to follow me and sprang over the wall, and running in zig zag fashion we all safely reached the barn."[7]

For three hours Private James Carver of Company A used the garret of a stone house as a sharpshooting perch. At first he traded ineffectual shots at long range with a Confederate counterpart lying in a hole. Then his attention was diverted by an officer to a brick structure standing west of Washington Street, where Rebels were firing from an upper window. Carver related: "The officer told me to dislodge them, but the window was at such an angle from me that I could not, and they threw a couple of shots ... into the gable. This same officer came again and pointed out a brick house on the east and north of the house I was in, where a rebel had punched out a brick between two windows and picked off two or three of our men going through the orchard [behind the 55th's position]. I must have done some execution, for the rebels sent a company of infantry over in the next lot under a grape arbor, and they fired two volleys into the house and I returned the fire. They then retreated with two wounded. In about two or three hours the rebels threw four shells at the house; the first one struck the chimney on the east of the house, the second struck the northeast corner, the third struck about six feet from the ground on the north side, and the fourth near the west end, about ten feet from the ground."[8]

Company I's section of stone fence sat almost five feet above the Taneytown roadbed. Private An-

J. B. Everts Collection

Private Moses Brown, Company F, 55th Ohio, was the son of German immigrants who settled in Crawford County. A cousin, Daniel Brown, and Moses' future brother-in-law, Solomon Sheller, also served in the regiment at Gettysburg. Moses spent much of July 2 and 3 on sharpshooter duty, "firing at dem Rebels in the town." Eight days later he wrote home that "Solomon and Daniel mad[e] it threw the battle wid but a scratch or two."

Left: A Confederate wood canteen used by Moses Brown at Gettysburg. Family tradition holds that Brown picked up the canteen in Virginia in 1862, and carried it for the next three years.

drew Sweetland, a Huron County farmer who served alongside his 41-year-old father Daniel, noticed the most accurate enemy sharpshooting came from a house situated to the 55th's right front. "We made a barricade of stone about four feet high, half-moon shape, for the protection of Colonel [Gambee] and staff, a few feet in rear of Co. I." When musketry fire from the building reached an intolerable level, "a brass six-pounder cannon was brought down the road from the south by hand ... and fired a shell into the upper part of the house, where it exploded, causing three or four Johnnies to jump from the upper rooms to the ground, taking the window sash with them." This cannon fire, a neighboring Ohio officer attested, only served to provoke "worse" sharp-shooting.[9]

Gambee apparently kept two companies out in shifts as pickets. Toward noon, as escalating gunfire seemed to presage a Confederate attack, the colonel ordered Company D under First Lieutenant Frederick H. Boalt to reinforce the skirmishers when Company H was driven from a fence line. Sergeant Luther Mesnard recalled: "Boalt drew his sword and we were out there in a jiffy, but my how the lead did fly. A half dozen men were sent to a small brick barn to the right. As I was kneeling in the grass capping my gun a ball from the right struck my gun-stock, stinging my little finger, bruising my knee severely, and spoiling my gun. I picked up another gun, and suggested to Boalt that we charge the post and rail fence behind which the rebs were, as I thought they were *too close*. The word was given and we got there. There was wheat standing on the other side of the fence. I raised up behind a post to look over as a bullet struck the edge of the post and glanced past my ear, sending splinters into my forehead."[10]

Twenty feet beyond the fence a large tree stump jutted from the

Second Lieutenant John R. Lowe, Company B, 55th Ohio, received a slight, unspecified wound July 2.

Brad L. Pruden Collection

ground, surrounded by a clump of elderberry. After removing a lower rail, Mesnard allowed Private Charles Stacey to crawl to the stump. "He did good work there as a sharpshooter," Mesnard stated. "It was a better, safer place than the rest of us had." Stacey, a 20-year-old English emigré, located several enemy positions and squeezed off two dozen carefully aimed shots from his nest over the next four hours. He finally left the stump when Company D expended its ammunition and was recalled to the

Private Charles Stacey, Company D, 55th Ohio. Many years afterward he reminisced: "Every time I would locate a Sharpshooter and fire at him, [a] whole line [of battle] would fire on me but I would drop down. ... I fired 23 shots in the four hours I was alone and during that time my company did not have a man touched during the time I was out and I destroyed the Sharpshooters. I don't believe any man ever had a line of battle fire at him as many times as I was fired at and live to tell of it."

Courtesy of John L. Harris

Born in 1841 to one of Huron County's most prominent families, First Lieutenant Frederick H. Boalt commanded Company D, 55th Ohio. The Norwalk businessman's meritorious service on July 2, wrote the regiment's historian, was performed "beyond the view of ordinary observers. It was one of many like incidents for which medals of honor were issued; but Boalt never made any claim for superior valor. He was as modest as brave," eventually becoming his company's captain in March 1864.

55th's main line. In 1896 the Norwalk farmer received a Medal of Honor for his actions.[11]

The day's work was not yet finished for Stacey and Mesnard. Late in the afternoon the 73rd Ohio's skirmishers, to the 55th's left, were driven back. Lieutenant Boalt's company again was ordered to reinforce the hard-pressed skirmish line, deploying to the right — "the worst place," Mesnard believed, "and my position was at the right of the Company. We went out clear to the fence, but could not stay as the rebs were on our side of the fence to the left and right. We fell back to where the [skirmish] line had been most of the day, but my boy it was a bad place. Rebs on both flanks and front and quite too close, and we laid close and fired as fast as possible. Soon I was wounded in the right arm. ..."[12]

Mesnard sprinted for the regiment's stone wall, bullets criss-crossing his path. When he reached it Colonel Gambee advised him to seek medical treatment at the rear. Boalt eventually returned with about 15 men. Ten others, including Second Lieutenant John P. Jones, Sergeant William C. Penfield and Charles Stacey, were captured. Imprisoned on Belle Isle in Richmond, Stacey was paroled September 22 and rejoined the regiment the following spring.[13]

As tough a position the 55th was delegated to defend, Lieutenant Colonel Long's 73rd Ohio next in line suffered much higher losses. During the day's skirmishing 18 men of the latter regiment were killed or mortally wounded as opposed to six in the 55th. A majority of these fatal casualties occurred near 6 p.m. when Confederate skirmishers from two brigades of Major General W. Dorsey Pender's division, A.P. Hill's corps, advanced to push Orland Smith's Federals from the fields west of the Emmitsburg Road. "Their skirmishers had been

Taken prisoner July 2, Sergeant William C. Penfield of Company D, 55th Ohio, spent nearly three months in captivity on Richmond's Belle Isle. He was paroled in late September and rejoined the regiment in May 1864. A native of North Fairfield, Ohio, and an Oberlin College graduate, he lost two brothers to wounds and disease during the war. This photograph was taken March 28, 1865 when Penfield was a second lieutenant in the 5th U.S. Infantry.

heavily reinforced," explained the 73rd's major, Samuel Hurst. "Our whole brigade line of skirmishers charged and drove them from [a swale, behind which ran a farm lane]; but, going too far, and the enemy being reinforced, they in turn charged and drove back our line again, with heavy loss." Half the regiment was sent forward at the height of the ebb-and-flow contest, which Hurst characterized as "especially deadly from its deliberateness of aim."[14]

Writing to *The Circleville Democrat,* Sergeant George Gephart, who was wounded in the left leg the following day, described the 73rd's fight from his viewpoint in Company E: "Skirmishers were sent out to strengthen the line already stationed, which was being overpowered. Two companies of our regiment having arrived and deployed behind those already engaging the enemy, were thrown forward on the double quick just as the line gave way under the rapid advance of the enemy. Our boys passed on, charging upon and completely routing the foe. Following this supposed advantage, they pressed on over a small hill and soon found themselves overpowered by the enemy's reserve, and were obliged to fall back to the brow of the hill. The scene was indescribable; wild, exciting and fearful. ... Till six o'clock none of our company was severely wounded; shortly after which ... our First

"The Skirmish Line." Colonel Orland Smith reported his brigade front "was covered by a line of skirmishers thrown out toward the enemy's lines, the right resting near the town and the left connecting with a similar line of the Second Corps. Though the situation was at times of the most trying character, never a man faltered, to my knowledge, or complained, but every man seemed inspired by a determination to hold his position, dead or alive."

First Sergeant William B. Davis, Company E, 73rd Ohio, was shot in the right shoulder July 2. The 19-year-old Pickaway County merchant from Williamsport was wounded again the following year, and promoted captain in February 1865.

Jackson County farmer George M. Waller served as a private in Company G, 73rd Ohio.

L. M. Strayer Collection

York skirmish companies connecting with the 73rd's left flank. "The boys marched off on quick time," related First Lieutenant Samuel Fellers, Company G's commander. "On arriving on the ground, I discovered that the rebel sharp shooters had a cross fire on us. At this time the companies from the 136th gave way, and fell back past our companies, which were lying down. We were then ordered to advance over the rise. The boys, who were deployed five paces apart, all sprang to their feet, and advanced as steadily as iron, and picked every rebel as fast as one showed his head above the wheat. I will here state that the rebels had advanced their line of skirmishers in the night, and dug holes in the field for each man to conceal himself in as he lay down to load. Both sides fought with determination not to give ground. In this charge Co. G suffered severely; we went in with thirty-six men, and lost twenty-three killed and wounded. Isaac J. Sperry, Sergt. Jasper C. Briggs, Sergt. [Isaac] Willis, James Ray and E[lisha] L. Leake were killed; Corporal G[eorge] B. Greiner lost his left leg; James Marshall lost his right arm; J[oseph] Barrett lost his right leg, and many others of Co. G were badly wounded. Not one of the company faltered from duty, but fought like tigers as long as they could stand, free from wounds." [17]

Captain Thomas Higgins' Company B was equally chewed up. [18] During the 30-hour period between 6 a.m. July 2 and noon July 3, it sustained 22 casualties:

• Sergeant Johnston Prior, killed.
• Sergeant Thomas H. Rice, skull fractured; died July 17.
• Sergeant Benjamin Shattuck, captured.
• Sergeant George Weisensa, gunshot to left arm.

Lieut. H[orace] S. Clark, fearing that our line would be heavily pressed, called out *'Stand fast boys, don't give a foot,'* at which juncture he nearly lost a leg, a piece of shell, of a half pound weight, passing through his left thigh, badly lacerating the flesh. He was carried from the field to the rear." [15]

Lieutenant Clark survived his serious injury. Two weeks later in a Baltimore hospital he displayed to Gephart "the piece of shell which struck him, it passing through the thigh fell down into his boot. A dear piece of iron indeed, and one of which this young and valiant officer may well be proud." [16]

Companies B and G were hit especially hard. Both had been ordered to support two 136th New

- Corporal Henry M. Lawson, captured.
- Corporal Joseph Reed, gunshots to right arm, left hip.
- Corporal Samuel Turner, killed.
- Corporal Samuel Ward, gunshot to right shoulder.
- Private William R. Call, wounded; died July 16.
- Private George England, gunshot to right abdomen.
- Private Samuel M. Hatfield, gunshot to right thigh.
- Private William E. Haynes, killed.
- Private Absalom Hissey, wounded.
- Private Michael Kennedy, gunshot to right hip.
- Private George W. McGehee, gunshot to right leg.
- Private William McLuen, killed.
- Private Warren Miller, wounded.
- Private Joseph Nelson, gunshots to right hip, left arm.
- Private Amos T. Reed, captured.
- Private Samuel A. Shattuck, wounded.
- Private John Terry, gunshot to left leg; amputated.
- Private George Nixon III, gunshots to right hip, side.[19]

Regarding the last-named casualty, Private Nixon, 42, was the father of nine children and farmed outside McArthur in Elk Township, Vinton County, when he enlisted in the 73rd Ohio at Wa-

verly. During the height of Company B's fight sometime after 6 o'clock, he was struck by two bullets and fell bleeding in the trampled wheat. For more than two hours Nixon called for help, his impassioned entreaties distinctly heard as far back as the Emmitsburg Road. Unable to bear them longer the company's drummer, Richard Enderlin, asked Captain Higgins for permission to bring in the wounded man. "No," the officer replied. "It will be sure death if you do." Enderlin persisted. According to one account Higgins eventually relented. Another version portrays the musician flatly ignoring the captain's order to remain put. In any event, after dark Enderlin removed his equipment and began crawling toward the source of the heartrending moans.[20]

Born January 11, 1843 at Eichsteten in Baden, Enderlin emigrated with his parents to Ohio in 1854 and settled in Ross County near Chillicothe. Like Nixon he grew up tilling the soil. Although 22 years separated them by age, both joined the same company in November 1861. When Enderlin finally reached the stricken man he discovered he was ly-

George Nixon III, mortally wounded July 2, had moved with his family to Vinton County from Pennsylvania in 1853. One hundred years later his great grandson, then Vice President Richard M. Nixon, visited and placed flowers on the 73rd Ohio private's grave in Gettysburg National Cemetery.

Richard Nixon Library & Birthplace Collections

Right: Musician Richard Enderlin, Company B, 73rd Ohio, received sergeant's chevrons for his battlefield heroism and in August 1897 was awarded the Medal of Honor. After Gettysburg he was detached for service with Orland Smith's brigade ambulances. Carte de visite by F.A. Simonds, Chillicothe.

Richard F. Carlile Collection

ing quite near the enemy's pickets. Slowly he dragged Nixon in the opposite direction, the faint noise of rustling wheat stalks masked by periodic rifle fire. At a point closer to the 73rd's line the musician draped his wounded comrade on his back and crawled the rest of the way to safety. Their regimental mates were astonished. Higgins at once promoted the 20-year-old drummer to sergeant, and Nixon was carried to the 11th Corps hospital. On July 8 he died there of his wounds. A little more than a century later his great grandson, Richard Milhous Nixon, became the nation's 37th president. As for Enderlin, he continued soldiering until May 1864 when a gunshot wound to his right foot at New Hope Church, Georgia, sent him home. In 1897 he was awarded the Medal of Honor for his Gettysburg gallantry.[21]

Some 250 yards south of the 73rd Ohio other Buckeyes also became involved in the escalating skirmishing west of the Emmitsburg Road. Earlier in the day Carroll's 2nd Corps' brigade reached

The engraved reverse side of Richard Enderlin's Medal of Honor (third design).

Cemetery Hill, then was moved at 8 a.m. across Taneytown Road to the rear of Ziegler's Grove in support of a Regular battery (Woodruff's). "Everything seemed unusually quiet, for a battle-field," recollected the 8th Ohio's commander, Franklin Sawyer. In the 4th Ohio, recalled Private William Kepler, "there was a disposition to get a glimpse across the hill, 'to see how the land lay' and the position of the enemy." Lieutenant Lemuel Jeffries of Company E noted Howard's 11th Corps was located to their right, while the 2nd and 3rd corps extended "the whole distance from our left to Round Top Mountain. Not much firing was going on at this time and the men generally lay down behind a stone wall and talked or slept, or in some way amused themselves." Others "fixed up their guns — put their cap and cartridge boxes in shape and ... prepared for the conflict they knew was coming." [22]

Lieutenant Galwey of the 8th was engrossed in making pencil sketches when his attention was drawn west to Seminary Ridge, where Rebel skirmishers debouched from a tree line and began advancing through the fields. Federal pickets stationed halfway between Seminary and Cemetery ridges, near the house and barn of farmer William Bliss, already were popping away. About 9:30 these Union skirmishers were strengthened, part of the detail being furnished by Captain Wells W. Miller's Company H, 8th Ohio, and a 4th Ohio battalion commanded by Major Gordon A. Stewart. Stewart led his four companies over the Emmitsburg Road to a fence line northeast of the Bliss buildings, while Miller hooked up with the southernmost skirmishers of Orland Smith's brigade. Their "brisk interchange of shots," however, could not have been very accurate. All five Ohio companies were armed with .69-caliber smoothbore muskets. Stewart's Buckeyes remained on the skirmish line for five hours until relieved at 3 p.m. by Companies G and I, jointly commanded by Captain Peter Grubb.[23]

A German immigrant born in 1833, Grubb was a Kenton merchant and good friend of the 82nd Ohio's colonel, James Robinson. Both had served seven months together in the 4th Ohio's Company G during 1861, Robinson as captain and Grubb his first lieutenant. When Robinson was promoted major of the 82nd in January 1862, Grubb replaced him as company commander. He was known as a highly efficient officer whose conduct at Fredericksburg and Chancellorsville was praised by regimental and brigade commanders. In the latter battle Grubb was shot behind his left knee, the bullet partially severing the inner hamstring, but he refused to leave the field. Although he recuperated quickly it is likely he walked July 2 with a limp.[24]

With Grubb overseeing both companies, Second Lieutenant Addison H. Edgar was in charge of Company G and Second Lieutenant Samuel J. Shoub commanded Company I. Their combined strength was 49 men. Just before setting off, the 24-year-old Edgar apparently was seized by a premonition of death. He requested comrades to return his watch and sword to his parents in Hardin County, and assure them "he had been true to his trust." The Ohioans crossed the Emmitsburg Road near Emanuel Trostle's farm buildings and occupied Major Stewart's former position, shielding themselves behind fence rails and a slight rise in the ground. The advance coincided with increasing Confederate pressure at the Bliss farm and against Orland Smith's beleaguered skirmishers off to their right. It was, to use the soldiers' euphemism, "a tight place."[25]

Early on, Lieutenant Shoub was killed by a shell. A piece of another soon sliced into Lieutenant Edgar, fatally wounding him in fulfillment of his fears. Before succumbing he gasped to Grubb, "Let us die like men, rather than run like cowards." Grubb had no intention of running, even though his small force was dwindling and enemy skirmishers bypassed his right flank all the way to the Emmitsburg Road. A bullet tore into the captain's left forearm, incapacitating him. He relinquished command to Company G sergeant Martin Longworth who, suffering from a hand wound himself, "was determined not to leave the field until he had received orders to do so."[26]

Colonel Carroll and his division commander, Brigadier General Alexander Hays, saw that Grubb's detachment was in imminent peril of being overrun. Hays told his subordinate to send reinforcements, and Carroll decided Lieutenant Colonel Sawyer's entire 8th Ohio was required to "clean out the nest of rebels," which by now was shooting at Union artillerymen and mounted officers on Cemetery Hill. It was an apt choice. Not only was the 8th Carroll's old regiment, but 11 years earlier Sawyer, as Huron County prosecuting attorney, successfully broke up a noted gang of horse thieves, counterfeiters and professional con men infesting the "Fire-

Captain Peter Grubb, Company G, 4th Ohio.

lands" region of northern Ohio.[27]

A week and a half shy of his 38th birthday, Sawyer was a Crawford County native but had lived in Norwalk since 1845. Two years later he received his law license and established "a respectable practice" in Huron's county seat. He was regarded as being "a man of strict integrity," as well as "an eloquent speaker and ready debater, and a thorough student of literature and history." Though not possessing any formal military training, he was persuaded by Governor William Dennison in 1860

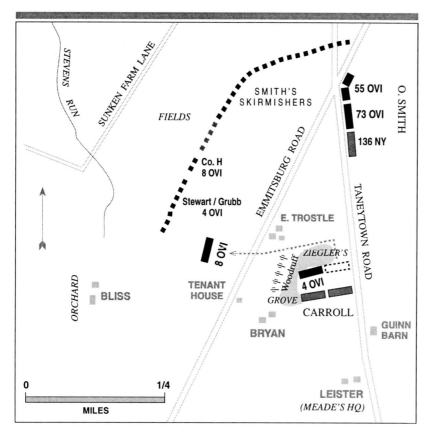

to organize the Norwalk Light Guard, a militia unit which became Company D of the 8th Ohio upon war's outbreak. By December 1861 Sawyer advanced from captain to lieutenant colonel, and commanded the regiment in three major battles prior to Gettysburg. One observer wrote of him: "His popularity with his men was unbounded, his ability as an officer was conceded, and his absolute bravery in battle unquestioned." At Antietam and Chancellorsville the horses he rode were shot beneath him.[28]

Sawyer received his orders from Carroll about 4 p.m. From his vantage point near Ziegler's Grove the Emmitsburg roadbed could not be seen, but it was enclosed on both sides by post-and-rail fences, "thus making the road in which these rebels were practically concealed a fair rifle pit." The regiment formed behind a low stone wall. Companies B and D, armed with Enfield rifle muskets, took position on the flanks; the other companies carried smoothbores. Seated atop his favorite horse "Old Sam," Sawyer cleared the wall with a bound, closely followed by his Buckeyes who dashed downslope at the double-quick. Recollecting the charge years later, he wrote: "The artillerymen as we passed them

mounted their guns, and waving hats and swords cheered us on. Our men soon began to fall, some killed, some wounded. We had about five hundred yards to make, but the on-set was so sudden and spirited that the rebels could not well escape, cooped up as they were between the fences. A squad of them made the attempt on the left, and were run down and captured by a corporal's guard from Co. B; and another lot, who got half way to town, shared the same fate; forty or fifty more surrendered, and were sent to the rear as prisoners. We found several of their dead and wounded in the road, victims of our fire, delivered as we advanced."[29]

The Ohioans' charge cost two men killed and 14 wounded, as well as "Old Sam." Dismounting, Sawyer discovered the horse bleeding from several wounds. He slapped its rump and the animal galloped back up the ridge, where the astonished officer found him alive late the next day.[30]

The 8th halted only briefly at the road. Company K under Captain Wilbur F. Pierce was sent forward to the right to join Captain Miller's Company H. Captain Azor Nickerson with Companies I and A moved to the left front as skirmishers, which must have been a welcome sight for Grubb's weary 4th Ohioans. The balance of the regiment pried rails from fenceposts and built a crude barricade above the road's west ditch. Sawyer admonished everyone to keep down. His own orders from Carroll were to hold the position "to the last man."[31]

Rearward, meanwhile, Confederate bullets and shells still searched for victims on Cemetery Hill, which had become a bit more crowded with new arrivals. By 8 a.m. Lieutenant Colonel William Bown returned from the Mechanicstown scout with most of his 104-man detachment of the 61st Ohio. The march to Gettysburg had been "very hard," according to First Lieutenant Anthony Grodzicki of Com-

Captain John Garrett, Company H, 61st Ohio, commanded the regiment in Georgia during the latter half of 1864.

Courtesy of Mac Schumm

pany F. "There was considerable straggling on account of the difficulty of finding our Corps." Once it was located, First Lieutenant Jacob F. Mader of Company H realized the Union line was "in the shape of a horse shoe[.] wee can reinforce either flank in fifteen minutes."[32]

The 61st remained reunited for only four or five

hours. At 1 p.m. 53 officers and men, including Grodzicki, were sent on picket. An equal number commanded by Company H's captain, John Garrett, was detailed to support Dilger's artillerymen near the cemetery gatehouse. Ninety others under Colonel McGroarty stayed in the regimental line. Abraham Bope, a Company K private who took part in the Mechanicstown expedition, was not very pleased drawing the battery assignment, as he informed his father: "I did not get to fire a shot this fight, and I did not like that fore when the rebels shoot at me I like to bee whare I can return the compliment."[33]

At about the same time, Captain James Huntington's four batteries of the 3rd Brigade, Artillery Reserve, arrived from Taneytown and parked just off Granite School House Road near Powers Hill. Piled high with bulging canvas bags, some of his vehicles resembled farmers' carts on their way to market. For two previous days the cannoneers had foraged corn, enough of it to fill a wagon per battery as feed for their horses. But when Huntington received his marching orders late in the afternoon of July 1, he learned that all extra wagons were to be sent to Westminster, Maryland. "This latter clause was embarrassing," he reflected, "as it involved parting with the reserve stock of corn, which we were loth to do in view of the impossibility of collecting forage while in position at Gettysburg. All the available sacks were filled and loaded on the caissons, and the wagons despatched as directed before sunset."[34]

Leaving Taneytown close to 5 a.m. on the 2nd, Huntington's brigade marched "rapidly" for the battlefield 13 miles away. It was "a close, murky morning, sultry and no air stirring," wrote Private William Parmelee of the 1st Ohio's Battery H. "The roads are rough and heavy from recent rains. It is very hard marching." Two miles south of the Round Tops the axle of one of the battery's ordnance rifles cracked, requiring it to be pulled off the road and repaired. Somewhere along the way Corporal John Merrell first heard the news of General Reynolds' death, and jotted in his diary, "General Mead[e] has command of this army now. Hooker is relieved for some cause or other unknown to me."[35]

Once in park Merrell and his fellow artillerists were allowed to brew coffee, eat dinner and rest for two hours. Toward 4 o'clock they were ordered to proceed to Cemetery Hill. Arriving there, Huntington was requested by Major Osborn, 11th Corps artillery chief, to detach a battery for service east of the Baltimore Pike. Union artillery on that side of the road was commanded by the 1st Corps' Colonel Charles S. Wainwright, while Osborn controlled the batteries on Cemetery Hill west of the pike. Huntington designated Captain R. Bruce Ricketts' combined Battery F & G, 1st Pennsylvania Light Artillery, for the duty. Ricketts replaced another Pennsylvania battery, rolling his six 3-inch rifles into pre-constructed earthen lunettes opposite Evergreen Cemetery's gatehouse. According to Huntington, Captain Wallace Hill's Battery C, 1st West Virginia Light Artillery, "was placed on the left of [Osborn's] line already formed on the northwesterly side of the [hill]." His own Battery H, under Lieutenant George Norton, "took position at an angle across the cemetery," and Captain Frederick Ed-

gell's 1st New Hampshire Battery "was placed in reserve in a field near by." [36]

Huntington's initial impression was that the "position of our army [was] peculiar, the line forming a triangle with the apex towards the enemy, whose line was in front around ours, we having the advantage of being able to throw troops across, while the enemy had to go round." He considered the cemetery "a position fine for artillery, yet quite exposed, being swept by rebel batteries in front and on our left flank." [37]

His cannoneers unlimbered their guns in the midst of heavy shelling that began at 4 p.m. At least five Rebel artillery battalions belonging to Ewell's and A.P. Hill's corps targeted Cemetery Hill and Culp's Hill. The closest Confederate batteries banged away from the open crest of Benner's Hill, a 100-foot-high elevation astride the Hanover Road just east of Rock Creek. Nearby, six 20-pounder Parrott rifles, the heaviest guns on the field, added to the din and explosive damage inflicted in the Union lines. Some projectiles landed or blew up in the cemetery, which Ohio artillery Private Orin G. Dority thought was "getting used rather rough. A great many of the tombstones are broken up by the shots and shells of the enemy." [38]

In Dilger's Battery I, Lieutenant Clark Scripture cheated death by mere inches. A 20-pounder solid shot glanced against his holster, mangling the revolver inside and bruising his left hip. Before burying itself in the ground the projectile took off Private Alonzo Silsby's left hand at the wrist, an injury that claimed his life three weeks later. Private Green Brockway was mortally wounded a short time afterward. Battery mate Darwin Cody wrote home that "I stood within ten feet of [fellow Clevelanders Silsby and Brockway] when they were shot. There was a place to try a mans courage. I

First Lieutenant George W. Norton of Lucas County assumed command of Battery H, 1st OVLA, when Captain Huntington was promoted in mid-June. Norton, 44, was the father of four children aged 2 to 12. He posed here following presentation of a new sword, belt, sash, spurs and field glasses by the battery's enlisted men in September 1863.

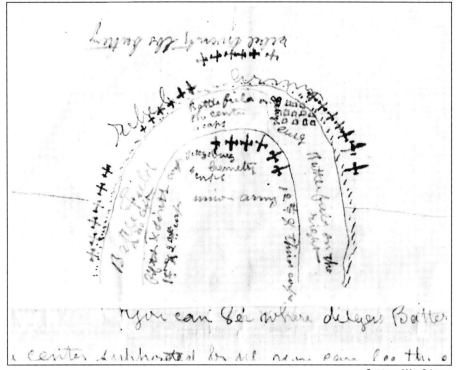

Courtesy of Mac Schumm

A crude sketch showing the battlefield's northern "horseshoe" shape was included in a letter sent home by Lieutenant Jacob Mader, 61st Ohio. Under the drawing he scrawled, "You can see where dilgers Battery was in the center supported by us. You can see the cross fire the rebel Batteries had on us while laying on the hill of Gettisburg Cemetry."

hope I never shall be in quite as close quarters again. I was hit once but soon got over it." Scripture's miraculous escape apparently made the rounds quickly, for Private Dority of Battery H mentioned in his diary that evening of seeing the lieutenant's weapon, its barrel broken in three places. By the end of July the relic revolver was on display in the Ravenna cigar store of Scripture's brother-in-law, L.T. Moses.[39]

"Their was not a spot in our line but what was reached by their canon," believed Lieutenant Mader, whose 61st Ohio detachment supported Dilger's artillerymen "under a cross fire of the rebels shott & shell which made the air hideious with the whizing. I am thankfull to the almighty God that I have escaped the iron hail. ..." Some in his regiment did not. Company B's captain, James M. Reynolds, was struck in the hip and died the next day. A bullet or piece of shell tore through acting Adjutant Daniel W. Williams' lungs. He was carried to a 12th Corps hospital, where the Miami County farmer passed away July 5.[40]

General Ames' aide Edward Culp, 25th Ohio, wrote several days after the bombardment that the air was "resonant with the angry shrieks of shells. The battle of Chancellorsville was a mere skirmish compared to the scene which now took place. Gen.

Gary Delscamp Collection

Second Lieutenant Daniel W. Williams, Company G, 61st Ohio, was acting regimental adjutant when he fell mortally wounded July 2. Carte de visite by C.A. Gale Photographer, Piqua.

Captain Benjamin Franklin Stone Jr., 73rd Ohio, acted as Orland Smith's brigade adjutant from May 24 through August 1863. After the battle Stone, a Ross County teacher, wrote his fiancée: "We were ordered to hold the hill at all hazards & promised to do it. On ... the 2d the fight opened by a furious cannonading of the enemy who brought all the pieces they could to bear on the cemetery hill. We felt the emergency & stood our ground without flinching for hour upon hour." Here, Stone sported a commercially produced, non-regulation sack coat with six buttons.

Ross County Historical Society

Hunt, chief of Artillery for the army, said it was the heaviest cannonading that ever took place on this continent. One shell burst within twelve feet of where Gen. Ames and staff were standing, killing four men and wounding eight." [41]

Ames' division near the base of East Cemetery Hill lay within easy range of the Confederate guns on Benner's Hill. Colonel Harris was impressed by the "heavy roar" mingling "with the shouts of the living and the groans of the dying. In the distance could be seen the smoke as it curled up at each discharge ... and in a few seconds the shells would come crashing among the locust trees in our front, bursting into fragments, and filling the air with deadly missiles and hideous noises." One of Harris' 75th Ohio privates, William Southerton of Company B, thought "A few too many shells on Benner's Ridge [sic] came our way, and a few too many balls from sharpshooters' rifles. Thunder and lightning! The Johnnies had a powerful battery there." [42]

Southerton related that a comrade, 18-year-old Private Andrew Jackson of Company D, grew "tired of dodging their shells" and slid over the stone fence lining Brickyard Lane. "Jack worked his way along [another] low stone wall that was edged with thick brush, and to a field and locust grove in the lowlands. There he disappeared among the trees. Every whiff of smoke [from] the rebel battery was sure to be followed by the crackle of Jack's rifle. We were amused. Then silence. We wondered what had become of Jack. In about half an hour he slithered back over our wall and dropped to the ground. 'Did you get your man, Jack?' Minutes passed and Jack hadn't said a word. 'I don't know whether I did or

not. A shell struck a tree right by my head, so I quit!' " [43]

A number of overshots from Benner's Hill landed among Orland Smith's troops on the northwest side of Cemetery Hill. Captain Benjamin F. Stone Jr., Smith's acting assistant adjutant general and commander of Company C, 73rd Ohio, rejoiced in a letter to his future wife back in Chillicothe: "I am by a great Providence — or so it seems to me — alive & unhurt. My escapes have been wonderful. I was struck only once & that by a twenty four lb. shell [sic] — which however only bruised me, its force being spent. I was standing under a tree in an orchard watching the line of infantry. In the midst of the cannonading a huge shell struck the tree just above me & fell striking me on the head & shoulder, stunning me for a few moments but in no way disabling me. Several times I have been covered with dirt & fragments by shell[s] exploding within a few feet — & bullets without number have whistled by me, some of them I know sent explicitly for me [but] I am entirely unharmed. The same is true of all of the staff." [44]

What Confederate gunnery may have lacked in accuracy was offset by sheer volume, judged Major Hurst of the 73rd. "Their shot and shell fell upon the hill like hail. The stone fence, behind which we had a partial shelter from their skirmish fire, was little protection now. Indeed, the cross-fire of the rebel batteries ... became so heavy as to induce a change of our battalion to the front [west] side of the wall. Still, there were few of our men injured by this heavy cannonade. ..." [45]

One member of Company F, 55th Ohio, was amazed he did not receive a scratch, "or even a hole in my clothes. The closest 'call' I had was from a

solid shot. It came directly from our rear ... and struck the ground perhaps six feet from where I was lying (throwing dirt and stones in a man's face sitting next to me, bleeding him quite profusely), ricochetted, and struck the stone fence behind which we were lying, directly over our heads, taking a stone or two from the top, and passed on. It's a 'peculiar' sensation a man experiences just as one of those articles is passing so close to him. It isn't to be described." [46]

The cannonade was not all one-sided. Within 10 minutes Federal gunners found the exact range of Benner's Hill. They began pasting their Rebel counterparts while enemy artillery on Seminary Ridge, though farther away, also received return fire. First Lieutenant William A. Ewing, commanding Battery H's left section of two ordnance rifles, informed readers of the *Toledo Blade:*

Although rather more elevated than that of the enemy, our position upon "Cemetery Hill" was so cramped that it gave their artillery an opportunity to concentrate their fire on a *mass of artillery* in a small compass, while their batteries were much scattered, causing us to divide our fire in order to silence the single guns and batteries that were pouring the missiles of death and destruction in upon us from a semi-circle which *completely surrounded our front and both flanks,* owing to the fact that the hill we occupied was the key or point of our line of battle, which was almost precisely like the two sides of a triangle, this hill being the apex of the triangle; if they fired upon our right the shot and shell would most of them pass over the line and land on our devoted heads, and *vice versa* on the left with the same result, so that the direct fire of the enemy's guns upon our immediate front became a mere accompaniment to the enfilading fires upon either flank. For *three mortal hours* the iron storm was howling around and over us. ...

This could not last long without casualties, and while standing between the two left guns of the battery, I saw a 20-pound[er] Parrott shell strike one of our men at the

USAMHI

"For three hours we were under a most terrific artillery fire," explained First Lieutenant William A. Ewing of Battery H, 1st OVLA, to his mother, "but never closed the mouth of a gun so long as rebels could be seen or heard to fire at."
Carte de visite by John Cadwallader, Toledo.

Private Wilkinson D. Perrin

Although Battery H private Orin G. Dority noted some destruction in Evergreen Cemetery wrought by enemy shellfire, he confided to his diary: "We don't get much time to look about for the Rebs keep sending their compliments. They fall faster than we wish to receive them." Among Dority's comrades on Cemetery Hill were the two Buckeyes pictured at left. Perrin was killed 11 months later at Cold Harbor, Virginia. In 1864 Covert was promoted corporal in the battery's Gun Detachment F.

Private Charles T. Covert

left piece in the calf of the leg, *completely severing the limb;* two hours after, Jacob Kirsch [*sic*] said "Tell the boys I died doing my duty," and breathed his last.[47]

Battery H's first casualty, ironically, was not even an Ohioan. Private Keirsh hailed from Pittsburgh and was one of two dozen cannoneers detailed after Chancellorsville from Pennsylvania Independent Battery F. These Pittsburghers temporarily served in Ewing's section. The center and right sections, commanded respectively by Lieutenant Norton (overall battery commander) and Second Lieutenant Frank B. Reckard, were composed of Ohio volunteers from Lucas, Washington and Monroe counties. Soon after Keirsh was hit, Reckard and Norton each lost a man to mortal wounds. Private Henry Schram of Marietta was struck in the shoulder by a 2.9-inch Parrott shell and died that night. Maumee native John N. Edmonds, a private in the center section, had his lower left leg almost torn away by another shell. At the time, Captain Huntington was standing a few paces to the rear, watching the effects of Battery H's fire through field glasses. He assisted applying an improvised tourniquet to the mangled limb. Lieutenant Ewing remarked, "... with his usual patience and endurance [Edmonds] bore it all, simply saying while being

carried to the rear, 'Boys, that was a pretty tough pull on me, wasn't it?' " He died in a field hospital 13 days later.[48]

Across the cemetery to the west, Captain Wallace Hill's four 10-pounder Parrott rifles of Battery C, 1st WVLA, sat between Wheeler's battery and a section of Wiedrich's, both belonging to the 11th Corps. Hill, 25, was a Washington County, Ohio, farmer who had commanded the battery since August 1862. It was christened the "Pierpont Battery" to honor Francis H. Pierpont, western Virginia's provisional governor prior to June 20, 1863, when West Virginia attained official statehood. Most of Battery C's men were Buckeyes, primarily residents of Washington and Morgan counties who originally served from April to August 1861 in Company B, 18th Ohio Infantry. The three-month volunteers guarded railroads in western Virginia until their muster-out, then reenlisted in September 1861 as a light artillery company. "Owing to a misunderstanding among those in authority in Ohio," recalled a former member, "the service of the battery was offered to Governor Pierpont, of West Virginia, and accepted, and was named by [original commander, Captain Frank Buell]."[49]

Eighteen-year-old William Jenvey was in charge of one of Hill's guns, which pointed toward

Seminary Ridge. Born in Hampshire, England, he had been a student in Marietta before enlisting as a bugler in March 1862, and subsequently served in the Shenandoah Valley campaign, Second Bull Run and Chancellorsville.[50] Adept at providing detail, Jenvey described part of Battery C's action:

All this time we had been actively engaged with the Rebel artillery in our front. They were strong in force, and had been tasking us pretty severely. The sharpshooters, too ... had been annoying us terribly, but as yet no casualty had taken place.

All were congratulating themselves when a shell too surely aimed came crashing through the air. Louis Fourgeres saw and avoided it, but poor Stephen J. Braddock, more unfortunate, was struck fair in the head, the shell taking as it went a portion off the top part of his head. If his body had been made of stone, he could not have fallen more rigidly. He threw out his arms, and with a gentle oh! returned his soul to Him who gave it. His death for a time threw a gloom over all, for no one knew but he would be the next. I am convinced from the suddenness of the blow that he never knew the cause of his death.

So hotly were we engaged that no one had a leisure moment to remove him; there he lay grim and ghastly. Although I was commanding the gun next to the one on which Braddock was killed, and was but a few feet from him, still I was ignorant of the fact until quite a time afterward, when Lieutenant Theis informed me. So you may imagine how actively we were engaged. A lull soon

Captain Wallace Hill, Battery C, 1st West Virginia Light Artillery.

L. M. Strayer Collection

occurred in the firing when Braddock's remains were carried off, and laid in their last resting place. Truly a soldier's burial was his, the noise of war resounding on all sides when we laid him in his grave. He was wrapped in his blanket, a good deep grave dug, and a head board with his name carved on by a comrade, placed at the head. We left his body, but carried away a just appreciation of his worth as a man and a soldier.[51]

Braddock, 26, was a pre-war Morgan County teamster. Eulogized as "a good, brave & reliable soldier" by Battery C's first sergeant, Theodore G. Field, he was buried across from Granite School House next to a stone wall and two hickory trees — very near where he had eaten dinner that afternoon. His wooden head-board was simply inscribed "S J B."[52] William Jenvey continued:

Under the renewed energy of the battle all else was forgotten, and little by little accidents happened; two of my horses had their forelegs cut off by one shell, and so close did it strike to Charley Boyce,

L. M. Strayer Collection   *L. M. Strayer Collection*

Sergeant Leonidas Miraben, *left,* and First Lieutenant John G. Theis, Battery C, 1st WVLA. The German-born Theis was a Marietta shoemaker prior to enlistment.

their driver, that it knocked the dust over him and stunned him for a time. Supposing him killed, I ran to his assistance, but found him safe and cool as if nothing had happened. I ordered to unharness his crippled horses, take them to the rear and have them shot, and am not positive that I did not see a glistening in the poor fellow's eyes, very much like a tear, when he received the order.

John Lehnhard and Martin Wendelkin, both cannoneers on my gun, were standing side by side, taking ammunition out of the chest, when a shell came thundering between them, tearing off half the axle, and burying itself in the ground. Each looked at the other, and grasped their legs, thinking one at least was gone, so close did the shell pass, but finding themselves intact, they laughed and went on with their work. Another of my boys, whilst leaning against a wheel, heard a dull *thud*. On looking around, he found a musket ball half buried in the wheel close by his head. Sergeant [David] Dorr seeing a shell coming too friendly a course, leaped aside and escaped death. Captain Hill, while walking up and down the line, encouraging all, nearly lost both his legs by a shell.

Seeing a shell coming bent on mischief, I called "Look out." L[ewis] R. Moore on my right, hearing me, fell to the ground and the shell passed so close to him across his back, that he thought he was wounded, and placed his hands on his back like one in intense agony; he looked towards me, and seeing me laughing, found himself uninjured. He laughed also, and went on with his duty. It was now getting on towards dark, and the fire of the artillery was beginning to die away, but still the sharpshooters kept up an incessant fire. I was standing by my gun when I felt a sharp stinging sensation in my throat. I clapped my hand to the spot, imagining myself badly wounded. I felt a second time, but found no blood, and came to the conclusion that it was nothing. The next morning, on mentioning the fact, I was told there was a red streak across my throat.[53]

While the cannoneers on Cemetery Hill dueled and infantrymen took shelter behind available cover, a spectacular drama unfolded nearly two miles to the southwest. Just after 4 p.m. two-thirds of General James Longstreet's corps attacked the Federal left flank, which the Confederates erroneously believed lay along the Emmitsburg Road near a peach orchard owned by John Sherfy. Earlier in the day Union 3rd Corps commander Daniel Sickles pushed his two divisions forward from positions Meade instructed him to hold, thereby creating a salient at the orchard. Sickles' line extended southeast through a wheatfield to boulder-strewn Devil's Den, behind which rose the unoccupied Round Tops. Longstreet's initial blows fell in this area.

First Lieutenant Charles E. Hazlett, commander of Battery D, 5th U.S. Artillery. The Muskingum Countian's death July 2 was cause for General G.K. Warren to reflect, "No nobler man fought or fell that day than he."

From Little Round Top's summit Meade's chief engineer, Brigadier General Gouverneur K. Warren, realized the hill's tactical importance and urgently requested troops to hold it. Sickles could spare none. Fortunately Sykes' 5th Corps, having reached the battlefield about 8 a.m., was at hand, and a brigade commanded by Colonel Strong Vincent was rushed to Little Round Top's rocky crest. It soon was followed by First Lieutenant Charles E. Hazlett's Battery D, 5th U.S. Artillery, and another infantry brigade led by Brigadier General Stephen H. Weed. [54]

Hazlett, 25, was born and raised in Zanesville, briefly attended Kenyon College in Gambier, and graduated early with the West Point class of May 1861. He had commanded his Regular battery for 11 months and bore the reputation of an accomplished instructor and disciplinarian, yet was possessed with a "kind, affectionate disposition." General Warren first thought Little Round Top was no place for efficient artillery fire, but Hazlett disagreed. "The sound of my guns will be encouraging to our troops, and disheartening to the [enemy], and my battery's of no use if this hill is lost." His 10-pounder Parrotts were partly driven, then manhandled to the crest, where they began firing across Plum Run valley. Warren later wrote of Hazlett: "There he sat on his horse on the summit of the hill, with whole-souled animation encouraging our men, and pointing with his sword toward the enemy amidst a storm of bullets — a figure of intense admiration to me, even in that desperate scene. ..." [55]

By the time Weed arrived on Little Round Top Vincent's brigade had suffered heavily and its ammunition was dwindling. Weed, promoted to general from captain less than a month before, was not on the hill long when he, too, fell — paralyzed from the shoulders down by a Confederate bullet that clipped his spine. He asked for his friend Hazlett, who rode over, dismounted and kneeled at Weed's side. Leaning closer to catch the general's words, the Ohio-born artillery officer suddenly slumped forward. A bullet struck his head, fatally wounding him. Weed died a few hours later. [56]

Prior to Hazlett's death Captain Frank Gibbs' Battery L, 1st OVLA, took position on Little Round Top's rough northern slope. Like Gibbs, most of his cannoneers were from Portsmouth and Scioto County. The battery of six 12-pounder Napoleons had been among the last 5th Corps units to arrive from Hanover, and the Buckeyes were dog-tired. While parked in reserve earlier in the afternoon, recalled First Sergeant James Gildea, "we were all asleep in a short time and did not arouse until the heavy cannonading at 4 p.m.[,] which brought everyone to his feet." [57]

When the battery was summoned it halted on the eastern side of Little Round Top. Gibbs could not find his corps' artillery chief, Captain Augustus P. Martin, who was watching the battle from atop the hill. Accompanied by Gildea, Gibbs rode west on the Wheatfield Road and found General Sykes with a portion of his old Regular division. He asked where he was needed. Sykes, according to Gildea, looked around for a moment, replying, "Captain, choose your own position to cover this front. I leave it to yourself." Gibbs made a cursory survey of the surrounding terrain, then told his subaltern to have the battery's left section under First Lieutenant

Captain Frank C. Gibbs, Battery L, 1st OVLA. His July 4 after-action report contained the earliest known reference of the hill his left section occupied as "Little Round Top." In order for the battery's Napoleons to cover Plum Run, Gibbs wrote: "The rocky nature of the ground compelled us to unhitch our horses and place our guns in position by hand."
Carte de visite by T.T. Garlic, Portsmouth.

Author's Photo

In a mural by Robert Dafford painted on Portsmouth's Ohio River floodwall, Lieutenant Guthrie's section of Battery L, 1st OVLA, is depicted firing from the north slope of Little Round Top. *Right:* Private Francis Marion Temple and an older brother, Corporal Joel T. Temple, served three years in Gibbs' battery.

Herbert Guthrie placed on Little Round Top's northern slope, south of the Wheatfield Road. Gibbs chose a position north of the road facing marshy Plum Run for First Lieutenant William Walworth's two guns. Gildea was ordered to take the center 50 yards behind the other sections. "Do not fire a shot until we are all captured," Gibbs admonished him.[58]

After Gildea showed Guthrie his location he saw to the placement of his own section. "I found the ground covered with scrub and brush[,] which I directed the men to cut down so as to give a clear view to the front." While hacking away at obstructing vegetation with his back toward the west, Gildea was interrupted by one of his corporals, who pointed to a body of troops not far off. "As there was considerable smoke and haze in the air, I could not see very clear and as the road was sunken so that nothing was to be seen but their guns and flag, which was furled up, I mistook it for an Irish flag,

Courtesy of Marian H. Andre

[thinking] that it must be the 9th Mass[achusetts, a regiment belonging to the 5th Corps' 1st Division]. I did not look further but the head of the column swung around and came on the regulars who did not see them until they received a volley[,] which sent the remainder of them up to my section where they formed a support." Gildea estimated the enemy was only 80 yards from his battery's four advanced guns.[59]

The Confederates were part of Major General Lafayette McLaws' division, Longstreet's corps. "Our front was hardly clear," Gibbs reported, "when the irregular, yelling line of the enemy put in his appearance, and we received him with double charges of canister, which were used so effectively as to compel him to retire. So rapidly were the guns worked that they became too hot to lay the hand on."[60]

In reality, only three of Battery L's forward guns were engaged. One of Walworth's Napoleons, recalled Gildea, "could not be fired on account of the rocks around it caused hot recoil and [it] jumped straight up." Since his center section was idle, "I directed my men to carry canister to the left section as the rapid fire now going on would soon exhaust the supply in the limbers, the caissons not being yet up."[61]

Guthrie's doses of double-shotted canister were instrumental in driving the approaching Rebels to ground. One gunner, Private Benjamin F. Reed of Ironton, remembered the left section's initial blasts "mowed them down. It was the fighting of demons there." He recalled that the battery's first casualty, Leonidas Pyles, received an injury through forgetfulness. "By failing to rise on his toes as the heavy pieces were fired [he] suffered the bursting of blood vessels in his head. ... There is a violent concussion of the air when a heavy piece of artillery is fired, and to counteract its effects on the body, the men are instructed to stand on tip-toes as the explosion takes place."[62]

From Gildea's vantage point "the rebs dropped on their faces behind the rocks which were here in plenty and never raised until driven out by the charge of the Penna. Reserves, Col. [Joseph W.] Fisher, commdg. When Fisher passed my guns, he became a little excited for fear that the rebs would get our front guns before he arrived, so his men fired one volley through our men by which 2 of our men, Harrison Massie and Asa Kline, were wound-

His jacket adorned with Russian shoulder knots, First Lieutenant Herbert F. Guthrie was Battery L's second-ranking officer at Gettysburg. Carte de visite by Hoag & Quick's studio, Cincinnati.

ed. Lieutenant Guthrie yelled to him to charge or cease firing, so he advanced and drove the rebs out of their holes which ended the fight there."[63]

Battery L expended 90 rounds of canister, most of it in Guthrie's section. Accolades quickly followed. Gibbs credited the battery's position "and the gallantry with which it was handled by the men." But for these things "I have no doubt the enemy would have accomplished his purpose of breaking our lines at this point, and possibly changed the for-

Tony Lemut Collection

The 5th Corps' two brigades of U.S. Regulars, which advanced past Gibbs' battery and fought briefly July 2 in the bloody Wheatfield area, contained a sprinkling of Buckeyes. One of them was Clevelander Patrick Tucker, a sergeant in Company G, 11th U.S. Infantry. The regiment's six companies sustained 120 casualties out of 286 officers and men present.

tunes of the day." Captain Martin, 5th Corps artillery commander, wrote that Guthrie and his cannoneers "deserve special mention for the splendid manner in which the section was served." The sentiment was echoed by the army's artillery chief, General Henry Hunt, who lauded the Ohioans' "excellent service, especially Guthrie's." Sergeant Gildea, who mustered as a second lieutenant three weeks later, was the beneficiary of the battery's initial battlefield praise. He explained: "When Fisher charged, I looked back for the first time and found 6 lines of battle in the rear of my guns. The Sixth Corps had arrived and Genl. [John] Sedgwick was standing between the two guns. When I saluted him he remarked that we had ... done splendid by holding the ground against such a force, an opinion which our Corps Commander, Genl. Sykes, corroborated that night by sending for Gibbs and told him he should have the credit of saving that part of the line in his official report." [64]

When Sykes' document was completed at the end of July the general drew attention to 21 officers in his command. Curiously, Gibbs' name was not

among them. [65]

About the same time that Battery L went into action, another Ohio-born artillery officer was hotly engaged to the northwest along the Emmitsburg Road. First Lieutenant Francis W. Seeley's Battery K, 4th U.S. Artillery, anchored the left-center of Brigadier General Andrew A. Humphreys' 2nd Division, 3rd Corps, near the Daniel Klingle house. Seeley, born April 12, 1837 in Ashtabula, had served in the Regular Army artillery since 1855, rising in rank from private. For the war's first nine months he was stationed at Fort Pickens, part of that time as the Department of Florida's adjutant general. In March 1862 he took command of Battery K, participating in the siege of Yorktown, the Seven Days battles and Fredericksburg. [66] At Chancellorsville, his combative nature earned high praise in a report issued by the Congressional Committee on the Conduct of the War:

At the conclusion of the battle of Sunday [May 3, 1863], Captain [*sic*] Seeley's battery, which was the last battery that fired a shot in the battle of Chancellorsville, had 45 horses killed and in the neighborhood of 40 men killed and wounded; but being a soldier of great pride and ambition, and not wishing to leave any of his material in the hands of the enemy, he withdrew so entirely at his leisure that he carried off all the harness from his dead horses, loading his cannoneers with it; he even took a part of a set of harness on his own arm, and so moved to the rear. [67]

One military scribe referred to Seeley as "that prince of battery commanders." A fellow Ohio artillerist, writing to the *Ashtabula Weekly Telegraph* several days after Gettysburg, informed its editor that "As an officer and a gentleman Seeley cannot

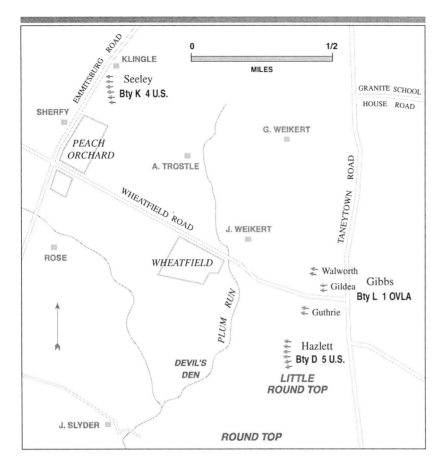

be exceeded. His battery has the reputation of being the best in the service, and I believe it fully maintained its reputation in this conflict." [68]

During mid-afternoon July 2 the lieutenant's six 12-pounders traded rounds of solid shot and spherical case with seven Confederate guns 800 yards to the west. According to Seeley's second in command, Lieutenant Robert James, these Rebel pieces were silenced and retired within 15 minutes. Shells from other enemy batteries continued falling in Humphreys' locale for two more hours, but at 5:30 the Federal line on both sides of the Klingle house was subjected to "a most destructive fire" — presaging the Confederate infantry attack here. Poised to assault was one of McLaws' brigades and two others belonging to Major General Richard H. Anderson's division, A.P. Hill's corps. [69]

At first, Seeley's gunners and those of another Regular battery 200 yards to their right replied to the incoming cannon fire. Battery K's guidon bearer, Edward I. Davis, understandably was concerned when he saw his commander fall. A shell fragment had contused his left thigh and the shock, Davis

wrote, "was so severe as to throw him down to the ground, he being at the time dismounted superintending the service of his guns." Seeley regained his feet, shrugging off the injury. When the Rebel infantry columns hoved into sight, reported Lieutenant James, "we turned our attention to them, firing as rapidly as possible shot, shell and spherical case." A dip in the ground momentarily hid Anderson's yelling men from view. Seeley's Napoleons fell silent while canister was rammed down their barrels. As soon as the oncoming enemy reappeared the 12-pounders' lanyards were yanked, spewing hundreds of iron balls into the closest Confederates like giant shotguns. After this and possibly another salvo, Seeley fell again. A bullet passed through his right thigh from side to side, taking with it a three-inch section of bone. Lieutenant James assumed command, ordering the stricken officer to be carried from the field and overseeing the battery's retirement to a new position 1,200 yards further east. [70]

By month's end Seeley returned to Ashtabula, where he was married August 5. Although he later performed quartermaster duty at Fort Washington, Maryland, his leg wound never healed properly and he was forced to resign August 31, 1864. Of his conduct at Gettysburg, General Humphreys wrote: "Lieut. F.W. Seeley's gallantry, skill, good judgment, and effective management of his battery excited my admiration, as well as that of every officer who saw him." [71]

From Cemetery Hill a panoramic view of Seeley's and much of the 3rd Corps' desperate fight was afforded to many of its occupants. "On went the great battle," recorded Lieutenant Jeffries of the 4th Ohio. "It raged all along the lines. The air was darkened with sulphurous smoke, deafening was the roar of cannon, shrieking of shell, and hiss of rifle ball. Fearful carnage was going on toward and in front of 'Round Top.' " Higher up the elevation Federal artillerymen watched in fascinated awe. William Jenvey believed the Confederate volleys pouring into General Sickles' 3rd Corps "made the earth quake; their whole line blazed with a sulphurous light. ... Mortal men could not stand such a fire. They wavered, then rallied, then wavered again, then broke, and with terrific and appalling yells the Rebel infantry pursued."[72]

For a while Captain Huntington was worried. "From our position on [Cemetery] hill, we had a full view of the plain in rear of the line. When, hard pressed, a portion of the [3rd] Corps gave way and came streaming back in disorder, while the exultant yells of the enemy rent the air, it seemed as if the Army of the Potomac were on the eve of another defeat. I met Gen. Warren, the Chief of Engineers on the general staff, and asked him if he thought it best to prepare to retire the batteries on the hill while it was practicable to do so. He replied, that 'If we were beaten here, the whole thing had gone up, and a few batteries more or less would make no difference.' "[73]

At the height of Huntington's anxiety the 5th Corps already was in action, as were portions of the 2nd, 6th and 1st corps, summoned by Meade to thwart the serious danger to the army's left flank. Huntington saw 12th Corps troops leave Culp's Hill

Major General Daniel E. Sickles' 3rd Corps was mauled July 2. In the process he lost his right leg.

and cross the Baltimore Pike, noting "the horseshoe shape of our position gave us the advantage of an interior line of communication. Erelong [the Confederates] were forced sullenly back, and our left was again intact. The line originally taken up by the 3d Corps was not, however, regained. It was better so, at least in the opinion of Gen. Meade, as that position was assumed by Sickles without his orders or concurrence. No proper connection had previously been made with the left of the 2d Corps, the next in line. This fault was now corrected."[74]

The 12th Corps regiments observed by Huntington probably belonged to the 1st Division, which vacated its entrenchments along the southern portion of Culp's Hill's defensive line. Thirty minutes later two brigades of General Geary's 2nd Division departed the hill as well, leaving only George S. Greene's New York brigade to hold the breastworks. Since little activity had occurred on the Federal right flank up to this point, Union commanders deemed it necessary to strip Culp's Hill of troops to bolster the endangered left. They did not know the fighting was about

Brigadier General John W. Geary.

Brigadier General George S. Greene.

Corporal Augustus Hively, *far left*, and Private John M. Hammel belonged to the 61st Ohio's Company C, recruited primarily from Montgomery County. Photographed early in his service, Hammel wore ornamental brass shoulder scales on his frock coat.

to shift in the opposite direction.[75]

The Confederate battle plan July 2 called for Ewell's Second Corps to assist Longstreet's main effort by attacking Culp's Hill and Cemetery Hill; doing so in tandem was intended to prevent Meade from moving troops to reinforce those opposing Longstreet. Delays postponed the simultaneous advance until late afternoon. Even then, as Longstreet's legions fought furiously at Little Round Top, Devil's Den, the Wheatfield and the Peach Orchard, Ewell's foot soldiers waited. Although his artillery bombardment made it quite hot for the occupants of Cemetery Hill, and to a lesser extent the Unionists on Culp's Hill, Ewell's infantry assault against the latter eminence did not begin until 7 p.m.[76]

Three Rebel brigades of Major General Edward Johnson's division crossed Rock Creek and moved west toward the hill's upper and lower slopes. Maintaining alignment was difficult in the fading daylight, and was further complicated by the area's rocky, tree-covered terrain. Johnson's Virginians, Louisianans, North Carolinians and Marylanders were unaware that most of the 12th Corps had just left the hill, but they knew defensive works of some strength faced them at the top.[77]

Bracing for the assault, General Greene ex-

tended his 1,400 men in fortifications from the hill's highest point south to the saddle connecting the lower hill. At the same time he urgently requested help. From Cemetery Hill General Howard sent four depleted regiments, including the 157th New York and part of the 61st Ohio, jointly commanded by the 61st's Colonel McGroarty. Three others were detached from Brigadier General James S. Wadsworth's 1st Corps division. Greene's skirmishers already had retired and their assailants were climbing the hill's slopes. Crashing volleys momentarily lit up the black woods. Behind their protective barriers the Federals aimed at the muzzle flashes and returned fire. Johnson's right and center brigades recoiled and reformed, making three fruitless attempts to storm the crest. His left brigade, however, fared better. Brigadier General George H. Steuart's five regiments and a Maryland infantry battalion managed to occupy the lower hill's abandoned trenches. But in the dark their success degenerated into trading random, ineffective shots with Greene's men and his supports.[78]

One of Wadsworth's regiments rushed to Greene's aid was the 6th Wisconsin, part of the 1st Corps' vaunted Iron Brigade, which had fought valiantly and suffered heavily the previous day west of

Gettysburg. The 6th's commander, Lieutenant Colonel Rufus R. Dawes, was a native Buckeye born on Independence Day in 1838 along the Muskingum River in Morgan County. Known as "Rufe" to family and friends, Dawes spent his youth near Marietta in the villages of Constitution and Malta, where he worked as a storekeeper and packer in his father Henry's wool and grain warehouse. According to an army subordinate, the 1860 Marietta College graduate "was a born leader of men, and we of the rank and file appreciated him as such. He never swore, drank or used coarse language when most of those around him were proficient in these traits."[79]

Hearing the crash of musketry off to the right, Dawes later described his regiment's combat role on Culp's Hill:

Soon a staff officer came along, calling: "Where is Colonel Dawes?" I answered, "Here." He said: "Take your regiment, sir, and report to General Greene." I said: "Where is he?" "He is right over in the woods where they are attacking." I commanded: "Attention, battalion, right face, forward by file right — march!" and we started for General Greene. Who he was I did not know, but the musketry showed where to go. The first mounted officer I saw proved to be General G.S. Greene, of the Twelfth Army

Lieutenant Colonel Rufus R. Dawes, 6th Wisconsin, photographed at the Marietta studio of Cadwallader & Tappan. His oldest son, Charles Gates Dawes, won a Nobel Peace Prize in 1925 and served as vice president under Calvin Coolidge.

Service with the Sixth Wisconsin Volunteers

Facing heavy musketry from Union breastworks above them, Confederate skirmishers took shelter behind boulders and trees at the base of Culp's Hill.

Battles and Leaders of the Civil War

Colonel William R. Creighton, 7th Ohio, was a native of Pittsburgh born in June 1837. At war's outbreak he worked in the *Cleveland Herald's* type composing room and belonged to the Cleveland Light Guard Zouaves. As the 7th Ohio's commander, observed First Lieutenant George McKay of Company A, Creighton was "an excellent officer, cool and recklessly brave in action [and] beloved by soldiers serving under him." Less than five months after Gettysburg he was killed leading a charge at Ringgold Gap, Georgia.

Corps. Taking from his pocket a card, he wrote in the darkness his name and command, which he handed to me. He then directed me to form my regiment, and go into the breastworks; to go as quickly as possible, and to hold the works after I got there. I did not then understand that the rebels already had possession of these works. Facing the regiment to the front, I ordered: "Forward — run, march!" We received no fire until we neared the breastworks, when the enemy who had possession of them, lying on the lower side, and who were completely surprised at our sudden arrival, rose up and fired a volley at us, and immediately retreated down the hill. This remarkable encounter did not last one minute. We lost two men, killed — both burned with the powder of the guns fired at them. The darkness and the suddenness of our

arrival caused the enemy to fire wildly. We had recaptured the breastworks on our front, and the Fourteenth Brooklyn, which came in on our right, also got possession of the works. We remained here till about midnight, when we were relieved by troops of the Twelfth Corps. ...[80]

Dawes' Badgers were replaced by Pennsylvanians of the 2nd Brigade, Geary's division, which had helped little if any that evening to stabilize the Federal left flank. Due to unclear orders and a great deal of confusion in the darkness, Geary's men marched all the way to the Baltimore Pike bridge crossing Rock Creek before it was realized they were heading in the wrong direction. Candy's 1st Brigade, in the lead, was posted east of the creek with instructions to picket its bank. This was easier said than done. To Private Joseph R. Lynn of the 29th Ohio the exercise consisted of "wandering through brush, briars and bowlders." For Private Henry Knapp, also of the 29th, it seemed "Our regiment was on the move all night long so we got little or no rest or sleep; we of the rank and file [knew] little of where we were at." The 2nd Brigade returned to Culp's Hill well before Candy's, which left Rock Creek sometime after midnight. An unidentified 7th Ohioan wrote to the *Cleveland Plain Dealer* four days later: "General Geary moved our [brigade] through the woods a mile and a half back on the road that we came in on. About 2 o'clock in the night we came on the road, and marched towards [Culp's Hill]. Hundreds of stragglers were strewn along the road, who asked us what was our corps, and told us all the news of the first and second days' fight. We affected ignorance of the whole. The whole army thought that Meade was being reinforced, and the weak-kneed became strong."[81]

Candy rearranged his brigade in a hollow to

the right rear of Greene's troops. In this position the 7th Ohio received a volley from Steuart's unseen line that wounded one man. Colonel Creighton was ordered to move the regiment farther right, forming behind a stone wall running perpendicular to the Baltimore Pike in the vicinity of Henry Spangler's orchard. Twenty men led by Sergeant Isaac Stratton of Company F were thrown out as skirmishers. They had not advanced far when more gunfire erupted. Stratton fell. A bullet fractured his left eye socket, destroying the eye. The 33-year-old Portage County boilermaker, injured in the head by a shell fragment two months earlier at Chancellorsville, was thought to be mortally wounded. But to his comrades' amazement he returned to duty late in October. A third wound suffered in the left foot at Ringgold, Georgia, the following month still did not dampen his ardor for soldiering. Finally, his luck ran out. In May 1864 at New Hope Church, Georgia, Stratton was killed in action.[82]

Some six hours prior to the 7th Ohio's harrowing moments on Culp's Hill much greater tension gripped the Buckeyes of Andrew Harris' 11th Corps brigade in front of East Cemetery Hill.

Not long after Johnson's initial assault on Culp's Hill had gotten underway, two brigades of General Early's division joined the attack with orders to storm Cemetery Hill. These Confederate troops — Isaac Avery's North Carolinians and Harry Hays' Louisianans — had smashed Coster's 11th

Corps brigade the previous day and captured two Napoleon guns from Battery K, 1st OVLA. Before sunup July 2 Hays' five regiments, nicknamed the "Louisiana Tigers," were moved from Gettysburg to a field near the town's southeast outskirts along Winebrenner's Run. Avery's men extended the line to the left of Hays. As day dawned the Louisianans discovered they occupied a perilously exposed position. Cemetery Hill, wrote one of Hays' staff officers, was about 500 yards away and "found to be crowned with strongly built fortifications and bristling with a most formidable array of cannon." For more than 12 hours "we had to remain there ... hugging the ground behind a very low ridge which only partially covered us from the enemy's fire. It was almost certain death for a man to stand upright and we lost during the day forty-five men in killed and wounded from the fire of the enemy's sharpshooters. ..."[83]

With escalation of musketry fire on Johnson's front, Hays, temporarily commanding his own and Avery's brigade, was told to advance a few minutes before 8 p.m. Notes from a lone bugle brought the Tigers and Tarheels to their feet. Automatically they formed ranks. "The quiet, solemn mien of our men showed plainly that they fully appreciated the desperate character of the undertaking," observed a Louisiana officer. Another serving in the 8th Louisiana commented after the battle: "I felt as if my doom was sealed and it was with great reluctance that I started my skirmishers forward."[84]

The Rebels' path of attack lay in the undulating fields and meadows north of Culp's Hill and east of East Cemetery Hill. Advancing south at first, both brigades had to wheel right in a 600-yard arc in order to face their objective frontally. Barring their way to the Federal batteries perched on the heights was Adelbert Ames' undermanned division of the 11th Corps, much of it posted along Brickyard Lane's low stone wall at the hill's base. Von Gilsa's 1st Brigade, reinforced by the 33rd Massachusetts of Orland Smith's brigade, occupied Ames' right. His left was held by Harris' three Ohio regiments and the 17th Connecticut of the 2nd Brigade. A late-afternoon shift of Harris' line brought the 25th Ohio downslope to the lane, while the 107th Ohio remained facing Gettysburg. Between the 75th Ohio on Harris' right and the 25th Ohio was sandwiched Major Allen Brady's Connecticut regiment, which had served all day on picket duty. Even with

Brigadier General Harry T. Hays, CSA.

Battles and Leaders of the Civil War

Louisianans of Hays' brigade assault East Cemetery Hill. Although this 19th-century illustration depicts artillery lunettes constructed to the east of Evergreen Cemetery's gatehouse, it fails to show any Federal infantry opposing the oncoming Confederates.

the shift Harris' line did not quite reach von Gilsa's left. Ames ordered Brady to support von Gilsa, and the 17th Connecticut was pulled from behind the wall to be posted right of the 75th Ohio.[85]

The redeployment strengthened the 1st Brigade, but it produced a gap at the right center of Harris' brigade that could only be closed by stretching part of the 107th and the tiny 25th Ohio to link up with the 75th's leftmost company. "This left my line very thin and weak," Harris stated. "All the men could get to the stonewall, used by us as a breastwork, and have all the elbow room he wanted." With his "Nutmeg brethren" gone, Harris was

forced to defend his brigade front "at all hazards" with fewer than 500 men. "Before I could make any arrangements to remedy this breach in the line the attack of the enemy on Cemetery Hill was made."[86]

Harris, a future Ohio governor, was stunned at first by the Rebels' appearance. "It was a complete surprise to us," he admitted. "We did not expect this assault as bravely and rapidly made. In fact, we did not expect any assault at all. We could not have been much more surprised if the moving column had raised up out of the ground amid the waving timothy grass of the meadow." His skirmishers and those in front of von Gilsa's brigade were the first to fire as the Confederates surged forward. Then, as the Union skirmish companies began retiring westward, six Napoleons of the 5th Maine Battery stationed on McKnight's Hill [later renamed Stevens' Knoll] roared to life. They were quickly followed by 15 ordnance rifles on East Cemetery Hill belonging to Wiedrich's, Ricketts' and G.H. Reynolds' batteries, the last-named commanded by First Lieutenant George Breck. "Our artillery," Harris continued,

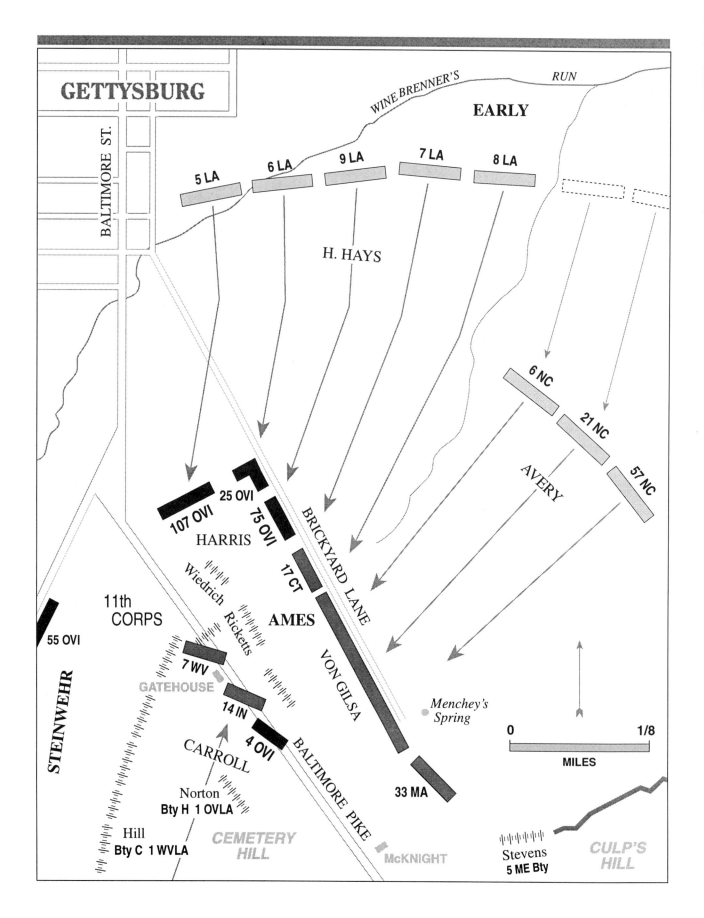

GETTYSBURG

WINE BRENNER'S   RUN

EARLY

BALTIMORE ST.

5 LA   6 LA   9 LA   7 LA   8 LA

H. HAYS

6 NC

21 NC

57 NC

AVERY

25 OVI

107 OVI

75 OVI

HARRIS

BRICKYARD LANE

17 CT

AMES

11th
CORPS

Wiedrich

Ricketts

55 OVI

VON GILSA

7 WV

GATEHOUSE

14 IN

STEINWEHR

4 OVI

CARROLL

BALTIMORE PIKE

Norton
Bty H 1 OVLA

Menchey's
Spring

33 MA

0   1/8

MILES

Hill
Bty C 1 WVLA

CEMETERY
HILL

McKNIGHT

Stevens
5 ME Bty

CULP'S
HILL

Caught up in the 25th Ohio's struggle on East Cemetery Hill were Private Ignatius Tillett, Company A, Corporal Oliver Hershey, Company E (pictured as a late-war lieutenant), and Private William Pancoast, Company G. All survived. Another regimental participant commented: "Within thirty minutes from the time the charge was made, the smoke had cleared away and the moon had risen with great brilliancy, flooding the battle field with mellow light. It was a ghastly battle field."

Private Ignatius Tillett.

Corporal Oliver P. Hershey.

Private William Pancoast.

"opened on them with all the guns that could be brought to bear. But on, still on, they came, moving steadily to the assault. They moved forward ... as though they were on parade far removed from danger." [87]

General Hays later made note of the "most terrific fire from the enemy's batteries" and offered an explanation for his troops' inexorable progress: "Owing to the darkness of the evening, now verging into night, and the deep obscurity afforded by the smoke of the firing, our exact locality could not be discovered by the enemy's gunners, and we thus escaped what in the full light of day could have been nothing else than horrible slaughter." [88]

Colonel Harris rode behind his extended ranks, shouting encouragement to the Buckeyes. "The infantry were loading and firing as rapidly as possible, keeping up a most galling fire." The right of the Louisiana brigade struck Harris' line first, at the junction of the 25th and 107th Ohio. "At this point," he remembered, "and soon all along my whole line the fighting was obstinate and bloody." Private George S. Clements of Company H, 25th Ohio, recalled that the charging Confederates "put their big feet on the stone wall and went over like deer, over the heads of the whole ... regiment, the grade being steep and the wall not more than 20 inches high." Edward Culp, the 25th Ohio lieutenant serving on

Sergeant Philip Scherhag, Company A, 107th Ohio, *right,* lost his Swiss-born brother-in-law, Private Samuel Maurer of the same company, to a mortal leg wound inflicted the evening of July 2. Born in the Rhine River city of Koblenz, Scherhag resided in Massillon. Nineteen years old at the time of the battle, Company I private Christian Van Guntian, *above,* was appointed corporal in December 1863.

Ames' staff, wrote a few days later: "On they came, with their wild, diabolical yells, up to our first line of stone fence ... and the carnage began. I cannot describe the scene that followed. Nothing could stay the progress of the rebels. ..." He later added, "The smoke of battle was so thick that with the increasing darkness it became difficult to distinguish friend from foe."[89]

With bayonets and clubbed muskets the Louisianans drove the 107th and 25th toward another low wall to the left of Wiedrich's guns. Somewhere on the slope Lieutenant William Maloney fell wounded, and command of the 25th Ohio devolved upon First Lieutenant Israel White of Company A. He became the regiment's fourth commander in less than

29 hours.

Adjutant Peter Young, still in command of the 107th Ohio, maintained afterward an order reached him to fall back to Wiedrich's battery and hold that position "at all hazards." Color Sergeant Christian Taifel, a Clevelander of Company E, defiantly waved the 107th's flag at the onrushing Confederates until a bullet mangled one of his hands and embedded itself in his arm. Young grabbed the flag before it could be captured and carried the banner out of harm's way. Sixteen days later Taifel died of his wounds in a Philadelphia hospital.[90]

"A regular hand to hand fight ensued," reported Company I's commander, Second Lieutenant George Billau, to an Akron newspaper. "The 'Louisiana Tigers' made a terrible bayonet charge upon us." Private Jacob McCormick was killed. Privates John W. Hall, John Corman, Frederick Trachsel, Samuel Braun and Caspar Schild fell with wounds, Braun losing his left leg. All were from Summit and Tuscarawas counties. Twenty-four others in Billau's company had been killed, wounded or captured the day before, including Captain William Speier of Tiffin, who suffered a grievous shoulder injury.[91]

Private Silas Shuler of Company A related to his brother how the Confederates "were all bent over as they charged up the hill. They kept coming [and] we opened up our fire on them. ... Then the Rebels took to using their bayonets." In the frantic melee someone behind him fell "and stuck me in the calf of the leg with his bayonet. That sent me to the hospital." Nearby, three of Shuler's company comrades also went down with leg wounds. Private Andrew Lahmiller was shot in a knee, Samuel Maurer in the right thigh. Private Lucas Strobel's right leg was fractured, probably when struck by a clubbed musket. None of them lived past July 15.[92]

The 107th Ohio was pushed "in some disorder" to the rear of Wiedrich's battery where a number of Louisianans, according to Lieutenant Young, were "yelling like demons at the [guns'] supposed capture." Corporal Frederick Nussbaum of Company C noticed a Rebel color bearer waving his flag near one of the battery's lunettes, while color guards grouped themselves at his sides. "I called the attention of Adjutant Young to this demonstration, and

there being about seven of us we at once, by command of the Adjutant, fired a volley and advanced toward them scattering the color-guards in every direction. The color-bearer being severely wounded, dropped on one knee holding to his flag with such a firm grip, that Adjutant Young who was trying to wrench it from him could not do it. The color-bearer had a large navy revolver in his right hand. I saw him pull the trigger and shoot the Adjutant through the shoulder blade; the Adjutant in turn planted his sabre in the color-bearer's breast. The color-bearer held on to the flag and sabre with a firm grip until he dropped over dead, never loosening his grasp until he drew his last breath."[93]

A somewhat different version of this incident was provided to the *Cleveland Herald* when Young was interviewed July 22 upon arrival in Cleveland to convalesce. His description was paraphrased two days later on the newspaper's front page: "The forces were within twenty paces of each other, when Young knew and felt the crisis, and knew how important it was to encourage his men. Right before him were the 8th Louisiana Tigers with the color bearer flaunting the rebel flag in the face of the 107th. Young drew his revolver, dashed forward, shot the rebel color bearer dead at his feet, when one of the rebel color guard caught the colors as the bearer fell, when Young snatched the colors ... and turned to go back to his men, when two of the rebel color guard fired at him. One ball entered Young's right breast at the center, and passed through his

Sixteen members of Private James Bowers' Company H, 107th Ohio, were killed, wounded or captured during the first day's battle north of Gettysburg. None were lost July 2.

Ron Chojnacki Collection

Corporal Conrad Deubel, a 19-year-old Cleveland varnisher originally from Bavaria, served in Company B, 107th Ohio. He succeeded John H. Brinker as sergeant major in January 1864, and that November was promoted first lieutenant of Company K.

Bob Albertini Collection

body, coming out behind the left arm. Young reached his men and was saved from falling, but he kept hold of the rebel colors."[94]

The adjutant finally collapsed in the arms of Sergeant Major Brinker, to whom Young entrusted the captured colors of the 8th Louisiana. He was conveyed to the Evergreen Cemetery gatehouse, "where refreshing water somewhat allayed the burning fever and saved my life." The following morning the flag was given to Company B first lieutenant Fernando C. Suhrer, who turned it over to 11th Corps headquarters. Young was succeeded in command of the 107th Ohio on July 3 by Company E's captain, John Lutz, who had been slightly wounded during the first day's battle. Several of his soldiers afterward examined the Louisiana color bearer's body, finding it riddled with seven bullet holes. Corporal Nussbaum appropriated the dead man's knapsack, "which was a very neat one, made of leather with a goat-skin cover, and which contained a single biscuit lately baked being yet warm; being minus my own knapsack, I carried it a while, but [my] Comrades made so much fun of me that I threw it away for which act I have been sorry ever since."[95]

The struggle at the entrenchments protecting Wiedrich's four rifled guns was savage if short-lived. The Confederate assault, recalled one of his New York artillerymen, "was so sudden and violent that the infantry in front gave way, and the enemy got within the battery; but only for a moment, for assistance was at hand, and the cannoneers, using sponge-staffs, handspikes, and stones, forced them back, following it up with doses of canister. One Rebel planted his colors on one of the lunettes of the first section (which was on the left), and demanded the surrender of the gun. He was promptly knocked down with a handspike. ..."[96]

Although the 107th and 25th Ohio were driven back, a majority of their brigade mates in the 75th Ohio and 17th Connecticut at the hill's base remained in place. Major Brady of the 17th succinctly reported: "When within 150 paces of us, we poured a destructive fire upon [the Confederates], which thinned their ranks and checked their advance. We fired several volleys by battalion, after which they charged upon us. We had a hand-to-hand conflict with them, firmly held our ground, and drove them back. Soon after, some of the troops on our [far] left giving way, the rebels succeeded in getting in our rear. We again drove them back and held our position." The enemy battle line was only seen at first by the flash of the 17th's Enfield rifle muskets. "We ... commenced firing," reflected Second Lieutenant Albert W. Peck, commanding Company D, "and did not cease until the enemy fell back. Not a member of my regiment left his position, unless he was wounded. ... A Captain from my regiment hauled a burly Johnny over the stone wall and captured him." Brady, whose right shoulder was contused by a shell fragment during the fight, wrote two days later that "The coolness and bravery displayed by the officers and men of Company D exceeded anything I ever saw."[97]

In Company B of the 75th Ohio, Private William Southerton had just settled down behind the Brickyard Lane stone wall "when a horrible screaming and yelling arose from the lowlands [west] of Rock Creek." He was further startled when Union

Major Allen G. Brady, 17th Connecticut.

First Lieutenant Oscar Derostus Ladley, Company G, 75th Ohio, was a Cincinnatian by birth but resided in Yellow Springs — site of Antioch College, where his father played a role soliciting funds for construction of the first building on its campus. Early in the war Ladley served as a private in the 16th Ohio's three-month organization. Carte de visite by E.P.H. Capron & Bros. Photographic Gallery, Springfield.

P. L. Dunbar Library Special Collections, Wright State University

guns to the regiment's rear suddenly unleashed their projectiles, the flare of bursting shells illuminating the advancing Confederates. "The screaming hordes came rushing at us. Frantic warnings couldn't be heard in that confusion. We didn't need warnings. We knew. The battery on the crest above us poured grape and cannister right in to the midst of the fiendish horde. The crackle of our rifle fire was incessant. What a furious gnawing of cartridge paper!" In what seemed to Southerton like seconds, the Rebels reached the wall. Private John North, standing beside him, was yanked over by a Louisianan. Corporal George C. Humphrey was shot and taken prisoner. A shell exploded overhead. Dodging, Southerton looked up and saw a Confederate officer standing on the wall with a flag in his hands. At that moment Private Lorenzo Fowler of Company B plunged his bayonet into the officer just as more grayclad soldiers bounded into their midst. Several others also were bayoneted while leaping down among the Ohioans.[98]

Near the 75th's left flank Captain Ben Fox, temporarily commanding the regiment, stood at a small gap in the wall, as he informed his father: "A 1st Lieut was first to enter. I had no pistol and not having my sabre drawn I hit him with a rock. He was not over ten feet at the farthest from me. A private of Co. D was ready for him with cold steel, or the bayonet, and making a lung[e] at him ran it through up to the hub, putting an end to the Lieut. The Reb Colors next came with a lot of mad men — and cursing us asking [us] to surrender. But they did not stop. Up and on they went, the battery was what they wanted." [99]

A similar rush of Rebels enveloped Lieutenant Oscar Ladley and Company G. Ladley had been in a melancholy mood since morning, when he learned

his good friend Captain James Mulharen of Company C died of wounds received the previous day. Having missed the July 1 battle, it was now his turn to fight. "They came on us ... yelling like demons with bayonets," Ladley wrote his mother and sisters on July 5. "We lay behind a stone wall and received them with our bayonets. I was standing behind the wall when they came over. A Rebel officer made at me with a revolver. ... I had no pistol[,] nothing but my sword. Just as I was getting ready to strike him one of our boys run him through the body so saved me. There was a good man killed in that way. ... The only one in my company who was killed was killed by a rebel bayonet thrust in the groin." [100]

This man, Private Wesley Raikes, was a 39-

year-old butcher from Camden in Preble County. In correspondence to the dead soldier's brother-in-law, Raikes' company commander consoled that "to talk of his home, his wife and children was his greatest pleasure. Not a day passed that he did not talk to me of his family. He fell in the second day's fight. The conflict was hand to hand; great confusion prevailed on both sides. In this struggle, which took place just at dark, when it was almost impossible to recognize friend or foe, he lost his life. He fell, as the true soldier falls — at his post. He had not moved a foot from the position in which he had been placed." [101]

For his part, Lieutenant Ladley was admonished two and a half weeks later in a letter from his mother. "You made a narrow escape," she told him, "when that rebel Officer came at you with his Revolver. Where was your own Gun and how came you to have no weapon but your sword[?] you ought never to go into battle without a good Revolver." [102]

Ladley made it through without injury, unlike many in his regiment who defied the Confederate onslaught at the wall. A wound dropped fellow Yellow Springs resident John Ginn, a private in Ladley's company. Nine others of Company G were overpowered and taken prisoner, including Sergeant Ira Curtner and Private Isaac Eby. In Company C — Colonel Harris' old command — brothers Joseph and Jeremiah Crubaugh were wounded, the latter dying the next day at the 11th Corps hospital. Privates Samuel P. Baughman and Thomas Pottenger were killed. A bullet smashed the right thigh of Color Sergeant William B. Spears and, as one member of his company phrased it, "We lost our flag." Spears died the following February at Dover, Ohio. [103]

Sergeant John A. Starrett of Company B feigned being wounded to elude capture. "I lay as limp as could be. One of the rebels yelled at me, 'Get up there! I'll run this bayonet right through you!' Just as I was getting up a shell burst overhead. The Tigers ran in every direction. I ran, too, back over the wall." [104]

Farther down Ames' division front the center of von Gilsa's line collapsed under pressure from Avery's attacking Tarheels, although Avery himself was mortally wounded. Two weak German regiments broke and retreated uphill, some of the New Yorkers apparently passing to the rear of the 17th Connecticut and 75th Ohio. Lieutenant Ladley later fumed. "They had driven back the dutch Brig[ade] on our right and had got behind us, and rebels & Yankees were mixed up generally. They (the 'dutch') commenced running back as usual. My sword was out and if I didn't welt them with it my name ain't O.D.L. It was the only good service it has done me yet, and if I live to see it home, I will have the satisfaction of knowing that if it never killed a reb it came mighty near laying out a dutchman!" [105]

Private Isaac Eby of Company G rejoined the 75th Ohio in October 1863 after imprisonment at Richmond. Promoted to sergeant, he was killed August 17, 1864 near Gainesville, Florida.

Brad L. Pruden Collection

Captain George Benson Fox, Company A, commanded
the 75th Ohio from the evening of July 1 to midday July 4.
Shortly after the battle he was promoted major,
his commission dating from June 11, 1863.

through the head. The rock crashed upon one of his screaming comrades." [106]

Captain Fox could not fathom how he escaped. "I was among them going up the hill. [It] was so smoky and dark one could hardly be distinguished. When we got to the top the adjutant of the 107th Ohio shot a color bearer and one of their Regt got the Reb's colors. The battery (1st NY) put the cannister into them heavy. The rebs came to the cannons mouth and demanded their surrender, the Cannoniers clubbing them with handspikes &c. Some in the german Regts gave them a few volleys and at last they were forced to retire but did not take or hurt the guns. I began to fear a panic in the 'Running half moons' but fortunately we whipped them with out assistance although reinforcements was at hand. ... All of us that got out safe were among the Rebs when they advanced up the hill — about 100 yards high — it being a clover field. Lieut Ladly [sic] and myself are the only Officers safe in camp." [107]

Four officers from the 75th Ohio were made prisoners that night — First Lieutenant David McCully of Company E and Second Lieutenants David B. Caldwell (Company I), John A. Mendenhall (Company B) and Joseph F. Potts (Company F). McCully later died in a South Carolina prison. [108]

Fox was incorrect about help not being needed or used to repulse Hays' Louisianans at Wiedrich's battery. When the assaulting Confederates' yells first were heard by Generals Howard and Schurz, the latter, at Howard's request, hurried two regiments from Krzyzanowski's command just north of the cemetery to Wiedrich's aid. Led personally by its Polish brigade commander, the 119th New York materially assisted in driving Rebels from the gun position and off the hill's crest. Three other regiments from von Steinwehr's division were summoned, but did not contribute to any great extent. [109]

Assistance also was required on East Cemetery

Despite the earlier vow to General Ames that its men would hold at all hazards, portions of the 75th were carried uphill. "My company was caught in the onslaught," recollected William Southerton, "[some] killed, wounded, captured. Others were lost in the crazed mob and were swept right up to [Wiedrich's] battery." Southerton chanced seeing comrade Andrew Jackson, the teenaged private from Company D who had been out sharpshooting that afternoon, "wriggle in reverse," slip over the wall and disappear. "The Johnnies, pushing, crowding, gained our first epaulements in spite of our efforts to block the way. It was almost impossible to distinguish who were Union, who were Confederate, to shoot and not kill our own men. Artillerists fought with ramrods, wielding them like ballbats. Our guns were not spiked. So infuriated were the Tigers that they jabbed with their bayonets. Fought with rocks. A tall rebel shoved right at my elbow, a huge rock raised ready to dash it at Major [sic] Fox. I jabbed with my bayonet. A burst of fire! The rebel fell, shot

Hill south of Wiedrich, where Captain Ricketts' Pennsylvania battery was assailed from the left and front. Clusters of Rebels from both Avery's and Hays' brigades swarmed into Ricketts' left and center sections. The short fight mirrored that taking place at Wiedrich's position. Handspikes, rammers, revolvers and rocks were used by the Keystone artillerymen to defend themselves and their guns, while the battery's right-hand pieces continued firing canister and fuseless case shot. The enemy succeeded in capturing and spiking one cannon, Ricketts reported. "If I had received no support, my men would have been overpowered." [110]

Salvation appeared behind the embattled artillerists in the form of a Union column double-quicking across the Baltimore Pike. Howard's appeal for help had produced an immediate response from General Hancock. He suggested to Brigadier General John Gibbon, temporarily commanding the 2nd Corps, to send Colonel Sprigg Carroll's "Gibraltar" brigade, three regiments of which were stationed along

the Taneytown Road near Ziegler's Grove. Carroll was told part of the 11th Corps was being driven back. Without any precise instructions he was ordered "to move immediately." At the head of the 14th Indiana "Old Bricktop" set off, followed in column by the 7th West Virginia and eight companies of the 4th Ohio. [111]

The "Gibraltar" soldiers entered Evergreen Cemetery, passing cannons and limbers parked amid the tombstones. Wrote Ohio artillery captain James Huntington: "Carroll, with his brigade of fire-eaters, came up just in the nick of time. Carroll sung out, 'Where's Huntington?' 'Here I am, General,' I said. 'I am sent here,' he continued, 'to support something or some one — where's the enemy?' I showed him their advancing line, and he commanded, 'Forward! double quick, march!' and in they went. ..." [112]

Once across the Baltimore Pike Carroll discovered "the enemy up to and some of them in among the front guns of the batteries [near] the road. Owing to the artillery fire from our own guns, it was

Members of the 4th Ohio's Company C included Private George W. Shearer, *left,* and Corporal Girard Welch, *right.* They were commanded by Captain Byron Dolbear, *above,* a Delaware clerk wearing the blue trefoil badge of the 3rd Division, 2nd Corps. He died in June 1864 from wounds suffered near Spotsylvania, Virginia. William Kepler of Dolbear's company maintained his regimental comrades "believed in less ammunition and more bayonet. 'Go in on your muscle,' was the motto of the 'Gibraltar Brigade.' Very many of the men would not carry more than forty rounds, because they would not be made pack-mules for the sake of any general."

impossible to advance by a longer front than that of a regiment, and it being perfectly dark, and with no guide, I had to find the enemy's line entirely by their fire."[113]

The 4th Ohio's fast pace through the cemetery, recalled First Sergeant Joseph L. Dickelman of Company D, "soon became a dead run, many of our men throwing away their knapsacks and blankets in order to keep up with the mad rush." At the pike the 14th Indiana, with the 4th Ohio to its right rear, passed the southern side of the cemetery gatehouse while transforming from column to battle line. The 7th West Virginia did likewise on the gatehouse's north side. Dickelman averred that Carroll's booming, "clarion voice" could be heard above the tumult — "Halt! Front face! Charge bayonets! Forward, double-quick! March! Give them hell!"[114]

Company C, the 4th Ohio's largest with two officers and 32 enlisted men, was closest to the Hoosiers as the regiment crossed the road. The Delaware Countians were led by 23-year-old Captain Byron Dolbear, who had been suffering painful headaches since June 20 as a result of sunstroke. One of his privates, William Kepler, later described their charge: "The position of the rebels [was] determined only by their fire; hastening toward them, now by the left flank ... through tanglements of retreating men, caissons and horses, up and along a slope, where maddened gunners of captured batteries raved and swore, or cried in very madness, vowing to meet death rather than give up their guns, striking the rebels with fist, rammer, ammunition and stones; greeting, echoing and re-echoing our cheer upon cheer, saying 'It's Carroll's brigade, there'll be no more running; give 'em hell, boys.' Bayonets and butts of guns at once joined the efforts of the heroic gunners, then infantry and gunner in a general melee, with flanks of regiments overlapping and every-man-in-as-you-can sort of way, drove the enemy from unhitching horses and spiking guns, down over the hill, under the crossfire of Stevens' [5th Maine] battery on our right, and captured a number of prisoners."[115]

Sergeant Dickelman remembered the regiment, commanded by Lieutenant Colonel Leonard W. Carpenter, was "yelling continually as we drove the Tigers before us." Kepler concurred, citing in large measure "the cheering and Carroll's mighty voice" for their success. Lieutenant Lemuel Jeffries, Com-

L. M. Strayer Collection

Lieutenant Colonel Leonard W. Carpenter, 4th Ohio.

pany E, tersely noted: "It was a headlong dash, a yell, and a few rounds fired and it was done." Only one man, Corporal John Debolt of Company B, was killed. Among the 4th's handful of wounded, Company A private James W. Harl of Knox County died a week afterward.[116]

By the time Carroll's three regiments arrived on East Cemetery Hill the Confederate assault essentially was spent. Helping to drive the North Carolinians and the Louisianans' left wing down the

First Lieutenant William W. Wallace, adjutant.

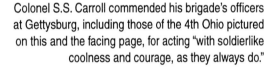

Colonel S.S. Carroll commended his brigade's officers at Gettysburg, including those of the 4th Ohio pictured on this and the facing page, for acting "with soldierlike coolness and courage, as they always do."

Captain Samuel L. Brearly, Company F.
Carte de visite by McIntire's Gallery, Canton.

hill's east face took 15 minutes or less, leaving the 4th Ohio and its brigade comrades "in the happiest mood." They did not know General Hays and other Rebel officers were attempting to collect scattered survivors and reform their lines while waiting for expected reinforcements. These never arrived. Finally, about 9:45 p.m., Hays ordered a withdrawal back to Winebrenner's Run. He reported his brigade's loss as 158 officers and men, but the actual count was probably twice as large. The North Carolina brigade suffered a similar number of casualties.[117]

The charge of Carroll's brigade carried the 4th Ohio to Brickyard Lane's stone wall, where the eight companies blindly sent a few volleys in the direction of the retreating enemy. With the order to

cease fire "an amusing incident occurred here," Dickelman recalled. From the darkness an Irishman's voice "called to us, 'Hould on, byes, I'm wan ov yoursilves. Don't shoot me!' Being told to jump over the Stone Wall, he did so; then slapping his thigh with his hand, exclaimed, 'Thank Jasus, I'm in the Union again.' "[118]

At least one other soldier recrossed the wall — before the shooting stopped. Private Andrew Jackson of the 75th Ohio was last seen slipping away when the regiment's left-flank companies were overrun. He decided to ride out the attack in a locust thicket where earlier in the day he narrowly missed being hit by a shell. Jackson explained to a comrade: "I saw my chance last night in all that yelling and screaming. My ammunition was gone. It

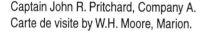
Tony Lemut Collection

Captain John R. Pritchard, Company A.
Carte de visite by W.H. Moore, Marion.

Tony Lemut Collection

First Lieutenant Channing L. Pettibone, Company E.
He was mortally wounded in 1864 at Spotsylvania.

was dark. No one could see me crawling through the brush along the fence where I went before. I knew there'd be a lot of dead Johnnies there. The place was thick with dead bodies. I pulled one dead Johnnie, then another, up against me for protection and went through [their] pockets. I got all these watches. And some money, too. [As] I started back I didn't know if I could make it or not. When I was part way up the hill the Tigers started to come back. Like wild beasts! They ran right over me. When I reached the wall I climbed over it in a hurry. I've been down there twice now. I'll never go again, never."

As for his battlefield spoils, Jackson soon "hated the sight" of them. He traded the pilfered watches for greenbacks.[119]

The 4th Ohio remained near the wall for the night and the rest of the battle. Lieutenant Colonel Carpenter threw out pickets "well to the front." He reported taking 34 prisoners and 200 stand of arms. "We were armed on going into the fight with the smooth-bore muskets, but these were exchanged for good Springfield rifles that we captured from the enemy."[120]

An hour before midnight with the sound of gunfire still emanating from Culp's Hill, Carpenter's men not on skirmish duty lay down for rest. "The moon rose and shed its sickly light over the field," Lieutenant Jeffries jotted in his diary. "None of the enemy could be seen, except the dead and severely wounded." About this time the remnants of detached Companies G and I returned to the regiment after spending seven arduous hours on the skirmish line west of the Emmitsburg Road. From a combined strength of 49, Captain Grubb's command suffered 24 casualties — 10 of them killed or mortally wounded. When all was quiet, wrote Private Kepler, a detail from both companies buried their dead, marked the graves and assisted the wounded to a 2nd Corps hospital.[121]

Other Ohioans on East Cemetery Hill were similarly occupied. "After the repulse of Early we gathered up the dead and cared for the wounded of both friend and foe," wrote Colonel Harris. "We lay down on our arms among the dead bodies and slept until 3 a.m." Captain Fox of the 75th realized that "Half an hour after the engagement many of the men are prisoners — or at least we did not find very many left on the field." One of his friends, Corporal Caleb Parent of Company A, was among the captives.[122]

Just at the close of fighting for the 75th, William Southerton heard his name called. "Bill, I've been shot!" The wounded man proved to be Private Norman Brooks of Company B. "I could scarcely distinguish his inarticulate words," Southerton reflected. "My gun was empty. Until ammunition could be brought up I was useless. I had only my bayonet. The Tigers were gone. We were instructed to help our wounded men when we could, and I could not fail Norman. Holding against his face a piece of pants leg he had torn from his own uniform, Norman bent forward as he walked. As he adjusted the cloth I saw that part of his jaw was shot away; many of his front teeth were gone. We made our way behind [Wiedrich's] battery, and were fairly safe. There was no mistaking the way to the hospital. Such a line of wounded men! Many on stretchers, many hobbling, trying to make it under their own power. To join the procession Norman and I had to cross a corner of the cemetery. Fences and monuments were blown to bits."

In the darkness the pair reached George Spangler's farm, site of the 11th Corps hospital located south of Granite School House Road between the Taneytown Road and Baltimore Pike. By lantern illumination and flickering candles stuck in bayonet sockets, Southerton found a surgeon in Spangler's large barn "working frantically near a wide open doorway. Other surgeons were working just as frantically, all by the light of a few lanterns hung on the walls. Hay was strewn about on the floor for beds for the wounded. At the doorway I saw a huge stack of amputated arms and legs, the most horrible thing I ever saw in my life. I wish I had never seen it. I sickened. I hurried outside [and] kept out of the way of the stream of wounded that flowed to the hospital." Southerton left Brooks in the surgeon's care and began the long walk back. On the way he encountered "dead horses strewn about in every shape. Some had been blown to bits. Bodies of our men had been gathered up and removed. [There was] seemingly no end to the battlefield." On arriving at East Cemetery Hill "I found what was left of my regiment, in almost the same spot it had occupied" before the Confederates' twilight assault.[123]

Doctors, hospital stewards, stretcher bearers and ambulance drivers obtained little if any sleep. "Going all night bringing off wounded," Sergeant Martin Buchwalter of the 73rd Ohio scribbled in his diary. He commanded a squad of 11th Corps ambulances. Another driver, Jacob Smith of the 107th Ohio, had spent the afternoon assisting wounded men back to the ambulance wagons. "From there," he wrote, "they were hauled to the different field hospitals to have their wounds dressed and to be cared for. The last comrade we took back in the evening we had to carry to the hospital [on a stretcher], a distance of more than a mile, the wagons having been driven away before we came. After hunting up our wagons we passed the night in them."[124]

At a temporary 2nd Corps dressing station established on the Catherine Guinn farm, Harry M. McAbee, Carroll's brigade surgeon, was swamped with casualties pouring in from the battlefield. McAbee, 36, was a native Pennsylvanian but had "adopted" Ohio as his home state. Several years after his 1851 graduation from Cleveland Medical College he entered the ministry, and at war's outbreak was pastor of a Methodist Episcopal church in Beaver, Pennsylvania. Leaving the pulpit, he was one of the first physicians to offer his services to Ohio Governor William Dennison, who appointed him surgeon of the 4th Ohio on May 1, 1861. A private in the regiment characterized the doctor as a hard worker possessed of "noble purposes, firm resolves, high ideals, and lofty conceptions of Christian duty. [He] was most assiduous in his attentions to the needs of those in his charge."[125]

That night Sergeant Franklin B. Nickerson of Company K, 8th Ohio, would have acceded whole-

At six feet nine inches, Charles M. Wright was perhaps the 75th Ohio's tallest soldier. The Company H private, a Morgan County farmer reduced to the ranks at his own request in January 1863, suffered a gunshot wound July 2 in the right hip. His convalescence took place in Harrisburg, Pennsylvania, and at Columbus' Camp Chase general hospital before he was transferred in December to the 124th Company, 2nd Battalion, Veteran Reserve Corps. Wright died 13 months later.

Number of Bed:

Ward 2

Name:
Charles M. Wright

Company:
H.

Regiment:
75 th O. V. I.

Disease or Injury:
G S Wd R. Hip (Con. Ball)

Date of Admission:
Oct 29 th 1863.

Date of Discharge:
Transfered to

Where Sent, and by what Authority:
2 Batt C. Corps
General Hospital
Camp Chase, Ohio.
Log Cabin
Morgan Co
Ohio

Transferred to 2 Batt 40.....

heartedly. A bullet fractured his left femur late in the afternoon, and it was midnight before McAbee examined the 22-year-old non-commissioned officer from Medina County. Nickerson recalled: "Having asked a few questions and promised to specially care for me at daybreak, he turned to a mere boy on my left — a Confederate — not more than seventeen years old; death's pallor was on his brow and the blood flowing from his mouth; he was moaning pitifully, in striking contrast to the silent way so many were suffering and dying all around. Dr. McAbee seemed touched with his youthful appearance and disquietude of mind, and said to him, 'My poor fellow, you cannot be helped; you can live but a little time.' The boy broke out in a despairing cry, 'My poor mother, what will she do? I cannot die, I cannot die. She will never know what became of me. I was shot on the skirmish line and no one knows it.' The Surgeon wrote into his notebook his name as a member of a Georgia regiment, and his mother's address, and promised, if possible, to write to his mother, and then knelt down by his side, holding the lantern in his blood-stained hand; with the other he took a pocket Bible from his pocket and read the first fourteen verses of the Fourteenth of St. John, and then offered up a prayer for the soul that was passing away. ..."[126]

The dying teenaged Rebel might well have belonged to one of Brigadier General Edward L. Thomas' four Georgia regiments, which joined others from A.P. Hill's corps by early evening in heavy skirmish fighting that engrossed the 8th Ohio. Some 270 yards west of the Emmitsburg Road the 8th's advanced position had been established by Lieutenant Colonel Sawyer, who kept six companies as support in the barricaded roadbed near a small tenant house owned by farmer Abraham Bryan.

"Hold to the last man," were the emphatic orders Sawyer received about 4 p.m.[127]

They coincided with the beginning of the Rebels' late-afternoon cannonade, which was promptly answered by Federal guns on Cemetery Hill. For more than two hours the 8th Ohio lay between opposing fires. "The scream and whistle of shot and shell was about and around us," Sawyer remembered, "and the clanger [sic] of battle reached us seemingly from every direction." An officer in Company B recalled that "The batteries on the hill behind us gave us good help, exploding their shells right in front of our skirmishers, but amongst the Confederates." Union gunnery caused at least one casualty in the regiment, however, when Second Lieutenant Lester V. McKesson of Company E was hit in the upper back. Two days later a comrade wrote to *The Sandusky Register*: "Lieutenant McKisson [sic] was wounded by a piece of shell, from one of our own batteries, striking him between the shoulders, producing a very painful wound. McKisson is a splendid fighting man, and it bores him the worst kind to be shot by our own men." The lieutenant recently had recovered from a Fredericksburg wound and would suffer a third one 10 months later in the Wilderness.[128]

As the cannonading continued and skirmishing intensified, Sergeant William W. Wells of Company D and several others sheltering in the road's ditch decided to put the Bryan tenant dwelling to further use. According to Sawyer, "There was an old unoccupied house on the rear [east] side of the road and to the left of where I had fixed my flag, to which the

Following 8th Ohio lieutenant Lester McKesson's muster-out in July 1864, he was presented with this silver badge from grateful residents of his hometown. The shield, wrapped by a scroll containing McKesson's name, is suspended from a pin-backed 2nd Corps trefoil inscribed with his company and regiment. Engraved on the reverse is the sentiment "Token of Honor from the Citizens of Sandusky, O. for three years distinguished service in the U.S.A. from 1861 to 1864. Winchester Antietam Fredericksburgh Chancelorsville Gettysburgh Wilderness Spottsylvania Coal Harbor Petersburgh & 65 other engagements."

Robert Everhart Collection

Firelands Historical Society

Lieutenant Colonel Franklin Sawyer, 8th Ohio, was educated in Huron and Licking counties prior to becoming a Norwalk attorney. His last of three wartime wounds was suffered in 1864 at Spotsylvania where a bullet passed through his abdomen, disabling him for further field service.

dead were carried and the wounded cared for, and a well near by that furnished us with water. Very soon some of the men had scrambled up into the garret of the old house, punched a hole through the roof, and commenced firing upon some rebels to our front. Their fire was instantly and fiercely answered, which soon made our daring fellows 'get out of that.' Sergeant Wells ... was of the garret squad, and hastened to inform me of the position of the rebels. Captain [Azor] Nickerson [commanding half of the 8th's skirmish line] was notified — but was already attacked by the troops who had been concealed in a sunken lane, and also from concealed troops toward town. In a few minutes Nickerson was hotly engaged. ..." Wells' company under Captain John Reid was sent forward to assist him. Sawyer claimed "Rebel officers could be heard yelling and swearing at their men [to] 'push on and clean out those yanks.' " [129]

Even with Reid's reinforcement Companies A and I were pressed hard and began to lose ground.

Seeing their predicament from the road, Sawyer "now led up nearly the whole remnant of the regiment, on a run, cheering and firing as we advanced near the skirmish line. The rebels must have believed that we had an ample reserve in the road, for on hearing our cheer and fire they dusted out of their hiding places and broke towards town with commendable agility." Captain David Lewis of Company G termed this action "a sharp little fight," which cost the regiment 18 casualties. Company C suffered the heaviest loss. Sergeants William M.N. Williams and John K. Barclay were killed. Of six others wounded, Private John McCillips died eight days later. [130]

With light of day fading Companies A, H, I and K were relieved from the skirmish line, replaced by Companies G and F under the joint command of Captain Lewis. Pickets and "look-outs" were established on the flanks. Most of the regiment, which apparently rotated skirmish companies during the night, was posted "several rods" west of the Emmitsburg Road where Sawyer, the color bearers, bugler and a few other men remained. Firing subsided in the immediate vicinity, but shortly after 8 p.m. a great deal of noise originating from the Buckeyes' rear could be heard. None of them knew the struggle for East Cemetery Hill and Culp's Hill had begun. Wrote Lieutenant Galwey of Company B: "Looking back we realized from the flashes of light, the roar of artillery, and the rattle of musketry, as well as by the much more convincing cheers that arose from time to time, that a desperate fight was going on behind us, over beyond the cemetery." In the meantime Sawyer dispatched a messenger to his brigade commander, Colonel Carroll, explaining the 8th's situation. Word returned from General Alexander Hays, division commander, that Carroll and his other three regiments had been sent to support the 11th Corps. Sawyer could not be afforded assistance, and again was told to maintain his position to the last.[131]

This unsettling news no doubt worried the Ohioan, but he dared not visibly show it. "A gloomier night than was now experienced by us can scarcely be imagined. We were a good way in advance of our division, without any direct support, with no knowledge whatever as to the event of the great battles of the day; ignorant of the hopes, probabilities or prospects of the morrow; threatened by a stealthy and skulking enemy, amid our dead and wounded, and too nervous if not too cautious to sleep."[132]

Corporal Thaddeus Potter of Company H did manage a few hours of sleep "such as none but soldiers can appreciate," though not before a bit of excitement occurred on the picket line well after nightfall. "We left our cramped positions behind our rail piles to take a stretch on the grass and have a smoke. As we lay there talking an officer rode up almost on to us. 'Hello! Who are you?' he said. 'Yanks,' was the answer. 'Well, by God, I'm a reb!' and away he went. We sent a few shots after him, which called forth a liberal response from the rebel pickets; it made us *git* for our rail piles in a hurry, but there was no more firing in our quarter during the night."[133]

Potter's comrades could be grateful for that, but they faced spending the next anxious hours with empty stomachs. Except for a few pieces of hardtack the regiment was without rations. Several Buckeyes began scavenging. Sawyer noted that "some bread, ham and cheese, taken from dead and wounded rebels, luckily fell into our hands, or we would have gone supperless. The rebels whom we had captured had secured ample forage from the *'Quakers,'* as they claimed, in the neighborhood." Second Lieutenant Thomas H. Thornburg of Company F reported "his men 'downed' a rebel soldier that evening who was actually fighting with four fair-sized hams strung on his shoulders, and another with a cheese as 'big as a grindstone,' all of which our fellows seized upon with avidity."[134]

While this food was divided among the 8th's tired ranks, hunger gnawed at another Ohioan back on Cemetery Hill. For Captain Huntington the day's fighting was over, but a good deal of labor remained unfinished. Most of his artillery brigade officers and men devoted attention to their horses. It was Huntington's responsibility to ascertain and provide for the needs of his four batteries, especially Ricketts', in the way of ammunition and materials. To replenish his guns' limber chests he rode down the Taneytown Road to Brigadier General Robert O. Tyler's Artillery Reserve headquarters, where ammunition wagons were parked nearby. Famished, Huntington found Tyler and his staff preparing for dinner. "The General kindly invited me to join. As I had given up all hope of getting anything to eat that night, this was a very agreeable surprise."[135]

At the same time the artillery officer was relishing the unexpected meal, General Meade convened his corps commanders to a council of war at the Leister house about three-quarters of a mile away. During the meeting it was concluded the Army of the Potomac would remain in place and await attack for one more day.[136] For many Ohio soldiers whose lives hung in the balance, it was a fateful decision.

FOUR

'A ghastly sight
to see men slaughtered so'

JULY 3

Stretched out on a blanket in Evergreen Cemetery, an exhausted Captain Huntington enjoyed three hours of "much-needed repose." His slumber instantly ended a little after 4:30 a.m. when "I became aware that a disturbance of some sort was going on, for the noise was loud enough to waken the seven sleepers. I soon found that a heavy infantry fight was in progress about a half mile off, on the easterly slope of Culp's hill."[1]

While Huntington was sleeping, preparations had been underway to retake the abandoned 12th Corps' defensive works on Culp's Hill occupied by some of Edward Johnson's Confederates the previous evening. To dislodge the enemy Brigadier General Alpheus Williams, acting 12th Corps commander, developed a plan whereby concentrated artillery fire and an infantry feint on the corps' right would be "followed by a strong assault by Geary's division from Greene's position on the left." Twenty-six 12th Corps and Artillery Reserve guns were in place or posted for the shelling, their muzzles aimed toward Culp's lower hill and the lowland leading to Rock Creek. The counterattack was ordered to begin at first light of day.[2]

Williams and his Federals were unaware their grayclad opponents also were preparing to attack at daybreak — with a force double that used the night of July 2 at Culp's Hill. To exploit modest gains al-

ready made, General Ewell reinforced Johnson with two brigades from Rodes' division and two regiments from Early's command. In addition, Johnson reacquired the services of the famed Stonewall Brigade, which had been detached from his division earlier in the battle. It was hoped increasing Johnson's strength would enable him to accomplish one of two things: smash through a weak spot in the Union line, or create a diversion to assist Longstreet, who was supposed to resume his assault on the Federal left flank. Before the Rebels could advance, however, Williams' guns opened with a concussive blast. Shells ricochetted and exploded among the trees and rocks. One Confederate officer, whose troops huddled behind a captured stone wall, thought "the whole hillside seemed enveloped in a blaze ... and the balls could be heard to strike the breastworks like hailstones upon the roof tops."[3]

Artillery fire continued at intervals for more than six hours, but the brunt of the Culp's Hill battle fell to the opposing sides' infantrymen. "Considering the numbers engaged," wrote Captain Huntington, it was "one of the stubbornest, bloodiest combats of the war. Until nearly eleven o'clock, the roar of musketry did not slacken for an instant. There was no rise and fall, alternate slacking and increase in the volume of sound, it was one steady infernal din." The heaviest fighting of the morning occurred along Geary's front, which was assailed three separate times by the Confederates. Once again General Greene's New York brigade, protected by breastworks running from the upper hill's summit to the lower hill's connecting saddle, found itself the primary target of these assaults.[4]

When shooting began in earnest at daybreak, Colonel Candy's Ohio and Pennsylvania brigade was positioned in support of Greene's right rear. Pre-dawn adjustments placed the 5th Ohio, 147th Pennsylvania and 7th Ohio to the right of Brigadier General Thomas L. Kane's small brigade, whose vacated entrenchments had been seized by Rebels during the night. This line connected with Greene's right flank at the saddle and angled southwest toward the Baltimore Pike along Henry Spangler's farm lane. The 7th did not stay long, being ordered by Candy to return to the hollow or shallow ravine north of Kane's position and 50 yards behind Greene's breastworks. It joined the 28th Pennsylvania and 29th Ohio as reinforcements for Greene.[5]

Candy's sixth regiment, the 66th Ohio, already had been sent to Greene's left flank and given a special assignment. Sometime before dawn Lieutenant Colonel Eugene Powell received orders to take his 300-man regiment to Culp's Hill's summit. There he was to cross the entrenchments between Greene and Wadsworth's right flank, push away any Rebels from his front, then face right (south) and enfilade the enemy opposing Greene's regiments. Powell, a 28-year-old Delaware County native who had attended Ohio Wesleyan and served in 1861 as a 4th Ohio company commander, knew nothing of what might confront him. At the top of the hill he halted the 66th, instructing the men to rest while he reported to the commanding officer there. Powell never was certain to whom he spoke, stating that in the darkness neither could distinguish clearly the facial features of the other. The officer probably was General Greene. According to Powell, "I told him what my orders were, to cross his line of works and drive the enemy off the side of the hill. His reply was: 'My God, if you go out there the enemy will simply swallow you!' He further said the enemy was out there and in force, and that he had been expecting and awaiting an attack all night, and that it might come at any moment. In reply, I merely repeated to him my orders, bade him good morning, and returned to the place where my regiment was. ..."[6]

New York State Library

Lieutenant Colonel Eugene Powell, 66th Ohio.

In a low tone Powell called the 66th to attention. "Instantly there was the jostle of soldiers arousing themselves from rest, together with the suppressed hum of voices, followed by the clatter of canteens and other utensils ... in addition to that of their arms, as these clashed together in the efforts of the men to get into ranks and go none knew where; forward meant into instant deadly conflict with the enemy, but to a man the regiment stood at attention and ready." By this time the Union artillery bombardment had begun, providing Powell with "assurance enough for me to know that my movement was well timed to help our comrades in their efforts to drive Ewell's forces out of our works. The command 'forward' followed, and my regiment was in motion. We rapidly crossed the intrenchments, but so close [was] the advance of the enemy that we received their fire before we were entirely over."[7]

The initial shots directed at the 66th Ohio came from alert Virginians of J.M. Jones' brigade. Among the first hit was Second Lieutenant Charles E. Butts of Company K. A minié ball passed through his right forearm, fracturing the bone before entering his right buttock and lodging near the anus. He previously had been wounded in the chest at Chancellorsville, and spent three months a prisoner after being captured in June 1862 at Port Republic, Virginia. The 25-year-old Delaware County carpenter also was embroiled in a fatal scandal that occurred early in 1863. Detailed for recruiting duty back in Ohio, Butts, a sergeant at the time, became romantically involved with a 17-year-old girl from Delaware County named Fidelia Oliver. Following a January 7 rendezvous with Butts at a Springfield hotel, the teenager, apparently betrothed to another man, placed a pistol to her right temple and pulled the trigger. The suicide prompted an Urbana newspaper to castigate the sergeant as a "dirty puppy, and infernal scoundrel." It claimed Butts "decoyed" the girl from her home, then abandoned her. "He pretended to be a Lieutenant. Why, such a vile pest as he is unworthy to bear an American musket."[8]

As Butts was assisted to the rear the 66th drove off those Virginians closest to the works. The regiment "pushed ahead over the great bowlders, stones and logs," Powell related, "and after a furious resistance by the enemy from behind such shelter, still not knowing but that this advance was that of a large Union force, they fell back, and gave up that side of Culp's Hill to us." Powell ordered his companies to fan out, facing south. The rightmost anchored itself at a 90-degree angle to the works at

While having his right arm injuries treated in November 1863, Second Lieutenant Charles E. Butts, Company K, 66th Ohio, sat for this portrait at Bishop's Photographic Gallery in Philadelphia. Earlier, he spent seven weeks hospitalized in Ward C at Gettysburg's Camp Letterman, where a bullet was removed from his nates. To help heal the entrance and exit wounds in Butts' arm, Assistant Surgeon E.P. Townsend prescribed "splints & cold water Dressings," followed with "Lead & opium dressings by day, Poultices at night." Butts, wearing here a 12th Corps badge pinned to his braided jacket, finished the war as a quartermaster captain in Murfreesboro, Tennessee.

Greene's extreme left. The regiment extended eastward some 60 yards to a massive rock outcropping, where Company B took position. Before crossing the entrenchments Powell believed the 66th stood a good chance of being annihilated. He was cautiously relieved "we were able to carry out a part of our orders and without the serious opposition that we had expected." He instructed his men to take "every advantage of the rough surface of the hill to protect themselves. ..."[9]

Company I's commander, First Lieutenant John T. Morgan, was seeking cover when, as he remembered, "we came to a large rock, and in order to get around it I exposed myself and was shot by a sharpshooter thru the left hip, and the stretcher bearers at once carried me back to a field hospital." Fire from Rebel marksmen stationed behind a fence at the hill's base accounted for a majority of the regiment's 17 casualties during the next six hours.[10]

One of these was Major Joshua G. Palmer, Powell's second in command. He no doubt made an inviting target standing near the 66th's left flank, and a sharpshooter's bullet ripped into his left lung. Earlier in the war the 34-year-old Urbana dentist had commanded Company B. When he slumped to the ground John W. Houtz and three other privates of his former company gently lifted Palmer to the crest's breastworks. "I saw he was breathing through the hole the ball had made," Houtz recalled. "I took a fine silk handkerchief I happened to have and wet it from my canteen and pressed it upon the wound." Palmer uttered, "Oh, that did me so much good," then said encouragingly, "Stay with them, boys! I will soon be back with you." It was the last time they saw him alive. A week later Palmer died in a 12th Corps hospital. "How we loved him," Houtz reflected years later. "He was the soul of honor and brave as steel."[11]

Returning to his company, Houtz soon exacted a measure of revenge for the major's wounding, although he nearly became a casualty himself. That night he wrote in his diary: "I kiled one Johnny this morn[.] he was a skirmisher[.] he shot a ball through my blous[e] and shirt sleeve above the elbo[w.]" For the next 50 years Houtz was convinced the Confederate he killed was the one responsible for Palmer's death.[12]

Private William Guy of Company F recollected that comrade Stephen Gray of Union County was a late arrival on the hill. "He had sore feet, due to

First Lieutenant John T. Morgan, Company I, 66th Ohio, hailed from the Champaign County town of Mechanicsburg. Seventeen days after his wounding he visited Ohio's statehouse and was handed a captain's commission by Governor David Tod.

Ohio MOLLUS

Civil War Library & Museum, MOLLUS

Following his death July 10, the body of Major Joshua G. Palmer, 66th Ohio, was shipped to his parents' home for burial in Parma, New York.

Company K private Mark Sweet joined the 66th Ohio in 1861 at his Marion County hometown of Waldo.

James C. Frasca Collection, USAMHI

long marching, and he came up with us on the line after we had been fighting for some time. But as soon as he reached the line he asked for ammunition, and taking his place between two big rocks began loading and firing. One of our men cautioned him against taking that position. 'Every man that has stood there this morning has been hit,' he was told, but he paid no attention to it. I remembered that I thought it was not lack of courage with that fellow that kept him back, and just then he fell dead, shot through and through." Gray actually was badly wounded. For four and a half months he lingered in various hospitals, expiring November 21 in Columbus at the age of 20.[13]

Nearly half the regiment's losses were absorbed by Company D. Two non-commissioned officers and five privates were wounded, one of them mortally. Private Guy noticed a man "walking back with his hands up to his face and the blood running through his fingers. The whole side of his face [was] shot off by a piece of a shell." Lieutenant Colonel Powell recognized the injured soldier as a Logan Countian nicknamed "Scottie" — Sergeant William Scott of Company D. "[He] received as severe a wound as I have ever known a man to live through or recover from," Powell avowed. "A shell burst over him, and some of the flying pieces striking him at the base of the jaw, broke these bones and drove the fragments and his teeth out at his mouth. As this man passed me on his way to the field hospital I noticed that as he breathed his cheeks seemed to meet, as there was not anything to keep them apart." Surgeons repaired Scott's face the best they could, though he was unable to speak for the rest of his life. More than two decades after the battle he was a member of the regimental committee that chose the 66th Ohio's monument site on Culp's Hill.[14]

Although Powell's men aimed some of their musketry across Greene's entrenched front, much of it was directed downslope during successive Confederate charges, and at enemy sharpshooters. A number of more daring Ohioans, including Corporal

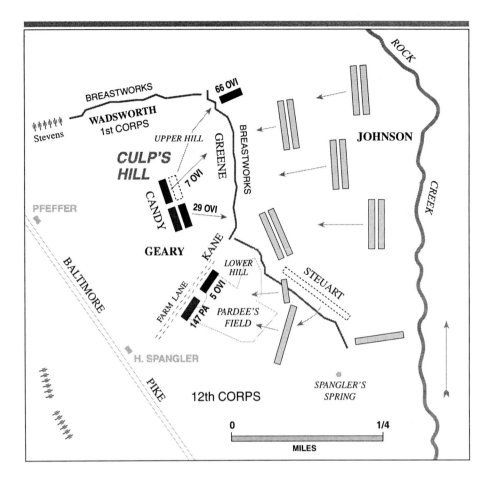

never saw boys take anything as cool as most of my company did. They just acted like they would in shooting squirrels [with] nobody to shoot at them." [16]

The regiment remained in its advanced location until sometime between 11 a.m. and noon, when it was directed to recross the breastworks and support a brigade of the 12th Corps' 1st Division. Enroute, Powell reported to Colonel Candy and was congratulated for his effective service and safe return. Years later Powell still retained a sense of incredulity about the 66th Ohio's mission. "It seems singular how it occurred that a single regiment was ordered out over the entrenchments on the top of Culps Hill to attack the enemy, but such an order was given. ... As we went over there before it was fairly daylight I did not know exactly what I was to do or where I was to go

James H. Corbin of Company K, found a way to increase the firepower. "We went out after the repulse of each assault on our works and gathered up dozens of rifles of fallen Confederates and bringing them in, loaded them and had them ready, so that when they came at us again each man of us had a half dozen guns ready loaded, waiting for them." [15]

The volume of lead thrown at the attackers was terrific. In a letter to his wife, Corporal George Milledge of Company I mentioned he fired 200 rounds. Company K private William M. Sayre informed relatives back on their Logan County farm that "the Rebs lay thicker than ever I saw them before." On one section of the hill 100 yards from the 66th's position he counted 25 dead Confederates lying in a space 80 feet wide. "Oh you had better think we give them what they needed this time if they never got it before. Well I could not say that I killed one myself. But I can say that I shot enough at them. I only fired upwards of ninety rounds at the Rascals. I done my best to kill to[o]." Captain Robert H. Russell, writing to his father, praised the Champaign and Clark county enlisted men of Company G. "I

Captain B.F. Ganson commanded Company B, 66th Ohio. Carte de visite by M.L. Albright, Urbana.

L. M. Strayer Collection

Battles and Leaders of the Civil War

except to get under fire with the enemy which was not difficult of doing on that morning." [17]

The soldiers of Candy's three other Buckeye regiments would have agreed with the last part of Powell's statement. In the 5th Ohio, Sergeant Joseph Gaul and fellow Cincinnatians of Company C managed to lay down and rest in the regiment's position along Spangler's lane. No breastworks were constructed here, though a worm fence, knocked over earlier, provided slight protection for the prone sleepers. To the 5th's left were the three Pennsylvania regiments of Kane's brigade. To its right was Lieutenant Colonel Ario Pardee's 147th Pennsylvania. From the lane both faced a strip of woods, beyond which sloped an open field (later named for Pardee) rising uphill to a stone wall and more trees. Sheltering behind them were troops of Steuart's Confederate brigade, having occupied the wall and Culp's lower hill just hours before. The presence of Steuart's veterans created a westward-pointing bulge in the Union line, a scant 500 yards or less from the Baltimore Pike. These Rebels were a

Confederates of Steuart's brigade renewed their Culp's Hill assault the morning of July 3. It failed. Steuart reported that "The [Union] position was impregnable, attacked by our small force, and any further effort to storm it would have been futile, and attended with great disaster, if not total annihilation."

prime target of the initial Federal bombardment beginning about 4:30. [18]

It was still dark when Gaul and his comrades "were aroused by the movement of artillery and horses. Generals Williams and Geary came upon the ground and took a position immediately in our rear. Gen. Geary's remarks were, 'Boys, be ready, we are going to shake them up.' We were soon in line [and] it was not long before the ball opened." [19]

Once the cannonade started the 147th Pennsylvania was advanced to the far edge of the wooded strip. From there it began shooting across the field at Steuart's skirmishers and others on the lower hill. Colonel Patrick's 5th Ohio, 300 strong, joined Pardee's men at the woodline, staying to the 147th's left and doubling its firepower. As visibility improved with daylight, Patrick decided to send a skirmish line forward off his left flank in order to achieve a cross fire. He called for Company F, whose acting commander was First Lieutenant Henry C. Brinkman of Company E. Patrick enthused the 24-year-old Cincinnatian "to fret the enemy as much as possible, for the purpose of drawing him from his intrenchments." [20]

Brinkman performed the task in a manner that was "most satisfactory" to the colonel. It probably was expected. Considered "a brave and gallant officer," he first displayed valorous behavior 13 months earlier as a color corporal in the battle of Port Republic. In the wake of defeat he saved one of the regiment's flags by wrapping it around his body and swimming the Shenandoah River's south fork under heavy musketry fire. At Culp's Hill, Patrick reported, the lieutenant's company "annoy[ed] the enemy so much that they were compelled to make a charge on our skirmishers, and either capture or drive them, neither of which was accomplished." A second attempt to push away the Ohioans also failed. Unfortunately, Company F's lone casualty in the fight was Brinkman, who was killed. [21]

Later in the morning (the time ranged between 8 and 10 o'clock) another advance ordered by John-

Sergeant Joseph L. Gaul, Company C, 5th Ohio, finished his four-year service as a brevet captain.

son was undertaken by Steuart's entire brigade against Patrick's, Pardee's and Kane's regiments. Also designated to attack was Brigadier General Junius Daniel's brigade of Rodes' division. Daniel's North Carolinians took position to Steuart's right and rear. Both generals, observed one of Steuart's staff officers, strongly disapproved making the assault. Prior to stepping off, a Maryland battalion commander remarked to a different member of Steuart's staff, "It was nothing less than murder to send men into that slaughter pen." [22]

There was apprehension as well in the 5th Ohio's ranks. Sergeant Gaul was especially anxious. Since the regiment's move to the woodline he had been eyeing a boulder situated to Company C's rear, and wished he was on the far side of it for protection. That would have been most "unmanly" for a non-commissioned officer, but its mere presence beckoned to him. He thought he could fight much better if only he was behind it. Gaul's reverie suddenly was interrupted, as he related:

The rebs were seen approaching in double line of battle with their arms at a right shoulder. ... They came on through the woods over the stone wall and into a large clear field, our [artillery] all the time playing upon them, but to me, apparently, without any effect. Their lines did not waver, though gaps were made in their ranks. The gaps were closed, and shoulder to shoulder they came on and on. We being at the foot of the hill in this strip of woods, were concealed from them, and as they came over the rise we saw how steadily they moved. All this time, which seemed an age to us, we were holding our fire. This is one of the trying times to a soldier. I became nervous, my knees began to shake and my body to tremble; then my eyes would turn longingly to that big rock. Finally ... the command was given to commence firing. Just as soon as we began firing I forgot my nervousness, and did not once think of the rock again. They were surprised, and we gave them a couple of volleys before it was returned. The firing was kept up for a short time, when their lines wavered and finally broke. [23]

Using the pseudonym "Corine," an unidentified 5th Ohioan (possibly Sergeant Peter A. Cozine of Company A), described Steuart's repulse in correspondence to the *Cincinnati Daily Times*:

The Rebels had to come over a hill and through a field before they could reach us. On they came, in fine order and with slow and measured tread. They were permitted to advance within seventy-five yards or so before a

L. M. Strayer Collection

Timothy R. Brookes Collection

Combat-tested in five major engagements prior to Gettysburg, the 5th Ohio's ranks included Private James Richey of Company E, *upper right,* Sergeant Henry Surles, Company H, *above,* and Sergeant Walter Elliott of Company K, *right.* All enlisted at Cincinnati, though Surles, a bricklayer, was a native of Steubenville. He and Richey displayed the 12th Corps star badge on their cap and coat, respectively.

Cincinnati Historical Society

gun was fired, when, as if by magic, the whole line flashed forth a sheet of flame, hurling death and destruction among them. For a time they strove manfully, but soon they broke and fled in the utmost confusion, while we accelerated their speed with a shower of bullets in their rear. Their dead and wounded were left in heaps, showing the accuracy of our aim and the effect of our fire.

There are many incidents, both ludicrous and amusing, that occur on the field during the hottest of the fight, but such places are not well adapted for the relishing of a joke, or the exacting of a smile; yet notwithstanding, he must have had a heart unused to the melting mood ... who could have seen Johnson's [*sic*] brigade skedaddling before three small regiments [5th Ohio, 147th and 111th Pennsylvania], without enjoying a good laugh. The way they dropped their guns was a caution. After they had lit out, our boys went out in squads of two and three, and brought in their wounded, who were exposed to our fire, and this while the Rebels were firing on them at the same time.[24]

Ashtabula County-born First Lieutenant Charles W. Kellogg, Company F, 29th Ohio, was an aide-de-camp on Candy's brigade staff.

Bob Willey Collection

"Corine's" account furnished to the Queen City newspaper also contained a cogent observation. "On the left of our regiment an American citizen of African descent had taken position, and with a gun and cartridge box, which he took from one of our dead men, was more than piling hot lead into the Graybacks. His coolness and bravery was noticed and commented upon by all who saw him. If the negro regiments fight like he did, I don't wonder that the Rebs and Copperheads hate them so."[25]

"Regular *bulldog* fighting" was how Major Henry E. Symmes phrased the 5th Ohio's successful action at Pardee Field. Colonel Patrick called attention to the "terrific slaughter" in his post-battle report, adding that "Very soon after this last repulse, we occupied the intrenchments." The correspondent "Corine" wrote, "Our regiment, for once, was fortunate in securing a position where we could do great execution without exposing ourselves." He correctly tallied the 5th's casualties as two killed and 16 wounded, although three of the latter afterward died.[26] One of these Sergeant Gaul knew well.

Twenty-one-year-old George Case was a native Pennsylvanian but worked as a Cincinnati upholsterer when he enlisted in Company C as a private in June 1861. A "venturesome fellow," as Gaul remembered him, Case either was ordered or took it upon himself to reconnoiter after the regiment regained a section of the 12th Corps' former defenses. Gaul explained: "[He] went out along the stone wall, which has been previously mentioned, for the purpose of locating the enemy. He found them rather sooner than he had expected, and they found him. This was immediately in our front, but at right angle with the left of our regiment. Case, in his effort to get back to our lines, was fired upon by a dozen rebels, but only one shot took effect, which laid him out, badly wounded. He lay there for a long time, and made repeated efforts to get back to us, but failed. Two others of my company resolved to rescue him. Throwing aside their guns they started.

The rebels seeing them, fired. They threw up their hands, and the firing ceased, and they allowed them to carry him off, cheering as they did so." Suffering from a spinal injury Case lived until August 2, expiring at Gettysburg's Camp Letterman hospital.[27]

Back in the shallow ravine behind Greene's works the northeastern Ohioans of the 7th and 29th regiments awaited their call to combat. All morning the troops on Greene's front used the area for rest, resupply and cleaning their weapons. As regiments in the works exhausted their ammunition, they exchanged places with those in the hollow. Moving forward or going to the rear required a "mad dash" to cover the intervening 50 yards of rocky ground. A large number of men were hit while making the crossing.[28]

Bullets zipped closely overhead and Captain Wilbur Stevens, commanding the 29th Ohio, discovered that safety for the supports in the hollow was only relative. An hour after the artillery bombardment opened he was struck in the neck by a spent ball. Giddy with pain, Stevens relinquished command to Captain Edward Hayes of Company C and

Company F's second lieutenant, Gurley G. Crane, a Cuyahoga Falls papermaker, temporarily led Company E, 29th Ohio, after its commander was killed in the Culp's Hill breastworks.

went to the rear. Fifteen minutes later Hayes received an order from Candy, through a staff officer, to relieve the 137th New York at the far right of Greene's brigade. The New Yorkers held a fortified traverse at the saddle connecting Culp's upper and lower hills, but Hayes was unsure exactly where to go. "I did not feel justified in taking the regiment into action without first looking at the ground," he reported a day later. The captain sprinted forward, found the 137th's commander, Colonel David Ireland, and discussed the situation and impending relief. He then returned to the hollow, explaining to his men what was expected of them. At Hayes' signal the 29th "moved over the ridge at a run without firing a shot until fairly in the trenches, when it opened a heavy fire upon the enemy, under cover of which Colonel Ireland was able to withdraw his regiment with but small loss."[29]

Fraught with danger, the scamper to the 137th's position was an exciting moment for Hayes' 308 Buckeyes. Private Orlando Gunn of Company E wrote that "We had to go up to the top of the ridge and then go down the other side about three rods, to the pits. When we got to the top of the ridge we gave

a tremendous yell and ran as fast as we could. ..." Private Henry Knapp remembered those in Company H hollered as loud as possible, "I suppose to keep our courage up. We were soon in the breastworks and everyone loading and firing as fast as we could for the rebels were close up. We fought behind very good breastworks which some other troops had made, but the rebels had only the rocks and trees for shelter."[30]

Hayes' and the two enlisted men's depictions of the dash were mirrored by Company D's captain, Myron T. Wright, who praised the 29th's acting commander. "Never was a regiment more ably handled or gallantly led," the Norton, Ohio, native told readers of *The Summit County Beacon*. "Capt. Hayes placed himself in front of the center of the regiment and said, 'Boys, we are going to advance. I don't want a shot fired until you are in the trenches. 29th, *forward, double quick,'* then facing about, commanded, 'march!' and with a shout that would have frightened a hundred Ciceroes from the field, we *did* forward, and thirty seconds later found us snugly ensconced in the trenches, with but a slight loss in killed and wounded."[31]

The regiment's first fatal casualty after reaching the breastworks was an officer. First Lieutenant George Hayward of Company E was shot through the neck and instantly killed while peering over a headlog. "I was close by him," wrote Private Knapp, "and with others called to him to keep down." Having commanded the company at Chancellorsville as first sergeant, Hayward was commissioned a lieutenant May 25, but did not muster at that rank prior to his death. "He was daring almost to rashness," observed the 29th Ohio's historian, "always at the front, unmindful of danger, while his tender solicitude for his men endeared him to all who knew him, and his death was sincerely regretted. The rebel who killed him was concealed in the crevice of [a] rock not more than twenty paces from our line." Corporal Nathan Parmater was nearby when Hay-

A wrist wound suffered July 3 ended Akron native Edward W. Farr's service with Company H, 29th Ohio.

John Gurnish Collection

ward fell, noting in his diary that most of the 29th's casualties in the entrenchments were hit in the head. Privates John Williams of Company C and Benjamin F. Pontious, Company D, died this way. Several others suffered less serious head, neck or shoulder injuries.[32]

A majority of the regiment's 38 killed and wounded occurred later in the morning. At 8 a.m. Hayes' men were relieved by the 28th Pennsylvania, which covered the Ohioans' withdrawal to the hollow to clean their Enfields and replenish cartridge boxes. After a two-hour respite an urgent request was brought to Hayes by one of General Greene's staff officers. He was asked to "take my regiment forward and relieve the troops in the pits in front of us, as they were being hard pressed and were getting short of ammunition. Ordinarily I should not have felt justified in moving without an order from the commander of my own brigade, but

the men in front were falling back by twos and threes, and there did not seem to be any time to lose. Besides, I had been informed by Lieutenant Hitt [Joseph W. Hitt, 66th Ohio], of Colonel Candy's staff, that we would soon be ordered forward. The regiment responded to the order in the most splendid manner, cheering as they charged; but, rapid as was the movement, it was not effected without severe loss."[33]

Hayes estimated that two-thirds of the 29th's casualties in the entire battle were cut down before it gained the breastworks. Company F was hit worst. Private Alpheus W. Hardy had his right thumb shot off. Five others were wounded and Private Josiah D. Johnson was killed. In Company I a bullet smashed Second Lieutenant John G. Marsh's right thigh, mortally wounding the "prompt, cool, brave and efficient" officer. Private Matthias Soden of Company K lurched to the ground clutching his abdomen. It took 12 days before an older brother serving in the 6th Ohio Cavalry discovered what happened to him. Corporal Edward Soden wrote home about Matthias' fate: "He lived about one hour after he was shot. He was carried off to the hospital but they could not do anything for him so he lie and died. He did [not] say anything to anyone that I could learn about. The ball went in on one side of his belly and come out up in his back almost against his shoulders. So he soon died." Edward last saw his brother June 30 near Taneytown. "I walked about one mile along with him and carried his gun for him for the roads was muddy and they was tired out. I [gave] him two cracker[s] and some butter and a piece of cows tongue for him to eat. He show[ed] me the last letter that he got from home. I was sorry to see him go. ..."[34]

The fighting in front of the 29th, as well as to its right and left, raged with "desperate fury." Firing volleys by files and ranks, or at will, each soldier tore off one end of a paper cartridge with his teeth, poured the load's black powder down his rifle musket's barrel, inserted a lead .577-caliber bullet,

John Gurnish Collection

Private David Thomas, Company C.

John Gurnish Collection

Private Oscar Brewster, Company D.

After the war a member of the 29th Ohio, several comrades of whom are pictured here, reflected on the "stubborn valor displayed on both sides by the common soldiers" at Culp's Hill. "The dauntless resolution exhibited in the attacks made it a terribly bloody and destructive conflict, and the unyielding and resolute front of the defence brought victory."

rammed the charge and projectile to the weapon's breech, cocked its hammer, placed a percussion cap on the barrel's nipple and was ready to shoot again. The procedure no doubt was performed in frantic haste, as Captain Hayes reported both sides' musketry between 10 and 11 a.m. as "heavy." Corporal Parmater described it being "terrific, nearly taking *all* the bark from the trees." Several members of Company D shot away more than 150 rounds each, their lips and chins coated charcoal gray from powder residue. Sometimes a man would forget to withdraw the ramrod from his weapon's barrel, sending it flailing through the air when he pulled the trigger.[35]

During the morning the regiment fired at Confederates belonging to five different brigades. "The rebels would yell and charge clear up to our line," declared Private Knapp. "One failure did not seem to discourage them, for they would reinforce, reform and with that demoniac rebel yell, come at us again and again. Instead of making one general heavy charge, they kept making many smaller ones, apparently hoping to find a weak place and break through. ..."[36]

In the midst of smoke and sense-numbing noise, Captain Wright could not help laughing at the antics of two Company D privates. "[Through]

L. M. Strayer Collection

Second Lieutenant Silas G. Elliott, Company A.

the entire action the men behaved with the utmost coolness, often even indulging jokes and funny sayings." As they reloaded their guns the comrades of Thomas G. Bare, noted for his wit and good humor, inquired of him nonsensically, "Domb, Domb, ish de *boat* on?" He invariably replied, "If it taint on now it won't get on at all." Wright was particularly amused by 19-year-old Ezra Spidel. "After having become weary with the loading and firing [he] would sit for a moment's rest until two or three balls from the sharp shooters would whiz close to him, then get up saying, 'Well, I guess I must fire *another* volley,' and cooly resume the business of the day. After the fight was over Lt. Curtiss, of the Pioneer Corps, was asked by some one how many rebels he had buried; he answered eighty-five. 'Just the number I killed,' says Spidel." [37]

By noon the shooting slackened considerably, giving five Confederates an opportunity to display a

white flag and surrender to the 29th. Private Joseph Lynn of Company E claimed they belonged to the 1st Louisiana of Francis T. Nicholls' brigade. "Both sides were watching the other sharply," Henry Knapp contended. "If a man exposed himself he was sure to get shot. Many of our boys would cautiously raise their caps on a ramrod and let the rebels shoot holes in [them], but they soon learned if there was a head in the cap." Sharpshooting continued all afternoon. Wrote Private Gunn: "We were not relieved again until ten at night; then we went to the rear and drew some rations, cooked our supper, drew a new supply of ammunition and then lay down to get some sleep; but we did not sleep much. We had to go up to the pits again at two, and no man was allowed to sleep, as we expected the rebels would make us an early visit." This time the regiment was led forward by Captain Stevens, who had returned with a bandaged neck and resumed command from Hayes at 4:30 p.m. [38]

For most of the day Colonel Creighton's 7th Ohio, the smallest regiment in Candy's brigade, shared experiences similar to those of the 29th Ohio, but suffered half the casualties. About 6 a.m. he was chosen to relieve the 60th New York at the left of Greene's line. One of the "Roosters" from Cleveland remarked, "Colonel Creighton gave the order to 'fix bayonets, and follow me!' In three minutes we were in the breast-works and firing. ... We had the most important position to hold, and the best for us, for it only required spirit to hold it." Second Lieutenant Harry M. Dean of Company G concurred, telling a Ravenna newspaper: "This is the first time that our Regiment ever fought behind breastworks or fortifications, and all agree that it is a pretty good way to fight." [39]

Sherman R. Norris of Company D found that "Our position was simply impregnable." Born at Windsor in Ashtabula County, the 22-year-old private was regimental clerk — a job for which he was

John Gurnish Collection

Captain Myron T. Wright, Company D, 29th Ohio. Outside Savannah, Georgia, in December 1864 he was shot in the lower left leg, which was amputated. The Wadsworth, Ohio, resident died less than three weeks later. Carte de visite by B.F. Battel's Gallery of Art, Akron.

Born in the German grand duchy of Saxe Weimar, Second Lieutenant Edward H. Bohm emigrated to America with his family in 1851. The Cleveland resident, sporting a stamped brass rooster device on his coat, commanded Company D, 7th Ohio, at Gettysburg.

range, when the command 'Front rank — Ready — Aim low — Fire!' was given and executed, and immediately the rear rank the same, and kept up as long as the line remained unbroken." [40]

Norris recalled the Rebel formation in the 7th's front "melted away before our volleys, and after they had been broken, numbers of the enemy [took] refuge behind trees and rocks. We put in the time while waiting for the next charge sharp shooting them. A spot of gray showing from behind a tree, or a hat above a rock, was sure to draw the fire of a dozen muskets. We took as deliberate aim at that line of gray coming up the hill as we would at a target." [41]

At 8 a.m. the 60th New York again exchanged places with the "Roosters," who reformed in the hollow for rest and ammunition replenishment. Two days earlier the 7th had received 5,000 rounds, and July 3 was issued "10,000 rounds elongated ball cartridges cal .574" by Geary's acting ordnance officer, Captain Gilbert M. Elliott. Other unreported ammunition may have been distributed, for Private James H. Merrell of Company H wrote on July 4 that "I shot about 100 rounds yesterday." Additionally, a 29th Pennsylvania private, David Mouat, remembered Lieutenant Colonel Orrin Crane of the 7th issuing cartridges to his regiment as well. Mouat related that Crane, referring to the Pennsylvanian's corps badge, told him, "Help yourself White Star and make good use of it for the prisoners say that Ewell is going to break through here if it takes every damn man he has." [42]

Creighton's Ohioans were back in the breastworks by 9:45 a.m., relieving an unspecified regiment to the left of the 29th Ohio. Company D had just taken its place when a shot laid out Corporal Charles Carroll, 27, a machinist from Lake County. Private Norris was nearby. "Being a tall man [Carroll stood five feet eleven], his head showed above

well qualified. Prior to enlistment in August 1862 he clerked for his brother's corset manufacturing firm in Cleveland. Norris wrote that rocks and logs "had been thrown up along the crest of Culp's Hill high enough to protect our bodies when kneeling, on top of which, leaving space through which to put our guns, a log was placed to protect our heads, and from the nature of the ground over which the enemy charged it was almost impossible for them to fire through this space until within short range, when they were too busy seeking shelter or the rear to do much execution. The enemy formed his line of battle at the foot of the hill and came up across the intervening space of woods and rock in splendid order, while we lay behind our solid breastworks, obeying the command to reserve our fire until the first line of battle was well up the slope and in easy

First Lieutenant Llewellyn R. Davis, Company E, 7th Ohio, served on Geary's division staff as aide-de-camp. Never short of words (the general's battle reports were among the army's longest), Geary praised his staffers: "From the peculiar nature of their duties, their untiring diligence and activity subjected them to severe drafts upon their physical endurance and to exposure to danger."

Brad L. Pruden Collection

the elevation in our front, and no sooner had he straightened up than a ball struck him and he was dead before he fell to the ground, killed by a rebel sharpshooter. These sharpshooters were stationed in trees out of range of our muskets, and every man who showed his head above the log on our fortifications was a sure candidate for the hospital or the [burial] trench."[43]

The regiment's only other known fatality was a former Oberlin College student, Private Joseph McCarran of Company C. He died July 22 at the 12th Corps hospital from a skull fracture. A third man, Private James J. Melton of Company F, was struck by a bullet above the right ear and taken to the rear for treatment. On July 6 Colonel Creighton listed him as "missing from hospital — deranged." Some speculated that, due to his head wound, Melton must have wandered off and was unable to give an account of himself. Two years later his whereabouts were still unknown.[44]

Author's Collection

Major General
Edward Johnson, CSA.

While the "Roosters" pulled their second, late-morning stint in the breastworks, General Johnson flung his last assault at Culp's Hill. Among the attacking Confederates this time were the five Virginia regiments of the vaunted Stonewall Brigade, once led by Stonewall Jackson. Its attempt to storm

the right center of Greene's line "was done with equally bad success as our former efforts," admitted Brigadier General James A. Walker, "and the fire became so destructive that I suffered the brigade to fall back to a more secure position, as it was a useless sacrifice of life to keep them longer under so galling a fire." Singly or in small groups, some Rebels became stranded on the hillside — unable or unwilling to retreat. About 11 o'clock Creighton noticed a makeshift white flag thrown out from behind rocks in front of the 7th Ohio's entrenchments. Anticipating a surrender, he shouted for his men to stop shooting. The Buckeyes then observed a mounted officer in gray uniform at the foot of the hill. He spurred his horse forward, evidently intent on preventing any capitulation. Partway up the slope the dramatic gesture ended in a fusillade of bullets. Rider and mount both tumbled to the ground, dead. The officer proved to be Major Benjamin W. Leigh, Johnson's chief of staff. His self-sacrifice went for naught as more than 70 Virginians gave themselves up to Creighton's men. According to Captain Mervin Clark of Company B, "There was three Captains, four Lieutenants and 66 non-commissioned officers and privates, who surrendered. Never were men more joyous over any thing than they to get inside of our breastworks." In Company G, Private Gilbert Bertholf professed that "One of the prisoners said he had been in many hard-fought battles, but this was the most destructive of any they had taken part in." Captain Clark was detailed with his company to guard the captives, "which I did, and delivered them over to the provost marshal, three or four miles in the rear. From a [Rebel] Captain I ascertained that nearly the whole of Ewell's Corps 25,000 strong, was engaged with us. They made several attempts to charge upon us, but we repulsed them with heavy loss. They claim to have never been under such a heavy and incessant fire. They fought with a desperation unparalleled." [45]

The next morning Company H corporal John Pollock, a Trumbull County carriage painter, climbed over the works and picked up the 4th Virginia's rumpled colors, one of three battle flags captured by Geary's division at Culp's Hill. The souvenir hunters and scroungers were especially drawn to Leigh's lifeless body. Papers he carried found their way into General Greene's hands. Gil Bertholf wrote that one of his comrades retrieved Leigh's sword, watch and diary, presuming they were turned over to brigade headquarters. Almost anything was considered a trophy — even the dead major's shirt studs, which were pocketed by Corporal Parmater of the 29th Ohio. [46]

For Federal participants writing about the battle it was a rare soldier who did not mention the cacophony of musketry and artillery fire that swelled from the slopes of Culp's Hill. Although curious as to what it meant, those stationed elsewhere on the battlefield were far more absorbed in what was happening in their immediate vicinity. Thirst and self-preservation, for instance, were paramount concerns of Frederick Nussbaum. His regiment, the 107th Ohio, furnished skirmishers of Harris' brigade but most of its depleted companies remained sheltering behind the stone fence off Wiedrich's battery's left flank. With daylight Nussbaum decided to search for water at a spring, possibly Menchey's, near the base of East Cemetery Hill. "The lane was covered with dead men from both sides, also a number of horses, cows and mules, so that it was impossible for me to get to the spring without stepping on

Sergeant Elias W. Morey, Company C, *right,* and Second Lieutenant Harlow N. Spencer, Company F, *far right,* were among those 7th Ohioans engaged at Culp's Hill. Morey eventually was promoted captain in the 9th U.S. Colored Troops. Spencer, a Geauga County resident later wounded at Ringgold, Georgia, was photographed by Peter S. Weaver of Hanover, Pennsylvania, and signed the carte de visite with date of July 23, 1863. The regiment's rooster device and 12th Corps' 2nd Division star badge adorned his coat and felt hat. At age 38, "He was like a father to his company," recalled a comrade.

Private Collection

L. M. Strayer Collection

Roger D. Hunt Collection

the dead. In the middle of the lane I stopped to pick up a rifle and exchange it for mine, when a bullet passed close by my ears; I dropped the gun and a few steps further on another ball went whizzing above my head, and so on until seven shots were fired at me by a Rebel sharp shooter from one of the windows of the [German] Reformed church [located at the northwest corner of East High and South Stratton streets in Gettysburg]. The sixth shot struck a gate post directly in front of my head, while the seventh touched the sole of my right shoe as I alighted on the ground, leaping over a gate to reach the regimental line. I succeeded in bringing eleven canteens full of water; these I left near the gate, telling the boys to go after them themselves. I had a very narrow escape. ..."[47]

Across the hill to the west, Orland Smith's Buckeyes in the 55th and 73rd Ohio experienced a harrowing night. About the time Harry Hays' assault on East Cemetery Hill peaked and sputtered out, Rodes' Confederate division advanced into the fields just southwest of Gettysburg, pushing Smith's skirmishers within 100 yards of Washington Street and the Emmitsburg Road. But Rodes did not press an attack on Cemetery Hill in the dark. Learning of Hays' failure, he pulled back 300 yards to what is known today as Long Lane. Two of his brigades were sent to reinforce Johnson at Culp's Hill. The other three fortified Long Lane with fence rails and earth. Skirmishers sent forward bolstered those of A.P. Hill's corps already in the fields. Both sides waited for daylight to renew the see-saw sharpshooting contest that characterized fighting July 2 and 3 in this area.[48]

Major Hurst of the 73rd Ohio found sleeping almost impossible. "During the night, we could hear the cries of hundreds of wounded and dying men on the field," he wrote. "It was the most distressful wail [I] ever listened to. Thousands of sufferers upon the field, and hundreds lying between the two skirmish lines, who could not be cared for, through

the night were groaning and wailing or crying out in their depth of suffering and pain. They were the mingled cries of friend and foe that were borne to us on the night-breeze, as a sad, wailing, painful cry for help."[49]

Resumption of shooting on July 3 drowned out the sounds of human anguish — but added to the 73rd's casualty list. "The enemy kept up a heavy skirmish fire in our front," Hurst continued, "and hundreds of rebel sharp-shooters poured down our line an enfilading fire that was cruel and deadly; and as we had no defense or covert whatever to screen us from this flank fire of the sharp-shooters, we suffered terribly. Again the enemy tried to establish himself on the [rise of ground] where he could annoy our artillerists; and again our line was compelled to charge and recharge his skirmishers, to hold them at bay. In one of these charges our regiment captured about twenty prisoners."[50]

Such duty in the open, exposed fields was performed at a high price. Nineteen in the 73rd were shot dead or mortally wounded between 5 a.m. and 1 p.m. First Lieutenant James C. McKell's Company H was punished severely on the skirmish line. Six of his men died while another eight were badly injured. The latter included Privates John C. Brown, 16, and Daniel Buckley, 47, the youngest and oldest soldiers in the company.[51]

Corporal Alonzo Keeler spent 12 hours on picket in Captain Henry Miller's Company C, 55th Ohio, until it was relieved at 11 a.m. Keeler scribbled in his diary, "heavy fighting all day[.] 7 men wounded[,] one Prisoner[.]"[52] His accounting of Miller's losses that day did not reflect the company's lone fatality, 20-year-old Private John R. Myer, whose death was described by an unnamed member of the regiment:

Companies from [the 73rd Ohio] and our regiment were on the skirmish line in front of our brigade ... and the skirmishing was very heavy in our front; and our line charged straight up a little declivity that was there, and drove the rebel line from behind rail piles they had for breastworks, and away they skedaddled. Soon they were reinforced, and came tearing down on us with a yell. Then was our time — to fall back, which we did in a hurry to the place we started from. Here the line faced about, and fought for a while, when we made another charge, driving the rebels pell-mell. There was "charge and countercharge," until, finally, we drove them out of their earth breastworks, way in rear of their rail piles. What made it worse for our skirmishers were the sharpshooters in the houses in town. They hit at least two-thirds of our men. On the line, their balls would strike our men in the right side. ...

It was on the second charge I speak of above, that Johnny Myer, of Co. C, from Milan [in Erie County], was hit. He was struck in the right side by a sharpshooter's ball, while running *toward* the enemy, and instantly killed. A braver or more obedient soldier than he never stood up in a fight; and in camp he was a general favorite with his officers and comrades. His body was buried in an orchard, near Gettysburg, and the spot marked, so that his grave can be easily found, should his friends ever desire to remove his remains.[53]

The pre-dawn hours also were anxious ones for the 8th Ohio, by now reduced to 165 officers and men. "Utmost vigilance" was impressed upon its

L. M. Strayer Collection

A Greenfield, Ohio, enlistee, Private Andrew Miller of Company I, 73rd Ohio, was killed July 3.

Karl Sundstrom Collection

First Lieutenant James C. McKell, Company H, 73rd Ohio.

Wounded July 3, Corporal Henry B. Warren of Company C, 55th Ohio, recuperated at Philadelphia's Satterlee General Hospital. The Huron County farmer was promoted Company D's first lieutenant in April 1865.

Brad L. Pruden Collection

skirmishers lying behind piles of stripped fencing 150 to 200 yards northeast of the Bliss farm buildings. Notwithstanding, Company B's Lieutenant Galwey fought hard to overcome falling asleep. "Two or three times it seemed to me that I had dozed off, and I would rouse myself and whisper something to one of my men, who would also appear to have been nodding." At 4 a.m. Galwey and his Clevelanders were relieved and withdrew to the Emmitsburg Road ditch, where nearly all of them flopped down exhausted.[54]

After daybreak Captain David Lewis reported enemy activity brewing to the front of Companies G and I. Lieutenant Colonel Sawyer reinforced him and Captain Azor Nickerson with parts of two other companies. Commanding the skirmish line, Lewis "advanced in fine style driving the enemies' [*sic*] skirmishers like chaff before the wind; but there is an end to all things[,] so there was to our driving the enemy." Just ahead of the Ohioans several hundred Confederates "arose from a ditch on our front and poured upon us a deadly fire. The enemy advanced on our flanks and gave us a severe cross fire — almost an enfilading fire. We were compelled to fall back. ..."[55]

Back in the road Sawyer already had his remaining companies on alert and in line. As the firing increased he ordered them forward to support the skirmishers. All the officers, including Sawyer, had dispensed with their swords and were carrying muskets. "We went without any well-defined lines

or well-defined companies," he explained. Individual Confederates were "all the way up to our line" with the main body 275 yards distant. "We dashed in among the skirmishers and poured into the rebels a most rattling volley." This broke the enemy advance, although Sawyer momentarily was unaware of it. "Just as I fired my rifle I plainly saw a rebel aim at me from behind a rock. I remember an hallucination of stars, the ball had knocked me down. I was soon helped to my feet with my head bleeding. The ball had pierced my corps badge, the trefoil on the front of my hat, cutting the scalp and stunning me by the concussion, but the wound was not very serious." Private John H. Jack of Company E noted that his commander simply cracked a joke about the incident. "Col. Sawyer, on having a minie ball pass through his hat, coolly lifted it from his head, looked at it, replaced it, and remarked that 'he had been wanting a ventilating hole in his hat for several days, and that he was much obliged for the favor.' "[56]

Captain Lewis, however, was in a sour mood. As part of the morning's fighting that swelled on the Bliss farm, the action cost the 8th Ohio another two dozen men, 10 from Company G. Lewis lost Sergeant John G. Peters, killed, and Sergeant Philip Tracy, badly hurt in the shoulder. A bullet also struck Company I's Captain Nickerson in the left arm, drilled through his right lung and exited under the right arm. Sergeant Benson Beamon and Corporal Edward H. Irish carried him in a blanket to the Bryan tenant house, where Beamon procured a stretcher before returning to the regiment. Irish stayed to care for the grievously wounded officer who, everyone thought, was a dead man. Command of Company I passed to First Sergeant Lucien Abbott. An hour later he was replaced by Lieutenant Thornburg of Company F.[57]

As recompense for its casualties the 8th had successfully driven back the Confederates in its front. "Several rebel dead and wounded were left on the ground," Sawyer related, "and a few of them had got so near us that they did not dare to run, and fell into our hands as prisoners." Later, "eight more of their dead were found in the lane and along the fences, who were undoubtedly killed at this time. When the prisoners were brought down to the road they were greatly disgusted to find we had no reserve or supports, and our flags actually in charge of a guard of wounded men. They declared 'if their men had advanced properly they could have knocked h—l out of us.' " The regiment's dead and wounded that could be recovered were moved to the east side of the Emmitsburg Road. A few of them, including Captain Nickerson, were taken up the slope and deposited on Cemetery Hill.[58]

Sawyer rectified his skirmish line, frequently rotating companies through the morning. When it was again Company B's turn Lieutenant Galwey's men "began to be scientific in our fire. In this way four or five neighbors in the line would load and, seeing a puff of smoke rise from some spot in front, would 'watch for it.' Being ready as soon as the smoke would rise, they would all aim at it and fire together. Generally, the poor 'Johnny' was hit by this device." Galwey continued:

The skirmishing was of that steady nature that comes from acquaintance with the ground and with the enemy's manner of fighting. The firing was rapid enough, and yet there was not much random work. It was almost as much as a man's life was worth to rise to his height

Courtesy of Dennis Frank

Private Jason J. Jack, Company G, 8th Ohio. The Fremont native was photographed at Benham's Studio in Clyde, Ohio.

from the ground. The advance of our line in the early morning had strewn the ground with our wounded, who ... were necessarily left where they fell, now between the two fires.

About thirty yards in front of my company stood a solitary tree which, I suppose, had been left as a shade for men in the harvest field. During the morning this tree became conspicuous on account of the well-aimed shots that came from it. We soon became aware that a couple of bold enemy sharpshooters had crawled up to it and were now practicing on any thoughtless man who offered himself as a mark. About the middle of the forenoon a cry of "Don't fire, Yanks!" rang out, and we all got up to see what was coming. A man with his gun slung across his shoulder came out from the tree. Several of our fellows aimed at him but the others checked them, to see what would follow. The man had a canteen in his hand and, when he had come about half-way to us, we saw him (God bless him) kneel down and give a drink to one of our wounded who lay there beyond us. Of course we cheered the Reb, and someone shouted, "Bully for you, Johnny!"[59]

Those companies of the 8th in the road's ditch were afforded time to prepare a belated breakfast of what remained in their haversacks. The temperature was climbing well on its way to the day's high of 87 humid degrees. Lieutenant Elijah Hayden's blood already was warm when he spoke with bravado to soldiers of Company H gathered around him. "Boys, to-day will probably decide the battle. We have held them pretty well so far, and to-day we must whip them; yes, I say we *must* whip them. I would rather be killed right here, than that they should whip us." [60]

The earnestness of Hayden's little speech might have surprised his listeners, for they had occupied their perilous position without relief for 18 hours and were dog-tired. But it produced an electrifying effect, as did the "incessant" and "annoying" Confederate sharpshooter fire emanating from the Bliss house and orchard off the regiment's left flank. Since morning of July 2 both sides disputed possession of the farm buildings. Much of that time the Buckeyes had a ringside seat to the ebb-and-flow fighting. Rebel bullets and shells frequently flew their way. By late morning of the 3rd, after several Federal attempts failed to completely evict the enemy, General Alexander Hays ordered the buildings torched by the 14th Connecticut. Flames quickly consumed the house and barn, provoking cheers in the Ohio ranks.[61]

Sawyer was just as glad to see Captain James Gregg of Company E turn up in the ditch. Gregg, acting inspector general on Carroll's brigade staff, was sent down "to see how we were getting along." He updated Sawyer about Carroll's "brilliant dash" the evening before and imparted what he knew about the 12th Corps' struggle on Culp's Hill. But Gregg also brought disappointing word that relief or reinforcements would not be forthcoming. Instead, a fresh supply of ammunition was delivered soon afterward. The Erie County captain lingered to chat further with Sawyer and the Sandusky soldiers of his company.[62]

At noon Captain Wilbur Pierce's Company K took its place as skirmishers. Company H under Captain Wells Miller extended south from Pierce's left flank. A third company, C, may have been next to Pierce on the right. Miller's men, according to Corporal Thaddeus Potter, "were farther to the left than the line we occupied the day before; we were deployed along a gentle rise of ground that ran parallel with Cemetery Ridge; we took our stations along a board fence." Company H received instructions to hold its fire unless the enemy advanced. But other troops, specifically a Federal picket detachment identified by Potter as belonging to a New York regiment, "kept up a constant fusillade" off Miller's left. Miller was told, possibly through orders from Captain Gregg, to have the firing cease, so Sergeant George Hitchcock was sent over to request compliance. "He soon came back," Potter wrote, "and reported that he could not stop them. They were Germans, and could not understand why they should stop firing. They pointed to the dead and wounded. 'Nein! nein! Seh' die Toden und Verwundeten, wir wollen schiessen!' and kept banging away. The sun beat down upon us fiercely as we sat or lay along the fence. Many a wistful thought went back to the old well and shade at home."[63]

On the company's extreme left Hitchcock and Corporal Henry A. Brotts, per Miller's orders, closely scanned the fields between Stevens' Run and Seminary Ridge for any sign of a Rebel advance. It was near 1 p.m. when Brotts observed movement. "Hello, what the devil are they up to over there?" He notified Miller. Corporal Potter recalled: "Instantly the line is alert, and all eyes are watching a stirring scene over on the opposite ridge. Battery after battery was wheeling into position. The guns were placed as close together as they could work

them. Several batteries came down into the field and unlimbered. Soon the ridge was lined with guns for a mile or more. We watched them as the gunners loaded, then stood at attention and awaited the signal."[64]

The battle's climax was set to begin.

Two days of bitter, bloody but inconclusive fighting had severely tested the resolve of both armies. For the Confederates the bright prospects of July 1 dissolved in frustration with the July 2 failure of Ewell's and Longstreet's attacks on the Army of the Potomac's flanks. Determined to drive the Federals from the field, Robert E. Lee, as his counterpart General Meade surmised, decided to strike the Union line at its center. His spearhead would be the all-Virginia division of Major General George E. Pickett, Longstreet's corps, supported by portions of two divisions belonging to A.P. Hill's command. To pave the foot soldiers' way, a two-hour cannonade of Cemetery hill and ridge was ordered to destroy or disable Union batteries stationed there and drive off the defending infantry. Accordingly, Confederate artillery commanders under Longstreet and Hill marshalled 150 guns for the bombardment and attack. Their positions stretched in an irregular line from Oak Hill south to the Sherfy peach orchard. It was some of these cannon and crews that Company H of the 8th Ohio saw preparing to fire.

Behind Cemetery Ridge about three hours earlier Captain Huntington, commander of the Artillery Reserve's 3rd Brigade, sauntered on horseback along the Baltimore Pike accompanied by Ohio Battery H guidon bearer William Parmelee. The intense fighting nearby at Culp's Hill was sputtering out, although Parmelee remembered that "For quite a long distance we were under fire — minie bumblebees humming around thickly. I was in a hurry, but Capt. Huntington was not. He rode leisurely along, stopping to talk whenever he met acquaintances. As he ranked me, I could not hurry him any."[65]

The pair eventually reached Battery H's position on Cemetery Hill. By then both noticed a distinct lull in the shooting. "From 11 o'clock till about 1 it [was] very quiet for a battlefield," wrote Parmelee. "Even the sharpshooters are not disposed to improve their opportunities. Most of the boys are resting in the shade of the trees near us. Horses go back on the Baltimore pike to water. The few around the

Captain James F. Huntington, a Marietta hardware store owner, led Battery H, 1st OVLA, before receiving command of the Artillery Reserve's 3rd Brigade. "He is made of the right kind of mettle," thought one of Huntington's Ohio cannoneers.

shot, Parrott, Schenkl, Hotchkiss and James shell, each with its peculiar nerve-cutting, blood-curdling screech, making discordant music that must have pleased the death angel."[67]

Battery H's ordnance rifles still faced Benner's Hill east of Gettysburg. Although 20 or so guns belonging to Ewell's corps added to the din, Huntington divined the weight of enemy fire came from the left, or west. He ordered Lieutenant Norton, battery commander, to change front. For a few moments his cannoneers stood stupefied, unable to move and seemingly unable to comprehend. "For the first time the men of Battery H hesitated to obey my orders," Huntington confessed. "[They] were nearly used up from labor in the excessive heat, and want of food. For an instant they hesitated and hung back, but only for an instant." With officers assisting, the guns were swung around and wheeled by hand a short distance to the left of Captain Wallace Hill's "Pierpont Battery." Huntington "opened one section to the left, another to the front, and the third I could not work for the want of men able to stand on their feet."[68]

The momentary lapse in promptitude by Huntington's Ohioans must have affected him deeply, for he mentioned it in a letter to his wife and again 18 years later while writing more in depth about Gettysburg and Chancellorsville. Private Parmelee, who ended the war as a second lieutenant, probably was stunned as well by his comrades' slow reaction. Years afterward he stated, "The battery ... [was] of-

guns are wondering what will come next." Lieutenant William Ewing, commander of the battery's left section, was among the artillerists pondering the sudden absence of noise. "The question whether the perfect silence of the army for [two] hours indicated that [the enemy] were retreating or preparing for a last grand effort to defeat us was being generally discussed."[66]

Shortly after 1 o'clock all doubt was dispelled when two guns on the Rebel right bellowed a signal to open the Confederate bombardment. "All at once there came a most terrible storm of iron," Huntington wrote. "The howling of shells, the deadly hiss of the solid Whitworth, and the crash of the 12-lb. spherical case, was awful, beyond description." Parmelee echoed his captain's words, employing a bit of hyperbole. "The racket was terrible — solid

ten taken for a regular battery, as they took personal pride in all the little details that go to make up good soldiers. High standards of drill and discipline [were] maintained from start to finish. [We] received [the] personal compliments of Generals Joe Hooker and D. Sickles on the battle field of Chancellorsville, [and] stood high in the opinion of Henry J. Hunt, chief of Artillery, Army of the Potomac." [69]

Ruffled feelings aside, the Marietta, Toledo and Pittsburgh cannoneers manning four of the battery's six guns now toiled with a vengeance. Even though late that morning General Hunt urged his artillery commanders to husband ammunition for an infantry assault expected to follow the bombardment, Norton's and Hill's crews fired projectiles "as lively as we could" at Rebel batteries little more than a mile away in McMillan's Woods. For Private Orin Dority of Battery H's Gun Detachment B, "the [enemy] shells came crashing through the trees and gravestones at furious rates. This is the heaviest cannonading I ever heard." Lieutenant Ewing agreed. "We thought we had endured hot fire before, but the terrific fury of the concentrated fire now brought to bear upon us beggars all description. ... The day had all along been intensely hot and sultry [and] the men were ready to fall down at their guns from sheer exhaustion. ..." Some Buckeyes stripped to their shirts. Diarist John Merrell, a corporal of Gun Detachment A, complained, "I took off my jacket and gave it to Lt. Norton to take care of for I was so warm that it was impossible to keep it on. Lt. kept it a few moments and then laid it down and when I found it someone had taken everything out of the pockets, a Bible and 3 letters ready to mail. The Bible was a capture of Fredericksburg." [70]

Next to Norton, the Ohioans of Hill's "Pierpont Battery" labored just as feverishly at their 10-pounder Parrott rifles from the edge of the smoke-shrouded cemetery. "The whole field was as convulsed as if an earthquake had occurred," recalled William Jenvey. "The air was alive with shrieking and bursting shells, guns discharging, men shouting, and [some] crying out in pain, horses rearing and neighing as they were being horribly mangled, caissons bursting ... until it appeared it was impossible for man to survive the destructive missiles. Still, although our position was higher and more exposed, it appeared as though some guardian angel was watching over us, for our losses were but few." Only two battery members suffered injuries. A spent iron shard hit Private James Loufman in the chest, bruising him. Charles Lacey, a driver for Sergeant Owen O'Neil's Parrott, was struck by a shell fragment in the right temple while trying to keep

A native New Yorker, Corporal John H. Merrell joined Battery H, 1st OVLA, while visiting Toledo in September 1861. Carte de visite by J.B. Smith, Utica, New York.

L. M. Strayer Collection

Private William E. Parmelee, 19, was Battery H's guidon bearer at Gettysburg. Born in Fulton County, he worked as a clerk and bookkeeper in Toledo prior to his August 1862 enlistment.

L. M. Strayer Collection

Private Frederick A. Regnier, Battery H, 1st OVLA, served as Captain James Huntington's orderly at Gettysburg. Rigorous campaigning sapped Regnier's strength, for he spent four months following the battle sick in a Washington hospital and at his home in Marietta.

L. M. Strayer Collection

his horses from bolting. He died that night.[71]

With the same number of men in Battery H just slightly wounded by Rebel shells, Captain Huntington thought "It seems strange that such a fire did not sweep us all, men, horses and guns, off the face of the earth, but it was due to their *over-shooting.*" After the battle he and Lieutenant Ewing inspected some of the positions where Confederate cannon had been firing at Cemetery Hill. At a mile's distance "I was surprised to see how much higher the hill seemed than when one looked down from it. This may account for their mistake in elevation. It was a lucky one for us, at all events; the bulk of the fire passed over our heads, apparently from one to twenty feet, some shells even bursting away to the right, on the wooded slopes of Culp's hill. Still, even as many came among us as were at all desirable. Every now and then a monument in the cemetery would be struck, and fragments sent flying in every direction. In a depression of the ground, in the rear of the cemetery, forming a partial cover from the fire of the preceding day, were massed most of the caissons of my brigade, as close as they could stand. Now they were entirely exposed. I watched them anxiously, as the shells burst all around; it seemed impossible that they should not be exploded. Fortunately, they escaped with the loss of a few horses."[72]

Contrary to General Hunt's instructions, Hill's battery fired with such rapidity that it exhausted its long-range ammunition after an hour. The Parrotts were withdrawn and replaced with the four 3-inch rifles of Edgell's 1st New Hampshire Battery, which had not yet been engaged. The barrel of Norton's Gun A had become so heated by now, wrote Corporal Merrell, "that we could not use it any longer and we run and got another gun and rolled it up in position and fired that until it was impossible to bear our hand[s] on it." Again Merrell's crew exchanged the piece for its original one. Firing re-

sumed. Soon "the vent got stopped up with a friction primer so that we could not get it off, but we had shot away nearly all our ammunition. ... Detachment B's gun was disabled by a shell which struck its axletree but we got it off the field."[73]

Seeing that Norton's supply of long-range ordnance was almost "played out," Huntington decided to obtain another battery at Artillery Reserve headquarters. He told Orderly Frederick Regnier of Battery H to accompany him. "I had just mounted for that purpose," the captain recollected, "when a shell struck the ground and burst in my right front. It scattered the dirt pretty freely, but I thought it had done no other damage, when I found that my right stirrup was missing. A fragment of the shell had cut the leather as clean as it could have done with a sharp knife; another severed the crupper of the saddle, while a third broke the leg of my orderly's horse, who was just behind me. I must say that this ride was about the most disagreeable I ever took. For more than a mile the road was swept by the various projectiles that came over the left and center of our line in great numbers. As I rode along, I noticed a colored boy holding the bridle of some officer's horse. He was ensconced behind a rock, perfectly covered, save that the hand that held the rein was raised above it. A shell burst just then and tore his hand to pieces." [74]

The unparalleled bombardment was endured by several thousand Ohioans caught in its path. Musician Henry Henney, a 55th Ohio stretcher bearer sheltering on the northwest slope of Cemetery Hill, thought "pandemonium seemed to break loose as thousands of shells passed over the place where our Regiment lay. Mainly the boys were hugging the stone fences for the little protection they offered from the flying fragments of exploding shells. The shots from both sides screamed overhead, some close to the ground and others high up in the air. Most of the shells were aimed at the guns on the hill back of where we lay, and passed far to the rear of their aim. Others fell short, striking in water between our regiment and the cemetery, blowing great furrows in the rain soaked earth. The suspense was very trying on those who had to lie still and take anything in the encounter, simply hugging the stone walls, not knowing what moment a shell would strike short and plunge through the slight barricade on its motion of death and destruction." [75]

Elsewhere in Henney's brigade along the Taneytown Road, Medina Countian George Metcalf followed his officers' instructions to the letter. "We were ordered to keep our heads down and lie flat on the ground. This was a useless order to me, for I was doing that pretty effectually without orders." Metcalf's regiment, the 136th New York, was only 75 yards below and in front of Cemetery Hill's line of guns. "During all this time these ... cannon were constantly being fired," he wrote. "The discharges came so rapidly, you could not distinguish one from the other. It seemed more like a settled roar than like a noise made by distinct pieces. The pieces of wood [sabots] that helped keep the flannel bag that held the powder attached to the ball, would fly down upon us and often struck us with such force as to produce great pain. Occasionally a shell would prematurely burst before it reached us, and our own troops would suffer the consequences. Aaron

Courtesy of Mary Kate Liming

Assistant Surgeon William S. Moore, 61st Ohio. During leave of absence three months before his death he visited his brother-in-law, a Methodist minister, in Xenia. "He assured us all," wrote William Fee, "that if this was his last meeting, he was endeavoring so to live each day as to have no fear of the future. He had been in several great battles, and met with many hairbreadth escapes."

Walker [a corporal in Company D], who lay just to my right as we sat with our backs against the wall, and we facing the cannon, was wounded by one of these shells prematurely bursting." [76]

Luther Mesnard intuitively felt the fate of the Union was at stake. Wounded in the right arm July 2, the 55th Ohio sergeant watched the spectacle behind Cemetery Ridge not far from the 11th Corps hospital. "Soon orders came for all that could walk to go to the rear as the shells came screeching through the air by the score. I went back some thirty rods to the shelter of a hillside[,] stopping on the way to comfort my old neighbor Wm. Pollock (of

Company C, 55th Ohio), who had been mortally wounded the night before. After the cannon shot had struck the ground once or twice they would ricochet along the ground[,] and looking the way they were going I could see a dozen at a time bounding along like foot-balls."[77]

At the George Spangler farm hospital location, Assistant Surgeon William S. Moore, 61st Ohio, was superintending removal of less seriously wounded men to the rear when a cannonball or large piece of shell shattered his left thigh. Moore, 33, was a native of Georgetown, Ohio, a graduate of Cincinnati's medical college and the father of two young children. Though wracked with pain, for two days he wrote messages to friends and his wife, Sarah, back in Clermont County. He died July 6. Grief stricken, Sarah never remarried and family tradition holds that she wore mourning black for the rest of her life.[78]

A good number of Confederate overshots fell in the vicinity of Culp's Hill. Sergeant William Tallman, 66th Ohio, recalled helping regimental Assistant Surgeon B.F. Ludlum at a temporary aid station established in a barn along the Baltimore Pike. Projectiles "in great numbers from the enemy guns [were] falling upon our barn, and exploding all around us," Tallman explained. "It was soon found that this place was untenable, and the wounded [were] as quickly as possible placed in an ambulance and moved to a safe place farther in the rear. I was much more exposed in going to the rear than I would have been with the Regiment in their works. I shall not deny that I made fast time in the direction of the rear, as I was in light marching order having only a blanket, canteen, haversack and a case of surgical instruments. In the general stampede from the barn I got lost from the surgeon and I did not see him again that day."[79]

Elisha B. Seaman of Company A, 66th Ohio, was detailed to fill canteens at nearby Spangler's Spring. The Logan County private, awarded a Medal of Honor 29 years later for gallantry at Chancellorsville, "had just got them filled when that great artillery duel burst out and you ought to have seen me getting back to the line, with the air full of things. But I got back safe and had every canteen with me." Not far away, Private Samuel W. Hart of Company H, 29th Ohio, imagined "that I was about as thin as a slapjack during the cannonading. The air seemed to be alive with screeching and howling

demons. Every now and then, some poor fellow among us would be hit with a piece of shell and would yell — if not killed outright."[80]

Having received some rations after its morning fight at Pardee Field, Company C of the 5th Ohio was boiling coffee when the bombardment began. "The enemy opened up several batteries," wrote Sergeant Gaul, "which brought the place where we were located directly in range. Cannon balls and shells skipped around, ploughing up the earth near where we were sitting. Some of our men quickly retired to places of safety, which the location afforded. I felt secure for a while, and said: 'I am not going to leave until I drink my coffee.' The next moment I changed my mind, as a shell about as large as a small sized camp kettle struck the ground close by, throwing the earth all over me, and upsetting my coffee. I then followed the other boys on a double quick."[81]

The heavy cannonading had lasted almost two hours by the time Captain Huntington returned to Cemetery Hill empty-handed. From General Tyler he learned that every Artillery Reserve battery was engaged. During his absence Battery H was visited in the cemetery by the Army of the Potomac's commander, who earlier had been shelled out of his headquarters at the Leister house. According to Private Parmelee, "Gen. Meade, attended by only one officer, appeared among our guns, on foot, saying to our officers that this point must be held at all hazards. When the cry went round that ammunition was getting short, Gen. Meade picked up a shell, stepped up to a gun, asking if that could not be used." Just then William H. Styer, a beardless 19-year-old corporal from Marietta serving as No. 6 with Gun Detachment C, rushed forward with several projectiles. "Seeing someone in his way," Parmelee continued, "he grabbed him by the arm, saying, 'Out of the way, you old fool,' and clapped a shot into the gun. Gen. Meade retired in good order, smiling, we supposed, at the boy's earnestness. Accidents of the battle gave him an Irish promotion to 'powder monkey' when this occurred. When told [later] how he had treated the commanding General he could not believe it." Styer finished the war as the battery's first sergeant.[82]

Five hundred yards to the west the diminished 8th Ohio lay beneath a "darkened, sulphurous canopy." For two hours "our little band of veterans withstood the heavy fire without a murmur," boast-

Gun Detachment C of Battery H, 1st OVLA, was photographed April 9, 1863 with its 3-inch ordnance rifle near Falmouth, Virginia. The artillerymen pictured included Private Edwin P. Hopkins, *second from left,* Lieutenant William A. Ewing, *fourth from left, wearing hat,* Sergeant William H. Perigo, *seventh from left,* Private William E. Parmelee, *behind wheel, holding battery guidon,* and Corporal William H. Styer, *third from right.* All were Toledo men except Styer.

ed Private Jack of Company E. On the skirmish line, Private William H. Clough and Company H endured the "terrible fire; the shot and shell flew around us like hail. Never had the 8th been called upon to stand such an ordeal of artillery fire — but not a man moved. We sat and watched the rebel gunners load and fire their pieces, although scarce-

ly a minute passed without some poor fellow near would be struck." Thaddeus Potter, close by, later wrote: "Boom! whiz! bang! whir-r-r-r, the air appears to be filled with the missiles of death. Shells burst all around us. Solid shot come ricochetting along the ground, boards are knocked from the fence into the air, splinters tear ghastly wounds, men are torn to pieces, but the skirmish line stand their ground." Among the skirmishers' first casualties was Stephen Strange, Company H's second lieutenant. The Elyria native suffered a painful concussion wound of the upper left hip.[83]

In the Emmitsburg Road ditch Lieutenant Colonel Sawyer sat on a fence rail conversing with Captain Gregg, who was unable to return to his staff duty on Cemetery Hill because of the shelling. "The air was filled with screaming, plunging, crashing missiles," Sawyer noted. As the pair talked a solid shot plowed into a rail pile to their front, passed under the seat between them and bounced away to the rear. Both officers were showered with wood splinters. A large piece hit Gregg in the head, momentarily stunning him.[84]

Incredibly, the artillery's roar became so monotonous to Lieutenant Galwey that he dozed off. Several others in Company B did likewise. One of them, Private Charles Gallagher, had crossed the road to lie down under a tree. While fast asleep he was wounded in the thigh by a piece of shell. "I slept for about ten minutes, then awoke," Galwey related. "Shortly afterwards I was struck in the foot by a spent shell fragment. After recovering from the pain of the impact, and whilst laughing at the matter, I was slapped in the thigh by a fragment of an enemy shell. This knocked me over, but I picked myself up." Private Joseph Lloyd remarked to his company commander that he feared the next hit would be a fatal one. Galwey rebuffed him. "Prophets of evil are always to be found."[85]

Those Ohioans with pocket watches noticed a perceptible drop in the rate of Union artillery fire around 2:30. Soon, by orders from Generals Meade and Hunt, it stopped completely. With the firing's cessation, thought Sawyer, "that of the rebels' seemed to redouble in its energy, and for a moment the very earth trembled amid this cyclopean effort for our utter destruction. Suddenly their fire also ceases, as if the rebels believed our line [was] annihilated. ... Indeed, as the smoke and dust lifted, this, to all appearances, seemed the case." Sawyer anxiously looked back toward Alexander Hays' division headquarters for a sign to withdraw from his precarious position. Instead he saw a bustle of activity on the 2nd Corps' front — infantry forming, batteries changing location or replacing crippled ones, generals and other mounted officers dashing along the line, shouting commands. "There had been no annihilation there. The whole line seemed now to spring up as from out of the earth. A grand line grimly awaiting the coming assault. An order just then recalling the Eighth would have been to us very pleasant. None came."[86]

At 3 o'clock the 8th's skirmishers caught sight of glimmering bayonets among the trees on Seminary Ridge. Captain Miller of Company H spoke aloud what his men already knew. "Boys, they are going to make a charge. See that your guns are in order."[87]

A half mile away Pickett's Virginia division formed ranks. To its left assembled six more brigades under the acting command of Brigadier General James J. Pettigrew and Major General Isaac R. Trimble. Some 12,000 Confederate infantrymen readied for the assault, their distant guide point being a small copse of oak trees growing near the right center of the Federal line. Pickett's three brigades were fresh, not yet having been engaged in the battle. The same could not be said for Pettigrew's and Trimble's troops, most of whom had experienced bloody combat July 1 west of Gettysburg. On the attacking columns' left flank the brigades closest to the 8th Ohio were those of Colonel J.M. Brockenbrough, temporarily led by Colonel Robert M. Mayo, and Brigadier General Joseph R. Davis, a nephew of the Confederacy's president. Both suffered severely in manpower and morale two days before, Brockenbrough's effective strength having dropped to just 500 men.[88]

The Buckeyes of the 8th's skirmish line watched in awe as Pettigrew's and Pickett's ranks appeared, fronted by skirmish-

Library of Congress

Major General George E. Pickett, CSA.

Battles and Leaders of the Civil War

Brigadier General James J. Pettigrew, CSA.

ers. "We saw emerge from the woods opposite us a long line of men," wrote Private Clough. In their excitement he and others in Company H thought the Confederate host was "a mile in length, and three lines deep." From Corporal Potter's view, "When they reached the fields they halted, then dressed ranks. They were ordered forward. It was a grand sight [as] they stepped off in quick-time, their flags waving and dipping." Clough related: "Lieut. Hayden jumped up and clapped his hands, shouting, 'hurrah, my boys, they are coming! Now be steady, boys!' The rebels advanced steadily across the plain, but suddenly our artillery opened fire on them. We saw huge gaps torn in their ranks which were immediately closed up by the living."[89]

A variety of ordnance was hurled at the oncoming Southerners, much of it from 41 Federal guns on Cemetery Hill. Brockenbrough's weak Virginia

Private Aaron M. Alvord of Company D, 8th Ohio, broke his right ankle in the regiment's July 3 dash when his foot wedged between two rocks and several comrades collided with him. The injury ended the Norwalk blacksmith's field service.

brigade, under Mayo, began crowding to its right, or south, and inadvertently formed a perfect target for the cannoneers. To Major Osborn, Union artillery commander in the cemetery, "the havoc produced upon their ranks was truly surprising."[90]

Further damage was inflicted on Mayo's men by the 8th Ohio skirmishers of Company H and Pierce's Company K. At 140 yards' distance both companies sent "a ripple of fire" into the enemy. According to Corporal Brotts, Captain Miller "ordered us to fire and fall flat on the ground, and as soon as they fired to retreat to the road. We followed his orders as given. ..." Reloading at trail arms, the skirmishers retired to the Emmitsburg Road a bit south of Sawyer's main reserve in the ditch, and were forced to sprint to regain their places in the regimental line. They were joined, as Corporal Potter recollected, by the German skirmish detachment which had been so boisterous earlier in the day. Without a commissioned officer the New Yorkers formed by themselves. The 8th Ohio's adjutant, Lieutenant John W. DePuy, a former member of Company H, stepped up and asked, "Will you follow me, boys?" They nodded assent.[91]

Cognizant of his orders to hold at all hazards, Sawyer by this time calculated the regiment's chances of survival and, as he wrote the following day, "we made arrangements to fight to the last man." With artillery fire blazing overhead he decided to strike the advancing Confederates in their left flank. "Every man who could stand on his feet was there, musket in hand, the officers thus armed as well." At Sawyer's command the 8th sprang to the top of the ditch, formed ranks and moved "at a run" toward the fence line its skirmishers held the previous day. The regiment's sudden appearance instantly caught the attention of Rebel skirmishers and troops of Thomas' Georgia brigade in the sunken road (Long Lane). "Their volley was simply terrific," Sawyer affirmed. As many as 20 Buckeyes crumpled to the ground, including Captain Miller

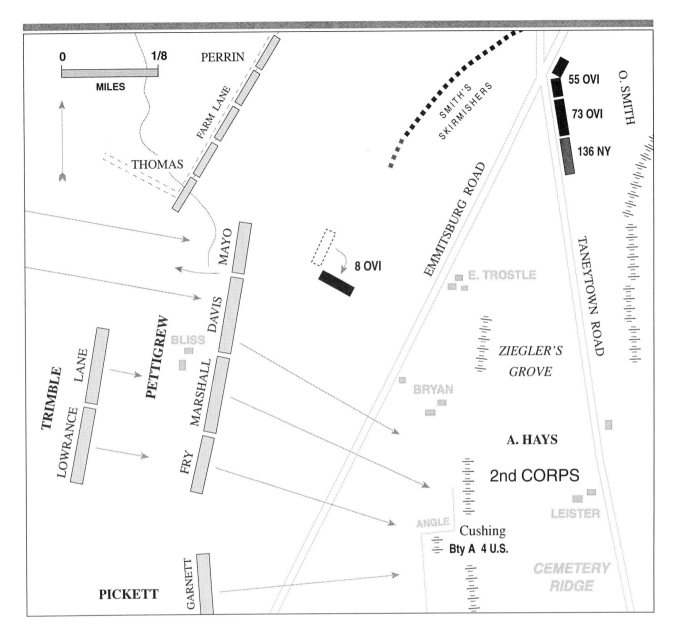

with a severe shoulder wound and Corporal Brotts, who would lose his right leg.[92]

In spite of these losses the 8th reached the fence and immediately loosed a volley of its own into Mayo's approaching brigade. The combined musketry and devastating shell fire were too much for the Virginians. Although some lay down, most broke and "skedaddled" rearward. Davis' brigade, next in line, already was passing the northern part of the Bliss farm orchard. Not hesitating, Sawyer changed front, wheeling his regiment nearly 90 degrees along a perpendicular fence to blast the Rebels' moving left flank. Again the combination of cannon and rifle fire threw the closest Confederates in-

to "the wildest confusion." Large portions of Davis' four regiments began drifting to the rear and the Ohioans turned their weapons on other targets, most likely the two brigades led by General Trimble.[93]

Officers shouted, "Come on boys, give it to them now!" Sawyer, with Captain Gregg at his side, stood transfixed behind his line and watched in "utter amazement." For a few moments "the whole rebel charging column was in plain view from our position," he recalled. "Our blood was up, and the men loaded and fired and yelled and howled at the passing column. Some of the wounded, and among them Capt. Miller, say the passing rebels came so close

First Lieutenant Finney R. Loomis, *above,* of Company K, 8th Ohio, had been wounded previously at Antietam. Company K's second lieutenant, Oramel G. Daniels, *left,* was the regiment's acting adjutant at Chancellorsville. Both officers were from Medina County.

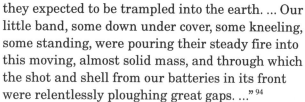

they expected to be trampled into the earth. ... Our little band, some down under cover, some kneeling, some standing, were pouring their steady fire into this moving, almost solid mass, and through which the shot and shell from our batteries in its front were relentlessly ploughing great gaps. ..." [94]

Even so, the 8th Ohio in its isolated position was not immune. Bullets splintered fence rails and smacked sickeningly into bodies. Amid the powder smoke Color Sergeants James Conlan of Company B and Romeo W. Foster of Company E flaunted their riddled regimental and national flags. Miraculously, both escaped injury, but Color Corporal William Welch of Company I was mortally wounded in the head. A ball struck Company A corporal Edward Jones in the face, gouging out his left eye. In Company K, Corporal Silas Judson rested his musket on the shoulder of his older brother Horace,

when an enemy skirmisher shot Silas in the upper right arm, the ball lodging in his chest. Their company commander, Captain Pierce, also took a hit in the shoulder. Within a few minutes every captain in the regiment was wounded except David Lewis and William Kenney, acting as major. For Lieutenant Galwey, commanding Kenney's Irish Company B, the damage brought tears to his eyes. His first and second sergeants, John G. Fairchild and James Kelly, each lost legs, Kelly dying July 7. One of Private George T. Upright's hips was shattered, and Private John Burk, 38, who had served two decades in the British army with the 18th Royal Irish, suffered a mangled foot. Corporal Bernard McGuire and Privates William Brown and George R. Wilson were killed. [95]

Though Sawyer's numbers were dwindling at an alarming rate, those unhurt continued shooting into the compacting mass of Confederates. "I do not see how I, or anyone else could go through such a terrible battle and come out without a scratch," wrote First Sergeant Lucien Abbott to a former comrade in Company I. Sergeant Beamon frankly admitted in a letter to his mother that "It was the hardest fight we have had. ... Men were swept down on all sides of me, but I did not get a clip. ... I tell you it looked a little serious when their whole force came on us in one black solid column, which we could see no end to, with demon yells, and fixed bayonets, but we met them on the run. ... The cannon mowed them down, and helped break them up as we rushed on."[96]

By now 2nd Corps infantry on Cemetery Ridge was shooting into the Rebels' front, adding measureably to destruction wrought by the artillery and Sawyer's Ohioans. The forwardmost batteries had switched to firing canister at a range of 500 yards or less, effectively transforming their cannons into giant shotguns. As they reached the Emmitsburg Road the ranks of Pettigrew's and Trimble's four brigades still advancing lost their symmetry. Some Confederates tumbled into the road just off the 8th Ohio's left flank, and began firing from the strong post-and-rail fence lining the roadbank. A majority continued on, breaking into the high-pitched Rebel

yell, charging upslope. To their right Pickett's battered regiments did the same. From the Bryan farm buildings south past the copse of trees, an "awful concussion" rent the air.[97]

With "bated breath," Sawyer stared as "a sheet of flame burst like a tornado upon the [Confederate] mass. 'Close up! Close up!' rung along their lines which were fast loosing [sic] their grand organic form and becoming indistinct amid the smoke and dust and debris of battle. The grand formation of a moment ago was soon utterly enveloped. ... Above the turmoil of battle we could hear curses, shouts, shrieks, and could see hats, guns, legs, arms and mutilated carcasses hurled out into the less murky atmosphere." To Company H's Thaddeus Potter, "It was a fearful, ghastly sight to see men slaughtered so. Our main line was pouring a hail of bullets into them, while the artillery was mowing

The Abraham Bryan house, looking west, was photographed by an M.B. Brady cameraman in mid-July 1863. Bryan, a free black, owned a 12-acre farm and lived in the house between 1857 and 1866. In restored form it still stands on the battlefield.

swaths through their ranks with shell and canister. Men were thrown into the air like chaff by bursting shells." [98]

Near the inferno's center sat two serviceable ordnance rifles belonging to First Lieutenant Alonzo H. Cushing's Battery A, 4th U.S. Artillery. The battery had been virtually demolished during the pre-assault bombardment with three limbers or caissons blown up and several guns disabled. Numerous horses had been killed and men injured. Cushing himself was painfully wounded in the lower abdomen by a shell fragment. Despite this he retained command, and when the oncoming enemy was 700 yards away he ordered the remaining rifles rolled forward to an angle formed by two low stone walls. The guns were charged with double loads of canister, stacks of it piled beside each piece. [99]

As many as a quarter of Cushing's artillerymen were Ohioans. The previous October, 39 members of the 4th Ohio transferred voluntarily to the battery, and at least 12 others joined prior to July 1863. Typical of these volunteers was Corporal Thomas Moon of Marion, commander of Cushing's caissons. After 16 months' infantry service he concluded he "did not like walking & carrying a gun and knapsack." The sentiment was shared by Private James H. Patterson, formerly of Company E, 4th Ohio. He became one of the battery's two buglers. [100]

It is not known just how many Buckeyes composed Cushing's gun crews at the wall. When Confederates to their front began scaling the Emmitsburg Road fence the lanyards were pulled, releasing a deadly torrent of iron balls into the moblike mass. The rifles were loaded again with double canister and fired. Before they could fully recoil a bullet smashed into Cushing's face, killing him. The battery's first sergeant assumed command and gave the Rebels another staggering blast from 90 feet away. Musketry disabled the left piece. As the enemy closed within point-blank range the right gun, stuffed with triple canister, exploded. Those cannoneers not taking to their heels found themselves fighting hand to hand with screaming Confederates scrambling over the wall. [101]

The struggle at the Bloody Angle and Copse of Trees — the culmination of what popularly became known as "Pickett's Charge" — lasted five, perhaps 10 minutes. Every Confederate who crossed the wall was killed, wounded or captured. Singly and in groups of varying sizes, the dazed grayclad survi-

Tony Lemut Collection

Private William H. Strode of Battery A, 4th U.S. Artillery, previously served in Company K, 4th Ohio. Although Strode was unscathed, six Ohio members of Cushing's battery were wounded July 3. Carte de visite by W.H. Moore Photographer, Marion.

vors on Cemetery Ridge's body-strewn western slope began drifting back toward their own lines.

All this time the 8th Ohio had continued shooting into the left flank and rear of the smoke-enveloped column, nearly exhausting its ammunition. The Buckeyes knew their comrades on the main line had held when scores of enemy soldiers emerged from the murk in obvious retreat. Sawyer wrote: "Men wounded and men half naked were teeming about over the field making the most frantic efforts to get somewhere — anywhere — but to get away from the scene of annihilation. ... Swarms of rebels came down upon us, not apparently any longer in fighting mood, for they had thrown away their guns, and were apparently more intent on safety than glory; pale, faint, and some with their tongues hanging from their mouths. Our line was extended in single file along the road as far back as it would possibly reach [in order] to capture all fugitives that came within reach. ..."[102]

Lieutenant Galwey observed that "They all seemed to extend their arms in their flight, as if to assist their speed. They threw away everything — cartridge boxes, waistbelts, and haversacks — in their stampede. We dashed in amongst them, taking prisoners by droves." Corporal Joseph Evans of Company B alone corralled 15 captives, including two lieutenants. German-born Corporal John Miller of Company G and Private James Richmond of Company F spied Rebel color bearers trying to save their banners. Each wrestled away trophies. Richmond secured an unidentified flag and Miller, of Sandusky County, captured those belonging to the 34th North Carolina and 38th Virginia. Both soldiers were given Medals of Honor in December 1864, although Richmond's award was posthumous. A Toledo resident, he died the previous June of wounds inflicted at Spotsylvania while on detached service with his brigade's pioneers. He was buried in Arlington National Cemetery.[103]

Sawyer's begrimed men rounded up about 200 Southerners before he finally received a verbal order from one of Hays' staff officers to "come in as soon as I pleased — and we prepared 'to come.' We threw ourselves into a formation that the men called a sandwich; that is, half the regiment in front with our colors and captured flags, then our multitudinous prisoners ... and our rear guard with fixed bayonets." But not everyone departed with Sawyer. Possibly on his own volition Lieutenant Hayden, in command of Company H since Captain Miller's wounding, remained behind with several others. One of them, Private Clough, afterward wrote to Hayden's wife, telling her they did not retire with the regiment because enemy sharpshooters were still firing, and the lieutenant wished to rout them. "He waved his sword over Sergeant [Elnathan M.] Smith, shouting 'hurrah, we have whipped them, they have got enough,' and turned to join the regiment, when a bullet from a sharp shooter struck him in the spine, and he hollowed oh! and fell dead." Clough further related that "We could not

bring his body from the field that night, as our wounded claimed all our attention. One of the boys went to him and got his things. His watch had been taken. The rest of his things we got. His revolver was stolen from me after the fight. ... He died much loved by his company, for he was a brave and good officer. ... I heard him say just before the fighting commenced that he had rather die right there, than to have the rebels whip us."[104]

Back in Elyria Hayden's young daughter, Ella, would never receive the photographs he promised to send her 12 days before.

The captured Confederates paraded by the 8th Ohio outnumbered its reduced strength two to one. Casualties suffered during the 24 hours it spent west of the Emmitsburg Road carved the regiment in half. Of 209 engaged, 27 were killed or died of injuries. Seventy-four were wounded badly enough to require extended medical treatment. One man, Private Alfred Smith of Company H, did not answer roll and was listed missing. Nearly everyone else obtained cuts, abrasions or bruises of some kind. All were dirty and lathered with sweat. A sergeant in Company I concluded, "The old 8th is pretty much used up this time. We lost terribly in men and officers. There were but 21 of our company in the fight, and only eleven left, and we came out as black as niggers."[105]

The exhausted Ohioans' spirits no doubt soared during the procession toward Ziegler's Grove. "Several Generals with their staffs rode forward and cheered us," wrote Sawyer. Second Lieutenant David S. Koons of Company C claimed General Meade himself "came down with a score or more of officers, jumped off his horse and, taking Col. Sawyer by the hand, exclaimed, 'Take your regiment to the rear, and tell them to stack arms and go wherever they please.' " According to Lieutenant Galwey, "As we ascended the hill down which we had come yesterday in gallant array, the artillery, who had seen us through all the fight, cheered us and spoke flattering words to us as we passed them." Captain John Madeira, a 73rd Ohio officer serving on Colonel Orland Smith's brigade staff, had watched the "distinguished work" of Sawyer's troops from the side of Cemetery Hill. Unaware of their identity, Madeira rode over to investigate. "I never was so proud of being an Ohio man in my life as I was when I found that the men whose gallantry I had never seen eclipsed on a battlefield was the Eighth Ohio. I felt

At Gettysburg, Captain John D. Madeira of Company H, 73rd Ohio, served as acting assistant inspector general on Orland Smith's brigade staff. Carte de visite by F.A. Simonds, Chillicothe.

like yelling out, 'I am from Ohio, too! Bully for Ohio!' "[106]

The 8th marched beyond Meade's former headquarters at the Leister house, its yard and adjacent Taneytown roadbed littered with dead horses. Crossing the Baltimore Pike, recalled Galwey, it halted in "a hollow, where we stretched ourselves out on the grass to rest." Apparently the location was not far from the other three "Gibraltar" regiments east of the pike. A 4th Ohioan wrote that Sawyer's regiment, with trophies and prisoners in tow, "soon made its appearance from the skirmish line … and was greeted with rousing cheers by their comrades." The 14th Indiana, noted several members of the 8th, "fell in and presented arms — a tribute we highly appreciated." Sawyer later stated that Colonel Carroll, venting his own excitement, climbed atop a cannon and exclaimed, "Look, you fellows, there comes my old Eighth with the balance of Lee's Army!"[107]

The prisoners were placed in custody of the brigade provost guard, commanded by Captain Alfred T. Craig of Company F, 8th Ohio, who in turn handed them over to different provost marshals. Craig's 32-man detachment then assisted Carroll's brigade pioneers by picking up discarded weapons, carrying the wounded and collecting the dead. One of these belonged to his own squad. Private Jacob Sheak of Company I, 4th Ohio, had been killed July 2 when a piece of shell ripped open his chest.[108]

While the 8th Ohio relaxed and received food, including a whiskey ration, Captain Azor Nickerson of Company I found himself in a harrowing predicament. Fearing himself mortally wounded with his own chest and arm injuries, he laid all day somewhere in or near Evergreen Cemetery. He survived the early-afternoon artillery barrage, but once the Pickett-Pettigrew charge was repulsed Confederate cannons again began firing to cover the infantry's retreat. Shells burst uncomfortably close to the captain, as Nickerson remembered: "Men lying near me were cut in two and others torn in pieces by the jagged missiles. I thought a change of location, no matter how slight, might take me out of their immediate range. Certainly it could not be worse, so I dragged myself a short distance only to find that I was in a worse place, if possible, than where I had been. Then, by a supreme effort … I struggled to my feet and started to run. I had taken but a few steps when the blood gushed from my mouth in a torrent, and I fainted and fell."[109]

Nickerson, born in Medina County in 1838, had been studying law in Elyria when he was commissioned second lieutenant during the summer of 1861. At Antietam he suffered a shoulder wound while leading Company I's assault on the Sunken Road, and consequently missed the Union debacle at Fredericksburg. Having rejoined the regiment prior to Chancellorsville, he was recognized there

Battles and Leaders of the Civil War

A column of Confederate captives being escorted south along the Baltimore Pike. Immediately after the battle dozens of Ohioans and other Federal soldiers erroneously wrote home that General James Longstreet was a prisoner, or dead. One of his subordinates, Brigadier General Evander M. Law, suggested a plausible explanation for the mistake. Among Confederate casualties "was Colonel [Robert M.] Powell of the 5th Texas regiment, who was shot through the body. ... Powell was a stout, portly man, with a full beard, resembling, in many respects, General Longstreet, and the first impression of his captors was that they had taken that officer. Indeed, it was asserted positively by some of the [Union] prisoners we picked up during the night [of July 2-3] that Longstreet was badly wounded and a prisoner in their hands, and they obstinately refused to credit our statements to the contrary."

for being "particularly conspicuous and attentive" to duty. Sawyer thought highly of him. When Nickerson was carried away bloodcovered and insensible early July 3, the 8th's commander was certain he'd never see the captain alive again.[110]

As Nickerson regained consciousness he discovered a hospital attendant daubing his face with water. An ambulance was parked a few feet distant, its driver helping to place the officer inside next to another wounded man. "Even while they were doing this," Nickerson continued, "a conical shell went crashing through one of the wheels of the vehicle. The driver very properly did not wait to see whether his wheel could hold together, or if the shell exploded, but went tearing over the fields at full speed. The ground was awfully rough and covered with debris, but he turned out for nothing." The captain and his injured companion were jostled so severely that both fainted. Nickerson was revived with brandy at a barn hospital and 4th Ohio Surgeon Harry McAbee soon was examining his wounds, including an ugly exit hole close to the officer's right armpit. Nickerson asked if there was any hope for his recovery. "No," replied the doctor, patting him gently on the forehead. "No, my boy, none whatever."[111]

□ □ □

At nearly the same hour McAbee gave Captain Nickerson his dire diagnosis, Sam Gillespie apprehensively watched as fellow cavalrymen from General Judson Kilpatrick's command spurred their mounts forward in a futile charge. The Buckeye bugler and comrades of the First Ohio Squadron, Kilpatrick's escort, had been in the saddle much of the time since witnessing the heavy cavalry skirmish with Jeb Stuart's Rebel troopers June 30 at Hanover. The next day the Cavalry Corps' 3rd Division marched to Berlin, Pennsylvania, where, Gillespie reflected, "we picked up a number of Stuart's stragglers as he passed around our front. ... This was a noted copperhead town, but now they were glad to see us, having had a visit from their Southern friends." [112]

Ordered on July 2 to move toward Gettysburg, Kilpatrick's division of two brigades under Generals Elon Farnsworth and George Custer rode westerly in the firing's direction. To Gillespie, a 23-year-old farmer and regular contributor to the newspaper in Washington Court House, Ohio, they "wander[ed] about all day through fields and lanes, listening to the [distant] battle and seeing the smoke, when we came to Hunterstown." Near sundown, "We had just taken off the bridles to feed our horses, after the advance had driven the enemy from the town, when the rebel yell came from the woods and hill beyond, like a pack of hounds in the chase. Then there was hurrying to get in line across the road, but our artillerymen were ahead of us and had two guns in position as they came down the hill and gave them a few doses of [canister], which sent them back faster than they came. One [Confederate's] horse ran clear around our line, the man, without hat, sawing on the bit trying to stop his horse. He was so frightened and so helpless that we felt more like laughing than shooting at him. There were repeated charges, and several shells came over the hill and burst near us before they gave it up and left us to eat our supper in peace." At 11 p.m. the division was ordered to Two Taverns, reaching the hamlet by daybreak July 3. [113]

With only two or three hours' sleep Kilpatrick's Ohio escort, commanded by Captain Noah Jones, accompanied the diminutive general when he left Two Taverns at mid-morning. Kilpatrick had received orders from Cavalry Corps commander Alfred Pleasonton to move the 3rd Division to the Army of the Potomac's far left. There, combining forces with a Regular cavalry brigade coming north from Emmitsburg, he was supposed to attack the Rebel army's right and rear. Kilpatrick rode with Farnsworth's brigade, unaware for several hours that Custer's command had been detached and sent to assist General David Gregg's 2nd Division off the Union right flank. In a sharp encounter occurring simultaneously with the cannonade preceding the Pickett-Pettigrew assault, Gregg and Stuart clashed three miles east of Gettysburg. Custer's Michigan brigade, partially armed with new Spencer repeating rifles, bore the brunt of the hardest fighting and suffered 219 casualties. The cavalry

At Hunterstown, Pennsylvania, George Armstrong Custer led a cavalry charge for the first time as a brigadier general, having a horse shot beneath him. For a short period prior to entering the U.S. Military Academy in 1857, Custer, born at New Rumley, Ohio, taught school in the Harrison County seat of Cadiz.

battle ended inconclusively, both sides claiming victory.[114]

Meanwhile, Kilpatrick and Farnsworth reached the vicinity of the John Slyder farm west of Big Round Top. Those present with the First Ohio Squadron were beginning to assimilate opinions of "Little Kil" and his leadership style. Bugler Gillespie remembered that at Hanover their commander had urged, "Boys, look at me. I am General Kilpatrick. I want you to know me, and where I go I want you to follow." Gillespie avowed the remarks were thoroughly characteristic of the officer. In time, troopers serving under the 27-year-old West Point graduate came to love or hate him. He was personally brave, flamboyant, often reckless and overflowing with ambition. On July 3, Gillespie inferred, he also was a man not to be trifled with when the cavalry approached Taneytown Road at Round Top's base. "As we were moving out to the battle line we met some ambulances returning with wounded, which General Kilpatrick ordered out of the road until his column could pass. A stubborn driver refused to turn out, when the General drew his sword and, the man still refusing, gave him a thrust and ordered us to lead the horses out of the way." [115]

Once in position Farnsworth deployed skirmishers, as did Brigadier General Wesley Merritt, whose 1st Division brigade of mostly Regular cavalry appeared to Farnsworth's left a little earlier via the Emmitsburg Road. Their thinly stretched opponents belonged to Hood's division, Longstreet's corps, supported by a smattering of Rebel cavalry. Skirmish firing was brisk until the early-afternoon Confederate cannonade commenced. Some Southern guns threw shells toward the Federal troopers, forcing them to seek shelter. Following the failed infantry assault on the Union center, Kilpatrick determined the moment was ripe for his cavalry to charge the Rebel right. Gillespie thought the general "was very anxious to carry this position, as he would then be able to reach the enemy's ammunition train." At 5:30 Merritt and Farnsworth were ordered to attack. Because of poor tactical judgment, however, Kilpatrick's effort was doomed almost from the start.[116]

Merritt's men, pushing up the Emmitsburg Road west of Kilpatrick, were dismounted and fought as infantry over relatively open terrain. Their Sharps carbines possessed neither the accuracy nor range of enemy rifle muskets. As a serious threat to the Confederate flank, Merritt soon was neutralized. Farnsworth, on the other hand, was told to charge from the saddle with sabers. His path just west of Plum Run lay over broken ground studded with rocks, thick underbrush, trees, fences and stone walls — hardly an ideal spot for cavalry to

Author's Collection

Brigadier General Hugh Judson Kilpatrick. An Ohio infantry officer who became acquainted with the cavalryman in Georgia in 1864, thought Kilpatrick was "the most vain, conceited, egotistical little popinjay I ever saw. He has one redeeming quality — he rarely drinks spiritous liquors, and *never* to excess. He is a very ungraceful rider, looking more like a monkey than a man on horseback."

Ross County Historical Society

operate. The incredulous brigade commander protested to Kilpatrick, insisting a mounted attack was utter folly. Both officers exchanged brief, heated remarks that no doubt were heard by many of the Ohio troopers. According to Gillespie, "General Farnsworth remonstrated with the General when ordered to make this charge against infantry and artillery posted behind what seemed to be insurmountable barriers. But General Kilpatrick was excited, saying, 'If you won't go I will go myself.' It appeared to us that he ordered Farnsworth to go on this charge to try him, and there certainly could be no greater test of a man's courage than to lead such a charge." [117]

As Farnsworth predicted, the desperate dash made by one of his regiments and supported by two others failed. He himself was killed, pierced by five bullets. One wounded participant sadly reminisced, "There was no encouragement of on-looking armies, no cheer, no bravado; each man felt, as he tightened his saber belt, that he was summoned to a ride to death." The gallant but fruitless charge accomplished none of Kilpatrick's envisioned goals. That night, wrote Bugler Gillespie, "we slept in the rear of the line of battle, amid the dead and dying, not knowing but what the next day we would be numbered with them." [118]

The battle of Gettysburg was over, though virtually no Buckeye on the field knew it. Sharpshooting, particularly in the areas of Culp's and Cemetery hills, continued until nightfall veiled the marksmen's targets. "The grand result was as yet unknown to us," reflected artillery Captain James Huntington. "As the fierce, discordant yells, the roar and rattle of combat died away, the defenders of [Cemetery] hill only realized that the enemy had been severely repulsed. That our troops had gained, at least in a certain sense, a decisive victory, we did not then consider by any means certain. ... After the

Brad L. Pruden Collection

Second Lieutenant Isaac N. Hawkins, *top,* and First Lieutenant James S. McCommon, *left,* of Company C, 73rd Ohio, survived the battle — Hawkins winning "laurels for bravery," according to a fellow regimental officer. Seventeen weeks later both were wounded in Tennessee. Another wound suffered in June 1864 required amputation of McCommon's left foot.

day's work was fairly over, with another officer, I spent some time in trying to ascertain the whereabouts and condition of our wounded men, who during the battle had been sent to the rear. We were only able to find a part of our men; those we saw were as well cared for as circumstances admitted. A grassy couch was never more welcome than on that night. The mental and physical strain of such a prolonged conflict is excessive. I do not remember ever feeling more utterly used up in my life. ... I went to sleep, thankful that I could do so, a possessor of what is vulgarly but expressively called 'a whole skin.'" [119]

After sundown at Culp's Hill, Sergeant Joseph Gaul was instructed to issue three days' rations to Company C, 5th Ohio. "As they were all asleep in and about the breastworks, it was necessary for me to get them up. I went along where I supposed they were, and gave a fellow a push with my foot, or pulled the blanket from his face to ask him who he was, and found, in a number of cases, that the man was dead. The dead and living were lying side by side, neither troubled at the other's presence." [120]

At dark, recounted Major Hurst of the 73rd Ohio, "the firing slackened, and soon entirely ceased. We were greatly worn and fatigued; and, that night, got a little uneasy sleep as we lay on our arms." Company G's commanding officer, Sam Fellers, pondered the human cost of the past 48 hours. One-fourth of the lieutenant's 36 Highland County men were gone forever, killed or mortally wounded. At least 14 others were prostrated with bloody injuries, three losing limbs. "I don't think language can express or describe the determination and daring bravery with which the fighting was carried on, on the 2d and 3d days of July — language cannot tell to those who have lost their fathers, husbands and sons, with what determination they faced the cannon's mouth, and all the deadly missil[e]s the rebels hurled at the Union army." Gettysburg was the 40-year-old Fellers last battle. Having been wounded himself at Second Bull Run, he resigned his commission August 16, 1863. [121]

George Metcalf huddled on Orland Smith's brigade skirmish line in a shallow hole he scraped out with his bayonet and frying pan. The night was unlike any the 19-year-old farmer had ever spent in his Ohio hometown of Liverpool, or during his entire army service. Twenty years later he vividly recalled:

Although Private George P. Metcalf was enrolled in the 136th New York, he was born and raised in Ohio on a northern Medina County farm. This portrait was made about 1876 when he served as Lorain County's prosecutor. "He not only was the acknowledged leading jury attorney of the bar," his law partner affirmed, "but while on crutches he served a term in the [Ohio] legislature. He was the most popular man in the county. Everybody loved him." Metcalf's death in 1887 at age 43 was attributed to dysentery and heart disease contracted in the army.

I found we were now among the dead and wounded that had not been carried from the field by their friends. I shall never forget this night. It made its memory fixed for all time to come. The night was black with darkness. A rainstorm was gathering in the west. The air was filled with groans, moans, shrieks and yells. Prayers were offered and curses pronounced. Piteous appeals were made for water, for help, for death. The sounds came from everywhere, distinctly heard [by] those near by, and growing fainter and more indistinct until lost in one constant low, far-away moaning sound. Occasionally, by the flashing of the lightning, you could see a dark form rise from the ground as some poor wretch by a superhuman effort would attempt to rise, and then it would disappear. ...

As the long night wore away and it seemed morning would never come, there came a drenching rain. The pit I had dug was filled with water, but still I sat in it, for it must be remembered we were not ten rods from a strong skirmish-line which at every opportunity took occasion to shoot at anyone whose form could be seen or guessed at. When the storm of the elements had abated, I found that the life-spark had gone out of many of those to whom death was a most welcome visitor. The battle-field was quieter now.[122]

In Gettysburg, Colonel James Robinson of the 82nd Ohio listened to Confederate officers talking in the street outside the house where he lay painfully wounded. From their conversation he learned of the enemy's mid-afternoon repulse, and that Ewell's corps was in the process of withdrawing from the Rebel left. The news acted like a restorative. Robinson asked a Union soldier who was hiding in the dwelling to open the back shutters and assist him to a window. North of town he glimpsed ambulances, caissons and ammunition wagons headed westward "in great confusion." The colonel fervently wished there was some way to relay his observations to General Meade.[123]

Not far away in the J.S. Crawford house along the Harrisburg Road, wounded 82nd Ohio captain Alfred Lee noted "The after-dark fighting of the previous night was not repeated, and, except for the rattling of moving caissons and wagons, all was quiet. During the evening a rebel soldier who had been slightly wounded in that day's battle came limping into the room where I lay, and, squatting on the floor beside me, began conversation. He belonged to Stonewall Jackson's old corps [now Ewell's], and it so happened that we had shared, on opposite sides, in most of the battles in which his command had been engaged." The two adversaries spoke at length about the war, until the Southerner concluded by remarking to Lee, "Well, I suppose we shall have another hard battle tomorrow, and I must go to my regiment. It won't take more than another day to decide this fight." With that he bade the officer goodbye and hobbled away.[124]

FIVE

'So fearful was the spectacle, it was too much for tears'

AFTERMATH

The rain, which so often followed a major battle as veteran soldiers quickly pointed out, continued falling at daybreak on July 4, Independence Day. It seemed unusually quiet to the men entrenched on Culp's Hill and the 11th Corps' skirmishers in the fields extending from East Cemetery Hill. Here and there reports filtered back to commanding officers that the Confederates were pulling out or had vanished. As early as midnight officers on Colonel Andrew Harris' brigade skirmish line informed him their opponents of Early's division were "drawing off." Harris imparted the news to General Ames, who ordered the colonel to advance his men with day's first light.[1]

At 5 a.m. Harris' troops, fronted by the remnants of the 25th Ohio strung out in skirmish order, moved toward Gettysburg in a line stretching from Baltimore Street to the brick kiln just east of town. Each man's bayonet was fixed. Silence greeted the soldiers, but once they entered southeastern Gettysburg's muddy streets and alleys they were told to move fast and cheer.[2]

The 75th Ohio, numbering 80 or fewer effectives that morning, was led by Captain Ben Fox. Only one other officer, Lieutenant Ladley of Company G, remained to assist the regiment's acting commander. Nearing the town square Fox divided his men, placing half under Ladley while he re-

tained control of the rest. Utilizing stationery found on the battlefield later in the day, Fox wrote to his father: "We charged through the town for a half mile in length — *double quick* — and yelling like demons. The people knew not what was up, only that the folks knew twas Yankees. The flags came out by the dozens and the women shook their handkerchiefs. We drove the enemy out of town and beyond it some three squares. We captured some 300 prisoners. The fact is that we surprised them. Many were sleeping around and in the houses. How *blue* they looked."[3]

Ladley explained in his own letter home that "we celebrated [the 4th of July] by chargeing into town which put an end to it, the fighting. We captured 300 prisoners. I arroused two out of sweet slumber myself, they did not know what to make of it. ... We went like a set of devils and raining as hard as it could pour down, and of all the waveing of handkerchiefs and smiling faces, you never saw the equal. I was ordered to take half of the 75th and secure all the rebels in the east part of town and Capt. Fox in the west. After we had made a clean sweep I posted the men around to keep a lookout. I went into a yard to see how things looked and while there I was invited to stay for breakfast[.] Accepted with many thanks for I was nearly starved."[4]

Colonel Harris was delighted. His small bri-

167

Colonel William H. Noble, 17th Connecticut.

Styled the "farmer statesman," Colonel Andrew L. Harris, 75th Ohio, grew up in Preble County and was an 1860 graduate of Miami University. In 1906 he became the state's 44th chief executive — the last of Ohio's Civil War veteran governors.

gade had "liberated" Gettysburg with barely firing a shot. A week later he gushed: "This was the proudest moment that ever passed over our heads — so long used to defeat, we felt sure of victory once. Even if we had been ever so desponding we could not have helped being cheerful with so many bright countenances surrounding us. We felt as though we had relieved so many innocent citizens from captivity. It was rather amusing to see the boys gather around the young ladies and hear their tales of rebel cruelty." The 25th Ohio's Edward Culp discovered "The inhabitants were overwhelmed with joy at what they called their delivery." As he rode down York Street, Culp noticed a familiar face from his regiment. "I found [Lieutenant] Wood gazing out of

a window and looking ridiculously happy. He is severely wounded in the arm. I went in the house, and he introduced me to a Mrs. Culp. She was taking care of half a dozen of our wounded men in her own house."[5]

While Harris, Ladley and Culp savored the foray's successful outcome, Fox's portion of the 75th Ohio was greeted by bullets at the western edge of town. His men located the enemy in some strength near the Lutheran Theological Seminary. A sharp skirmish ensued. After an hour Fox was relieved by troops from von Steinwehr's division, and on Ames' order reassembled his regiment in the vicinity of Gettysburg's railroad station. About this time the 17th Connecticut's colonel, William H. Noble, appeared in town. He had been recovering from a Chancellorsville wound and missed the Gettysburg fight. Since he ranked Harris the Ohio officer asked Ames to assign Noble to the brigade's command. When the request was granted Harris reassumed command of the 75th.[6]

Gettysburg was again in Union hands. As the gloomy morning wore on the Federals discovered General Lee had abandoned the ground east and north of town, and pulled back his army's right wing. But the Confederates still maintained a potent force in the woods along Seminary Ridge, apparently inviting an attack which never materialized. Although the 6th Corps had not been heavily engaged in the battle, much of the Army of the Potomac was exhausted and part of it battered. Content with Gettysburg's occupation, General Meade opted to keep his infantry and artillery in place. The cavalry received different orders.

July 4 passed much like the previous two days for the Ohio skirmishers of Orland Smith's brigade. Sharpshooting and sporadic volleys between opposing skirmish lines kept Smith's men on edge, and close to cover. Private Wilmont A. Mills of Company G, 55th Ohio, informed his father: "I will tell you how I spent the Fourth. In the forenoon we were stationed behind a stone wall, and in the [afternoon along] the skirmish line, when we took our place in a corn field and layed down. The ground was soft, and I took my bayonet and dug a hole deep enough to lay in, which screened me from the rebel balls. I could load laying on my back, and then raise up and fire. The rebels were in plain sight from my position, but too far off to shoot with accuracy. After a few hours, I changed my position, as every man was allowed at this time to play sharp shooter with the rebels at a distance of about 40 rods. We made them keep very close. ..."[7]

Stiff and soaked to the skin, George Metcalf reclined in a muddy hole of his own. He also furnished a description of his morning's activity:

When the morning light came, orders came to advance our line. This order included only our skirmish line. I crawled out of my pit, wet as a drenched muskrat. I straightened up. I had no sooner got upon my feet than a volley was fired from the enemy in front. The minie-balls went whistling by my head, and before I had time to take any second thought I was back in my pit of water. Upon peering out to see what had become of the rest of the line,

I found every man had obeyed the instinct of self-preservation and dodged behind his improvised breastwork the same as I had done.

The order was renewed and we again started, this time with a full realization that danger was ahead in the shape of a strong skirmish line of rebels. We started for them on the run, yelling at the top of our voices. I remember placing the butt of my gun in front of my face and holding my trusty old frying-pan and knapsack up, so as to stop any unfriendly bullet that might be calling my way. I ran down the line of a board fence, or rather what had been a board fence, for nothing but the posts stood now. As I hurried along I heard the rifle-balls strike these

An unspecified wound allowed Second Lieutenant Edward Bromley of Company G, 55th Ohio, to recuperate at his Republic, Ohio, home. The visit proved to be his last. In November 1863 he was shot through the heart and killed in fighting just outside Chattanooga.

posts and expected every second to be taken for a post and killed. We ran about sixty [yards] forward, but before we had gone half that distance the first line of rebel skirmishers broke and ran before us.

I saw about ten [yards] ahead of me a rail-pile made into a sort of breastwork. I made up my mind to reach this pile and stop whether the rest of the company did or not, for the bullets came too thick to expect to escape much longer. I ran or tried to run as I never ran before. It seemed I would never reach the place, and in my anxiety to get there my head wanted to go faster than my feet could carry it. As a result, I fell forward when within ten feet of the rail-pile. As I fell my cheek struck the leg of a dead man who had been stripped of his clothes and had lain all night in the rain. I was going so fast that when I fell on my face I slid the whole length of this dead body, and a sort of slimy matter peeled off and stuck to my face.

I found myself now with two other comrades, who put in their appearance at about the same time I did, and three dead men behind this pile of rails, which was about two feet high. I was near the right of our company, and I found all those to the left of me stopped when this old fence was reached, the same as I had. On my right was a company from the 55th Ohio. They did not stop, but climbed over the fence and ran down nearer the enemy who were hid away in a grove of low bushes. Before they were ten [yards] in advance of us a volley was fired into them. They halted, turned and came back in line with us; but several of them were shot before they got back.

We stayed in this place until nearly noon. I counted out fifty-four [percussion] caps and laid them on a rail, so as to be handy when loading, for I did not dare rise over the top of the rail-breastwork to load, so loaded my gun lying on my back. When I first undertook to fire my gun it would not go off, as it had lain under water all night. I primed it by pricking in fresh powder which I got from a cartridge, and hastily sitting up pointed it towards the rebels. Just as I was about to fire, a bullet struck the rail my gun lay on and I jumped back. The gun was discharged, the bullet striking in a wheat-field, or what had been a wheat-field, not more than twenty feet from where I was.

I began to load and shoot, and the two comrades with me did the same. I took deliberate aim and discharged my gun fifty-three times — at a rebel every time. We three would shoot together, often by calling "One, two — fire," and watch for the result. Whether we actually hit anyone or not we could not tell. The one fired at would drop almost every time; but whether it was because he had heard the bullet whiz by or because he was hit we could not tell. Often, after dropping to the ground, in a second he would jump up and run away.

Sometimes four rebels would come together from back in the woods, each at the end of a stretcher, as if after some wounded comrade. We had a rule among us not to fire upon anyone while taking off the wounded; but we soon learned that they were not after the wounded, but had their guns concealed in the stretcher and took this way to get down near us without being shot at. After we discovered this we made no distinction, but shot at any fellow who showed himself. [8]

Elsewhere in Metcalf's brigade the 73rd Ohio lost one man during the day, but not by enemy fire. Thirty-five-year-old William Ackerman was a farmer and native of Germany. For 10 months the Company D private had served in relative safety as a brigade headquarters' teamster, but after Chancellorsville he rejoined the ranks. On July 4 Ackerman was instantly killed "by an accidental discharge of a musket." [9]

Meanwhile, more troops from the 11th and 1st corps were ordered or filtered into Gettysburg. They rounded up Confederate stragglers missed by Harris' men and began the onerous job of collecting wounded and dead comrades. Ambulance squad leader Martin Buchwalter, 73rd Ohio, noted in his diary: "All quiet this morning. We bring wounded out of town[.] 2 loads[,] then go down in a field when it rained very hard and orders came to hitch up and bring another load — We went 2 miles beyond town and brought in a load. They are left in the ambulances — No feed for our horses." [10]

Another ambulance driver, Jacob Smith of the 107th Ohio, was "kept very busy hauling wounded soldiers to the field hospitals where their wounds could be dressed and they be properly cared for. The badly wounded of the first day's fight fell into the hands of the enemy when our forces retreated back to the line on Cemetery Hill. They had all been put into buildings, but no care or attention had been given them at all, and their wounds had become badly inflamed and were in a very sore condition. Owing to the hot weather many of their wounds had begun to gangrene, thus rendering their recovery far more doubtful than if attention had been given them when first wounded. The fourth of July we spent in moving those wounded who had fallen into the enemy's hands, and a very busy day we had of it before our work was completed there. To add to the disagreeableness of our task, about noon it began to rain and during the afternoon we had several hard, heavy, violent showers. Indeed for severity and violence the times were few and far separated

82nd Ohio surgeon Jacob Y. Cantwell treated scores of injured 11th Corps soldiers, which included more than 85 from his own regiment. A native of Richland County, he had been severely wounded himself at the 1862 battle of Cross Keys, Virginia, taking a round musket ball in the thigh. Cantwell ended the war as superintendent of hospitals at Columbus. An older brother, James, was killed rallying the 82nd Ohio as its colonel in the battle of Second Bull Run.

when there were any rain showers to exceed those of today." [11]

As the number of Union troops swelled in Gettysburg's streets, the 82nd Ohio's colonel, James Robinson, was elated to hear familiar voices outside the house where he lay grievously wounded for nearly three days. Robinson faced a six-month re-

covery. Despite a desire to resign his commission for health reasons just a month before Gettysburg, he returned to the army in 1864 and led a 20th Corps' brigade in Georgia and the Carolinas, finishing the war as a brevet major general. For years afterward Robinson suffered from the effects of his July 1 shoulder and chest wound. It largely contributed to his death in January 1892. [12]

About 7 a.m. a Union ambulance sergeant entered the Crawford house on the Harrisburg Road, announcing to the inhabitants and injured occupants that the Rebels had withdrawn to Seminary Ridge. His orders were to remove all wounded from the house immediately. Among them was Captain Alfred Lee, who recalled:

Accordingly, we were hurriedly carried to the ambulances and driven to a field-hospital established in a large barn a mile or more from Gettysburg. In and around that barn were gathered about fifteen hundred wounded soldiers, Union and Confederate. They were begrimed, swollen, and bloody, as brought in from the field, and, for the most part, had received as yet but little surgical treatment. Some were barely alive, others had just died, and many were in a state of indescribable misery.

In the centre of the barn stood an amputating table, around which two or three surgeons were busily performing their dreadful offices. A handsome young German captain, whose leg had been shattered by a musket-ball, was placed upon the table and chloroformed. After the operation of removing his injured limb was complete, he was brought to where I lay and placed beside me. The pallor of his face betokened great loss of blood and extreme weakness. After some minutes, he opened his eyes, and, turning languidly toward me, inquired, "Is my leg off?" Being told that it was, he gazed intently at his hand, and, observing that a ring had been removed from his finger, he remarked, "I would not care for this, were it not for a little friend I have down there at Philadelphia." He could not say much more, for his remaining vitality was fast ebbing away. In a few hours it was gone. [13]

Several hundred wounded or dead Buckeyes were retrieved from the first day's battlefield and the town itself. Like Alfred Lee, Captain William J. Rannells of Company I, 75th Ohio, had been shot in the hip. That he was not killed July 1 seemed almost miraculous, for his uniform was perforated by a number of bullets, his sword scabbard bent and its belt hanger severed by a passing missile. Unable to walk, he was carried to a Confederate field hospital and suffered there with scant if any attention until found by comrades July 4. He joined Captain Lee and a growing throng at the 11th Corps hospital where a brother, Doctor C.S. Rannells, arrived within a few days to accompany him to their family farm north of McArthur, Ohio.[14]

From the evening of July 1 when he was deposited badly injured in the Benner farmhouse east of Rock Creek, Lieutenant Colonel Benjamin Morgan of the 75th Ohio was convinced he faced death. Charles L. Wilson, the 75th's surgeon, thought so, too. Captured at the Almshouse while tending wounded men of Ames' division, the doctor was permitted on July 3 to visit Morgan, remove his bloody clothing, and wash and dress his shoulder and chest wounds. Wilson determined the officer's left lung was severely contused, perhaps damaged beyond repair. Late that night Confederate soldiers departed the house and Morgan was aware of hurried activity outside. He related: "I called Josiah Benner and asked what was up. He answered 'Oh! Oh! Thank God they are retreating.' Then I asked him if he could get through the lines and acquaint our forces. He demurred. I then offered him $100.00 which I fortunately had in my pocket, to go, but he refused. Lieutenant [Charles H.] King of the 25th O.V.I. who was lying beside me badly wounded offered him another $100.00 but he still persisted in his refusal."[15]

The next morning Morgan and King were in friendly hands, but the former's critical condition precluded moving him to a field hospital. He remained in the Benner home for a month, nursed during the last two weeks of July by his wife. A few days before the couple's return to Warren County, Morgan wrote to relatives: "I have every reason to be thankful, for had the ball passed an inch or two either way it would have been fatal; likewise that the Rebels conveyed me here so soon, where I had shelter and attention. I only laid about 5 hrs. on the Battlefield, but during that time was under a heavy fire of Grape, shells and musketry, expecting momentarily to be blown to pieces."[16]

Physical evidence of the conflict's fury seemed to radiate from Gettysburg in all directions. An unidentified Buckeye in Captain Hill's "Pierpont Battery" prophesized in a July 4 letter to *The Marietta Register:* "This place will hereafter occupy a prominent historical position for here during the three past days has progressed one of the hardest fought

Captain William J. Rannells, Company I, 75th Ohio.

battles of the war." William Jenvey of the same battery observed the destruction from atop Cemetery Hill. "Some of the boys, on going over the field to our front and left, said that fully three acres could be traversed without touching the ground, so thickly were the bodies strewn. I was content to take a view from our position."[17]

Writing to Norwalk relatives several weeks later, a member of the 55th Ohio stated that "One needs to *hear* and *see* a battle to know anything about it; and he will and can know nothing of the *horrors* of war unless he has walked over a battle-

Sarah Xalissa Morgan, *far left,* assisted with her husband's medical care while the 75th Ohio officer recuperated at Gettysburg. His severe wounds, combined with six months' imprisonment following capture in Florida a year later, markedly aged Benjamin Morgan in appearance. Compare this 1865 portrait with his earlier photograph on Page 52.

field like that of Gettysburg, before the dead have been removed. The dead there lay in rows, as they advanced in line of battle. On one spot, about three rods square, were counted between thirty and forty dead rebels. ... [T]he wounded filled every house and barn, for miles. At one barn, in the shed part, I saw a gray back lying under the sill, stiff as a mackerel; and occasionally, along the road, could be seen a dead rebel, who had probably been brought in wounded, and died in hospital. The stench for miles was almost unbearable." [18]

For the Ohioans who fought on Culp's Hill, and those who visited its badly scarred eastern slopes immediately following the fight, the scene was stunning. The 66th Ohio's lieutenant colonel, Eugene Powell, related:

Probably no battlefield ever presented more evidences of a severer struggle than did that part between our fieldworks and Rock Creek. The face of the space that the enemy had advanced over was very rough, covered with rocks, logs and forest trees; these had afforded shelter to the enemy and were thereby made objects of our wrath, and upon which we vented our vengeance in hopes of striking the men behind them. For two days and nights volleys of lead and iron were hurled from foe to foe until bodies of trees of large size were actually cut in two by these missiles, and falling with their outspreading

branches upon the living or dead beneath buried them, for the time, as in a sepulcher; the faces of the rocks fronting these foes were marred and battered by bullets until a line of dead lay in a shapeless heap beneath. Logs were splintered and torn, so as no longer to afford shelter to human beings. The earth alone was proof against that carnival of destruction, as the seams and rents made in its surface were filled by the dirt and dust falling back into them, and the sears and rents thus made soon became imperceptible. ...

The Confederate wounded were gathered up, and their dead prepared for burial. The burial of the dead upon the field of battle has a form, but no ceremony. Pits or trenches take the place of the separate grave, and into these the bodies of the dead soldiers are laid to await the final trumpet call. [19]

William Tallman, also of the 66th, watched as dozens of bluecoated soldiers scoured the hillside. He remembered seeing "two young Johnnies who, although badly hurt, were plucky and independent, saying they would have better luck next time. The ground was thickly strewn with dead and wounded, of all ages and conditions of men. ... Most of the dead had laid upon the field since early in the previous day and [were] badly swollen and blackened. About this time occurred one of those ludicrous panics that sometimes took place on the field. ... The woods was full of men who were there from curiosity and maybe in a few cases for the purpose of plunder (I was among the crowd but not for the plunder). A Regiment to our left quite a distance away had moved back from the front to fire away the dampened powder in their guns, as it had been raining for several hours. At the first report some one yelled out that the Johnnys were coming back, and then commenced a stampede for the Breastworks; although considerably excited I could not help laughing as the fellows went headlong over the works and grabbed their guns. Soon afterwards details were made from each Brigade and Division to bury the dead and remove the wounded from their fronts."[20]

Sergeant Joseph Gaul was in charge of a 5th Ohio detail ordered to inter dead Confederates littering the hill's slopes. "There were many such

L. M. Strayer Collection

squads for that purpose, sent out that day," he reminisced. "I do not know how the other squads operated, but mine dug three big trenches. One after the other was filled, and in each we put about thirty bodies, making ninety-two in all. I scored the trees close by, and marked thereon the number in each. ... This burial was a most trying task upon me, as well as many others engaged in it. The bodies were so badly decomposed that they had to be gathered up carefully, by placing strips or sticks beneath them and by rolling, pushing and carrying them, they would be dropped in the trenches and when full would be covered up."[21]

Sherman Norris of the 7th Ohio inscribed his diary for July 4: "I have just returned from being one of the 'pall bearers' to the largest funeral I ever attended, having been detailed to help bury the rebel dead in front of our brigade; and we dug a trench, into which we piled about 200, and carried off 2,000 stand of arms." Afterward Norris wrote, "As long as reason holds her sway, until all else is forgotten, I shall remember that day and its ghastly dead. We took them from perfect lines of battle as they had fallen; we dragged them out from behind rocks; we found them behind logs or lying over them, with eyes and mouths distended, and faces blackened by mortification. We found them everywhere in our front, from within a few feet of our fortifications to the foot of the hill."[22]

After inspecting former Rebel gun positions on Benner's Hill, Ohio artillery officers James Huntington and William Ewing were among Culp's Hill's sightseers. According to Huntington, "The burying parties were busy at their repulsive task though from the appearance of the ground in front of our line, one would have thought their labors scarce begun. A long trench already packed with bodies of the slain bore evidence to the contrary. I never saw the dead lie so thick on any field, as on that stony hillside, and the bullet-scarred trees, with leaves prematurely scattered by the leaden tornado that had swept through their branches. Bodies in gray

Second Lieutenant Edward T. Curtiss, Company B, 29th Ohio, commanded a burial detail of 12th Corps pioneers on July 4. His detachment interred 85 Confederates killed on Culp's Hill.

lay within two yards of our breastworks. Some lay dead behind little walls of stone thrown up as a protection from the fierce fire that consumed them. In one place I traced the line of a company, lying dead where they had stood, with the captain at his post." A fellow member of Battery H, Corporal John Merrell, recorded in his diary that he viewed "dead rebels by the hundred. There was 40 in one place all laying close together so that they completely covered the ground. It was the hardest sight that I ever saw in my life." [23]

Equally appalling to the senses was the agony of thousands of men clogging makeshift field hospitals. "Our wounded are having the best care circumstances will admit of," wrote Chaplain Lyman Ames, 29th Ohio, to the *Conneaut Reporter* on July 5, though that care in many cases was woefully inadequate, or too late. The flood of injured soldiers simply swamped overtaxed surgeons and hospital attendants. Federal wounded presented enough of a problem, but medical personnel also were confronted with a large number of Confederate casualties. Captain David Lewis reported that at one site alone adjacent to the 8th Ohio's bivouac, "Hundreds of wounded Rebels are laying at a barn near where I am writing and many are now being brought off the field where they have lain since day before yesterday. Their groans and yells are distressing." [24]

Charles Merrick had been the 8th's hospital steward since January 1863, previously serving in the regiment as a musician and private. A 35-year-old doctor from Elyria, he wrote frequent letters following the battle to his English-born wife, Myra, who is credited as being Ohio's first female physician.[25] For the first two weeks of July Merrick toiled at three 2nd Corps hospital locations. Excerpts from his correspondence home are highlighted by lurid, sometimes acerbic observations:

Disillusioned by wretched conditions encountered in the field hospitals, 4th Ohio surgeon Harry M. McAbee resigned from the army in September 1863. Writing to the secretary of war, he complained: "After the battle of Gettysburg, with but three assistants, I was left in charge of a thousand badly wounded men, not a few of whom, I fear, absolutely died for want of appropriate and good professional care. And it is my deliberate opinion that the failure to furnish a sufficient number of medical officers on that occasion has cost the country more good men than did the charge of any rebel brigade on that severely contested field." During a snowstorm January 19, 1864, McAbee was killed in a railroad accident near Painesville, Ohio.

July 6th 1863

My dear Min

It pleased me much to get a letter from you yesterday and I was glad to lie down away from the sounds and sight of misery to read it. Such a time as we have had and are having still. There are from our Reg. alone ninety six wounded men, many of them seriously wounded. Since the battle four have died, making our killed sixteen. Two more will die to night. ... We have several hundred rebels here to feed and take care of which adds much to the horror of the scene. Dr Brinton [*sic*] was ordered to the Reg.

this morning and he left me to take care of our wounded. I have about fifteen [orderlies] to help me but for all that the work is very great and I can scarcely get a moments rest. Loads of rebel wounded still come in and they say the field is just covered with dead. ... We are shut out from all news. But I suppose the papers are full of rejoicing. They ought to be for I believe the "army of the Potomac" has gained *one* victory and a great one too. ...

Tuesday July 7th 1863

Dear Min

I wrote to you yesterday and have but little to say to day. I know you will be glad to hear almost daily from me and the poor boys so I will write again. We have not so many to care for now — some have died and the slightly wounded have been sent away. I have 40 now who need constant care. When I wrote day before yesterday we had about 1,200 lying around here. I think we have about 800 now. This includes about 300 rebels. In our Reg. 18 have been killed or died since the battle. James Kelly [of Company B], whose mother lives in Cleveland cannot live long. I thought sure he would die last night. I wish you would see her or see Capt Kenny's [sic] folks and tell them to see her. I told him there was no hope of his living. He said "All right; I am willing and reconciled to what ever be my fate." His leg is badly shattered and has never rallied from the shock sufficient to warrant an operation. He speaks of his mother often and says she is all he has to care for. I feel almost alone here with the boys. No one to boss me or no one to run to for advice. Many times I have wished you could be here, but I know it would be more than you could endure. It is pleasant though to see now and then a woman flitting around among the sufferers. ...

I have one awful case. [Corporal William] Welch Co. I was shot in the cheek, the ball went diagonally down, lodged in the lower jaw, or below the Jaw in the throat. This morning some of the arteries broke and fresh blood run in streams from his mouth and nose. I ran to him and placed my thumb on the carotid when the blood stopped. We fixed a tourniquet so as to hold the artery for the time but what can be done — nothing but tie the carotid and that you know seldom if ever succeeds in saving life. To cut out the ball is equivlent to cutting his throat and sure death. But it is hard to see a healthy man lie and bleed to death. ...

I fear it will be several weeks before I can join the Regiment. Not because I tire of taking care of the boys but I cannot expect any letters from you. They will all follow the Regiment. Since I wrote that last word "Regiment" we have buried Kelly. Our boys get [a] better burial than some. We bury them within ten minutes after they die. I counted 19 in one row who have been lying three days above ground. I have wished some of these Chaplains instead of preaching and praying around here nights when men want to sleep would take a shovel and bury our dead. Perhaps I am uncharitable towards army Chaplains but my conviction is strong that they as a whole are a humbug and a burning shame to their profession. ...

'Deserving of especial praise'

The attentive ministrations of volunteers like Cornelia Hancock, a 23-year-old nurse from New Jersey, were gratefully appreciated by at least two Ohioans in the 2nd Corps hospital. Badly injured 8th Ohio captain Azor Nickerson met Hancock July 7. "She carried writing materials, envelopes, and postage stamps, and wrote letters to the friends of those who were too desperately wounded to do so themselves. She took down just what each wanted to say, without abridgment, and in this manner many a mother, sister, and sweetheart received their first, last, and only message from their loved ones, whose lives ebbed out on this fatal field. It was a thoughful, sensible, and delicate service, faithfully performed."

On July 13 the 8th Ohio's hospital steward, Charles Merrick, observed: "We have an abundance of help now and plenty to eat. The ladies old and young take hold with a hearty good will. One, Miss Hancock, is deserving of especial praise. She is a frail looking woman although possessed of a ruddy healthy face. She is on the go *all* the time. How she endures it I cannot understand. She is chatty and cheerful and the only one I have noticed yet who is not everlastingly asking that indelicate question of the men 'Where are you wounded.' "

July 10th 1863

We had a great time here yesterday. The mean little creek [Rock Creek] got mad and rose over seven feet. It flooded our Camp so quick we had to wade in the water to remove the wounded. It was an awful thing to hurry out several hundred wounded and dying men — the rain falling in torrents all the time. How I *did* work and how the poor fellows did suffer. But we are comfortably situated again and I am most *broken backed*. Some of our slightly wounded are gone. I still have forty who need constant care. About six of them I have no hope of saving. ...

July 12th 63

I have been the rounds among my patients and report to you their condition. I have only about twenty left — most of them I have sent away — some of them have died. I have eight very serious cases yet, two of them I have no hope for. Since I [last] wrote to you two have died which makes seven since the battle. The two cases I refer to are both shot through the nates [buttocks] — the ball coming out near the ospubis. One has the rectum and bladder both wounded — the other the rectum. We have plenty of help as far as *dressers* are concerned but no Surgeon at all to look after the boys.

Our boys are very indignant at the conduct of the "Christian Sanitary Commission." They devote almost their whole time to the rebels — give them everything to eat and wear — preach and pray with them — but pay very little attention to *our* men. ... Our boys have not had their share of the comforts, the delicacies, the attention they bestow on the rebels. The 14th Ind[iana] Sutler sent a lot of wine to their boys. The "Christian Commission" took it and gave every drop to the rebels.[26]

One of Merrick's patients during this period was 8th Ohio captain Azor Nickerson. Shot through the left arm and right lung, he spent his second night at the 2nd Corps' 3rd Division hospital on the ground, unprotected and drenched by rain. In spite of a downpour Nickerson craved a drink of water "as I had never before wanted it. I called, and called again and again, but no one came. Those who were not disabled were sleeping too soundly for one feeble voice to awaken them." Finally Philip Tracy, a sergeant in the 8th's Company G whose shoulder was mangled July 3, answered the captain. Lying nearby, Tracy said he would try to retrieve some water from Rock Creek. Nickerson "heard him get up and the rattling of his canteen, as he started down to the creek for the coveted drink, but he did not return. He had been badly wounded himself, and daylight showed that in his effort to succor his fellow-soldier, he had fallen near the banks of the stream and there bled to death. 'Greater love hath no man,' than was here shown by poor Sergeant Tracy."[27]

For several successive days Nickerson was delirious, his conscious moments filled with "wild phantasmagoria that always accompanies hours like these." He was tended by Corporal Edward Irish of Company I, who saved the captain from drowning July 9 when Rock Creek, swelled by heavy rains, overflowed its banks. As Nickerson related, the corporal, "finding that he could not, alone, carry me to higher ground, cut some stakes, drove them into the ground, placed poles on them, and then breaking up an old barrel, took the staves

and laid them across the poles, thus making quite a comfortable bunk, several feet above the water. Upon this, after great labor on his part, and no little anguish on my own, this faithful man succeeded in placing me out of reach of the angry waters that swept through our camp and under my cot. The overflow was probably not over two feet in depth, but to men who could not raise their heads, this ... was enough — it sufficed. The few attendants there worked like Trojans, but it was impossible to save all."[28]

Captain Azor Howett Nickerson, Company I, 8th Ohio. Although his Gettysburg wounds never completely healed he remained in uniform for two decades, serving 12 years as adjutant and aide-de-camp (as pictured here in 1875) to General George Crook. In 1878 Nickerson was appointed the U.S. Army's assistant adjutant general.

Seated in front of a painted backdrop, 8th Ohio commissary sergeant Lemuel Snover, *far left,* and Corporal Edward Jones, Company A, posed in healthier times. On July 3 Jones, a 23-year-old Seneca County farmer, was shot in the face, losing his left eye. "The blow," wrote an attending physician, "rendered the patient unconscious for about 20 minutes immediately after its reception but except this he suffered no symptoms of concussion until about 14 days afterward." Jones received treatment at five different Gettysburg and New York City hospitals (achieving promotion to sergeant on November 1) before transfer to Camp Dennison's 2,300-bed hospital complex outside Cincinnati on December 30. There, his condition worsened until February 10, 1864, when he sank into a coma. On the 16th Assistant Surgeon W.C. Cole operated to decrease brain compression and remove bone particles oozing from the eye socket, discovering in the process that Jones' skull was fractured. For the next 10 days, Cole reported, "all the functions of life were harmoniously performed," but on February 27 he again "sank steadily, and died on the afternoon of the 28th." After Jones' burial in Dennison's cemetery, his brother-in-law claimed his effects — an overcoat, blouse, trousers, wool shirt, hat, blanket and pair of boots.

L. M. Strayer Collection

The captain's precarious balance between life and death was a shared experience of dozens of injured Buckeyes in the battle's aftermath. Some survived, some did not.

On July 10 Nickerson's father arrived from Elyria, learning that Merrick and other 2nd Corps doctors entertained little hope for the officer's recovery. The elder Nickerson was surprised to find a wounded Mississippi soldier lying on a cot just a few feet from his son. Azor Nickerson recalled: "I was quite proud that, from this time on until all the Confederates were removed from among the Union troops ... my father showed the man even more attention than he did me, so anxious was he to demonstrate that he made no difference because he might have 'shot his boy.' " [29]

Another arrival from Ohio was George G. Washburn, 41-year-old editor of *The Elyria Independent Democrat.* The newspaperman was a longtime friend of the Nickersons, having assisted organizing Company I in Lorain County during the summer of 1861. He was among the 8th Ohio's most visible benefactors, remembered Lieutenant Colonel Sawyer, visiting the company "at various times while it was in the field, and each time he brought with him from friends at home many things to make the men comfortable and happy. His many kindnesses to the men will not be forgotten by those who survived the ravages of battle, pestilence and disease." [30]

Washburn came to the battlefield with a heavy heart. Less than a month earlier his only brother, Captain Frederick S. Washburn, had died of head and neck wounds suffered in May while leading the 9th Iowa Infantry in an assault outside Vicksburg. [31]

Once in Gettysburg, the editor immediately sought the 2nd Corps' 3rd Division hospital site. "I began to experience the effects of war," he wrote, "in the almost sickening effluvia which arose from the bloody field, and all the way to this place the stench is unbearable. On entering the field where the wounded of the 8th lay, I proceeded to the tent occupied by Capt. Nickerson, who was so overjoyed at seeing me so unexpectedly, that for some time he could not be composed, and I thought best to leave him for a time, and look after others of the 8th." [32]

That evening, July 12, Washburn observed surgical procedures in a large tent "where the amputating tables were placed and in the course of an hour [I] witnessed a large number of operations, the patients being entirely insensible from the use of chloroform. The legs and arms, as fast as cut off are thrown in a heap at the side of the tent, and one would think he was in a slaughter house, at the extent of the pile. During my stay here, the scene was beyond any description. The rain was pouring down in torrents, the thunder was rolling incessantly, and from the poor rebels on the side of the hill there came up a constant moan, distinctly heard above the noise of the raging elements, and mingling with the chorus of many voices, singing and praying in the adjacent tents. No language can portray the horrors of the scene. At the same time the surgeons were plying their knives and saws, in almost unbroken silence, for scarcely a loud word was spoken, while I remained in the tent. As soon as one was finished another was brought in on a stretcher and placed on a table, and the other carried away to his quarters, many of them to linger a few hours and die. May God, in his infinite mercy spare me from ever again beholding such an aggregation of human misery." [33]

Washburn finished composing his first day's dispatch "on my knee, by the side of Capt. Nickerson's couch. He is sleeping under the effects of opiates I have administered; and I fear will soon fight his last great battle. He says he is ready to die, and has every attention he needs. ... In the next tent are eight Union soldiers with only eight legs — They are doing well, but the moans that even now, at midnight, come up from them are truly distressing." [34]

The newspaperman stayed on the field nine days, departing for Elyria July 21. When he left only Nickerson and seven 8th Ohio enlisted men remained in the 2nd Corps hospital. They were:

• Private Charles C. Sewald, Company A, Tiffin, shot through a leg below the knee.

Tents of a 2nd Corps field hospital, photographed one week after the battle. Loaves of soft bread were stacked atop the barrel at right.

Private William Jones of Company F, 82nd Ohio, was shot in the back of his left knee joint on July 1. He was admitted eight days later to a Baltimore hospital, where Assistant Surgeon D.C. Peters summarized Jones' case: "[He] was very cheerful. Stimulants [of] wine & beef tea were administered but he sank and died from exhaustion on the 25th July. Autopsy 24 hours after death." Jones' damaged knee bones were preserved in the U.S. Army's anatomical collections.

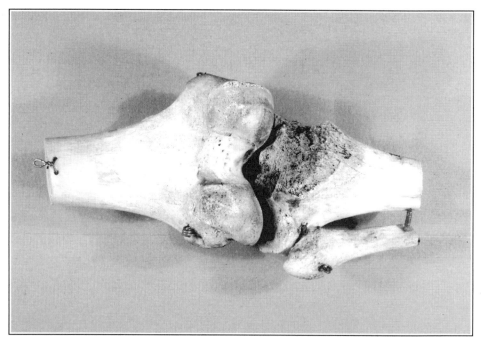

National Museum of Health and Medicine

- First Sergeant John G. Fairchild, Company B, Cleveland, shot through leg [amputated] and right shoulder.
- Corporal William Gridley Jr., Company D, Franklin Mills, shot through a knee and sick with typhoid fever.
- Corporal Oscar E. Bacon, Company E, Bedford, shot in the chest.
- Corporal Henry A. Brotts, Company H, Seville, shot through the right leg below the knee [amputated].
- Private John C. Biggs, Company I, Elyria, shot in the upper right arm.
- Private Jonathan E. Meyers, Company K, Homer, shot through the lower abdomen and hip.[35]

Sewald succumbed to his injury August 16 at Gettysburg's Camp Letterman hospital, and Bacon passed away April 11, 1864 in the U.S. General Hospital at Baltimore. Gridley died the same day as Washburn's departure. His father reached the 2nd Corps hospital just two hours after the 23-year-old corporal was buried. The body was exhumed and Mr. Gridley had it reinterred in nearby Evergreen Cemetery.[36]

His sad sojourn was by no means the only one experienced by Ohioans rushing to Gettysburg following reports of the tremendous battle. Newspapers in the state's largest cities carried lengthy, detailed wire accounts of the fight by July 4, and within seven days even small-town weeklies began publishing fairly reliable casualty lists. Scores of concerned family members and friends traveled east to search for wounded loved ones, many fearing the worst. Some already knew the soldier's fate, like Thomas Mulharen, a Chancellorsville convalescent and older brother of Captain James C. Mulharen, 75th Ohio, who died July 2 of a wound received the previous day. His body, retrieved from a shallow grave, was transported to Preble County and buried July 25 in Eaton's town cemetery. Nine days earlier Lieutenant Ladley had written home remorsefully, "I send you another picture of Lt. Mulharen lately promoted to Captain. ... He was my comrade[.] he and I were always together and I can hardly believe that he is dead."[37]

Similar sentiment was felt by survivors of Company H, 8th Ohio. Their lieutenant, Elijah Hayden, had been killed July 3 west of the Emmitsburg Road. Private William Clough wrote Hayden's newly widowed wife Deborah: "On the morning of the fourth we went to the field and got his body and brought it up to where the regiment was encamped. Our Colonel had selected a beautiful knoll [south of the Catherine Guinn house], shaded by a walnut tree, as a burial place for the dead of the 8th regiment. It was impossible for us to send the body of Lieut. Hayden home, being so far from any R.R., and all the ambulances and wagons that could be got were carrying off the wounded (which took them nearly a week). So we dug him a grave, and after we had washed him and cleaned the dust of battle

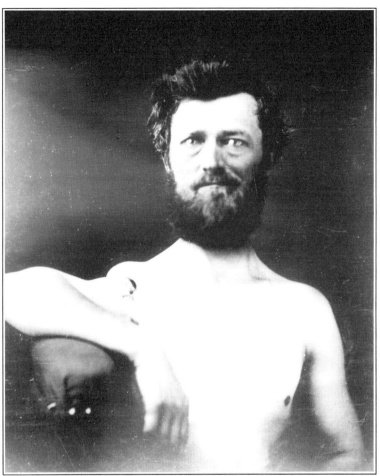

Thirteen years after a bullet fractured his right shoulder July 3, former Private Eldridge Sherman of Company G, 55th Ohio, exhibited the wound's scars. Instead of amputating, 55th Ohio assistant surgeon Henry K. Spooner removed three inches of the arm's humerus. Sherman spent more than two months recuperating at Gettysburg's Camp Letterman, and was discharged at Columbus in January 1864. The lifelong resident of Seneca County never regained use of his limb.

from his clothes, we wrapped him in a blanket and buried him. A simple board with his name, rank, company and regiment, marks the place where we laid him; so if you ever wish to get his body, you would not have much trouble. He died much loved by his company, for he was a brave and good officer."[38]

Less charitable words were penned by Hospital Steward Merrick, though Deborah Hayden never read them. On July 14 he and George Washburn visited the officer's grave. "Lieut Hayden sacrificed himself almost foolishly," Merrick surmised in a letter to his own wife. "He did not use ordinary caution but to give his men courage exposed himself needlessly."[39]

Charles Parmely, a former private in Company I recently discharged for wounds suffered at Fredericksburg, volunteered to bring Hayden's remains back to Ohio for permanent burial. They reached Lorain County July 25, and with "a vast concourse of sympathizing friends present to witness the sol-

emn rites" were laid to rest the next day in Elyria's Ridgelawn Cemetery.[40]

A few days after the battle the parents of Private Hiram C. Hill, Company G, 29th Ohio, received "mournful intelligence" of their son being fatally wounded. Harlan Hill of Mogadore hurried to Gettysburg and was informed that on the afternoon of July 3 a shell struck Hiram's right leg below the knee, tearing it off. Fully conscious, he was carried to an aid station but expired several hours later. His father accompanied the body home, where it was interred in Tallmadge Cemetery. The Hills' bereavement was magnified by the fact a second son, John, also of the 29th, had been missing since the battle of Chancellorsville and was presumed dead.[41]

George Helmich's body was returned to Sandusky and buried in that town's Oakland Cemetery. A 34-year-old cabinet maker originally from Baden, Helmich had left a wife and six children to enlist as a private in Company F, 107th Ohio. He was a man of strong religious convictions, a class leader in Sandusky's German Evangelical Association, and was elected to act as chaplain for his company. Early July 2 while on picket duty, Helmich was killed.[42] In 1884, his widow decided to have him exhumed and moved to a new section of Oakland Cemetery reserved for former soldiers. The process created quite a stir, as reported in 1920 by the *Sandusky Register*:

"The grave diggers found that the coffin was in [a] good state of preservation, but imagine their great surprise, when upon moving the lid they found Helmich's remains, which had been in the grave for nearly 22 years, in as perfect a state of preservation as though buried but the day before. Helmich had been buried in his soldier's uniform and so perfect was the preservation that the brass buttons shone as though recently polished, the uniform retained that bright blue color so familiar in the days of 61-65 and the flesh of the dead man remained unchanged and the remains were most wonderfully the same as though deposited in the grave only the day before. ... [T]he case of the body of Soldier Helmich is believed to be without parallel here."[43]

Word of William Moore's death generated decades-long grieving in Felicity, Ohio, for his 28-year-old wife, Sarah. The 61st Ohio assistant surgeon had been mortally wounded by shellfire July 3 at or near the 11th Corps hospital. Sarah's two brothers, William and John Fee, arrived at Gettysburg July 8. William, a Xenia minister, was shocked by the

Courtesy of
Mary Kate Liming

Kate Moore, two-year-old daughter of Doctor William S. Moore. The 61st Ohio assistant surgeon was carrying this photograph when he was mortally wounded July 3.

battlefield's expansive destruction, as well as the large numbers of dead men still lying unburied. Years later he reminisced: "We soon found the grave of Dr. Moore, and, after obtaining the liberty to transport his remains through the lines, we disinterred them, and had them hermetically sealed in a tin case. We spent nearly two days in passing over the battle-ground. Multitudes of people were there to secure the remains of their departed friends, or to comfort those who were wounded and dying. I passed by many places where near relatives, fathers, mothers, brothers, sisters were disinterring their friends. So fearful was the spectacle, it was too much for tears. I never saw a tear shed by any person on that historical battle-field."[44]

Although Fee's mission to locate and bring home a fallen relative was fraught with melancholy, he and many others doing so within four weeks of the battle were fortunate. On July 31 a Department of the Susquehanna general order was issued through Gettysburg's post commander, which read: "During the months of August and September no corpse will be allowed to be disenterred [sic] from any of the burying grounds, cemeteries, or battle-grounds of Gettysburg. The health of the wounded soldiers and citizens of this community requires the stringent enforcement of this order, and any violation of it reported to these headquarters will meet with summary and severe punishment." The temporary ban was lifted October 1.[45]

Another clergyman, W.D. Siegfried of Zanesville, was a member of the Christian Commission assigned to provide food, beverages and physical and spiritual comfort to wounded at the 11th Corps hospital. His duty began late on July 10, at which time he listed 14 officers and 32 non-commissioned officers from Ohio among more than 1,000 patients there. Before reaching the hospital, however, Siegfried spent most of that day traipsing over the "awful field." His observations, condensed here, were dispatched July 14 to the *Zanesville Daily Courier:*

Fences were gone, trees which had braved successive storms, lifted their broken arms towards heaven to show what war can do. Crops were destroyed, here and there a few stalks of wheat and corn afforded some nourishment to broken down and wounded horses, wandering about uncared for.

[The battlefield] stretched away 10 miles in length, by 4 to 6 in width, taking out the very heart of Adams

Effects of William S. Moore brought back to Ohio by his brother-in-law included the officer's sash, a shoulder strap, coat buttons and a sewing housewife made of sky blue kersey wool.

county. On every hand were guns, canteens, shells, balls, and all the implementa and accoutrements of the men who fought there so desperately a few days before. Crowds of people were driving and walking across that bloody plain, no fences to obstruct them, and various roads made by cavalry and artillery, during the fight, led them around to spots revealing notoriously bloody deeds. Dead horses were lying about on every side, some heaps of them burning sent up a volume of smoke, and gave out a stench horrible to endure. Indeed the whole field was horribly oppressive, and parties traveling over it had to carry hartshorn, camphor &c as a relief from the horrible atmosphere of the plain. Clots of blood, pieces of limbs of the poor men, and other horrible sights met the eye at every turn. Some of the rebel dead yet lie unburied, though they will all be buried to-day, as parties of rebel prisoners are compelled to render that sad service. Yonder are three men burying a dead horse; they have just buried two rebel horses. Ah! they *have to do this,* as a *penalty* for having tried to pass the guard with some bayonets and ramrods as trophies of the battle. Nothing of this kind is allowed.

A loud report of an explosion attracts our attention. A man driving off the field with a dead body has driven against a shell and it exploded — fortunately, no one was hurt. A poor fellow carelessly kicked a shell this morning, as he passed along, and it exploded, tearing off his foot.[46]

Scavengers and gawkers appeared with astonishing speed. Major Hurst of the 73rd Ohio was repulsed by those he encountered early July 5. "Today there were hundreds of well-dressed citizens

Cincinnati Historical Society

Sergeant Henry C. Koogle, Company E, 5th Ohio, was promoted to hospital steward of the regiment July 1, 1863. Carte de visite by Pein & Co. Photograph Gallery, Washington, D.C.

across their shoulders, provide us a good deal of amusement. Most of them have come from a good distance at the news of the battle, and have gained permission to journey to the field by representing themselves as volunteer nurses for the wounded. Some of them are medical men, some clergymen, and what not. But their innate curiosity is their main motive in visiting the places where anything remarkable occurred during the battle, and to gaze with ludicrous horror at the black and mutilated dead who are strewn everywhere. Cannon balls were especially sought for by these people."[48]

Even Galwey's regimental benefactor, newspaperman George Washburn, could not resist an opportunity to sightsee and collect a small cache of souvenirs. The editor pressed Charles Merrick into service as an impromptu guide, who related: "I spent the whole day yesterday [July 14] in showing Washburn over the battle field and explaining the different positions. We went over a good portion of both lines to see the effect of the artillery on both sides. He loaded himself with various relics of the field and took notes of many remarkable things. ... We measured one tree for [the] 'fun of it' where one of our balls had gone clear through *twenty two* inches of green oak and the tree [was] nearly a mile from our Battery. Washburn could hardly believe it. Another good sized tree near one of their Batteries was hit 19 times, so you may know it must have been rather dangerous working their guns. But O, such piles of dead men and horses. The whole plain beyond their battle line is one vast grave. 'My God!' says Washburn — 'Lee must have sacrificed half his army here.'"[49]

□ □ □

The Ohio newsman's conjecture about Confederate casualties was not far off the mark. General Lee lost one-third of his engaged forces at Gettysburg. After three days of ferocious fighting the Rebel commander decided to return his embattled survivors to Virginia. First to leave, during the rainy afternoon of July 4, was his army's long train of supply wagons and ambulances, filled with campaign booty and as many wounded as were fit to travel. Protected by cavalry, the column crawled over South Mountain via Cashtown and Greenwood, then south toward Hagerstown and Williamsport, Maryland, where only the Potomac River sep-

coming in to *see* the battle-field. They were talking about what a noble battle 'we' had fought, and what a splendid victory 'we' had won; but they said not a word about helping to bind up the wounds of our suffering thousands — not a word about making a cup of coffee or a pallet of straw for a single bleeding patriot. They had come to *see* merely."[47]

That same morning, noted Lieutenant Galwey of the 8th Ohio, "the civilian souvenir hunters are scattered over the field, picking up relics of the battle. ... The relic hunters, with their satchels slung

arated it from "home" soil. Lee's infantry and most of his artillery took a more direct route for Hagerstown via Fairfield, Pennsylvania.[50]

Just outside that village on July 3 a sharp melee had occurred between the 6th U.S. Cavalry and a Virginia cavalry brigade. The Regulars were overwhelmed — losing 60 percent of their force, a majority taken prisoners. Among those wounded and captured was Second Lieutenant Adna R. Chaffee, a 21-year-old native of Orwell in Ashtabula County. Chaffee refused to accept a battlefield parole, so the Confederates simply abandoned him with other Federal wounded. For "gallant and meritorious services" in the Fairfield fight, he was breveted first lieutenant. Four decades later Chaffee was promoted to lieutenant general and appointed the U.S. Army's chief of staff.[51]

Second Lieutenant Adna R. Chaffee, Company K, 6th U.S. Cavalry, was one of four brothers who served during the war. Sheburn H. Chaffee was a private in Company I, 6th Ohio Cavalry. Truman E. Chaffee was killed in battle at Shiloh with the 14th Ohio Battery. Having moved to Alabama prior to 1861, Orestes P. Chaffee fought for the South.

Ken Lawrence Collection

While the bulk of General Meade's army remained inert until the afternoon of July 5, his cavalry was busy, having received orders to strike the enemy's rear and communication lines so as to "harass and annoy him as much as possible in his retreat." During the next 12 days Ohio troopers belonging to the Cavalry Corps saw plenty of action. It came none too soon for Private Thomas M. Covert of the 6th Ohio Cavalry, which spent most of July 1-3 camped in reserve at Manchester and Westminster, Maryland. "I feel as though I want to let out the pesky rebles blood more than I ever did," he announced in a letter to his wife. "You need not worry for I will come out all right for I will be doing my deauty."[52]

Covert's regiment, reduced from 12 to 10 companies, was part of Colonel Pennock Huey's brigade, Gregg's division. It reached Emmitsburg about noon July 4 and was attached temporarily to Kilpatrick's command. A Confederate wagon train was reported to be nearby on South Mountain just north of the Maryland-Pennsylvania line at Monterey. According to one of Covert's comrades, "Kilpatrick was bound to capture it if possible." His troopers, "soaked thoroughly to the skin" by a thunderstorm, headed for Monterey with Huey's brigade protecting the column's rear. Before all the 6th Ohio town guards vacated Emmitsburg, elements of Jeb Stuart's cavalry swooped in and snatched 11 Buckeyes from Companies C, E and G as prisoners. Three of them later died in captivity.[53]

Bugler Sam Gillespie rode near the division's van with the First Ohio Squadron, Kilpatrick's escort. Darkness descended on the column. "The night was very dark and raining as we wound slowly up the mountain along the narrow dug way," remembered Gillespie. "On one side was the dark forest, overhanging the road, and on the other a fearful precipice. ... On such a night it would have been dangerous for the ordinary traveler to have ventured over that mountain, but for a whole division of cavalry, with artillery, it was perilous. ..."[54]

Near the summit Kilpatrick's advance was met by sudden small arms and artillery fire. Almost simultaneously Confederate cavalry shot at the Federal rear guard. For a while, thought Gillespie, prospects seemed "rather gloomy," until Custer dismounted his Wolverine troopers and threw out skirmishers. The Ohio-born general "then sent forward a squadron of the Fifth Michigan to charge upon the enemy and clear the road, but as soon as the rebels opened on them with their artillery they turned and came scampering down the road like a drove of frightened cattle." The Michiganders rode pell-mell into the First Ohio Squadron, which happened to be guarding the boxed-in ordnance rifles of

Ken Lawrence Collection

Battery M, 2nd U.S. Artillery. Kilpatrick, at the front with Custer, mistakenly heard that his escort had given way. He came back roaring mad, questioning the Ohioans' courage. Lieutenant Alexander C.M. Pennington Jr., the battery's commander, tried to assuage Little Kil's anger by explaining the Buckeyes actually held their ground in the midst of the confusion.[55]

"Then," Gillespie continued, "one of the boys in the company spoke up and said: 'Only give us a chance, General, and we will show you whether we are cowards or not,' when he replied, with an oath, that he would give us the chance." The squadron's commander, Captain Noah Jones, stated Kilpatrick "jumped his horse over [a] stone wall at the left of the road and began giving commands in a loud voice as though ordering a large force. 'Advance the infantry on the right. Bring forward the battery. Prepare to charge,' etc. On hearing this the enemy fell back ... and the column moved forward to the

level ground at the summit."[56]

Just ahead, a train of wagons and ambulances from Ewell's corps was trying to escape. It was shielded by a polyglot force of cavalry, staff officers, one gun crew and a few infantrymen who managed in the inky blackness to keep Kilpatrick's division at bay for two hours. After midnight the impatient general ordered a charge, this one spearheaded by the First Ohio Squadron and the 1st West Virginia Cavalry. Bugler Gillespie noticed the moon "had now risen and dispelled enough of the darkness to distinguish whether a man wore a cap or a hat, as the enemy all wore hats and we wore caps, but the thick clouds still shut out the stars from witnessing the mortal strife. Slowly and quietly we advanced to [a] little bridge where our pickets were placed, and then Captain Jones gave the order: 'Forward! Charge!' "[57]

Sabers drawn, the 40-man squadron spurred its mounts ahead. First Lieutenant Albert E. Chester's yells were drowned by the "unearthly screaming" of his Company A comrades. Pennington's battery fired overhead, its shells crashing into wagons as they rolled along the muddy road. A Confederate eyewitness, Brigadier General William E. "Grumble" Jones, reported the Yankee onslaught "swept everything before it. The led horses, wagons, straggling infantry, and camp followers were hurled down the mountain in one confused mass." General Jones barely escaped capture, as did Captain Jones of Kilpatrick's escort. The Ohioan's horse was shot in five places, but remained afoot. Half the squadron's mounts fell wounded or killed, their riders sprawling with bruises. Sergeant William McMasters and Private L. Campbell Thomas were shot in the legs. At one point Captain Jones found himself alone and surrounded by Rebel wagon guards. In the darkness he bluffed his way back to his own men, then resumed the attack in company with the

West Virginians and Custer's troopers.[58]

By daybreak the wreckage strewn from Monterey pass to the mountain's base "was a sight to see." The 6th Ohio, bringing up Kilpatrick's rear, did not take an active part in the nighttime charge, but its members cheerily reveled in what their fellow cavalrymen accomplished. "Daylight came on as we began the descent," wrote Sergeant Wells A. Bushnell of Company A, "when objects began to assume shape. The road and ditches was littered with the contents of the wagons; bales of cloth, boots and shoes, everything imaginable was scattered around. The wagons lay in the ditch with wheels broken, and some were burning. ... 100 wagons were captured and destroyed, 1000 horses and 1000 prisoners were captured." Captain Norman Barret of Company D hypothesized that "The frightened teamsters attempted to run off their wagons, but

An August 1862 recruit, Private Samuel Rodgers of Company A, 1st Ohio Cavalry, displayed the full array of weapons carried by the First Ohio Squadron at Gettysburg — M1860 light cavalry saber, Colt Army revolver and .52-caliber Sharps carbine. During 1864's Atlanta campaign Rodgers was detached to General William T. Sherman's headquarters staff as an orderly.

A History of Co. A, First Ohio Cavalry

wheel locked with wheel and the road was soon impassable. We captured the entire train and guard. Some of the wagons contained arms, but most of them contained the plunder extorted by the rebels from the farmers of Pennsylvania. A more heterogeneous mass of articles it would be difficult to find. Boots, shoes, hats, caps, clothing of all kinds, even women's under clothing, cooking utensils, school books, &c. Nothing seems to have escaped their rapacity. All this was soon reduced to ashes." Private Jacob A. Sager crowed in a letter home: "We ... had a big time chasing the rebs wagon train. I tell you but we made them get — dont know for certain how many wagons and prisoners we did capture but I know we done a good job."[59]

The affair at Monterey, in reality, proved to be a pinprick in the Confederate army's effort to return to Virginia. Pursuit by Meade's troops at Gettysburg did not begin until the afternoon of July 5, and it was not directed in the Rebels' tracks. Instead, the Army of the Potomac was sent south into Maryland along three different routes similar to those traveled by many of the Unionists just a week earlier. While this move screened Baltimore and Washington, for a time it kept Catoctin and South mountains between the Federal infantry and Lee's retreating main force. But veteran soldiers like Lieutenant Harry Dean of the 7th Ohio believed they possessed a powerful trump card, one provided by nature. "There has been a heavy rain for the last two days — very heavy last night," Dean wrote July 5 before departing Culp's Hill. "The creeks are all unusually high, and we hope the Potomac is *bank full,* so we can get another fight out of the Rebs this side."[60]

Sergeant Mathias Schwab Jr. of Company K, 5th Ohio, left the Keystone State near Littlestown in a disgusted mood. The Cincinnati native had lost his diary during the battle, although that angered him less than the collective attitude of most Adams County residents he apparently encountered. Schwab opined to his parents: "I must say that the part of Pennsylvania that the Rebels invaded deserved the invasion. The meanest and dirtiest copperheads [live] in that part of the Union that I ever saw or heard of. Farmers charging damages done to their fields and the troops were fairly camped, charging double amount for bread and butter because they were good Union people. If I wished to mention all these little incidents of Copperhead, it would make a complete novel." He acknowledged, "It is true that there were a few who did try and help along as much as possible but such as they were indeed very few. The best of the thing is that the Rebel Sympathizers lost most property by the invasion. ... I got sick and tired of Pennsylvania and was heartily glad to get out of it."[61]

William Tallman of the 66th Ohio was more tolerant in recalling the same subject. "As we marched away we hardly knew whether to claim a victory or not, our losses had been so heavy, and we had not been able to follow Lee at once. The people of the country did not seem to have the same spirit of Liberality that was exhibited as we marched to the defense of their homes, but I afterwards felt like forgiving them for their seeming lack of this quality for the soldiers had helped themselves liberally to their milk[,] butter and yellow legged chickens. There was not a rooster left to tell them when to get up in the morning; this is one of the great calamities of having a war carried on in your own country as the citizens suffer alike from friend and foe. It was a fact fully developed in the war of the Rebellion that all soldiers were not perfect Gentlemen."[62]

As the campaign entered its fifth week a fair number of Tallman's fellow infantrymen also resembled armed vagabonds. Hard marching, exhaustive combat and exposure to the elements had worn out uniforms and footwear. Buckeyes in the 11th Corps were particularly affected. "Everybody was in high spirits & bodily misery," affirmed Captain Benjamin Stone of Orland Smith's brigade staff. "When we reached [the] Md line over 300 of our soldiers were absolutely barefooted & many more as good as shoeless. We had no time to stop & get up supplies from the depots." Writing July 9 from Boonsboro, Maryland, the 75th Ohio's Oscar Ladley told his mother "The men are nearly all barefoot and have

marched over 50 miles in that condition. They get shoes to day." Lieutenant Jacob Mader's company in the 61st Ohio was bereft of brogans, too, as he informed his fiancée: "For my part I have had no change of clothing since this campaign commenced. I made one days march entirely bare footed. Wee could not get shoes or boots for love or money, but am glad to say their was several waggon loads came up to us from Frederick City a fiew days ago & supplied us with the necessary articles which pleased us very much."[63]

Those in Smith's brigade may not have been so fortunate, as some lacked proper dress well into the month. An unidentified member of the 55th Ohio whimsically observed: "Since we left Brooke's Sta-

First Lieutenant Jacob F. Mader, Company F, 61st Ohio. Carte de visite by Marshall's Ambrotype & Photograph Gallery, Circleville.

tion [June 12], no clothing, except a few shoes and stockings, has been furnished the men, and you can imagine how they look. In this corps — and especially in this brigade — and more particularly in this Reg't — they are devilish[ly] ragged. For instance there are some completely *non est.* More than half of the men in the Reg't are without that part familiarly known as the 'seat.' But the boys say they are better off than they were before, as a hole will last the longest. Indeed, if clothing is not furnished us soon, they ought to transfer the seat of war farther south, where it's fashionable to wear, in warm weather, a shirt collar and pair of spurs! For in a few days all that it will be necessary to furnish, to thus fit us, will be the *collar and spurs!*"[64]

For several days Ohioan George Metcalf noticed that "Scattered along our entire line of march and under every meeting-house shed and every shade tree were the state militia with their new, bright guns and clean uniforms. They made a wonderful contrast to us. We were ragged, smoky, grimy and dirty. We had not seen water enough (except rain) in five days to wash our faces even once. I had on only one shoe, the other foot was bare. My pantaloons were minus one leg below the knee, leaving the leg without any covering from there down."[65]

Metcalf was puzzled by the pursuit's spasmodic pace. "We proceeded cautiously. Sometimes we would be hurried along for a few hours, and then swing around into line of battle, build up breastworks and lie behind them for an hour or so, and then move on and repeat the same thing again." In his diary, Henry Henney of the 55th Ohio questioned the logic of making fatiguing marches that seemed to be followed by protracted delays. "I don't know why we halted so long, probably our Generals know. Now there's more than lice and nits in our heads." When the 55th slogged from Emmitsburg to Middletown, Maryland, Henney noted "the roads were awfully bad. There was a great deal of straggling in other regiments. It makes me sorry to see how unsoldierly the boys conducted themselves, wantonly destroying much valuable property. This demoralized me more than anything else in the army." On July 8 "We had a very severe tramp ... over the mountains in a very heavy rain, which contributed to dis-spirit the boys. I was nearly bushed as I had no supper or breakfast." That morning news of Vicksburg's surrender circulated in the 11th Corps' camps. Henney didn't believe it.[66]

Trials and Triumphs

Corporal Moses Pugh of Company H, 55th Ohio. The Seneca County native previously was wounded at Second Bull Run.

One of his comrades landed in hot water with Colonel Charles Gambee during the 55th's first overnight halt. Company H corporal Moses Pugh was carrying a new Richmond rifle musket appropriated from a dead Rebel outside Gettysburg. He explained: "We were ordered to sleep on our arms, and, as it was raining slightly, I greased my precious gun with a piece of bacon rind. When I awoke in the morning my first act was to remove the [percussion] cap from the tube. Pressing the greasy hammer with my thumb, I accidentally let it slip, whereupon my first Johnny ball went through the blouses of three of my comrades and killed my colonel's horse, which was tied to a stake about twenty rods away. The boys laughingly told me my gun would turn traitor, and at that terrific report I began to believe it. Colonel Gambee was incensed at the death of his faithful horse. He ordered my corporal's stripes to be taken off, and demanded pay for the horse."

Gambee never collected restitution. He was killed the following May at Resaca, Georgia, but not before promoting Pugh to sergeant and absolving him of his debt. Pugh retained the "traitor gun" until the 1865 battle of Bentonville, North Carolina, where "it was struck while I was loading it by a piece of shell, and maimed so severely that I pronounced it unfit for duty and turned it [back] over to the Southern Confederacy." [67]

Another potentially catastrophic accident occurred July 10 at Boonsboro in an artillery camp close to Battery H, 1st OVLA. Corporal John Merrell recorded, "There was some men in a Battery joining us got fooling with one of their guns pulling off friction primers when all of a sudden the gun went off and the shell struck the caisson, wounding two men. The men did not know that the gun was loaded, but it appears that it had been loaded ever since the battle of Gettysburg. It created considerable excitement in camp." [68]

The army's Ohio cavalrymen, meanwhile, needed no such artificial arousal. Their branch of service saw constant action in the attempt to thwart Lee's southward withdrawal. July 6 was a particularly exciting and trying day for the Buckeye horsemen. Kilpatrick's division, with Huey's brigade still attached, headed to Hagerstown to attack Stuart. Brigadier General John Buford's cavalry division rode from Frederick for Williamsport, about seven miles southwest of Hagerstown, its mission being the destruction of Lee's main wagon train. Half a mile from the Potomac River town the train's determined defenders stopped Buford, fighting him to a standstill. "The enemy was too strong for me," he admitted, "but he was severely punished for his obstinacy. His casualties were more than quadruple mine." [69]

One man Buford lost was an Ohio native son, Major William H. Medill of the 8th Illinois Cavalry. This regiment was among the first to fire Gettysburg's opening shots the morning of July 1. Medill, born at Massillon in 1835, was the younger brother of Joseph Medill, owner-editor of the *Chicago Tribune* and an organizer of the Republican Party. Having grown up on the family's Stark County farm,

Major William H. Medill, 8th Illinois Cavalry.

William also entered the news business and in the 1850s held various positions with papers in Cleveland, Coshocton and Canton. He founded the *Stark County Republican* in 1858, and during his short tenure as publisher it was considered "a pungent and attractive sheet, handsomely printed, and filled with interesting matter. In politics, like its proprietor, it was radical Republican." [70]

Medill was in Chicago when war erupted in 1861, enlisting four days after Fort Sumter's capitulation as a private in Barker's Chicago Dragoons. When the 8th Illinois Cavalry was raised late that summer he was unanimously elected captain of Company G and served with distinction in the Peninsula, Antietam and Chancellorsville campaigns. As major, he temporarily commanded the regiment in the June 1863 cavalry battles at Aldie and Upperville, where, according to an 1866 biography, he "behaved with a bravery, a skill and a gallantry that won the admiration of all who witnessed his conduct. His favorite weapon, in making a charge, was the revolver. He would dash his men right up to the rebel squadrons, who, in the melee, would unhorse scores of them with their sure and deadly six-shooters. He considered a sabre no match for two revolvers in a close encounter either with cavalry or infantry." After Gettysburg, Medill hoped the Potomac's steadily rising water level would stop Lee's retreat. He believed the Rebels were cornered, that the Army of Northern Virginia was close to receiving its "death-wound." His men were urged to strengthen their resolve.[71]

During Buford's advance outside Williamsport, Medill borrowed a Sharps carbine from one of the 8th's troopers. He never got the chance to use it. The following day Captain John M. Waite of Company L wrote: "Three squadrons of our regiment were dismounted to fight on foot. The other three squadrons were kept mounted as a support for them, and also for a section of artillery. The Major went to the front with the dismounted men, and took charge of those three squadrons. They moved out to deploy as skirmishers at a quick step, and with a 'hip,' 'hip,' in the very best of spirits. In a few minutes, the sad news came back to us that Major Medill was badly wounded, and soon several of the boys came slowly back bearing the gallant Major from the field. A ball had entered his stomach. ..." Suffering intense pain, Medill was conveyed to Frederick, where his brother Joseph arrived after being summoned by telegraph from Chicago.[72]

Buford was joined late in the afternoon July 6 by most of Kilpatrick's division, which faced more than it could handle in Hagerstown. Confederate cavalry, supported by infantry, pushed out Little Kil in what one Ohio trooper called "very brisk skirmishing." Sam Gillespie of the general's escort recorded that "We found the streets barricaded and rebel sharpshooters in the houses and in the cupolas of the churches." The First Ohio Squadron was "left for some time drawn up in front of a large church exposed to the aim of the rebels posted in a cupola about three squares away. To remain standing in line as the mark of sharpshooters, with their bullets whistling about our ears or going thug into a horse and seeing it tremble and fall or rear and plunge with its rider, and we still remain in line, was even harder

than to go on our charge at Monterey." Private John L. Reese of Company A lost his mount in this manner.[73]

Leaving one brigade to protect his rear, Kilpatrick withdrew and set off to cooperate with Buford. There was little he could do. Increasing numbers of Confederates converging in the Williamsport area soon threatened his front, right flank and rear. "We came very near being surrounded," Private Covert of the 6th Ohio told his wife. Covert's company commander, Captain Delos Northway, related: "We fought them until dark, but we were finally compelled to give way and fall back. ... It was warm work yesterday. The squadron under my command was drawn up to support [a] battery which covered our retreat. The Rebels advanced one of their batteries to within three hundred yards of where we were and poured into us a perfect storm of shell and grape shot. The shells burst above us, before us and behind us. Nothing but the darkness, which prevented accuracy of aim, saved us from being badly cut up. As it was we only had one man wounded. But I was not sorry when night came."[74]

The injured trooper was Private Morris Tobin of Company C, whose left arm was drilled by a bullet that creased his chest and lodged in his right arm. He survived. Private Robert Tweedale of the First Ohio Squadron did not. Listed among the engage-

A teacher born in Orwell, Captain Delos R. Northway of the 6th Ohio Cavalry was among 11 related Northways from Ashtabula County to don the Union's blue uniform, nine of them in the Company A commander's regiment. Married during veteran furlough in March 1864, he told his tentmate upon returning to Virginia he would not live to see his wife again. Two months later Northway was killed in the battle of Haw's Shop, a major's commission folded in his pocket.

Ken Lawrence Collection

Captain John C. Tidball commanded the Cavalry Corps' 2nd Brigade of Horse Artillery. Born in 1825, he was raised on a Belmont County farm before entering West Point in 1844. The professional soldier extolled his artillerymen in the wake of Gettysburg, reporting that "Never in the Army of the Potomac has such arduous service been required of batteries, and in every instance in marching and in fighting they proved themselves equal to all requirements, and received the well-earned commendation of those with whom they served. As the operations of the cavalry are mostly on the exterior of the army and out of view of the greater part of it, but an imperfect knowledge exists of the importance and arduousness of its service. So also of the batteries of horse artillery serving with the cavalry. ..."

ment's missing, Tweedale was captured and ended up in Georgia's Andersonville prison. He died there April 24, 1864.[75]

Some measure of retribution was exacted July 8 and 9 when Buford's and Kilpatrick's commands again fought near Boonsboro and Funkstown. About 3 p.m. on the 8th, recalled Sergeant Wells Bushnell, the 6th Ohio "was ordered on the skirmish line dismounted. Taking our position on the extreme left of the line, we drove the rebels three miles over a rolling open country, the only cover being numerous stone fences which [were] utilized by the rebels in their defence. But our determined attack drove them from cover to cover until darkness ended the fight." Captain Northway more modestly estimated the distance their opponents were pushed at two miles. "We ... killed and wounded many and captured three pieces of artillery," he wrote. A Buckeye foot officer who watched the affair, however, was not overly impressed. Lieutenant Ladley of the 75th Ohio mockingly informed his mother: "Yesterday I witnessed a cavalry fight. There is a mighty difference between cavalry & Infantry fighting. If we fought like they do there would be nobody hurt at all scarcely."[76]

The horse soldiers, of course, would have disagreed vociferously. Confidence levels and morale, especially among Ohio's cavalrymen, soared during this period. "I never saw our soldiers feel in such good spirits," thought 6th Ohioan Jacob Sager. "Some are (or appear so) really anxious to fight." Northway believed "the boys went in with a will," inferring that Little Kil's leadership — criticized by some contemporaries and a fair share of postwar writers — was a motivating source of their inspiration. "Gen. Kilpatrick has great confidence in our regiment," the captain boasted, "and whenever there is any wavering in our lines, the 6th Ohio is called for. His old regiment, the 2nd N.Y., and ours, usually fight together, and where we go, the Secesh 'just climb' as the boys say."[77]

Ohio bugler Sam Gillespie did not mince words about his division commander. By July 9 he considered Kilpatrick "the most daring and skillful officer we have yet met. He fights the rebels as we expected to fight them when we enlisted. His ability to get his men out of tight places, as at Monterey and Williamsport, has won the confidence of all his men."[78]

Real or imagined, high spirits sagged somewhat during the next three days as rain, from driz-

Robert Van Dorn Collection

Due to heavy post-battle rainfall, teamsters and artillery drivers for both armies were confronted with muddy and deeply rutted roads in Maryland. One of them was Private Joseph O. Hess, a 25th Ohio wagoner belonging to Company E. Carte de visite by Thomas & Shell, Artists, of Fostoria.

zle to drenching downpours, retarded the Union army's progress. "They move very slow," wrote Sergeant Bushnell. "On every side you hear such remarks, 'why don't Gen. Meade hurry up? Lee will get away. Their line of battle [is] in plain sight, and Meade does not attack. Why this delay?' " Gillespie observed that Kilpatrick bristled with impatience, but that did not help pull wagons and artillery caissons out of the mud or put new shoes on footsore infantrymen. Without orders on July 11 Little Kil drove enemy pickets to the banks of Antietam Creek above Funkstown, which afforded an open view to Hagerstown. Howard's 11th Corps finally moved up to act in concert with Kilpatrick early the next morning. Orders were issued to advance on Hagerstown, with General Ames' 1st Division selected to support the cavalry.[79]

Two Ohioans provided perspectives of this operation. One was penned by Sam Gillespie two weeks later in a report to his hometown newspaper:

Gen. Kilpatrick moved his division immediately forward, sending one brigade to the right. We moved forward with such impetuosity that the few pickets at the [creek] were principally captured; and as soon as we had gained the opposite bank, there was Stewart's [*sic*] cavalry forming in a wheat-field, and several companies of dismounted men trying to escape across a cornfield to their horses. Gen. Kilpatrick ordered Gen. Custer, three times, distinctly, to send a regiment forward and pick up the dismounted men; but he as often refused, saying that they had artillery planted on the hill, and were preparing to charge upon us. Gen. Kilpatrick then called for his escort, ordering us to rush down on those dismounted men, and use our pistols freely. Away we went across the field, and brought back twenty-seven men and one 1st Lieutenant, who stated that we had taken every one of his company.

As soon as we started, our artillery opened on the enemy in the wheat-field, which kept them from charging upon us, and we brought back some of the prisoners from a short distance of their lines.

The brigade which was sent around to the right then charged, and captured a number of them, scattering the rest to the four winds. At the same time, one regiment was sent into town on the charge, which cleared the place of stragglers and bushwhackers, from which we had suffered severely the Monday previous, chasing the enemy behind their hastily constructed line of earth-works which stretched away toward the Potomac from the outskirts of the town. Several companies were completely surrounded, and surrendered horses, arms, and equipments entire. We had about five hundred prisoners altogether from this day's work.[80]

Captain Ben Fox, having relinquished command of the 75th Ohio to Colonel Harris before leaving Gettysburg, counted just five enlisted men present for duty in Company A on July 12. The next afternoon he updated his parents:

I wrote you last I believe on the 9th or 8th inst while in the gap through South mountain. Since then we have advanced and now are at Hagerstown — the Cavalry of the Enemy very stubbornly disputing every part of the ground. Again our Brigade has had the honor of chasing the Rebels from cities or towns on northern soil. Yesterday morning at 3 a.m. our Brigade was put in motion with Kilpatricks Cavalry. By the way[,] the 1st Ohio Cavalry (2 companies) are Kilpatricks body guard and I find one of my old Delaware chums is a Lieutenant in it. We made a very roundabout way coming upon them very suddenly from a north westerly direction. Kilpatrick charged upon their lines — it was a Magnificent sight. I never saw anything to equal it. The first charge was upon their pickets by the two Companies of the 1st Ohio, the body guard. 40 of them (Rebs) were captured and some dozen killed or wounded while we lost but three wounded. We then went some little distance — 3/4 mile when our Cavalry made this handsome charge — you just ought to have seen it — our Brigade had just got upon a high elevation with one battery of flying artillery in time to see the whole of it, it being a perfect surprise. They were totally routed. ...

Taking the advantage we marched right into the town taking many prisoners. Two majors were riding round through the town and came right upon us. Many of them took to the houses — and when we came from the town last night our boys were still getting them from the houses — the whole brigade but our Regt were thrown as pickets about the town — the fact is we easily could all have been taken but their alarm was too great.

The Rebs yesterday morning were here strongly intrenched on their side of Antietam Creek but when we came in their rear they lit out nicely. By our move we have the pike now from here to our line of battle of day before yesterday, while the Rebs held it here yesterday morning — and an attack from the front would have been a very severe one to have gained it. We were received splendidly by the people of Hagerstown. When the Rebs were in the town (half an hour before) there was not a thing to eat, so the Rebs say. When we came in nearly every house had a few loaves of bread cut up and spread with applebutter &c. Our Regt remained in the centre of the town as a kind of reserve should our boys around the town be pressed too hard.[81]

The captain concluded his letter by offering a shared opinion and posing a question. "If the Rebs do not recross the Potomac they will be pretty nearly used up. Old Lee however is keeping his eyes & ears open and gone to digging ahead here. Is it the last ditch, or will he fall back on Richmond?"[82]

The Confederates already were in the process of effecting their escape. Before Fox even opened his ink bottle July 13 to write home, Lee's engineers were fashioning a makeshift pontoon bridge over the river at Falling Waters, where Longstreet's and A.P. Hill's corps were to cross that night and the fol-

Writing home July 12 from Jones' Crossroads, Maryland, Private Jacob Sager of Company A, 6th Ohio Cavalry, declared that "if it hadent been for the rain we would have attacked them this morning. A hard battle will be fought here in a few days if the rebs dont steal a march on us." Sager was seriously wounded the following May at Haw's Shop, Virginia.

lowing morning. Ewell's troops would wade the Potomac at Williamsport, where the water level had subsided enough to permit passage. For his part, General Meade announced in a message to Washington that he intended to assault the Rebels on July 13. It was called off when a majority of his corps commanders expressed opposition. Meade then promised to "hazard an attack" after additional reconnaissance. By then it was too late.[83]

On July 14 the formidable Williamsport-Hagerstown line of Confederate earthworks was discovered abandoned. Union cavalry arrived near Falling Waters in time to surprise Lee's rear guard, taking some 1,500 prisoners, but that was little solace to those Northerners who felt certain they were on the verge of crushing their opponent. At Williamsport ford, stated a frustrated Sam Gillespie, the First Ohio Squadron "swung our hats at them and taunted them upon leaving 'My Maryland.' We did not fire at them, except one shot [Private] Jacob Miller fired over their heads when we first rode down to the water, saying, 'take that, you damned rebels!' In a very few minutes there was no rebels to be seen."[84]

Fellow enlisted Buckeyes were deeply disappointed, many of them wagging accusing fingers at their army commander in reproach. For two weeks 6th Ohio trooper Thomas Covert remained livid, venting his unveiled disgust in letters home. "It made every body look downhearted to find the rebles gon. All was anxious to fight them, and if Mead had attacted them yesterday we could now have them all. ... It makes me mad every time I think of Mead letting Lee get away from Williamsport. He could just as well as not have destroyed the Reble army and every soldier felt that he was letting him get away. I beleave it was one of the most shameful things that has happened during the War, and no one but Mead to blame."[85]

Twenty-ninth Ohio private Henry Knapp, whose right arm was shattered 10 months later in Georgia, agreed. "It seemed as if every circumstance after the battle of Gettysburg favored the capture or destruction of the rebel army. But our commander ... exhibited [a] spirit of over caution, and our lines were formed at a goodly distance from theirs, and then we stood still or sat down and rested as we liked. Some of our boys said if we were allowed to jump on them with both feet ... we would stand a good chance of stamping the life out of them then and there, but here we waited for three days and were finally ordered to fortify our line, which we did. When we were finally ordered to advance we found the rebels gone. They had been allowed to escape, either purposely or from lack of courage to attack, and as we turned back we felt that a great opportunity had been lost. ..."[86]

Officers, too, voiced their frustration. Lieutenant Colonel William G. LeDuc, the 11th Corps' chief

Born in 1823 at Wilkesville, Ohio, Lieutenant Colonel William G. LeDuc was educated in Lancaster and Gambier, graduating from Kenyon College in 1847.

Ron Chojnacki Collection

quartermaster and a southeast Ohio native, observed: "The soldiers were anxious to go in and make an end of the war, and go home. They could not understand such generalship, and became very impatient." LeDuc claimed many in the ranks regarded Meade "an accidental victor" at Gettysburg, who now was "afraid he will lose some reputation." Captain Benjamin Stone, 73rd Ohio, entertained no doubts July 17 that "cautiously feeling our way" and Meade's decision "to feel the position, arrange his lines & get more certain information" prevented a major grapple with the Confederates. "The men were furiously angry," Stone confirmed. "They had almost closed to meet the foe. They had felt assured of another conflict & another victory. They had marched & suffered excessively to secure it, then to have the coveted prize elude them was a bitter pill. They all knew the significance of the enemy's escape. It meant more marching & campaigning in the desolate mountains & thickets of Virginia — which they hate beyond expression."[87]

Lying grievously wounded in a Frederick hospital, Major William Medill begged his brother to tell him whether Meade had yet ordered an attack. An account likely furnished by Joseph Medill recorded the cavalry officer's reaction. "His mind was in a state of feverish anxiety for the assault to begin, lest the enemy would escape across the river. Lee's army, he said, was wholly in our power, and it only required a little daring and enterprise on the part

Looking south, a Federal wagon train at Berlin, Maryland, prepared to cross the swollen Potomac River spanned by two pontoon bridges.

of Meade to capture or kill every rebel composing it. Oh! for Joe Hooker, he would say; if he commanded now, not a rebel would escape. [Late July 14] the bad news was brought to him that the rebels had escaped without a blow being struck at them. He was in agony at the information. 'I wish I had not heard it,' he exclaimed. 'I am going to die without knowing that my country is saved and the slave-holders' accursed rebellion crushed. The capture of Lee's army would have ended the war in sixty days; now it may drag on for years. It was cowardice or weakness that let the rebels escape.' He was greatly consoled, however, by the news that reached him of the capture of Vicksburg and Port Hudson. 'Ah!' said he, 'blood will tell; it takes the *Western* boys to handle the rebels.'"[88]

Medill died 36 hours later. His brother accompanied the body to Canton, Ohio, where it reposed at their parents' residence July 20 before receiving a military funeral in Chicago. He was buried in Graceland Cemetery dressed, as he desired, in the same uniform he wore July 6 when wounded near Williamsport.[89]

Unfortunately Meade, who remained the Army of the Potomac's chief for the rest of the war, never inspired in his men the adulation of former com-manders like McClellan or Hooker. Most of the army's Ohioans, though they did not know it, soon would be scattered to other faraway theaters of the conflict, serving under other generals. Full realization of the magnitude of their — and Meade's — achievements at Gettysburg only came with time. The cost of victory, however, was felt immediately and keenly. Nearly 30 percent of those Buckeyes mustered June 30 were gone two weeks later. Their surviving comrades, before crossing the Potomac July 18 and heading south once more, attempted to rejuvenate themselves.

"Never was rest more welcome," thought Franklin Sawyer of the 8th Ohio. "We had been making rapid marches, or engaged in battle for about four weeks. Our tents were put up and the men were soon quietly enjoying a morning nap. Even our horses, when they saw our tents up, manifested their appreciation of a quiet camp once more, and lay down with as much satisfaction as the soldiers." Near Berlin, Maryland, on the Potomac, artillerist John Merrell occupied himself writing, washing and searching for food. At a country dwelling he found bread, butter and the sociable company of "a very fine young lady of some 18 years of age" with whom he flirted for more than an hour — an enjoyable respite from the war.[90]

In contrast, comfort was denied 82nd Ohio commander David Thomson as he composed a somber letter July 16 to his daughter. "I am in the field sitting on the ground," he wrote, "weary and hungry and dirty. This has been a hard campaign. Rain and mud. Yet our men are healthy, but our ranks are much thinned." He mentioned the 82nd's casualties, the fatal wounding of his faithful horse "Charly" and the death of a "good and honest" friend, Adjutant Stowel Burnham.[91]

The lieutenant, more than anyone else lost at Gettysburg, was mourned by the sensitive officer long after the battle and his regiment's return to Virginia's familiar ground. In August, Thomson addressed his feelings home in a knot of contemplative emotions. At his feet lay a reminder of his dead comrade — a linen and wool rug. "Night has come. I am in my little tent. The crickets sing all around and an old toad is hopping over my brussells carpet. Burnham and I tented together and had our floor carpeted with his and my carpet. Now I claim the carpet. He would give it to me if he could come back, I know. How much I miss Burnham. Glorious good fellow was he, and most generously did he live.

"The bugles sound, telling me it is the hour for retiring. The bands and bugles and drums, Katie-Dids, grasshoppers and crickets keep up a merry music. The soldiers sing over the camp. Yet I feel lonesome. ..."[92]

□ □ □

Beads of perspiration clung to Elizabeth Sykes' brow as she scrubbed clothes on her family's Richmond Township farm in Huron County. The weather in northcentral Ohio during the first three days of July 1863 was oppressively hot and sultry, making any kind of outdoor activity uncomfortable. The heat was especially irksome for her two small children, three-year-old Flora and William, a blond-haired toddler of 14 months. Little Willie became so

ornery he fell from a bed on July 5, breaking his collar bone. The accident was cause enough for anxious concern, but Elizabeth's thoughts that week were focused more intently on her husband's welfare. Word of a great battle raging in Pennsylvania already had reached the nearby villages of Centerton and New Haven. She was apprehensive, fully aware that her children's father belonged to a regiment that no doubt was immersed in the fighting.

Twenty-four-year-old Andrew J. Sykes was a sergeant in Company I, 55th Ohio. He had never seen his son, the boy being conceived just prior to his September 1861 enlistment. Affectionately nicknamed "Tip" by his wife, the dark complected Sykes was a veteran of five Virginia battles, including Second Bull Run and Chancellorsville. Gettysburg was his sixth, spent at the town's southern limits trading shots with enemy skirmishers and concealed sharpshooters. Company I emerged from the fight with relatively few casualties — one man

Tony Lemut Collection

Sergeant Andrew J. Sykes, Company I, 55th Ohio.

'My thoughts wander back to other days'

The late-July 1863 homecoming of 55th Ohio sergeant Andrew Sykes brought unbridled joy to his wife, Elizabeth, pictured here with the couple's children, Flora and William. Before Sykes' leave of absence expired their third child, Libbie, was conceived on the family's Huron County farm.

Soon after Sykes' return to his regiment it was sent to Chattanooga to be amalgamated in the Army of the Cumberland, and he was appointed Company I's first sergeant. On May 2, 1864, the 55th marched off to begin General W.T. Sherman's drive toward Atlanta. In the campaign's first major battle at Resaca, Georgia, the regiment suffered severely, losing its colonel and major. Sykes was among the casualties, as he related to his parents from a field hospital May 20: "I was shot through [the] left lung, the ball passed through and came out through the Shoulder blade. I am doing as well as could be expected and with proper care I think I will recover." It was misplaced hope. Three days later he was dead.

For two subsequent weeks Elizabeth Sykes frantically waited again for an encouraging letter. But on June 6, exactly one month following

Tony Lemut Collection

Libbie's birth, she wrote in anguish in her diary: "The great blow fell on me. The news came ... that my beloved Husband had died on the 23rd of May at the Hospital at Resaca. Oh God my heart seems to be bursting. Sometimes my thoughts wander back to other days, happy days that I spent with him in our dear little home and at other places, happy scenes that have passed by never more to return and then Oh merciful God, the great weight of my woe comes back rushing upon me like a mountain as though it would crush me down forever. Oh Tip, my darling Tip, I cannot believe that you are gone never more to return to me, never more to whisper words of hope and happiness in my willing ear. Oh no, it cannot be, it cannot, cannot be."

After a decade of grieving Elizabeth married Andrew's younger brother Otis Sykes, a disabled veteran of the 123rd Ohio. They had two daughters.

killed and four wounded.

Like hundreds of other Ohio soldiers' wives, Elizabeth Sykes worried. She busied herself with chores, visited her father-in-law and neighbors, watched the cutting of the summer wheat, picked cherries. News came July 7 that Union forces had prevailed at both Gettysburg and Vicksburg. "Oh, I pray it is so," she confided to her diary, "but victory

First Sergeant Lorenzo D. Anderson, *right,* Company I, 82nd Ohio, and Private John N. Delameter, *below,* of Company B were captured July 1. A Hardin County farmer, Delameter was marched to a Richmond prison, paroled in September and returned to duty March 1, 1864. Anderson apparently accepted a battlefield parole, for a company comrade mentioned him working at the 11th Corps hospital July 22. Carte de visite by W.H. Furbish, Delaware.

Brad L. Pruden Collection

has been bought with fearful cost. I know not but my own Dear One is among the slain. God help me if so." Another week passed and Elizabeth remained in the dark. "At home all day, very unhappy," she wrote on the 15th. "No letter from Tip yet since the battle. ... it seems as though I should go crazy."

Finally, on July 17 her worst fears evaporated. An envelope arrived containing a few hastily scribbled lines "from Dear Tip telling of life and health. He was at Gettysburg." The next eight days brought four more letters from Sergeant Sykes, who crossed the Potomac with his regiment on the 19th. Near the end of the month her husband received a furlough and traveled to Huron County in company with a regimental recruiting detail. His sudden appearance on the farm July 29, Elizabeth's diary related, was completely unexpected. "Oh joy and Happiness. Dear Tip has come. I was washing and all dirty. Saw him coming down the hill. Willie [k]new him. There was a great many come in to see Tip. He looks as natural as life. Oh I am so happy."[93]

The post-battle uncertainty experienced by Andrew Sykes' wife, while temporarily unnerving, was eclipsed in many Ohio households when a loved one was listed a prisoner. In several cases the soldier was never heard from again. Army of the Potomac casualty returns for Gettysburg show 183 officers and 5,182 enlisted men as missing or captured. Of these totals, 363 were Ohioans — 94 percent belonging to 11th Corps regiments. Before withdrawing from the battlefield the Confederates paroled between 1,500 and 2,000 Federals, a good portion of them wounded and too badly hurt to travel. The rest were marched south with Lee's retreating troops. A few escaped enroute. Most were herded to prisons scattered from Virginia to Georgia.[94]

Bob Albertini Collection

A month and a half elapsed before Alfred Goodin's father in Hardin County positively learned what happened to him. From Richmond's Libby Prison the 82nd Ohio lieutenant ended the suspense. "I am at present in the above-named place, a prisoner. I was taken at Gettysburg, Pa., July 1. On the 4th, we started for Richmond, and arrived here on the 19th. My health is tolerably good. My feet are almost ruined from marching on the hard pike up the [Shenandoah] valley. Write to me and let me know the news you have from the Regiment. There are about 60 from the Regiment here — only two commissioned officers." [95]

Lieutenant Colonel Jeremiah Williams, 25th Ohio, was incarcerated eight months in Libby. On August 1 he informed his wife, Flora, of his first 10 days locked up in the converted nine-room warehouse. "I am still in this notorious prison, with the prospect for getting away but slightly improved. There is a report that the commissioners of exchange will meet next week, when something may be done. I have had a troublesome diarrhoea, but am about well. Our room is large and airy, but the water is wretched. I have heard nothing from the regiment since I left it. ... You need feel no uneasiness about me. I am quite as safe from disease here as in camp. We have become tolerably comfortable, but I am anxious to join my regiment again. I am allowed to write on one side of the paper only." Williams was released in March 1864, and discharged from service three months later. [96]

Lieutenant Joseph Potts, 75th Ohio, was more direct in his opinion of confinement at what he disparagingly called the "Hotel de Libby." In November he penned Lieutenant Colonel Benjamin Morgan, his former company commander, a lengthy note that was smuggled out by the regiment's paroled assistant surgeon. "As Dr. W[ren] is about to leave the old 'Rebel Bastile' for Gods country," Potts explained, "I send you the following lines by him. Would send a letter but they are contraband. We of the 75th are all well[,] that is all that remains of us after a four months contest with C.S.A. 'greybacks.' I heard you were in hospital in Gettysburg after you were wounded & looked through there on the evening of the 2d after I was taken but failed to find you. We have had a mean time of it here. I would rather fight every other day in the week than ever be taken prisoner again by Jonnies. ... Please write soon. Give my respects to the company. I would like

to be with them again. Louie Eckerlie [Private Louis Eckerly, Company F] is the *only* one of our company who came through to Richmond. I have not seen him since I arrived here. I am glad no more of our men are here, for the enlisted men received horrible treatment." [97]

Alphonso Davis of the 75th considered himself lucky to spend just a month in captivity. The sergeant had been induced to surrender on Blocher's Knoll with four others from Company G, but was exchanged early in August. His parents, living in West Alexandria, Ohio, were the first beneficiaries of the good news he supplied by letter upon reaching Camp Parole, Maryland. Davis described his experience: "[On July 1] I was taken to the rear of the rebel army where we lay for three days. On the 4th we were started for Richmond, about four thousand of us. On that march we went four days at one time when they only gave us a half pint of flour and about three ounces of beef. We had to march 166 miles after we were take[n] to Staunton. When we went through Martinsburg [W.] Va., the ladies came out and gave us bread and water and did all they could for us, the rebles cursing them all the time, and swerring [sic] they would kill some of them. We lay at Staunton four or five days, and then started for Richmond. I forgot to tell you that my shoes gave out at Harrisonburg and I had to march 30 miles barefooted; for two weeks I had no shoes.

"We arrived at Richmond on the 23rd and were put on Belle Island where we remained until the 1st of Aug. Our rations on the island were four ounces of bread and 1/2 ounce of meat at ten o'clock, and 4 ounces of bread and a little soup at 4 in the afternoon. We are now with Uncle Sam again, after an absence of 32 days and I must say I like his boarding better than uncle Jeff's. ... I am getting all right again, and am anxious to hear from home. Give my love to all and keep a large share for yourself." [98]

One of Davis' Company G comrades imprisoned on Belle Isle in the James River never made it home. Private Levi Westfall, 22, died in Richmond January 31, 1864. [99]

Ninety-six members of the 75th Ohio were captured at Gettysburg, the highest number of any Buckeye regiment engaged. Unlike Potts, Davis and Westfall, Private Elias Clear of Company C opted for a battlefield parole instead of prison. By July 13 the Preble County shoemaker was back home in

Newark native Horace B. Smith was an 18-year-old student when he enlisted at Kenton in February 1862. By Gettysburg he had been promoted to first sergeant of Company B, 82nd Ohio. Wounded and captured July 1, Smith was incarcerated six months on Belle Isle at Richmond before transfer to Andersonville's stockade in southwest Georgia. There, on March 14, 1864, he died of typhoid fever in the prison hospital. Grave #44 in Andersonville National Cemetery contains his remains.

Richard W. Fink Collection

Eaton, reunited with his mother and sisters. Clear was a veteran of McDowell, Strasburg, Cross Keys and Second Bull Run. At Chancellorsville he carried the regimental colors. To family and friends he was a hero.[100]

Others in the community, however, viewed soldiers like Clear as representatives of a despotic Union government. Sizeable numbers of Northern politicians and ordinary citizens were opposed to Lincoln administration policies and the war by mid-1863. "The pressure of its burdens displeased some," observed journalist Whitelaw Reid, "[and] gloomy prospects in the field discouraged many more." A handful of Ohio counties teemed with disaffected residents, most notably Montgomery, which borders Preble. The Peace Democrats, derisively labeled Copperheads or Butternuts by pro-Lincolnites, already chafed at enactment of a new national conscription bill. They were further outraged in May by the arrest of their chief spokesman, Clement L. Vallandigham, a Dayton attorney, former Ohio congressman and acid-tongued Lincoln critic. In retaliation, Dayton's Republican newspaper offices were ransacked and torched by a mob. Proclamation of martial law followed in Montgomery County. Vallandigham was tried in a Cincinnati military court and found guilty of "expressing ... sympathy for those in arms against the Government of the United States, and declaring disloyal sentiments and opinions, with the object and purpose of weakening the power of the Government in its efforts to suppress an unlawful rebellion." Fearing the verdict and imprisonment might exalt Vallandigham in public estimation as a martyr to the cause of free speech, some officials urged Lincoln to banish him to the Confederacy. The presi-

Born in Columbiana County in 1820, Clement L. Vallandigham was the Midwest's most prominent Copperhead and vocal critic of Lincoln administration policies. Stories of his arrest, trial and banishment to the South by order of the president filled news columns in papers across the state on the eve of battle at Gettysburg. When Federal officers escorted him to Confederate lines in Tennessee, the Ohio politician was given a chilly reception. According to an account furnished to a Buckeye soldier from Trumbull County, "Vallandigham ... was under no great restraint, surely not in irons, and was received without ceremony or with but little dignity. He treated the matter as a joke or farce in which he was the central figure. He was sent out under a flag of truce and an escort. An officer from [General Braxton] Bragg's army met them who, being informed of the business at hand, replied: 'We don't want him. We have no use for him.' Here was a transaction without precedent, a dilemma hard to solve. But without further ceremony the escort came back and reported the goods delivered with no receipt asked for or given."

dent acceded, but Vallandigham soon was ejected from the South as well. He sailed a blockade runner for Canada, and there on July 15 accepted nomination as Ohio's Democratic gubernatorial candidate. That same evening in Preble County, in a climate simmering with potential political turmoil, Elias Clear strolled into an Eaton saloon.[101]

Citizens, soldiers and local militiamen returning from duty in Butler County packed the drinking establishment. Clear joined a group of acquaintances, several of whom were fellow 75th Ohio parolees. One facetiously asked a comrade if he was a Butternut, and received an equally jocose, affirmative answer. The soldier, asking another man in the crowd the same question, began pummeling him playfully with his fists. During the feigned scuffle a bystander named Philip Reichard walked over, pulled a knife and slashed the joking soldier's arm. According to an eyewitness, "Reichard then ran into the street, where stones were used very freely for a time by two or three soldiers — one of them striking Reichard a tremendous blow on the head. He then went to Minor's Corner, the soldiers pursuing. ..." Clear and two companions confronted Reichard, who flailed at them with his knife, stabbing all

three. John McGregor, a newlywed from Virginia, and Clear crumpled to the ground, blood spurting from deep gashes. Both died the following day. Just two weeks after surviving battle at Gettysburg, the 22-year-old veteran returned home only to be murdered.[102]

More than 1,000 mourners gathered July 17 to see Clear and McGregor buried side by side. The town's Democratic paper announced that the joint funeral "was the most solemn and imposing that we have ever witnessed in Eaton," adding, "As the man who used his knife so fatally, is now in jail, and will be tried by the law of his country, the Editors of newspapers are not at liberty to make any particular remarks until the law has pronounced its sentence."[103]

That never happened. On July 25, while much of Eaton's population was absent attending similar obsequies for Gettysburg casualty Captain James Mulharen, the alleged attacker skipped town. Friends of Reichard, a known Southern sympathizer, bailed him from jail. He then disappeared. Indignant citizens and soldiers scoured the countryside in a fruitless search that merely succeeded injuring two of Reichard's "butternut neighbors" sus-

SOLDIERS' FUNERAL.

Died—*Near Eaton, on the 16th inst., from stabbing, inflicted by Philip Reichard, on the 15th,* **ELIAS CLEAR**, *aged 22 years. The deceased was a member of Co. C, 75th O. V. I., had been in eight battles; was the Standard-bearer at Chancellorsville, and was taken prisoner at Gettysburg, when he came home on parole.*

On the same day, from a wound inflicted by the same hand, as above, and at about the same time, **JOHN T. McGREGOR**, *aged 27 years. The deceased was a native of Virginia, and had been impressed into the rebel service, from which he escaped over 6 months since.*

The funerals, one from the residence of Mrs. Margaret Clear, the other from that of David Clear, will take place at 3½ o'clock, P. M. to-day. Processions will meet at the Depot, and proceed under the direction of the comrades in arms of the former, to the Cemetery, where services will be held by Dr. J. W. Weakley, former Chaplain of the 75th.

July 17, 1863.

Funeral card circulated in Eaton and Preble County for murder victim Elias Clear of the 75th Ohio.

pected of helping him. Eaton's Republican newspaper editorialized: "The circumstance was an outrage on the people and an insult to the dignity and majesty of the law. It would seem that human life is an exceedingly cheap article when a man can kill two men and stab two others with intent to kill and then go free in ten days after the commission of the bloody and murderous deed by the payment of the paltry sum of $800."[104]

Back in Virginia, the opposing armies of Meade and Lee resumed positions near the Rappahannock River not far from those occupied two months earlier. Summer's dog days descended upon the Union camps, and once again army reshuffling brought change for most of Ohio's noticeably depleted regiments and artillery companies. In mid-August the 4th and 8th Ohio were shipped to New York City to assist enforcement of the draft. Deadly rioting had erupted with its July implementation, although the seething unrest was all but quelled by the time the Buckeyes arrived. Instead, "we went into camp, and had a grand time for a few days," remembered the 8th's commander, Franklin Sawyer. "We had no duties to do. The riot squelched itself when the blue coats appeared, and we enjoyed a continued ova-

tion." William Kepler of the 4th Ohio recalled that "Wherever our troops were quartered the people would gather about them, ask many curious questions concerning our mode of life, watch our cooking and eating, and expressed great surprise that a single one had survived 'sleeping on the cold ground.' It was soon evident to all that our services were no longer needed, discipline became lax, men and officers roamed throughout the city seeing the sights, many indulging to their heart's content, some even beyond moderation." Lieutenant Colonel Sawyer, apparently, was among them. On August 28 one of his lieutenants found him "quite tipsy" in a Brooklyn saloon. "He was surrounded by a lot of privates, some drunk, and some, who were sober, rejoicing in his discomfiture."[105]

The 4th and 8th Ohio returned to the Army of the Potomac in September, maintaining ties with the 2nd Corps until they mustered out in the summer of 1864.[106] By then, only three Buckeye units that played significant roles in the Gettysburg campaign — Batteries H and L, 1st OVLA, and the 6th Ohio Cavalry — remained in Virginia. The 12th Corps and the 11th Corps' 2nd and 3rd divisions were transferred west in late September 1863 to reinforce the Army of the Cumberland after its defeat at Chickamauga. The subsequent spring both organizations were consolidated and redesignated the 20th Corps. Its Ohio contingents thereafter followed the fortunes of another native Buckeye, Major General William Tecumseh Sherman.

Just five weeks after the gunsmoke cleared at Gettysburg the 25th, 75th and 107th Ohio's association with the 11th Corps and Army of the Potomac ended. For these regiments that suffered so severely July 1 and 2 the news arriving August 6 came like a sudden thunderclap. Their division, now commanded by Brigadier General George H. Gordon (who replaced Adelbert Ames), was ordered to the Department of the South. Barely one week later Gordon's soldiers were battling flies and sand fleas within cannonshot of Charleston, South Carolina.[107]

"Who would have thought of a Regiment the size of the 75th being sent away down here," wondered Colonel Harris as he wrote from an oceanside tent on Morris Island. "We have but about one hundred and fifty men with us. It looks as though it was the intention to entirely annihilate the four old Regts of this Brigade — they are all just about like us in size." To his Ohioans it seemed like a backwater assignment, literally and figuratively, one far removed from the picturesque hills of the Shenandoah Valley, the plains of Manassas or the fertile fields and fruit-laden orchards surrounding Gettysburg. But the accuracy of an old adage was quickly demonstrated: The more things change, the more they stay the same. "I suppose all eyes are turned upon this place now since there is nothing doing any where else," Harris continued. "I must confess it aint very pleasant walking around among the shells thrown from James Island. They contest, in true rebel manner, every inch of ground. ..."[108]

For Harris, his regiment and all the far-flung Ohio veterans of Gettysburg, the war churned on.

SIX

'Gettysburg, by-and-by, will become an American Mecca'

EPILOGUE

Despite long odds, Captain Azor Nickerson did not die of his Gettysburg wounds. Four months after the battle the 8th Ohio officer was in Washington, partly convalescent but still not permitted by surgeons to rejoin his regiment. While waiting for a medical decision in his case, Nickerson read an announcement about ceremonies scheduled November 19 to dedicate a soldiers' national cemetery at Gettysburg. He resolved at once to attend.[1]

The previous July Gettysburg attorney David Wills conceived the idea of establishing a permanent burial ground for Union dead. With Pennsylvania Governor Andrew G. Curtin's authorization he purchased 17 acres adjacent to Evergreen Cemetery. Governors of Northern states whose soldiers fought in the battle were asked to cooperate. According to Wills' vision the dead would be buried in separate sections and the entire expense apportioned among the cooperating states — each assessed according to its population as indicated by number of representatives in Congress. The governors also were requested to appoint agents to assist in carrying out the reburial project. Although Ohio Governor David Tod "heartily" approved these measures, he waited until October 25 to name Daniel W. Brown as state agent. Brown, a Republican judge from Columbus who earlier served as warden of Ohio's penitentiary, was instructed to remain in

Gettysburg as Tod's representative until the cemetery's dedication.[2]

Brown arrived there the next day and on October 27 attended funeral services for Private Enoch M. Detty of Company G, 73rd Ohio, who died of chronic diarrhea at Gettysburg's Camp Letterman general hospital. Detty was the first known Union soldier interred in the new cemetery. Transfer of remains from their battlefield burial sites began the same day. Gettysburg's Samuel Weaver superintended the exhumations, which eventually took five months and totaled 3,512 bodies. Of these, 979 could not be identified in any way by name or state designation. Another 1,000 or so bodies, mostly Union, already had been removed for reburial in hometown cemeteries prior to October 27. This somewhat aggravated Weaver, who reported in 1864: "Before we commenced our work, the battle field had been overrun by thousands of sorrowing friends in search of lost ones, and many of the graves opened and but partially or carelessly closed. Many of the undertakers who were removing bodies, also performed their work in the most careless manner, invariably leaving the graves open, and often leaving particles of the bones and hair lying scattered around."[3]

It was Weaver's responsibility to identify remains exhumed by the contractor's work crews, record all items found in the graves and oversee that

TRIBUTE TO THE MEMORY
OF
CORP. THOMAS DUNN
Company K, 25th Ohio Volunteer Infantry.

Camp near Warrenton Junction, Va., July 27th, 1864.

EDITOR COMMERCIAL—It is once more, with feelings of regret, that we have to announce the loss of another comrade in arms—CORPORAL THOMAS DUNN, of Co. K, 25th O. V. I., a native of England—as a soldier, brave and intrepid; as a man of high moral worth he was not excelled.— When the dark cloud of rebellion overshadowed our country, and our Nation's Flag and Constitution seemed on the point of being blotted from existence, it was then the brave DUNN shouldered his gun, with many others of kindred spirits, and flew to the rescue of his adopted country. He left tyranny and oppression, and sought a land of freedom and pleasure. Like other adopted freemen he offered his life freely at the shrine of liberty. While nobly facing the enemy, he fell, like a hero. Well may our nation shroud herself in mourning when noble hearts like the brave Corporal THOMAS DUNN shed their blood in defense of our country's rights. His was a kindred spirit of the brave Herbert, Serg't L. E. Viers and others, who nobly fell at Chancellorsville, Va., and gave their lives in our enemy's country, the last by the peaceful and domestic fireside, in a State that upholds the honor of our nation. He met his death on the 2d of July at Gettysburg, Pa.

The death of brave Corporal THOMAS DUNN, should strengthen our arm and give us courage to avenge the death of our comrades who fall by traitor's hands. He died in a land foreign from the country that gave him birth, but, thanks to God, he died among friends, and those friends will cherish the memory of the brave. Of the gallant 25th but a handful remains to tell the sad tale of the many, many engagements they have had; when the brother falls his loss is heavy. May Ohio, the pride of the West and the star of the nation, long remember her sons that have strewn the soil of Virginia with her dead. When the gallant deeds of her sons shall be forgotten, may her honor and glory disappear forever; but let us not dishonor that glory of our homes and the State that gave us birth, so long as a vestige remains of the traitor's oppression. Let not an arm drop 'till it is driven from the land. Let us all follow the example of the gallant "Dunn," Herbert, Viers and others, 'till the work shall be accomplished.

At a special meeting of the members of Company K, 25th Regiment, O. V. I., held this day, the following Preamble and Resolutions were unanimously adopted:

WHEREAS, It has pleased Almighty God to remove from our midst, by death, our friend and brother soldier, Corporal THOMAS DUNN, therefore,

Resolved, That we tender to his parents, friends and acquaintance, our heartfelt sympathies in their hour of grief.

Resolved, That, in the loss of our brother and beloved friend, we are deprived of the association of an honest and brave soldier.

Resolved, That as a testimonial of our respect for our late brother soldier, the commissioned officers and men of this Company wear the usual badge of mourning for the space of thirty days.

SERG'T JOHN H. KEEN,
SERG'T PETER TREIQUART.

P. S.—Corporal THOMAS DUNN was in every engagement in which the gallant 25th Ohio took part, including the following battles: Greenbrier, Cross Keys, Allegheny, Huntersville, Montery, McDowell, sixteen days fighting on the Rappahannock, Bull Run No. 2, Chancellorsville, Va., and finally at Gettysburg, Pa. He lost his life like a hero and true soldier.

This memorial for Gettysburg casualty Thomas Dunn, 25th Ohio, was submitted to the *Cincinnati Daily Commercial* for publication less than four weeks after the battle. The 1864 dateline was a typesetter's error. Killed the evening of July 2 during the East Cemetery Hill assault of Hays' Louisiana brigade, Dunn was buried in Gettysburg National Cemetery's Ohio plot.

L. M. Strayer Collection

the bodies were carefully placed in wooden coffins before reburial. Previously erected headboards helped tremendously with identification. Other names were determined by personal items found in uniform pockets. In some cases money and jewelry were discovered. Weaver removed all such relics. When finished he had accumulated 287 separately labeled packages. The contents of 13 belonged to Ohio soldiers, including Private Lewis Davis, Company D, 75th Ohio (a Testament and letters); Corporal Thomas Dunn, Company K, 25th Ohio ($4 and a gold locket); First Sergeant John W. Pierce, Company C, 25th Ohio (a pipe); and Private Asa O. Davis, Company G, 4th Ohio (gun wrench, comb and a ring).[4]

In Columbus, meanwhile, Governor Tod invited a host of Ohio officials, members and members-elect of the legislature, newspaper editors and military officers to join him at state expense to witness the cemetery dedication. More than 100 acceptance letters were received. The list included Tod's predecessor William Dennison and Governor-elect John Brough of Marietta, who had soundly thrashed exiled Democratic candidate Clement Vallandigham at the polls October 13. Encouraged by the response, Tod began arranging for a special "Ohio program" to be held in Gettysburg following the dedication. For the oration he chose Colonel Charles Anderson, the state's lieutenant governor-elect and an outstanding public speaker. He was the younger brother of General Robert Anderson of Fort Sumter fame, and, as commander of the 93rd Ohio, had been severely wounded in the battle of Stones River, Tennessee.[5]

As the solemn occasion drew closer David Wills invited President Lincoln, his Cabinet and members of Congress to attend as well. With Lincoln's acceptance Wills asked him to "formally set apart these grounds to their sacred use by a few appropriate remarks." Despite the president's urgings only Secretaries William H. Seward, John P. Usher and Montgomery Blair decided to go. The Cabinet's two native Ohioans, Secretary of War Edwin M. Stanton and Treasury Secretary Salmon P. Chase, found excuses to stay in Washington.[6]

On November 16 Governor Tod's large delegation boarded cars for the rail journey to Gettysburg via Steubenville (Stanton's hometown), Pittsburgh, Harrisburg and Hanover Junction. Unforeseen delays dogged the party the entire trip. At Harrisburg Tod met Andrew Curtin and boarded a special train also carrying Governors Oliver P. Morton of Indiana and Horatio Seymour of New York.[7] During a short layover at Hanover Junction the dignitaries inadvertently were joined by two more Ohioans — Captain Nickerson and a Lieutenant McDowell, who was serving on General E.B. Tyler's staff at Baltimore. Nickerson explained:

When our train stopped we immediately boarded another that was standing on the Gettysburg track. We had barely gotten inside when a guard was placed at the entrance to each car to prevent outsiders from crowding into it, as it was a special train carrying the governors of the several States who were the guests of Governor Curtin, of Pennsylvania. Being locked in, as it were, we concluded not to try to break out, and proceeded to find the delegation from our native state, Ohio. McDowell went toward the head of the train and I toward the rear. In the first car I entered I saw Governor Todd [sic], while near him were ex-Governor Dennison and the Governor-elect, Brough. Thinking, perhaps, I might know some of his staff or retinue, I asked where the other members of the delegation were. He pointed to a group on the opposite side of the car, which upon joining, I found to contain several old acquaintances and one general officer, whom I had known as colonel of the Fourth Ohio, and who, when promoted, had afterward commanded our brigade, General John S. Mason [of Steubenville]. He knew the circumstances attending my former visit to Gettysburg, and insisted upon presenting me to the governor, although I said I had just spoken with him.

In introducing me, the general told the governor that I had a better right to be there than any of them, with many other equally flattering things which a soldier most likes to hear of himself. The governor then told me that he would like to arrange it so that I could see and hear everything that transpired at the dedication ceremonies, and that he could best insure that if I and my friend were to accept the positions of aides-de-camp on his staff, which he then tendered. Of course we gratefully accepted the proffered honor. The governor further informed us that although he had sent an agent ahead to secure accommodations for himself and staff, the latter had so increased in numbers since he started that he did not know whether all would have "downy pillows" to rest upon, but as we were soldiers he presumed we would not be troubled on that score.[8]

The train reached Gettysburg's station November 18 about 11 p.m. Nickerson, McDowell, George A. Benedict, editor of the *Cleveland Herald,* and another newspaperman found lodging in a private residence. Rooms for Tod and most of his entourage had been reserved by agent Brown in hotels or houses, but not all Buckeyes enjoyed deluxe accommodation. William Coggeshall of *The Springfield Republic,* for example, was forced to sleep "upon boards laid upon trussels, in the kitchen of a 'hospitable' Gettysburger."[9]

Before retiring, Tod was briefed by Brown on his activities. Twenty-four of 1,188 bodies reburied in the new cemetery by November 14 had been identified as Ohioans. He reported that the ceremony's chief marshal, Ward H. Lamon, had convened a meeting with the assistant marshals who were present to provide instructions regarding protocol during the next day's procession. Since Ohio's two assistant marshals, Colonel George B. Senter of Cleveland and Colonel Gordon Lofland of Cam-

bridge, had been aboard Tod's train they missed Lamon's briefing. Brown informed them that the various states' governors and staffs had been placed near the procession's front directly behind the speaker of the day, Massachusetts statesman and orator Edward Everett. The Ohio delegation's position, however, was near the rear. Brown also told Tod he had arranged use of the Presbyterian church on Baltimore Street for the special "Ohio program" that would follow the cemetery dedication ceremonies.[10]

November 19 dawned with rain showers. But by 8 a.m. the skies cleared and as Isaac J. Allen of the *Ohio State Journal* wrote, "the sun rose upon the scene with unclouded brightness." Allen and Martin D. Potter, editor of the *Cincinnati Daily Commercial,* wandered over to Cemetery Hill to sightsee several hours before the procession began. Gazing south along Cemetery Ridge, Allen noticed the ground was "even yet grim and ghastly with the mute memorials of strife and carnage. Soiled fragments of uniforms, in which heroes had fought and died, remnants of haversacks and cartridge-boxes and other mementoes of that terrible conflict, still lay strewn about." Potter observed decaying debris, too, commenting: "Patches and shreds of clothing, old hats, soleless boots, toeless shoes, mouldy bayonet-sheaths, rotten knapsacks, and rusty cartridge-boxes are to be found in every direction." He also was mildly amused to see "little stands on every street in Gettysburg where grape-shot, solid balls, and shell of all shapes can be purchased. A perfect percussion shell sells for $2 or $3, and other articles in proportion."[11]

Born at Youngstown, Governor David Tod (1862-1864) was the son of a decorated War of 1812 veteran. After the fall of Fort Sumter he was among the state's first public officials to advocate vigorous prosecution of the war "till every Rebel was cut off or surrendered."

National Archives

David Neuhardt Collection

William Dennison, *far left,* was Ohio's chief executive from 1860 to 1862. A Cincinnati native and Miami University graduate, he served in Lincoln's and Andrew Johnson's cabinets as postmaster general. John Brough, *left,* a former state auditor and owner-editor of the *Cincinnati Enquirer,* succeeded Governor Tod in 1864. A large, corpulent man, his health eroded rapidly with the strain of "arduous labor." He died in office August 29, 1865.

Focusing attention on the new burials, Potter discovered the cemetery was "laid out in semi-circular form, each State being allotted ground in proportion to its dead. The lines dividing these allotments are the *radii* of a common center, where a flag-pole is now raised, but where it is proposed to erect a national monument. The [burial] trenches follow the form of the circle, and the head of each is walled up in a substantial manner. The bodies, enclosed in neat coffins, are laid side by side, where it is possible, the fallen of each regiment by themselves, the heads toward the center. Boards bearing the name, regiment and company are put up temporarily." [12]

About 11 o'clock both newspapermen heard approaching strains of martial music, and soon the procession's leading elements entered the grounds. The parade began at Gettysburg's square, its various components first forming on Carlisle, York and Chambersburg streets. Ohio's citizen delegation had been rounded up and directed to its starting place on Chambersburg Street by Colonels Lofland and Senter, who, like all the assistant marshals, were bedecked with "straw-colored satin sashes, fastened at the shoulder with mourning rosettes, and on the breast full rosettes of the national colors. Their saddle-cloths were of white cambric bordered

with black." The column proceeded south along Baltimore Street, turning on the Emmitsburg Road [today's Steinwehr Avenue], and then to the Taneytown Road, which skirted the new cemetery quite close to Ohio's plot. [13]

Potter and Allen, standing near the specially erected speakers' platform, watched as a military escort of infantry, cavalry and artillery marched by, halted and saluted President Lincoln, next in line. The Union's chief executive, Allen wrote, "joined in the procession on horseback; and thus mounted on a splendid black steed [his] tall and upright figure becomes commandingly conspicuous, and is the observed of all observers." Riding near the president was Major General Robert C. Schenck, a Franklin, Ohio, native who had been wounded at Second Bull Run. Two weeks after the dedication the general claimed the seat in Congress formerly held by Lincoln's arch-critic Clement Vallandigham. Over the next seven years Schenck chaired congressional committees on military affairs and ways and means. [14]

After Lincoln dismounted, Ward Lamon escorted him toward the platform. Dozens of persons, including Ohio's ex-Governor Dennison, exchanged greetings and handshakes with the president. This provided time for the remainder of the long procession to reach the hilltop. Some members of the Ohio delegation, realizing their tail-end place probably would prevent them seeing and hearing the speakers, "broke ranks and charged indiscriminately upon the crowd in front of the stand." Only a few secured good vantage points.[15]

Slowly the distinguished guests were seated on the platform. Members of Ohio's large press corps, serving "pro tempore" to Governor Tod, took places in the back rows. Dennison and General Schenck were seated toward one of the stand's flanks separated from Tod and Brough, who sat, respectively, to the left and behind Lincoln's chair. A number of officials, among them Ohio's state treasurer, auditor and librarian, claimed seats, as did some of the state legislators and other temporary Tod aides. Captain Nickerson was quite pleased when he found "I had a seat on the platform within a few feet of the speakers."[16] No other state could boast an ex-governor, governor, governor-elect and lieutenant governor-elect present on the stand during the ceremony. In fact, Ohio citizens seated on the platform and journalists in attendance outnumbered those from any state.

When Lincoln finally made his way to his chair in the front row, Tod spoke to him. "Mr. President, I want you to shake hands with me." Lincoln cordially did so. Tod presented Governor-elect Brough to the president, who quipped, "Why, I have just seen Governor Dennison of Ohio — how many more governors has Ohio?" Just before the formal program began Lincoln acquainted Tod and Brough with Secretary of State Seward, who in turn introduced them to Postmaster General Blair.[17]

Sixty-nine-year-old Edward Everett's keynote speech consumed the next two hours. It was delivered, wrote Martin Potter, "with a clear voice, but not audible to the tenth part of the vast concourse." The Cincinnati journalist believed that "for beauty of language" and "formal eloquence" it was "unsurpassed by any previous effort of his life." Potter keenly scrutinized the president while Everett spoke. Lincoln possessed "a thoughtful, kindly, care-worn face, impassive in repose, the eyes cast down, the lips thin and firmly set, the cheeks sunken, and the whole indicating weariness, and anything but good health. Occasionally a smile passes over his face, as some forcible remark of the orator arouses him, and once he placed his hand quickly on the shoulder of the gentleman at his left [Sew-

ard], and spoke an approving word."[18]

Azor Nickerson also was impressed with Everett's "masterly" oration. "When finished it seemed as though the subject had been exhausted and there was absolutely nothing more to be said." A hymn followed. Then Lincoln was introduced to provide his "few appropriate remarks." As the president rose from his chair the wounded Ohio captain thought "he was the tallest and most awkward man I had ever seen."[19]

The now-famous Gettysburg Address, lasting just three minutes, stunned Nickerson. He listened transfixed as Lincoln uttered the words "we can not dedicate, we can not consecrate, we can not hallow this ground. The brave men, living and dead, who struggled here, have consecrated it far above our poor power to add or detract. The world will little note, nor long remember, what we say here, but can never forget what they did here." Thirty years afterward Nickerson declared: "Others have differed as to the immediate effect of his remarks. In this ... I give the impressions received at the time, which were also identical with those of all with whom I spoke. I thought then, and still think, it was the shortest, grandest speech, oration, sermon, or what you please to call it, to which I ever listened. It was the whole matter in a nutshell, delivered distinctly and impressively, so that all ... could hear him. My own emotions may perhaps be imagined when it is remembered that he was facing the spot where only a short time before we had had our death-grapple with Pickett's men, and he stood almost immediately over the place where I had lain [July 3] and seen my comrades torn in fragments by the enemy's cannon-balls."[20]

A dirge and benediction closed the proceedings, which concluded with marshal Lamon's announcement that Colonel Anderson would be speaking in the Presbyterian church at 5 p.m. Tod, Dennison and Brough repaired to David Wills' home in Gettysburg for dinner and an hour-long reception. Lincoln greeted guests as they entered. He also attended the "Ohio program" with Seward, Secretary of the Interior Usher and John Burns, a local resident who voluntarily fought and was wounded with Union troops west of town during the battle's first day. Burns, "a grave and venerable old man of seventy, clad in the common costume of a country farmer," sat with "perfect composure" between Lincoln and Seward while Anderson delivered his 40-minute

discourse. According to Isaac Allen, the president "expressed great satisfaction with Col. Anderson's effort, and complimented the Ohio delegation upon the spirit and energy displayed by the earnest manner in which they had joined in the work of securing and dedicating the National Cemetery."[21]

The exhumation of battlefield remains and their reinterment were completed March 18, 1864. Ohio's six-section plot contained 131 bodies — three of them officers and four unknowns. The state's share of the expense needed to finish the cemetery came to $7,834. Judge Daniel Brown, appointed to the cemetery's memorial committee, helped select the design for the national monument, which was dedicated July 1, 1869. Later, individual Northern states erected monuments at appropriate locations across the battlefield. In April 1886 the Ohio General Assembly set aside $40,000 and established a Gettysburg memorial commission for the purpose of commemorating its soldiers' deeds there in stone and bronze. James S. Robinson, Ohio's secretary of state and the 82nd Ohio's colonel at Gettysburg, served on the three-man commission. Alfred E. Lee, also of the 82nd and wounded in the battle, subsequently was added as secretary. The commission members shared a unanimous opinion "that each of the Ohio organizations which participated in the battle should have its own special memorial; that no two or more of these memorials should be of the same pattern or design, and

that none of them should be duplicates of any of the memorials already erected on the field."[22]

Although not all the state's monuments, tablets and markers were in place beforehand, they were dedicated September 14, 1887 and formally entrusted to the Gettysburg Battlefield Memorial Association's care. The official ceremony again was held in the National Cemetery with various addresses delivered from the grounds' stone rostrum. Among the speakers was Governor Joseph B. Foraker, who had served with the 89th Ohio in the Army of the Cumberland as a teenaged officer. Foraker, at the time, was at odds with President Grover Cleveland over the chief executive's recent request to return captured Confederate battleflags to the South. "No rebel flags will be surrendered while I am governor," Foraker emphatically replied, and many in the crowd came to see this obdurate Buckeye who so adamantly defied the president.[23]

At the conclusion of Samuel H. Hurst's keynote address a military homage to Ohio's dead closed the exercises. The 14th Regiment Ohio National Guard from Columbus was drawn up with inverted arms around the Ohio plot, each grave marker decorated with small national flags and flowers. Nearby, a section from Battery E, 1st Light Artillery O.N.G., began firing a 19-gun salute — one shot for every Ohio unit that participated in the Gettysburg campaign. Before the fifteenth could be fired the borrowed cannon went off prematurely, badly wounding and burning Corporal Orris Grisso, a Springfield pattern maker and four-year veteran of the battery's Gatling gun squad. "Grisso was engaged in ramming the charge," wrote an eyewitness, "and was nearly in front of the piece, when it was discharged without warning. His left eye was blown out and his left hand so badly mutilated that amputation will most likely be necessary." James Ogden, the lieutenant commanding, blamed the accident on "carelessness of the authorities at Gettysburg for allowing a condemned gun to be used." Grisso died of his injuries and lockjaw six days later in Philadelphia.[24]

While the tragic mishap marred an otherwise "most beautiful and appropriate ceremony," hundreds of attending veterans tramped the battlefield or socialized. Special reunion and dedicatory exercises were held at the 4th and 107th Ohio monuments. Members of the 29th Ohio Infantry Association set up an encampment in the woods near the regiment's memorial on Culp's Hill. Veterans of the 5th Ohio, when first reaching Gettysburg by train, found their 12-foot-high granite monument — surmounted by two inclining knapsacks and a carved owl, the regiment's unofficial badge — still crated

Middle-aged veterans of the 4th Ohio (opposite page) gathered the afternoon of September 14, 1887 for the regiment's East Cemetery Hill monument dedication. Samuel Sprigg Carroll, the 4th's brigade commander at Gettysburg, delivered the exercise's memorial address.

L. M. Strayer Collection

in a freight car at the depot. Some of them stayed three extra days, "took off their coats and assisted the contractor to get the shaft in position [on Culp's Hill] ... and went home happy in the success of their work."[25]

Visits to the sites of their regiments' or batteries' fighting on July 1, 2 and 3, 1863 only slowed as surviving ex-soldiers, over the next decades, passed away or were transformed into old men. In 1913, nearly 750 Ohio veterans traveled to Gettysburg to commemorate the battle's 50th anniversary, including 77-year-old Andrew L. Harris, the state's last governor with Civil War service.[26]

Some were drawn there singly, often for personal reasons not associated with reunions or state-sponsored ceremonies. "My own feeling in 1863 was one of indifference to ever seeing [Gettysburg] again," confessed former Ohio artilleryman William Parmelee. But well before monuments began dotting the landscape "the desire was so strong that I made a trip on purpose to go over the battlefield."[27]

It has remained a powerful magnet for millions of tourists since then. As early as November 1863 Cleveland journalist John S. Stephenson correctly predicted that "Gettysburg, by-and-by, will become an American Mecca." Ohio's troops at Gettysburg, wrote James S. Robinson, "All fought for American nationality. ... Here the tide of invasion was rolled back after the bloodiest and most stubborn contest of the war. With our soldiers it was a struggle for mastery on Northern soil. It was a victory of the rank and file."[28]

APPENDIX A

Ohio troops at Gettysburg

	Organization	Commander	Corps
Infantry	4th Ohio	Lieutenant Colonel Leonard W. Carpenter	2nd
	5th Ohio	Colonel John H. Patrick	12th
	7th Ohio	Colonel William R. Creighton	12th
	8th Ohio	Lieutenant Colonel Franklin Sawyer	2nd
	25th Ohio	Lieutenant Colonel Jeremiah Williams	11th
		Captain Nathaniel J. Manning	
		Lieutenant William Maloney	
		Lieutenant Israel White	
	29th Ohio	Captain Wilbur F. Stevens	12th
		Captain Edward Hayes	
	55th Ohio	Colonel Charles B. Gambee	11th
	61st Ohio	Colonel Stephen J. McGroarty	11th
	66th Ohio	Lieutenant Colonel Eugene Powell	12th
	73rd Ohio	Lieutenant Colonel Richard Long	11th
	75th Ohio	Colonel Andrew L. Harris	11th
		Captain George Benson Fox	
	82nd Ohio	Colonel James S. Robinson	11th
		Lieutenant Colonel David Thomson	
	107th Ohio	Colonel Seraphim Meyer	11th
		Captain Otto Weber	
		Lieutenant Peter F. Young	
		Captain John M. Lutz	
Artillery	Battery H, 1st OVLA	Lieutenant George W. Norton	Artillery Reserve
	Battery I, 1st OVLA	Captain Hubert Dilger	11th
	Battery K, 1st OVLA	Captain Lewis Heckman	11th
	Battery L, 1st OVLA	Captain Frank C. Gibbs	5th
Cavalry	First Ohio Squadron*	Captain Noah Jones	Cavalry Corps
	6th Ohio**	Major William Stedman	Cavalry Corps

* Companies A and C, 1st Ohio Cavalry.
** At Manchester and Westminster, Maryland, July 1-3, 1863.

APPENDIX B

Buckeyes buried in the Ohio plot at Gettysburg National Cemetery

* Denotes soldiers mentioned in the text or photo captions.
Unless a rank is given, all individuals listed were privates.

Section A

Enoch M. Detty*	G	73rd Ohio
2nd Lieut. George W. McGreary	C	82nd Ohio
Martin Jacobs	D	82nd Ohio
Eli A. Hain	H	82nd Ohio
William H. Bush	H	82nd Ohio
Jacob Warner	H	82nd Ohio
Elmer L. Ross	C	82nd Ohio
Francis H. Blough	C	82nd Ohio
Unknown		
Unknown		
Unknown		
John McClary	D	66th Ohio
George R. Wilson*	B	8th Ohio
Orville A. Warren	K	8th Ohio
Ozro Moore	I	8th Ohio
William Brown*	B	8th Ohio
Sergt. John K. Barclay*	C	8th Ohio
Corp. Frank Shaffer	D	8th Ohio
Danford Parker	K	8th Ohio
Jeremiah W. Crubaugh*	C	75th Ohio
John N. Edmonds*	H	1st OVLA
Frederick Meyer	I	1st OVLA
Andrew W. Houck	F	82nd Ohio
Joseph Klinefelter	F	55th Ohio

Section B

Corp. Edward T. Lovette	I	25th Ohio
William Williams	I	73rd Ohio
Henry Opher	E	55th Ohio
William Ackerman*	D	73rd Ohio

John R. Myer*	C	55th Ohio
Sergt. Caleb Dewese	F	73rd Ohio
Ai Maddox	G	73rd Ohio
Ozias Ford	A	55th Ohio
William Whitby	H	73rd Ohio
Joseph R. Blake	I	73rd Ohio
Andrew Miller*	I	73rd Ohio
William McLuen*	B	73rd Ohio
Corp. James H. Lee	H	73rd Ohio
William E. Haynes*	B	73rd Ohio
Corp. Allen Yaple	A	73rd Ohio
Henry C. Stark	I	4th Ohio
James W. Harl*	A	4th Ohio
Corp. Bernard McGuire*	B	8th Ohio
John McCillips*	C	8th Ohio
George H. Martin	G	4th Ohio
Sergt. Philip Tracy*	G	8th Ohio
Color Corp. William Welch*	I	8th Ohio
Samuel Maurer*	A	107th Ohio
Corp. Edward G. Ranney	D	61st Ohio
Unknown		1st OVLA

Section C

Anthony Murville	G	5th Ohio
John Lenhart	D	5th Ohio
Charles Reinhardt	I	1st OVLA
George Nixon III*	B	73rd Ohio
August Raber	F	107th Ohio
Elisha L. Leake*	G	73rd Ohio
Lucas Strobel*	A	107th Ohio
John Davis*	K	75th Ohio
Thomas Gilleran	F	61st Ohio

Corp. George B. Greiner*	G	73rd Ohio	Corp. John Debolt*	B	4th Ohio
Jacob Swackhamer	G	73rd Ohio	Haskell E. Farr	G	55th Ohio
Isaac J. Sperry*	G	73rd Ohio	Corp. William Myers	A	8th Ohio
Jacob Mitchell	C	55th Ohio	Jonathan Laraba*	E	75th Ohio
Chauncey Haskell	F	82nd Ohio	Perry Taylor*	G	75th Ohio
William E. Pollock*	C	55th Ohio	Tallis E. McCain	G	29th Ohio
Benjamin F. Hartley*	E	75th Ohio	George Case*	C	5th Ohio
Sergt. Thomas H. Rice*	B	73rd Ohio	Isaac Johnson*	K	1st OVLA
Joseph Barrett*	G	73rd Ohio	Asa O. Davis*	G	4th Ohio
Andrew Lahmiller*	A	107th Ohio	William Overholt	I	73rd Ohio
William R. Call*	B	73rd Ohio	Lewis Davis*	D	75th Ohio
Isaac Richards	A	82nd Ohio	1st Sergt. John W. Pierce*	C	25th Ohio
Adam Snyder	H	107th Ohio	Hiram H. Hughes	H	25th Ohio
Corp. James Goodspeed	D	75th Ohio	Wesley Raikes*	G	75th Ohio
William Miller	G	25th Ohio	Samuel P. Baughman*	C	75th Ohio
Nathan Heald	F	73rd Ohio	Joseph Juchem	G	107th Ohio
			Jacob Bise	K	107th Ohio
			Henry Schram*	H	1st OVLA

Section D

Sergt. Charles Ladd*	E	25th Ohio
Caspar Bohrer	G	107th Ohio
Jacob Hoff	E	107th Ohio
Joseph W. Cunningham	I	25th Ohio
John Aeigle	K	107th Ohio
Balts Beverly	C	107th Ohio
George Richards	D	75th Ohio
Sergt. Philip Shiplin*	F	75th Ohio
Samuel L. Connor	E	82nd Ohio
Corp. Carl Gebauer	K	107th Ohio
William McVey	H	73rd Ohio
Asa Hines	K	82nd Ohio
Sergt. William M.N. Williams*	C	8th Ohio
David W. Collins	G	4th Ohio
William Bain	G	4th Ohio
2nd Lieut. Addison H. Edgar*	G	4th Ohio
Andrew Myers	G	4th Ohio
1st Lieut. George Hayward*	E	29th Ohio
John Myer	G	107th Ohio
John C. Owens	G	75th Ohio
Ira L. Brigham	H	8th Ohio
Lemuel W. Walker	F	82nd Ohio
John Glouchlen	H	25th Ohio

Section E

Corp. Thomas Dunn*	K	25th Ohio
Benjamin F. Pontious*	D	29th Ohio
George H. Thompson	G	5th Ohio
Benjamin F. Sherman	G	61st Ohio

Section F

1st Sergt. Jasper C. Briggs*	G	73rd Ohio
Sergt. John C. Kipka	A	8th Ohio
Andrew J. Dildine	A	8th Ohio
Jacob I. Rauch	A	8th Ohio
Josiah D. Johnson*	F	29th Ohio
Sergt. Isaac Willis*	G	73rd Ohio
Daniel W. Palmer	D	107th Ohio
James Ray*	G	73rd Ohio

NOTE — Several burial anomalies exist in the Ohio plot. William Folk, Company D, 82nd Ohio, is listed in Section A, but according to the Ohio Adjutant General's Office he died August 14, 1864 at Andersonville prison and is buried there in Grave #5625. John Weiser and Richard Bradler, Company D, 82nd Ohio, also are listed in Section A. There is no record in the Ohio AGO for Bradler. Weiser was captured at Gettysburg July 1 but later exchanged. The Ohio AGO lists him as being wounded in Georgia in 1864, and discharged July 3, 1865 for disability. In Section B, Corporal Edward T. Lovette supposedly was reinterred at Harriettsville, Ohio. Remains buried in Grave #16, Section B, were listed as A.M. Campbell, Company E, 185th Ohio. This body likely was Andrew M. Campbell, Company E, 105th Pennsylvania. In Section D, John Glouchlen is not listed in Ohio AGO reports as belonging to the 25th Ohio. Mistakes in name spellings and regimental designations also occurred on stone markers in the Ohio plot. They have been corrected here.

NOTES

Prelude

1. Elijah Hayden to Ella Hayden, June 21, 1863, courtesy of Donald Lingafelter, Mentor, Ohio.

2. Ibid.

3. William H. Clough to Deborah Hayden, July 22, 1863, in *The Elyria Independent Democrat,* August 5, 1863.

4. Henry J. Hunt, "The First Day at Gettysburg," *Battles and Leaders of the Civil War,* vol. III (New York: The Century Company, 1888), p. 255, 256.

5. Edwin B. Coddington, *The Gettysburg Campaign: A Study in Command* (Dayton: Morningside Bookshop, 1979), p. 26.

6. Milo M. Quaife, editor, *From the Cannon's Mouth: The Civil War Letters of General Alpheus S. Williams* (Detroit: Wayne State University Press, 1959), p. 178.

7. William E. Parmelee to Samuel P. Bates, December 9, 1882, Bates Collection, Pennsylvania Division of Public Records, Harrisburg. At age 18 on August 5, 1862, Parmelee enlisted in Battery H at Toledo.

8. James F. Huntington quoted in John Bigelow Jr., *Chancellorsville* (New York: Konecky & Konecky, 1995), p. 480.

9. Luther B. Mesnard memoir, Civil War Miscellaneous Collection, U.S. Army Military History Institute (USAMHI), Carlisle Barracks, Pa. At Chancellorsville, the 55th Ohio's losses numbered 153 — nine killed, 87 wounded and 57 captured or missing. *The War of the Rebellion: A Compilation of the Official Records of the Union and Confederate Armies* [unless otherwise noted, assumed to be Series I], (Washington: Government Printing Office, 1880-1901), vol. 25, pt. 1, p. 182. Hereafter referred to as *Official Records.*

10. Oliver O. Howard, *Autobiography of Oliver Otis Howard, Major General* (New York: Baker & Taylor Co., 1907), vol. I, p. 370; Bigelow, p. 296-297. Howard had lost his right arm while commanding a brigade in the battle of Fair Oaks, Va.

11. Coddington, p. 32.

12. James S. Robinson to Lester T. Hunt, May 17, 1863, J.S. Robinson Papers, Ohio Historical Society, Columbus.

13. William D.W. Mitchell to his sister, May 10, 1863, courtesy of Stanley R. Burleson, Yukon, Okla.

14. Bigelow, p. 305; Augustus C. Hamlin, *The Battle of Chancellorsville* (Bangor: privately published, 1896), p. 78.

15. Isaac W. Gardner to his parents, undated May 1863 letter, Harrisburg Civil War Round Table–Gregory A. Coco Collection, USAMHI.

16. Bigelow, p. 296; Oscar D. Ladley to his family, May 4, 1863, in Carl M. Becker & Ritchie Thomas, editors, *Hearth and Knapsack: The Ladley Letters, 1857-1880* (Athens: Ohio University Press, 1988), p. 121. Hereafter referred to as Ladley.

17. Bigelow, p. 297; Benjamin Morgan memoir, courtesy of Jacqueline Ann Lane, Lebanon, Ohio.

18. Benjamin Morgan to Sarah Xalissa Morgan, May 14, 1863, courtesy of Jacqueline Ann Lane. The 75th Ohio's losses at Chancellorsville amounted to 140. Morgan's pet name for his wife was "Lissa."

19. See the *Cleveland Morning Leader,* August 18, 1855. Also, Jörg Nagler, "The Lincoln-Fremont Debate and the Forty-Eighters," in Charlotte L. Brancaforte, editor, *The German Forty Eighters in the United States* (New York: Peter Lang, 1989); Wilhelm Kaufmann, *Die Deutschen im Amerikanischen Bürgerkrieg* (München: R. Oldenburg, 1911); Constantin Grebner, *We Were the Ninth: A History of the Ninth Regiment, Ohio Volunteer Infantry April 17, 1861, to June 7, 1864* (Kent, Ohio: Kent State University Press, 1987), p. 4-5; and Carl Wittke, "Ohio's Germans, 1840-1875," *The Ohio Historical Quarterly,* vol. 66, no. 4, October 1957.

20. *Knoxville Register,* June 12, 1863, republished under the headline "Rebel Opinion of German Soldiers" in the *Mahoning Register* [Youngstown], July 16, 1863.

21. Bigelow, p. 478.

22. Ladley, p. 121-122; David Thomson to Mary Thomson, May 7, 1863, courtesy of David G. Thomson, Edina, Minn.

23. *Official Records,* vol. 25, pt. 1, p. 182-183; Nathaniel J. Manning, May 9, 1863, in *The Spirit of Democracy* [Woodsfield, Ohio], May 20, 1863; Benjamin Morgan memoir.

24. Seraphim Meyer military service and pension records, National Archives, Washington, D.C.; *Cleveland und sein Deutschthum* (Cleveland: German-American Biographical Publishing Co., 1907), p. 441.

25. Jacob Smith, *Camps and Campaigns of the 107th Regiment Ohio Volunteer Infantry from August, 1862, to July, 1865* (n.p., 1910), p. 9. Hereafter referred to as Smith; 107th Ohio descriptive book, Record Group 94, National Archives.

26. William H. Perrin, editor, *History of Stark County,*

with an *Outline Sketch of Ohio* (Chicago: Baskin & Battey, 1881), p. 264; Herbert T.O. Blue, *History of Stark County, Ohio* (Chicago: The S.J. Clarke Publishing Company, 1928), vol. I, p. 879; Smith, p. 9.

27. These and other descriptions of Meyer's "peculiarities" can be found in his court-martial transcript, July 22-August 5, 1863, File #nn163, RG 153, Records of the Office of the Judge Advocate General (Army), Court-Martial Case Files 1809-1894, National Archives.

28. *Official Records,* vol. 25, pt. 1, p. 182, 644. Surgeon Charles A. Hartmann was killed May 2.

29. Samuel H. Hurst, *Journal-History of the Seventy-Third Ohio Volunteer Infantry* (Chillicothe: n.p., 1866), p. 62; John Kratz to his parents, May 29, 1863, courtesy of Ron Chojnacki, Medina, Ohio.

30. A. Wilson Greene, "From Chancellorsville to Cemetery Hill: O.O. Howard and Eleventh Corps Leadership," in Gary W. Gallagher, editor, *The First Day at Gettysburg* (Kent: Kent State University Press, 1992), p. 61, 63; Ezra J. Warner, *Generals in Blue* (Baton Rouge: Louisiana State University Press, 1992), p. 5-6, 18-19; Blanche Butler Ames, compiler, *Chronicles from the Nineteenth Century: Family Letters of Blanche Butler and Adelbert Ames,* vol. I (privately printed, 1957), p. 16, 17; Francis C. Barlow to his mother and brothers, May 8, 1863, Massachusetts Historical Society, Boston.

31. *Official Records,* vol. 25, pt. 1, p. 182-183; vol. 27, pt. 1, p. 164.

32. Coddington, p. 41; *Official Records,* vol. 27, pt. 1, p. 162, 165, 168.

33. *Official Roster of the Soldiers of the State of Ohio in the War of the Rebellion, 1861-1866* (Akron, Cincinnati, Norwalk, 1886-1895), vol. III, p. 167; vol. V, p. 39; vol. VI, p. 207. Hereafter referred to as *Ohio Rosters;* Dwight L. Smith, "Andrew L. Harris" in *The Governors of Ohio* (Columbus: The Ohio Historical Society, 1969), p. 148; Benjamin Morgan to Lissa Morgan, June 6, 1863.

34. *Ohio Rosters,* vol. X, p. 424; Unpublished biography of James Freeman Huntington and history of Battery H, 1st Regiment Ohio Light Artillery, courtesy of Edward Browne, Pomfret, Conn.; John H. Merrell diary, courtesy of Barbara Linderholm, Davis, Calif. Battery H lost four of its six 3-inch ordnance rifles at Chancellorsville when the limber horses were killed or disabled. One gun was recovered May 4. A captured Confederate rifle was given to Huntington May 9, but not until June 8 was the battery fully reconstituted when two new 3-inch rifles were issued.

35. *Official Records,* vol. 25, pt. 1, p. 1123; *Ohio Rosters,* vol. X, p. 430; Samuel S. Cox to David Tod, May 24, 1862, in Correspondence to the Governor and Adjutant General of Ohio, 1861-1866, series 147, vol. 39, folder 1, Ohio Historical Society; James Gildea memoir, Western Reserve Historical Society, Cleveland.

36. *Official Records,* vol. 25, pt. 1, p. 4; *Ohio Rosters,* vol. XI, p. 311.

37. *Official Records,* vol. 27, pt. 1, p. 166-167; pt. 3, p. 805; Samuel L. Gillespie, *A History of Company A, First Ohio Cavalry 1861-1865* (Washington Court House, Ohio: Press of Ohio State Register, 1898), p. 147.

38. **Mark M. Boatner III,** *The Civil War Dictionary* (New York: David McKay Company, Inc., 1959), p. 332. The Army of Northern Virginia's actual strength at Gettysburg was about 80,025. See John W. Busey & David G. Martin, *Regimental Strengths and Losses at Gettysburg* (Hightstown, N.J.: Longstreet House, 1994), p. 118-129.

39. Boatner, p. 332; E.B. Long, *The Civil War Day by Day: An Almanac 1861-1865* (Garden City, N.Y.: Doubleday & Company, Inc., 1971), p. 366.

40. Coddington, p. 48-49; *Official Records,* vol. 27, pt. 1, p. 34, 35.

41. Coddington, p. 70-71; *Official Records,* vol. 27, pt. 1, p. 38.

42. Ladley, p. 141; Henry C. Henney diary, *Civil War Times Illustrated* Collection, USAMHI; Stowel L. Burnham to Luther Burnham, June 19, 1863, in Roderick H. Burnham, *The Burnham Family; or Genealogical Records of the Descendants of the Four Emigrants of the Name, Who Were Among the Early Settlers in America* (Hartford, Conn.: Press of Case, Lockwood & Brainard, 1869), p. 256.

43. Joseph L. Brenton deposition, December 28, 1876, in James K. O'Reilly pension file, National Archives. Brenton also was 3rd Brigade surgeon, 2nd Division, 2nd Corps.

44. Martin L. Buchwalter diary, courtesy of Jeffrey J. Kowalis, Orland Park, Ill.; Anthony W. Ross to Sarah Ross, June 23, 1863, Ohio Historical Society; Samuel Fellers to William Millikin, July 12, 1863, in the *Fayette County Herald* [Washington Court House, Ohio], July 30, 1863.

45. Nathan L. Parmater diary, Ohio Historical Society; Lawrence Wilson, *Itinerary of the Seventh Ohio Volunteer Infantry* (New York: The Neale Publishing Company, 1907), p. 250.

46. Benjamin Morgan to Lissa Morgan, June 21, 1863.

47. James F. Huntington, "Notes of Service with a Light Artillery at Chancellorsville and Gettysburg," in the *Marietta Sunday Observer,* June 30-August 18, 1918. Hereafter referred to as "Notes of Service." Huntington's memoir originally was composed prior to 1881. He contributed it to Seymour J. Hathaway, who at the time was writing a military history of Washington County, Ohio.

48. Ladley, p. 141-142.

49. Warner, p. 73; William Kepler, *History of the Three Months' and Three Years' Service of the Fourth Regiment Ohio Volunteer Infantry in the War for the Union* (Cleveland: Leader Printing Company, 1886), p. 107. [Reprinted as *4th Ohio Volunteers* in 1992 by Blue Acorn Press]. Carroll had commanded the 1st Brigade, 3rd Division of the 2nd Corps since mid-April 1863. Between June 14-28 the brigade's acting commander was Colonel John Coons, 14th Indiana.

50. Thomas F. Galwey, *The Valiant Hours,* edited by W.S. Nye (Harrisburg: The Stackpole Company, 1961), p. 1, 91-92. One of Galwey's best friends in the 8th Ohio was Lieutenant O'Reilly, the sunstroke victim of June 15. The two had enlisted together April 15, 1861.

51. Jason H. Silverman, " 'The Excitement Had Begun!' The Civil War Diary of Lemuel Jeffries, 1862-1863," *Manuscripts* (Fall 1978), p. 273-274; George F. Laird to his brother, June 21, 1863, courtesy of Barry L. Cornell, Rittman, Ohio.

52. Samuel L. Gillespie, June 27, 1863, to the *Fayette County Herald,* July 9, 1863. Gillespie corresponded to this

newspaper using the pen name "Lovejoy."

53. Coddington, p. 76-79.

54. Norman A. Barret, July 13, 1863, in the *Western Reserve Chronicle* [Warren, Ohio], July 22, 1863. Major William Stedman of the 6th Ohio reported 40 Rebel soldiers were captured in the ravine. *Official Records*, vol. 27, pt. 1, p. 972. Those killed in the regiment were First Sergeant Augustus S. Reckard, Company H, and Corporal George Cutchan, Company K. Private William S. Bruce, Company H, died of wounds June 22.

55. *Western Reserve Chronicle,* July 22, 1863.

56. Delos R. Northway, June 23, 1863, in "Extracts from the Diary of Major Delos R. Northway, Co. A, Sixth O.V.C.," *Souvenir Fiftieth Annual Reunion of the Sixth Ohio Veteran Volunteer Cavalry Association held at Warren, Ohio, October 5th, 1915* (n.p., n.d.), p. 118.

57. *Official Records,* vol. 27, pt. 3, p. 192; Wilson, p. 251; Horace Mewborn, "The Operations of Mosby's Rangers," *Blue & Gray* (April 2000), p. 19; Coddington, p. 79-80.

58. John H. Merrell diary; Galwey, p. 93; Nathan L. Parmater diary.

59. Nathan L. Parmater diary. Two of the deserters shot belonged to the 46th Pennsylvania. The third was a member of the 13th New Jersey.

60. Coddington, p. 121, 122; *Official Records,* vol. 27, pt. 3, p. 305.

61. Kepler, p. 122, 123.

62. Leonidas M. Jewett, "From Stafford Heights to Gettysburg in 1863," *Sketches of War History 1861-1865,* vol. 5 (Cincinnati: The Robert Clarke Company, 1903), p. 215.

63. William B. Southerton reminiscences, Ohio Historical Society.

64. Henry Henney diary; Hurst, p. 64.

65. George P. Metcalf, "Recollections of Boyhood Days," typescript of unpublished memoir, Ohio Historical Society. Metcalf had been visiting relatives in Wyoming County, N.Y., when he and a cousin enlisted August 22, 1862, in the 136th New York.

66. *Official Records,* vol. 27, pt. 1, p. 58-61. For a more detailed description and analysis of the Halleck-Hooker controversy and the latter's removal from Army of the Potomac command, see Coddington, p. 130-133.

67. Galwey, p. 96; Jewett, "From Stafford Heights to Gettysburg in 1863," p. 218, 219; Franklin Sawyer, *The Eighth Ohio at Gettysburg* (Washington: E.J. Gray Printer, 1889), p. 3; Huntington, "Notes of Service."

68. *Official Records,* vol. 27, pt. 3, p. 373, 376; Warner, p. 108; Gillespie, p. 147-150.

69. Coddington, p. 225.

70. Sawyer, *The Eighth Ohio at Gettysburg,* p. 3; Galwey, p. 97-98; Charles H. Merrick to Myra Merrick, July 1, 1863, Merrick Papers, Western Reserve Historical Society; George F. Laird to his brother, June 30, 1863.

71. Nathan L. Parmater diary; Lyman D. Ames diary, *Civil War Times Illustrated* Collection, USAMHI.

72. Luther B. Mesnard memoir.

73. Henry Henney diary; Smith, p. 85.

74. John H. Merrell diary.

75. *Official Records,* vol. 27, pt. 3, p. 415-417; Harry W.

Pfanz, *Gettysburg – The First Day* (Chapel Hill: The University of North Carolina Press, 2001), p. 45-46.

76. Smith, p. 85; Henry Henney diary; Albert R. Barlow, *Company G: A Record of the Services of One Company of the 157th N.Y. Vols. in the War of the Rebellion* (Syracuse: A.W. Hall, 1899), p. 125; *Official Records,* vol. 27, pt. 1, p. 723. Colonel Orland Smith, 73rd Ohio, reported that before half the distance between Brooke's Station, Va., and Gettysburg was covered by his brigade, "the shoes began to fail, thus leaving many men to march barefooted sometimes over very rough roads."

77. William B. Southerton reminiscences; Jewett, "From Stafford Heights to Gettysburg in 1863," p. 219.

78. *Official Records,* vol. 27, pt. 3, p. 417; David Thomson to Mary Thomson, July 16, 1863; Alfred E. Lee, "Reminiscences of the Gettysburg Battle," *Lippincott's Magazine* (July 1883), p. 54.

July 1

1. Alfred E. Lee, "Reminiscences of the Gettysburg Battle," p. 54.

2. *Official Records,* vol. 27, pt. 1, p. 701.

3. *Ibid.,* p. 715, 733, 738, 739; George B. Fox to his father, July 4, 1863, Cincinnati Historical Society; Andrew L. Harris, July 11, 1863, in the *Eaton Weekly Register,* July 23, 1863. One hundred men each from the 82nd Illinois and 58th New York also were sent on scouts toward Fairfield, Pa., and Creagerstown, Md., respectively.

4. *Official Records,* vol. 27, pt. 1, p. 701; Gary Kross, "The XI Corps at Gettysburg July 1, 1863," *Blue & Gray* (December 2001), p. 10, 12; Alfred E. Lee, "Reminiscences of Gettysburg July 1st, 1863," *Delaware Gazette,* February 26, 1864. Lee wrote this article under the pen name "A.T. Sechand."

5. Greene, "From Chancellorsville to Cemetery Hill," p. 68; *Official Records,* vol. 27, pt. 1, p. 727.

6. Alfred E. Lee, "Reminiscences of Gettysburg July 1st, 1863"; *Official Records,* vol. 27, pt. 1, p. 701-702, 727; Warner, p. 423.

7. Louise W. Hitz, editor, *Letters of Frederick C. Winkler 1862-1865* (privately published, 1963), p. 68-69.

8. Alfred E. Lee, "Reminiscences of Gettysburg July 1st, 1863."

9. George P. Metcalf memoir.

10. *Official Records,* vol. 27, pt. 1, p. 702, 727; D. Scott Hartwig, "The 11th Army Corps on July 1, 1863," *The Gettysburg Magazine* (January 1990), p. 33.

11. Ibid., p. 36-37.

12. *Official Records,* vol. 27, pt. 1, p. 754; David G. Martin, *Gettysburg July 1* (Conshohocken, Pa.: Combined Books, Inc., 1996), p. 200.

13. *Official Records,* vol. 27, pt. 1, p. 754; Stanley P. Wasson, editor, "Civil War Letters of Darwin Cody," *The Ohio Historical Quarterly* (October 1959), p. 387.

14. Kenneth M. Kepf, "Dilger's Battery at Gettysburg," *The Gettysburg Magazine* (January 1991), p. 50; John S. Applegate, *Reminiscences and Letters of George Arrowsmith of New Jersey* (Red Bank, N.J.: John H. Cook, 1893), p. 211-212; Pfanz, *Gettysburg – The First Day,* p. 220-221.

15. *Official Records,* vol. 27, pt. 1, p. 738; Whitelaw Reid, *Ohio in the War: Her Statesmen, Generals and Soldiers,* vol. I (Cincinnati: The Robert Clarke Company, 1895), p. 974-975; Busey & Martin, p. 205. The Ohio counties included Belmont, Clinton, Cuyahoga, Hamilton, Knox, Madison, Miami, Montgomery, Perry, Pickaway and Wyandot.

16. Alfred E. Lee, "Reminiscences of Gettysburg July 1st, 1863" and "Reminiscences of the Gettysburg Battle," p. 55.

17. Ibid., p. 55; Joseph Gillis to his sister, July 22, 1863, courtesy of Joseph H. Gillis, Youngstown.

18. Alfred E. Lee, "Reminiscences of the Gettysburg Battle," p. 55.

19. Ibid., p. 55; A.E. Lee alumnus file, Ohio Wesleyan University, Delaware, Ohio.

20. *Official Records,* vol. 27, pt. 1, p. 702, 728; Hartwig, "The 11th Army Corps on July 1, 1863," p. 37, 39.

21. *Official Records,* vol. 27, pt. 1, p. 752, 754.

22. *Ibid.,* p. 754; *Ohio Rosters,* vol. X, p. 415; William Wheeler to his family, July 26, 1863, in *Letters of William Wheeler of the Class of 1855, Yale College* (Cambridge: H.O. Houghton & Co., 1875), p. 409-411. Hereafter referred to as Wheeler.

23. William B. Southerton reminiscences.

24. Martin, p. 271-272; Hartwig, "The 11th Army Corps on July 1, 1863," p. 40.

25. Ibid., p. 41; Busey & Martin, p. 82; Seraphim Meyer military service records, National Archives.

26. Seraphim Meyer pension records, National Archives; Meyer to Theodore A. Meysenburg, July 14, 1863, in Meyer's military service records.

27. John F. Tescher military service records, National Archives.

28. *Official Records,* vol. 27, pt. 1, p. 717; pt. 2, p. 468.

29. Martin, p. 274; *Official Records,* vol. 27, pt. 1, p. 719; Edward C. Culp, July 5, 1863, in the *Norwalk Reflector,* July 21, 1863.

30. Edward C. Culp, *The 25th Ohio Vet. Vol. Infantry in the War for the Union* (Topeka: Geo. W. Crane & Co., 1885), p. 77. Hereafter referred to as Culp. *Official Records,* vol. 27, pt. 1, p. 756; Isaac W. Gardner to his parents, July 5, 1863; Charles J. Gillis to his father, July 5, 1863, in *The Portage County Democrat,* July 15, 1863.

31. *Official Records,* vol. 27, pt. 2, p. 468, 492, 582; Busey & Martin, p. 158, 167.

32. Edward C. Culp, "Gettysburg: Reminiscences of the Great Fight by a Participant," *The National Tribune,* March 19, 1885.

33. Ibid.; *Official Records,* vol. 27, pt. 1, p. 719.

34. Adelbert Ames and John M. Brown quoted from testimony given by them July 27, 1863 during Meyer's court-martial, File #nn163, RG 153, National Archives.

35. Ibid. Lutz's testimony at Meyer's trial was given July 30, 1863.

36. *Official Records,* vol. 27, pt. 1, p. 728; Carl Schurz, *The Reminiscences of Carl Schurz,* vol. III (New York: The McClure Company, 1908), p. 9.

37. Hartwig, "The 11th Army Corps on July 1, 1863," p. 44; Francis C. Barlow to his mother, July 7, 1863, Massachusetts Historical Society.

38. *Official Records,* vol. 27, pt. 1, p. 756; Andrew L. Harris, July 11, 1863, in the *Eaton Weekly Register,* July 23, 1863; William B. Southerton reminiscences; Edward Marcus, editor, *A New Canaan Private in the Civil War: Letters of Justus M. Silliman, 17th Connecticut Volunteers* (New Canaan, Conn.: New Canaan Historical Society, 1984), p. 41.

39. Frederick Nussbaum quoted in Smith, p. 225; Charles Harrison quoted from Meyer court-martial testimony given July 30, 1863.

40. Smith, p. 91-92; Augustus Vignos and Barnet T. Steiner military service records, National Archives; Steiner to his brother, July 8, 1863, courtesy of Brian Zimmerman, Canton; *Ohio Rosters,* vol. VII, p. 640-643; John W. Busey, *These Honored Dead: The Union Casualties at Gettysburg* (Hightstown, N.J.: Longstreet House, 1996), p. 229-231; *Cleveland Herald,* July 24, 1863. A short description of Mueller's wounding can be found in *The Tuscarawas Advocate,* July 17, 1863. A resident of New Philadelphia, Mueller resigned October 22, 1863 due to disability.

41. Busey, *These Honored Dead,* p. 222; Culp, p. 78, 80-81. Carroll's and Ladd's amputations are mentioned respectively in George A. Otis, *The Medical and Surgical History of the Civil War* (Wilmington, N.C.: Broadfoot Publishing Co., 1991), vol. X, p. 763 and vol. XI, p. 262; Nathaniel J. Manning military service records, National Archives; Jeremiah Williams to John B. Bachelder, June 18, 1880, in *The Bachelder Papers,* vol. I (Dayton: Morningside House, Inc., 1994), p. 668.

42. Martin, p. 289-290.

43. Andrew L. Harris to John B. Bachelder, March 14, 1881, in *The Bachelder Papers,* vol. II, p. 744; William B. Southerton reminiscences.

44. Alonzo Ford and Emanuel M. Shultz military service records, National Archives; William A. Frassanito, *Early Photography at Gettysburg* (Gettysburg: Thomas Publications, 1995), p. 404.

45. Harris to Bachelder, *op. cit.,* p. 744.

46. Alphonso C. Davis to Josiah Davis, August 7, 1863, in the *Eaton Weekly Register,* August 27, 1863.

47. Benjamin Morgan diary.

48. Irene Morgan Lane, "Lieutenant Colonel Ben Morgan 1823-1898," unpublished biography written by Morgan's granddaughter, courtesy of Jacqueline Ann Lane.

49. Benjamin Morgan diary.

50. Harris to Bachelder, *op. cit.,* p. 744.

51. *Official Records,* vol. 27, pt. 1, p. 712; John T. Wood and William L. Hubbell military service records, National Archives; *Cleveland Morning Leader,* July 10, 1863. Hubbell was paroled August 25, 1863.

52. Harris to Bachelder, *op. cit.,* p. 744; *Official Records,* vol. 27, pt. 1, p. 712-713. Ames' decision to give command of the 2nd Brigade to Colonel Harris can be found in his July 27, 1863 testimony at Meyer's court-martial, File #nn163, RG 153, National Archives. Colonel William H. Noble, 17th Connecticut, was senior to Meyer, but had not yet returned to duty following recuperation from a Chancellorsville wound.

53. *Official Records,* vol. 27, pt. 1, p. 728; Alfred E. Lee in the *Delaware Gazette,* February 26, 1864.

54. David Thomson to Mary Thomson, July 16, 1863.

55. Alfred E. Lee, "The Eleventh Corps. The Disadvantages Under Which It Fought at Gettysburg," *Philadelphia Weekly Press,* January 26, 1887.

56. Ibid.; William C. Layton military service records, National Archives.

57. James S. Robinson quoted in *Report of the Gettysburg Memorial Commission of Ohio,* 2nd edition (Columbus: Press of Nitschke Bros., 1889), p. 74. Hereafter referred to as *Ohio Memorials at Gettysburg.*

58. James S. Robinson obituary, January 21, 1892, *The Democrat* [Kenton and Hardin County, Ohio].

59. David Thomson to his son, July 5, 1863; Burnham's wounding is described in *The Hardin County Republican,* July 31, 1863. See also Alfred E. Lee, "Reminiscences of the Gettysburg Battle," p. 57.

60. David Thomson to James S. Robinson, February 28, 1888, in *The Bachelder Papers,* vol. III, p. 1529.

61. *Ibid.,* p. 1529-1530; Alfred E. Lee to John B. Bachelder, February 16, 1888, in *The Bachelder Papers,* p. 1526; *Official Records,* vol. 27, pt. 1, p. 745.

62. *Ohio Memorials at Gettysburg,* p. 74; Hartwig, "The 11th Army Corps on July 1, 1863," p. 45; *Official Records,* vol. 27, pt. 1, p. 183; *The Hardin County Republican,* August 7, 1863; Emily B.T. Souder, *Leaves From the Battle-Field of Gettysburg, A Series of Letters Written From a Field Hospital and National Poems* (Philadelphia: Caxton Press, 1864); William D.W. Mitchell military service records, National Archives. Alfred Lee in 1883 and the 82nd Ohio Gettysburg monument give the regiment's engaged strength as 258. Busey and Martin list it as 312.

63. Busey, *These Honored Dead,* p. 228-229; *Ohio Rosters,* vol. VI, p. 532-537. Four of the seven enlisted men captured July 1 from Lee's Company E, 82nd Ohio, later died in captivity.

64. Alfred E. Lee, "Reminiscences of the Gettysburg Battle," p. 56-57.

65. Hartwig, "The 11th Army Corps on July 1, 1863," p. 47; A.R. Barlow, p. 127.

66. *Official Records,* vol. 27, pt. 1, p. 183; Busey, *These Honored Dead,* p. 224; Edmund V. Brent, James H. Bell, Henry R. Bending and Joseph R. Mell military service records, National Archives.

67. Wheeler, p. 410; *Official Records,* vol. 27, pt. 1, p. 754; Alfred E. Lee to John B. Bachelder, February 16, 1888, in *The Bachelder Papers,* vol. III, p. 1527; *Sketches of War History,* vol. V, p. 221.

68. Daniel B. Wren to Benjamin Morgan, November 27, 1863, courtesy of Jacqueline Ann Lane.

69. *Official Records,* vol. 27, pt. 1, p. 729; pt. 2, p. 469.

70. *Ibid.,* pt. 1, p. 748, 755.

71. *Ibid.,* pt. 2, p. 479; Cecil C. Reed, July 13, 1863, in the *Cleveland Morning Leader,* July 24, 1863.

72. Mark H. Dunkelman, *The Coster Avenue Mural in Gettysburg* (Providence: privately printed, 1989), p. 2-3; Hartwig, "The 11th Army Corps on July 1, 1863," p. 49; *Official Records,* vol. 27, pt. 1, p. 755.

73. *Cleveland Morning Leader,* July 24, 1863. In their after-action reports, Colonel Archibald C. Godwin, 57th North Carolina, and Major Samuel M. Tate, 6th North Carolina, stated the latter regiment was responsible for capturing Heckman's two Napoleons. General Harry T. Hays claimed his brigade's skirmishers took the guns.

74. *Official Records,* vol. 27, pt. 1, p. 748; *Cleveland Morning Leader,* July 24, 1863; Busey, *These Honored Dead,* p. 232; Charles M. Schiely and William H. Cobbledick military service records, National Archives; *Columbus Evening Dispatch,* July 3, 1913.

75. David Thomson to John B. Bachelder, February 28, 1888, in *The Bachelder Papers,* vol. III, p. 1528; Henry Howe, *Historical Collections of Ohio,* vol. I (Cincinnati: C.J. Krehbiel & Co., 1904), p. 883.

76. Coddington, p. 295-296; *The Bachelder Papers,* vol. III, p. 1527; Andrew L. Harris, July 11, 1863, in the *Eaton Weekly Register,* July 23, 1863.

77. Joseph Gillis to his sister, July 22, 1863; Sylvanus Young military service records, National Archives.

78. Smith, p. 87-88.

79. Culp, in *The National Tribune,* March 19, 1885.

80. William B. Southerton reminiscences.

81. John H. Brinker testimony given July 30, 1863 at Meyer's court-martial; Seraphim Meyer to Theodore A. Meysenburg, July 14, 1863.

82. The verbal exchange between Meyer and the unnamed messenger is from Lieutenant Charles Harrison's testimony July 30, 1863 at Meyer's court-martial. Captain Weber was taken prisoner May 2 at Chancellorsville while serving on General Nathaniel McLean's staff, and had returned to the regiment June 8.

83. Adelbert Ames' and Charles H. Howard's testimony given July 27, 1863 at Meyer's court-martial. Additional testimony from 107th Ohio privates Philip May and Conrad F. Hornung, July 30, 1863; Edward C. Culp, "From the 25th Ohio," *The National Tribune,* June 4, 1885; Seraphim Meyer to Theodore A. Meysenburg, July 14, 1863; Findings of Department of the South examining board, November 25, 1863, in Meyer's military service records. Among the judges at Meyer's court-martial was Colonel Harris, 75th Ohio.

84. Frederick Nussbaum quoted in Smith, p. 225; *Official Records,* vol. 27, pt. 3, p. 461; pt. 1, p. 723; Orland Smith quoted in Hartwell Osborn, *Trials and Triumphs: The Record of the Fifty-fifth Ohio Volunteer Infantry* (Chicago: A.C. McClurg & Co., 1904), p. 97; Andrew F. Sweetland, "The 55th Ohio at Gettysburg," *The National Tribune,* September 9, 1909.

85. Schurz, *Reminiscences,* vol. III, p. 14.

86. Hurst, p. 66; George P. Metcalf memoir; Henry Henney diary.

87. Harry W. Pfanz, *Gettysburg: Culp's Hill and Cemetery Hill* (Chapel Hill: The University of North Carolina Press, 1993), p. 146; Adin B. Underwood, *The Three Years' Service of the Thirty-third Mass. Infantry Regiment 1862-1865* (Boston: A. Williams & Co., 1881), p. 122. [Reprinted as *33rd Massachusetts* in 1993 by Blue Acorn Press]. Busey & Martin, p. 84.

88. *Official Records,* vol. 27, pt. 1, p. 724; George W. Gephart, July 25, 1863, in *The Circleville Democrat,* August 7, 1863.

89. Frederick Nussbaum quoted in Smith, p. 226; Peter F. Young to John B. Bachelder, August 12, 1867, in *The Bachelder Papers*, vol. I, p. 310-311; Peter F. Young military service records, National Archives; Pfanz, *Gettysburg: Culp's Hill and Cemetery Hill*, p. 244; Kross, "The XI Corps at Gettysburg July 1, 1863," p. 50.

90. Pfanz, *Gettysburg: Culp's Hill and Cemetery Hill*, p. 242; *Official Records*, vol. 27, pt. 1, p. 718; George B. Fox to Andrew L. Harris, November 14, 1885, in *The Bachelder Papers*, vol. II, p. 1144; George B. Fox to his father, July 4, 1863.

91. New York Monuments Commission for the Battlefields of Gettysburg and Chattanooga, *Final Report of the Battlefield of Gettysburg*, vol. III (Albany: J.B. Lyon Company, 1900), p. 1246-1247. Hereafter referred to as *New York at Gettysburg*.

92. William B. Southerton reminiscences.

93. Busey, *These Honored Dead*, p. 226-228; Benjamin Morgan to Lissa Morgan, July 12, 1863; Howe, *Historical Collections of Ohio*, vol. I, p. 883.

94. *Delaware Gazette*, July 10 and 17, 1863.

95. Alfred E. Lee, "Reminiscences of the Gettysburg Battle," p. 57; Busey, *These Honored Dead*, p. 228-229; *Mansfield Daily Herald*, July 15, 1863; John Costin military service records, National Archives.

96. Stowel L. Burnham obituary, *The Hardin County Republican*, July 31, 1863; David Thomson to Luther Burnham, August 8, 1863, in Roderick H. Burnham, *The Burnham Family ...*, p. 256-257.

97. Alfred E. Lee to Lester T. Hunt, August 4, 1863, in *The Burnham Family ...*, p. 258-259.

98. *Official Records*, vol. 27, pt. 1, p. 115, 165; David T. Thackery, *A Light and Uncertain Hold: A History of the Sixty-sixth Ohio Volunteer Infantry* (Kent, Ohio: Kent State University Press, 1999), p. 26-29; Charles Candy assorted wartime correspondence found in his military service records, National Archives.

99. Reid, *Ohio in the War*, vol. I, p. 1001; William F. Fox, *Regimental Losses in the American Civil War 1861-1865* (Dayton: Press of Morningside Bookshop, 1985), p. 311, 312, 319; Steven H. Ward, *Buckeyes All: A Compendium and Bibliography of Ohio in the Civil War* (Dayton: privately printed, 1999), vol. I, p. 118, 124; vol. II, p. 203.

100. William H.H. Tallman memoir, Gettysburg National Military Park library.

101. Ibid.; Henry J. Knapp, "Gettysburg by a Soldier in the Ranks," *Jefferson Gazette*, February 12, 1912.

102. William H.H. Tallman memoir.

103. *Official Records*, vol. 27, pt. 1, p. 825, 836, 839; Charles P. Horton to John B. Bachelder, January 23, 1867, in *The Bachelder Papers*, vol. I, p. 292. Horton was General Greene's assistant adjutant general.

104. Harry W. Pfanz, *Gettysburg: The Second Day* (Chapel Hill: The University of North Carolina Press, 1987), p. 49-52; James Gildea memoir.

105. Kepler, p. 124; Galwey, p. 98, 99, 100.

106. Martin, p. 569; Henry J. Knapp, "Gettysburg by a Soldier in the Ranks."

107. Smith, p. 88-89.

108. Benjamin F. Stone Jr. to Olivia Allston, July 4, 1863, Ross County Historical Society, Chillicothe, Ohio; Henry Henney diary.

July 2

1. Sawyer, *The Eighth Ohio at Gettysburg*, p. 3; Azor H. Nickerson, "Personal Recollections of Two Visits to Gettysburg," *Scribner's Magazine* (July 1893), p. 21.

2. Thaddeus S. Potter, "The Battle of Gettysburg," *The National Tribune*, August 5, 1882; Busey & Martin, p. 42; William Wallace diary, Ohio Historical Society.

3. Pfanz, *Gettysburg: Culp's Hill and Cemetery Hill*, p. 111-112; *Official Records*, vol. 27, pt. 1, p. 836, 855-856; Warner, p. 187.

4. Joseph L. Gaul, "The Fifth Ohio Volunteer Infantry at Gettysburg," *The Ohio Soldier and National Picket Guard*, March 24, 1894; *Official Records*, vol. 27, pt. 1, p. 840; William H.H. Tallman memoir.

5. Edward C. Culp, July 5, 1863, in the *Norwalk Reflector*, July 21, 1863; Andrew L. Harris to John M. Brown, April 7, 1864, in *The Bachelder Papers*, vol. I, p. 138; George B. Fox to his father, July 4, 1863; Harris, July 11, 1863, in the *Eaton Weekly Register*, July 23, 1863.

6. Simon Hubler reminiscences, Civil War Miscellaneous Collection, USAMHI.

7. Ibid.

8. James Carver, "At Gettysburg," *The National Tribune*, April 30, 1914.

9. Hurst, p. 73; Andrew F. Sweetland, "The 55th Ohio at Gettysburg." Sweetland was wounded at noon July 3 behind the stone wall.

10. Luther B. Mesnard memoir.

11. Ibid.; Benjamin T. Arrington, *The Medal of Honor at Gettysburg* (Gettysburg: Thomas Publications, 1996), p. 25.

12. Luther B. Mesnard memoir.

13. Ibid.; *Norwalk Reflector*, July 14 and August 4, 1863; Charles Stacey military service records, National Archives.

14. Busey, *These Honored Dead*, p. 223, 224-226; *Official Records*, vol. 27, pt. 2, p. 663, 665; Hurst, p. 70. The Confederates battling Orland Smith's skirmishers belonged to Colonel Abner Perrin's South Carolina and Brigadier General James H. Lane's North Carolina brigades. The Rebel advance was spearheaded by a provisional battalion of sharpshooters commanded by Captain William T. Haskell, who was killed.

15. George W. Gephart, July 25, 1863, in *The Circleville Democrat*, August 7, 1863.

16. *Ibid.*

17. Samuel Fellers to William Millikin, July 12, 1863, in the *Fayette County Herald*, July 30, 1863. George Greiner and Joseph Barrett died of their wounds July 15 and 18, respectively, at the 11th Corps hospital.

18. *Ohio Rosters*, vol. VI, p. 131-135.

19. Military service and pension records, National Archives, for all named. Lawson, Ben Shattuck and A.T. Reed were confined at Richmond's Belle Isle and paroled in September 1863. All three eventually rejoined Company B.

20. Raymond M. Bell, *The Ancestry of Richard Milhous*

Nixon (Washington, Pa.: privately printed, 1970), p. 21; *Colonel Richard Enderlin* (Chillicothe: Scholl Printing Company, 1925), p. 53; Pfanz, *Gettysburg: Culp's Hill and Cemetery Hill,* p. 151.

21. *Ibid.,* p. 151; *Colonel Richard Enderlin,* p. 11, 53; Arrington, p. 4; Richard Enderlin and George Nixon III military service records, National Archives. One month after Nixon's death his sixth child, nine-year-old William Francis, died of an unspecified illness. Nixon's wife Margaret passed away March 18, 1865 at the age of 38. She was buried in McArthur, Ohio, while her husband's remains were interred in Ohio Plot C-4, Gettysburg National Cemetery.

22. Sawyer, *The Eighth Ohio at Gettysburg,* p. 4; Kepler, p. 126; Lemuel Jeffries diary, *Manuscripts* (Fall 1978), p. 274.

23. Galwey, p. 102; Elwood W. Christ, *"Over a Wide, Hot ... Crimson Plain": The Struggle for the Bliss Farm at Gettysburg July 2nd and 3rd, 1863* (Baltimore: Butternut and Blue, 1994), p. 13-18; *Official Records,* vol. 27, pt. 1, p. 456-457, 460; Thaddeus S. Potter, "On Skirmish," *The National Tribune,* January 24, 1895. Colonel Carroll reported Stewart was relieved by Grubb at noon. Lieutenant Colonel L.W. Carpenter, 4th Ohio, stated the time was 3 p.m.

24. *Ohio Rosters,* vol. II, p. 109; *Official Records,* vol. 21, p. 293; vol. 25, pt. 1, p. 366, 372; Peter Grubb military service and pension records, National Archives.

25. Kepler, p. 270. The effective strength of Grubb's force was extrapolated from figures in 4th Ohio adjutant William Wallace's diary. On July 2, Company G was composed of two officers (Grubb and Edgar) and 28 men, while Company I consisted of one officer (Shoub) and 18 men.

26. Busey, *These Honored Dead,* p. 219; *The Hardin County Republican,* July 10, 1863; Kepler, p. 127; Peter Grubb pension records, National Archives.

27. *Official Records,* vol. 27, pt. 1, p. 457; Sawyer, *The Eighth Ohio at Gettysburg,* p. 4; William W. Williams, *History of the Firelands, comprising Huron and Erie Counties, Ohio* (Cleveland: Press of Leader Printing Company, 1879), p. 135.

28. *Ibid.,* p. 135; Franklin Sawyer, *A Military History of the 8th Regiment Ohio Vol. Inf'y: Its Battles, Marches and Army Movements* (Cleveland: Fairbanks & Co. Printers, 1881), p. 82, 115. [Reprinted as *8th Ohio Volunteer Infantry* in 1994 by Blue Acorn Press].

29. *Ibid.,* p. 15; *Official Records,* vol. 27, pt. 1, p. 461; Sawyer, *The Eighth Ohio at Gettysburg,* p. 4.

30. *Ibid.,* p. 4.

31. *Ibid.,* p. 4; *Official Records,* vol. 27, pt. 1, p. 461.

32. *Ibid.,* p. 738; Anthony Grodzicki quoted from February 4, 1864 testimony during court-martial of Private Valentine Kline, Company I, 61st Ohio, File #nn1430, RG 153, National Archives; Jacob F. Mader to Mary L. Hartmeyer, July 5, 1863, courtesy of Mac Schumm, Circleville, Ohio.

33. *Official Records,* vol. 27, pt. 1, p. 738; Mader to Hartmeyer, July 5, 1863; Abraham Bope to his father, July 16, 1863, courtesy of Tony Lemut, Parma, Ohio.

34. Huntington, "Notes of Service."

35. William E. Parmelee, "At Gettysburg. The Experience of an Ohio Artilleryman," *The National Tribune,* September 2, 1886; "The Civil War Diary of Orin G. Dority (Part 1)," *Northwest Ohio Quarterly* (Winter, 1964-1965), p. 16; John

H. Merrell diary.

36. Ibid.; *Official Records,* vol. 27, pt. 1, p. 894; Huntington, "Notes of Service."

37. James F. Huntington to Ellen Sophronia Huntington, July 6, 1863, in *The Marietta Register,* July 17, 1863.

38. Pfanz, *Gettysburg: Culp's Hill and Cemetery Hill,* p. 177-179; "The Civil War Diary of Orin G. Dority (Part 1)," p. 16.

39. Ibid., p. 16; *The Portage County Democrat,* August 5, 1863; Wasson, "Civil War Letters of Darwin Cody," p. 389.

40. Jacob F. Mader to Mary L. Hartmeyer, July 5, 1863; Busey, *These Honored Dead,* p. 224; Daniel W. Williams military service records, National Archives.

41. Edward C. Culp, July 5, 1863, in the *Norwalk Reflector,* July 21, 1863.

42. Andrew L. Harris, July 11, 1863, in the *Eaton Weekly Register,* July 23, 1863; William B. Southerton reminiscences.

43. Ibid. Seven weeks later Jackson was seriously wounded at Fort Wagner on Morris Island, S.C., and remained hospitalized until January 20, 1865.

44. Benjamin F. Stone Jr. to Olivia Allston, July 4, 1863.

45. Hurst, p. 69.

46. Unidentified 55th Ohio correspondence, July 26, 1863, in the *Norwalk Reflector,* August 14, 1863.

47. William A. Ewing, July 11, 1863, in the *Toledo Blade,* July 18, 1863. Ewing used the pen name "Wanderer" for his newspaper correspondence.

48. Samuel P. Bates, *History of Pennsylvania Volunteers, 1861-5,* vol. V (Harrisburg: B. Singerly, State Printer, 1871), p. 898; William A. Ewing to his mother, July 4 and 11, 1863, in the *Toledo Blade,* July 11 and 18; Huntington, "Notes of Service." The evening of Edmonds' death a hospital attendant wrote: "One poor fellow who occupied this tent has left this world of suffering and gone to Jesus in whom he trusted. He was a fine intelligent man, was superintendent of the sabbath school in the town at which he enlisted, his name is John Edmonds, Co H 1st Ohio light artillery. He leaves a mother and sisters to whom he a short time previous had dictated a letter. He had his leg amputated twice." [Marcus, *A New Canaan Private in the Civil War: Letters of Justus M. Silliman, 17th Connecticut Volunteers,* p. 45].

49. Pfanz, *Gettysburg: Culp's Hill and Cemetery Hill,* p. 171-174; *The Marietta Register,* July 17, 1863; Wallace Hill military service records, National Archives; Martin R. Andrews, editor & compiler, *History of Marietta and Washington County, Ohio and Representative Citizens,* vol. III (Chicago: Biographical Publishing Company, 1902), p. 619.

50. William Jenvey military service records, National Archives.

51. William Jenvey quoted in Andrews, p. 625-626.

52. Gregory A. Coco, *A Strange and Blighted Land, Gettysburg: The Aftermath of a Battle* (Gettysburg: Thomas Publications, 1995), p. 96, 97; Stephen J. Braddock military service records, National Archives.

53. William Jenvey quoted in Andrews, p. 626.

54. Boatner, p. 336.

55. Charles E. Hazlett obituary, *Zanesville Daily Courier,* July 11, 1863; Eugene E. Taylor, *Gouverneur Kemble Warren: The Life and Letters of an American Soldier* (Boston: Hough-

ton-Mifflin Company, 1932), p. 129.

56. Pfanz, *Gettysburg: The Second Day,* p. 227, 228, 240; George W. Cullum, *Biographical Register of the Officers and Graduates of the U.S. Military Academy* (Boston: Houghton, Mifflin and Company, 1891), p. 784.

57. James Gildea memoir.

58. Ibid.

59. Ibid. The U.S. Regulars Gildea mentions probably belonged to Colonel Hannibal Day's 1st Brigade, 2nd Division, 5th Corps.

60. *Official Records,* vol. 27, pt. 1, p. 662.

61. James Gildea memoir.

62. Benjamin F. Reed quoted in the *Columbus Sunday Dispatch,* June 29, 1913.

63. James Gildea memoir. In the 5th Corps' 3rd Division, Colonel Fisher commanded the 3rd Brigade while Colonel William McCandless led the 1st Brigade, Pennsylvania Reserves. Privates Massie and Kline recuperated and rejoined the battery, mustering out when their service terms expired in the fall of 1864.

64. Ibid.; *Official Records,* vol. 27, pt. 1, p. 662, 661, 237.

65. *Ibid.,* p. 594.

66. *Ibid.,* p. 584; Francis W. Seeley pension records, National Archives.

67. *Report of the Congressional Committee on the Conduct of the War,* 1865 series, vol. 1, p. 9.

68. "Historical Sketches of the United States Army," *Journal of the Military Service Institution* (September 1890), p. 861; *Ashtabula Weekly Telegraph,* July 18, 1863.

69. *Official Records,* vol. 27, pt. 1, p. 590, 591.

70. *Ibid.,* p. 591; Francis W. Seeley pension records, National Archives.

71. Ibid.; *Official Records,* vol. 27, pt. 1, p. 534. After the war Seeley was a longtime resident of Lake City, Minn., where he flourished as a merchant and postmaster. He also served a term in the Minnesota legislature, and in 1887-1888 was the state's adjutant general. He died December 30, 1910 at Sawtelle, Los Angeles County, Calif.

72. Lemuel Jeffries diary, *Manuscripts* (Fall 1978), p. 274; William Jenvey in Andrews, p. 625.

73. Huntington, "Notes of Service."

74. Ibid. Sickles was seriously wounded when a Confederate cannonball or shell struck his right leg, necessitating its amputation just above the knee.

75. *Official Records,* vol. 27, pt. 1, p. 773-774, 826.

76. *Ibid.,* pt. 2, p. 446-447.

77. Pfanz, *Gettysburg: Culp's Hill and Cemetery Hill,* p. 206, 207, 211.

78. *Ibid.,* p. 213-221; *Official Records,* vol. 27, pt. 1, p. 738, 856.

79. William E. Roe, "Brigadier General Rufus R. Dawes: A Biographical Sketch," in Mary W. Ferris, compiler, *Dawes-Gates Ancestral Lines: A Memorial Volume Containing the American Ancestry of Rufus R. Dawes,* vol. I (privately printed, 1943), p. 3, 56; L.J. Kozlowski, "To Stand For All They Won: Rufus Dawes of the Iron Brigade," *Timeline* (March-April 1995), p. 4; Rufus R. Dawes, *A Memoir: Rufus R. Dawes* (New York: Devinne Press, 1900), p. 12, 20.

80. Rufus R. Dawes, "With the Sixth Wisconsin at Gettys-burg," *Sketches of War History 1861-1865,* vol. 3 (Cincinnati: Robert Clarke & Co., 1890), p. 386-387.

81. Pfanz, *Gettysburg: Culp's Hill and Cemetery Hill,* p. 223, 204; *Official Records,* vol. 27, pt. 1, p. 836; Joseph R. Lynn, "At Gettysburg. What the 29th Ohio did During the Three Days' Fighting," *The National Tribune,* October 7, 1897; Henry J. Knapp, "Gettysburg by a Soldier in the Ranks"; "Man Round the World" (7th Ohio), July 6, 1863, in the *Cleveland Plain Dealer,* July 14, 1863.

82. *Official Records,* vol. 27, pt. 1, p. 836, 840-841; Isaac Stratton military service records, National Archives.

83. *Official Records,* vol. 27, pt. 2, p. 480; Terry L. Jones, editor, *The Civil War Memoirs of Captain William J. Seymour: Reminiscences of a Louisiana Tiger* (Baton Rouge: Louisiana State University Press, 1991), p. 73.

84. *Ibid.,* p. 75; *Official Records,* vol. 27, pt. 2, p. 480; Terry L. Jones, *Lee's Tigers: The Louisiana Infantry in the Army of Northern Virginia* (Baton Rouge: Louisiana State University Press, 1987), p. 172.

85. Pfanz, *Gettysburg: Culp's Hill and Cemetery Hill,* p. 244-249.

86. Andrew L. Harris to John B. Bachelder, March 14, 1881, in *The Bachelder Papers,* vol. II, p. 746; Harris to John M. Brown, April 7, 1864, in *Ibid.,* vol. I, p. 138; Harris, July 11, 1863, in the *Eaton Weekly Register,* July 23, 1863.

87. Andrew L. Harris to John B. Bachelder, March 14, 1881, in *The Bachelder Papers,* vol. II, p. 745.

88. *Official Records,* vol. 27, pt. 2, p. 480.

89. Harris to Bachelder, *op. cit.,* p. 746; George S. Clements, "The 25th Ohio at Gettysburg," *The National Tribune,* August 6, 1891; Edward C. Culp, July 5, 1863, in the *Norwalk Reflector,* July 21, 1863; Culp, *The 25th Ohio Vet. Vol. Infantry,* p. 79.

90. Peter F. Young to John B. Bachelder, August 12, 1867, in *The Bachelder Papers,* vol. I, p. 311; Busey, *These Honored Dead,* p. 231.

91. George Billau, July 18, 1863, in *The Summit County Beacon,* July 30, 1863; *Ohio Rosters,* vol. VII, p. 654-657.

92. *Ibid.,* p. 630-633; Silas Shuler to Asa Shuler, July 16, 1863, in William T. Parsons & Mary S. Heimburger, "Shuler Family Correspondence," *Pennsylvania Folklife* (Spring 1980), p. 112.

93. Peter F. Young to John B. Bachelder, August 12, 1867, in *The Bachelder Papers,* vol. I, p. 311; Frederick Nussbaum quoted in Smith, p. 226.

94. *Cleveland Herald,* July 24, 1863. Young's attending surgeon at Cleveland's military hospital, writing September 3 to have the lieutenant's medical leave extended, explained that the bullet "entered the thorax, to the *left* of the sternum between the third and fourth ribs and passed out at the axilla, and from there through the left arm, the wounds being healed up, but leaving partial paralysis of the left arm." Young rejoined the army in October, briefly served on General Ames' staff and was promoted captain of Company G, 107th Ohio, on December 1, 1863. He resigned his commission 12 months later.

95. *The Bachelder Papers,* vol. I, p. 311, 312, 149; Frederick Nussbaum quoted in Smith, p. 226-227. During Colonel Seraphim Meyer's court-martial, Captain Lutz testified that

on July 1, when the 107th Ohio was ordered to retreat to Gettysburg, he "was struck by a ball & carried from the field."

96. Frederick Smith, Battery I, 1st New York Light Artillery, quoted in *New York at Gettysburg*, vol. III, p. 1247.

97. *Official Records*, vol. 27, pt. 1, p. 718, 719; Albert W. Peck, "Gettysburg. The Part Taken by the Eleventh Corps," *The National Tribune*, December 12, 1889.

98. William B. Southerton reminiscences.

99. George B. Fox to his father, July 4, 1863.

100. Ladley, p. 142-143, 147. An account of James C. Mulharen's death and funeral was published in the *Eaton Weekly Register*, July 30, 1863.

101. Wesley Raikes military service records, National Archives; Henry L. Morey to J.W. King, date unknown, in the *Eaton Weekly Register*, August 20, 1863. Raikes was buried in Ohio Plot E-18, Gettysburg National Cemetery.

102. Ladley, p. 148.

103. *Ohio Rosters*, vol. VI, p. 238-242, 222-226, 221; William B. Southerton reminiscences; *Cincinnati Gazette*, July 17, 1863.

104. John A. Starrett quoted in W.B. Southerton reminiscences

105. Ladley, p. 143, 147.

106. William B. Southerton reminiscences.

107. George B. Fox to his father, July 4, 1863.

108. *Ohio Rosters*, vol. VI, p. 216, 231, 246; Joseph F. Potts to Benjamin Morgan, November 22, 1863, courtesy of Jacqueline Ann Lane.

109. Pfanz, *Gettysburg: Culp's Hill and Cemetery Hill*, p. 263, 272; *Official Records*, vol. 27, pt. 1, p. 743.

110. *Ibid.*, p. 894; R. Bruce Ricketts to John B. Bachelder, March 2, 1866, in *The Bachelder Papers*, vol. I, p. 236.

111. Pfanz, *Gettysburg: Culp's Hill and Cemetery Hill*, p. 263; *Official Records*, vol. 27, pt. 1, p. 457; Kepler, p. 128.

112. James F. Huntington, July 6, 1863, in *The Marietta Register*, July 17, 1863.

113. *Official Records*, vol. 27, pt. 1, p. 457.

114. Joseph L. Dickelman, "Gen. Carroll's Gibraltar Brigade at Gettysburg," *The National Tribune*, December 10, 1908; Gary G. Lash, *The Gibraltar Brigade on East Cemetery Hill* (Baltimore: Butternut and Blue, 1995), p. 83, 86.

115. Kepler, p. 129; Byron Dolbear military service records, National Archives. Company C's total strength was given as 34 in 4th Ohio adjutant William Wallace's diary.

116. Dickelman, "Gen. Carroll's Gibraltar Brigade at Gettysburg;" Kepler, p. 130; Silverman, p. 275; Busey, *These Honored Dead*, p. 219.

117. Kepler, p. 129; *Official Records*, vol. 27, pt. 2, p. 481, 485, 486; Pfanz, *Gettysburg: Culp's Hill and Cemetery Hill*, p. 275, 282.

118. Dickelman, "Gen. Carroll's Gibraltar Brigade at Gettysburg."

119. Andrew Jackson quoted in W.B. Southerton reminiscences.

120. *Official Records*, vol. 27, pt. 1, p. 460.

121. Dickelman, "Gen. Carroll's Gibraltar Brigade at Gettysburg"; Silverman, p. 275; Kepler, p. 130; *The Hardin County Republican*, July 10, 1863. Four of Company G's

dead, including Lieutenant Edgar, were buried in a cornfield opposite the Abraham Bryan house. All were reinterred in Gettysburg National Cemetery.

122. Andrew L. Harris to John B. Bachelder, March 14, 1881, in *The Bachelder Papers*, vol. II, p. 747; Harris, July 11, 1863, in the *Eaton Weekly Register*, July 23, 1863; George B. Fox to his father, July 4, 1863.

123. William B. Southerton reminiscences; *Ohio Rosters*, vol. VI, p. 207, 218; Gregory A. Coco, *A Vast Sea of Misery: A History and Guide to the Union and Confederate Field Hospitals at Gettysburg, July 1–November 20, 1863* (Gettysburg: Thomas Publications, 1988), p. 105. Norman Brooks survived his facial wound and transferred to the Veteran Reserve Corps in February 1864.

124. Martin L. Buchwalter diary; Smith, p. 103.

125. Coco, *A Vast Sea of Misery*, p. 61; Kepler, p. 192, 193.

126. Franklin B. Nickerson quoted in Kepler, p. 193-194; F.B. Nickerson military service records, National Archives. The sergeant recovered and transferred to the Veteran Reserve Corps in March 1864.

127. Christ, p. 41, 42; *Official Records*, vol. 27, pt. 1, p. 461.

128. Sawyer, *The Eighth Ohio at Gettysburg*, p. 5; Galwey, p. 103; James E. Gregg, July 4, 1863, to *The Sandusky Register*, reprinted in the *Cleveland Morning Leader*, July 14, 1863; Lester V. McKesson military service records, National Archives.

129. Sawyer, *The Eighth Ohio at Gettysburg*, p. 4-5.

130. *Ibid.*, p. 5; David Lewis, July 5, 1863, in the *Bucyrus Weekly Journal*, July 17, 1863; Busey, *These Honored Dead*, p. 221.

131. Sawyer, *The Eighth Ohio at Gettysburg*, p. 5; Galwey, p. 105. According to two other 8th Ohio accounts, Companies B and H also spent time on the skirmish line during the night of July 2-3.

132. Sawyer, *The Eighth Ohio at Gettysburg*, p. 5.

133. Thaddeus S. Potter, "The Battle of Gettysburg."

134. Sawyer, *The Eighth Ohio at Gettysburg*, p. 5.

135. Huntington, "Notes of Service."

136. John Gibbon, "The Council of War on the Second Day," *Battles and Leaders of the Civil War*, vol. III, p. 313-314.

July 3

1. Huntington, "Notes of Service."

2. *Official Records*, vol. 27, pt. 1, p. 775; Quaife, *From the Cannon's Mouth*, p. 230; Pfanz, *Gettysburg: Culp's Hill and Cemetery Hill*, p. 285-287.

3. *Ibid.*, p. 287, 290-291.

4. *Ibid.*, p. 291-292; Huntington, "Notes of Service."

5. Kevin E. O'Brien, " 'A Perfect Roar of Musketry': Candy's Brigade in the Fight for Culp's Hill," *The Gettysburg Magazine* (July 1993), p. 87; *Official Records*, vol. 27, pt. 1, p. 841.

6. Eugene Powell to John B. Bachelder, March 23, 1886, in *The Bachelder Papers*, vol. II, p. 1248-1249; Powell, "Rebellion's High Tide: Dashed Against the Immovable Rocks of Gettysburg," *The National Tribune*, July 5, 1900.

7. Ibid.

8. Charles E. Butts military service records, National Archives; *Urbana Citizen and Gazette,* January 15 and 22, 1863. Butts recuperated and rejoined the regiment for a time, receiving promotions by July 1865 to first lieutenant, captain and major, though he never mustered at the latter rank.

9. Eugene Powell to John B. Bachelder, March 23, 1886, in *The Bachelder Papers,* vol. II, p. 1249; Powell, "Rebellion's High Tide."

10. John T. Morgan, "Wounded at Gettysburg," *The National Tribune,* May 22, 1924; *Official Records,* vol. 27, pt. 1, p. 844.

11. *Ohio Rosters,* vol. V, p. 524; Busey, *These Honored Dead,* p. 224; Robert T. Pennoyer & Mark Omvig, editors, *Diaries of Pvt. John W. Houtz, 66th Ohio Volunteer Infantry 1863-1864* (Homer, N.Y.: privately published, 1994), p. 1.

12. *Ibid.,* p. 26, 1.

13. William Guy quoted in the *Columbus Sunday Dispatch,* June 29, 1913.

14. *Ibid.;* Charles Candy, July 4, 1863, in the *Urbana Union,* July 15, 1863; Powell, "Rebellion's High Tide"; William Scott military service records, National Archives.

15. James H. Corbin quoted in the *Columbus Sunday Dispatch,* June 29, 1913.

16. George Milledge to Mary Milledge, July 7, 1863, Robert L. Brake Collection, USAMHI; William M. Sayre to his family, July 5, 1863, Civil War Miscellaneous Collection, USAMHI; Robert H. Russell to his father, July 5, 1863, courtesy of L.M. Strayer, Dayton. Milledge and Sayre were killed in Georgia within three weeks of each other during 1864's Atlanta campaign.

17. John T. Mitchell to Alfred E. Lee, August 15, 1887, in *The Bachelder Papers,* vol. III, p. 1508; Eugene Powell to John B. Bachelder, March 23, 1886, in *Ibid.,* vol. II, p. 1249.

18. Pfanz, *Gettysburg: Culp's Hill and Cemetery Hill,* p. 298; Gaul, "The Fifth Ohio Volunteer Infantry at Gettysburg."

19. Ibid.

20. *Official Records,* vol. 27, pt. 1, p. 846, 839.

21. *Ibid.,* p. 839; "Regiments Furnished by Cincinnati and What They Did in the War," *Cincinnati Enquirer,* September 9, 1898; Henry E. Symmes to his brother, July 4, 1863, in the *Cincinnati Daily Commercial,* July 9, 1863.

22. *Official Records,* vol. 27, pt. 1, p. 846; pt. 2, p. 511, 568; Pfanz, *Gettysburg: Culp's Hill and Cemetery Hill,* p. 313, 314.

23. Gaul, "The Fifth Ohio Volunteer Infantry at Gettysburg."

24. "Corine" (5th Ohio), July 6, 1863, in the *Cincinnati Daily Times,* July 14, 1863.

25. *Ibid.*

26. *Ibid.;* Henry E. Symmes to his brother, July 4, 1863, in the *Cincinnati Daily Commercial,* July 9, 1863; *Official Records,* vol. 27, pt. 1, p. 840.

27. George Case military service records, National Archives; Gaul, "The Fifth Ohio Volunteer Infantry at Gettysburg."

28. Pfanz, *Gettysburg: Culp's Hill and Cemetery Hill,* p. 299.

29. *Official Records,* vol. 27, pt. 1, p. 842, 843.

30. Orlando Gunn, July 12, 1863, in the *Ashtabula Sentinel,* August 5, 1863; Henry J. Knapp, "Gettysburg by a Soldier in the Ranks."

31. Myron T. Wright to S.A. Lane, date unknown, in *The Summit County Beacon,* July 30, 1863.

32. *Official Records,* vol. 27, pt. 1, p. 843; Knapp, "Gettysburg by a Soldier in the Ranks"; John H. SeCheverall, *Journal History of the Twenty-ninth Ohio Veteran Volunteers, 1861-1865* (Cleveland, 1883), p. 72; Nathan L. Parmater diary; George Hayward military service records, National Archives. Nearly complete lists of the 29th Ohio's casualties and their injuries were provided by Captain M.T. Wright in *The Summit County Beacon,* July 30, 1863, and by Chaplain L.D. Ames on July 5 for the *Conneaut Reporter.* Ames' list was published July 18 in the *Cleveland Morning Leader.*

33. *Official Records,* vol. 27, pt. 1, p. 843.

34. *Ibid.,* p. 843, 844; "Losses of the 29th Ohio," *Cleveland Morning Leader,* July 18, 1863; Edward Soden to his siblings, July 27, 1863, Ken Lawrence Collection, Orwell, Ohio.

35. *Official Records,* vol. 27, pt. 1, p. 843; Nathan L. Parmater diary; Myron T. Wright in *The Summit County Beacon,* July 30, 1863.

36. Knapp, "Gettysburg by a Soldier in the Ranks."

37. Myron T. Wright to S.A. Lane, date unknown, in *The Summit County Beacon,* July 30, 1863. Thomas Bare was killed in action May 7, 1864 at Dug Gap, Georgia.

38. *Official Records,* vol. 27, pt. 1, p. 843, 842; Joseph R. Lynn, "At Gettysburg"; Knapp, "Gettysburg by a Soldier in the Ranks"; Orlando Gunn, July 12, 1863, in the *Ashtabula Sentinel,* August 5, 1863.

39. *Official Records,* vol. 27, pt. 1, p. 184, 841; "Man Round the World" (7th Ohio), July 6, 1863, in the *Cleveland Plain Dealer,* July 14, 1863; Harry M. Dean, July 5, 1863, in *The Portage County Democrat,* July 15, 1863.

40. Sherman R. Norris military service records, National Archives; Norris, "Ohio at Gettysburg," *The National Tribune,* June 9, 1887.

41. *Ibid.*

42. *Official Records,* vol. 27, pt. 1, p. 841; 7th Ohio invoice of Ordnance and Ordnance Stores, William R. Creighton Papers, Western Reserve Historical Society; James H. Merrell to his uncle, July 4, 1863, in the *Western Reserve Chronicle,* July 15, 1863; David Mouat, "Three Years in the 29th Pennsylvania Volunteers," unpublished memoir, Historical Society of Pennsylvania, Philadelphia.

43. *Official Records,* vol. 27, pt. 1, p. 841; Norris, "Ohio at Gettysburg"; Charles Carroll military service records, National Archives.

44. Busey, *These Honored Dead,* p. 220; George L. Wood, *The Seventh Regiment: A Record* (New York: James Miller, 1865), p. 159. A list of the 7th Ohio's casualties for July 2-3 accompanies a handwritten copy of Creighton's Gettysburg after-action report dated July 6, 1863, and is part of the William R. Creighton Papers at Western Reserve Historical Society library. The *Ohio Rosters* list Private Melton as being wounded July 3, but transferring to Company G, 5th Ohio, on October 31, 1864.

45. *Official Records,* vol. 27, pt. 2, p. 519; pt. 1, p. 841; Mervin Clark to relatives, July 4, 1863, in the *Cleveland Herald,* July 10, 1863; Gilbert D. Bertholf, "The Twelfth Corps. The Part They Took in the Big Battle of Gettysburg," *The National Tribune,* May 11, 1893. Colonel Creighton reported 78 Confederates surrendered to the 7th Ohio.

46. *Ibid.;* Nathan L. Parmater diary; *Official Records,* vol. 27, pt. 1, p. 841, 858.

47. Frederick Nussbaum quoted in Smith, p. 227; *Official Records,* vol. 27, pt. 1, p. 720.

48. Pfanz, *Gettysburg: Culp's Hill and Cemetery Hill,* p. 279-280.

49. Hurst, p. 72-73.

50. Ibid., p. 73.

51. Busey, *These Honored Dead,* p. 224-226; *Ohio Rosters,* vol. VI, p. 156-160.

52. Alonzo Keeler diary, Civil War Miscellaneous Collection, USAMHI.

53. Unidentified 55th Ohio correspondence, July 26, 1863, in the *Norwalk Reflector,* August 14, 1863. Originally buried in James Pierce's orchard, Myer was reinterred in Ohio Plot B-5, Gettysburg National Cemetery.

54. Galwey, p. 107-108.

55. David Lewis, July 5, 1863, in the *Bucyrus Weekly Journal,* July 17, 1863.

56. Sawyer, *The Eighth Ohio at Gettysburg,* p. 6; John H. Jack, July 6, 1863, in *The Sandusky Register,* July 14, 1863.

57. David Lewis, July 5, 1863, in the *Bucyrus Weekly Journal,* July 17, 1863; Sawyer, *The Eighth Ohio at Gettysburg,* p. 6; Busey, *These Honored Dead,* p. 221; *The Elyria Independent Democrat,* July 22, 1863; Benson E. Beamon to his mother, July 4, 1863, in *The Elyria Independent Gazette,* July 15, 1863; Lucien Abbott testimony given at Edward H. Irish court-martial, File #ll1150, RG 153, National Archives; Azor H. Nickerson military service and pension records, National Archives. In two postwar narratives of the battle Sawyer erroneously gave July 2 as the date of Nickerson's wounding. Accounts by Lucien Abbott, Benson Beamon and Edward Irish in 1863 all agree Nickerson was hit the morning of July 3. Nickerson himself indicated the latter date in an 1893 magazine article.

58. Sawyer, *The Eighth Ohio at Gettysburg,* p. 6.

59. Galwey, p. 109-111.

60. Thaddeus S. Potter, "The Battle of Gettysburg"; Frassanito, *Early Photography at Gettysburg,* p. 330-331.

61. *Official Records,* vol. 27, pt. 1, p. 454, 467; Galwey, p. 109.

62. Sawyer, *The Eighth Ohio at Gettysburg,* p. 6; Galwey, p. 113.

63. Thaddeus S. Potter, "The Battle of Gettysburg"; Potter, "On Skirmish. Gallant Behavior of the 8th Ohio at Gettysburg," *The National Tribune,* January 31, 1895; Horace Judson to John B. Bachelder, October 17, 1887, in *The Bachelder Papers,* vol. III, p. 1515.

64. Henry A. Brotts, "Repelling Pickett's Men," *The National Tribune,* September 1, 1910; Potter, "On Skirmish."

65. William E. Parmelee, "At Gettysburg."

66. Ibid.; William A. Ewing, July 11, 1863, in the *Toledo Blade,* July 18, 1863.

67. William E. Parmelee, "At Gettysburg"; James F. Huntington to Ellen Sophronia Huntington, July 6, 1863, in *The Marietta Register,* July 17, 1863.

68. *Ibid.;* Huntington, "Notes of Service."

69. William E. Parmelee, September 1, 1918, to the *Marietta Sunday Observer.*

70. *Official Records,* vol. 27, pt. 1, p. 238; "The Civil War Diary of Orin G. Dority (Part 1)," p. 17; John H. Merrell diary.

71. William Jenvey quoted in Andrews, p. 626; "Outis" (Battery C, 1st West Virginia Light Artillery), July 4, 1863, in *The Marietta Register,* July 17, 1863.

72. James F. Huntington to Ellen Sophronia Huntington, July 6, 1863, in *The Marietta Register,* July 17, 1863; Huntington, "Notes of Service."

73. Ibid.; John H. Merrell diary.

74. Huntington, "Notes of Service."

75. Henry Henney diary.

76. George P. Metcalf memoir.

77. Luther B. Mesnard memoir. William E. Pollock died July 5. Private Sumner A. Wing of Company D, 55th Ohio, tended Pollock at the 11th Corps hospital. "He was torn by a piece of shell — a terrible wound. I remember just how he looked, with his pale, pleading face. Poor fellow, we could do but a little for him." [Osborn, *Trials and Triumphs,* p. 252].

78. William I. Fee, *Bringing the Sheaves: Gleanings from Harvest Fields in Ohio, Kentucky and West Virginia* (Cincinnati: Cranston & Curts, 1896), p. 445, 447. Moore family records were provided to the author by Mary Kate Liming, Felicity, Ohio.

79. William H.H. Tallman memoir.

80. Elisha B. Seaman quoted in the *Columbus Sunday Dispatch,* June 29, 1913; Samuel W. Hart, "At Gettysburg with the Twelfth Corps," *The National Tribune,* June 23, 1927.

81. Gaul, "The Fifth Ohio Volunteer Infantry at Gettysburg."

82. William E. Parmelee, "At Gettysburg"; *Ohio Rosters,* vol. X, p. 409.

83. John H. Jack, July 6, 1863, in *The Sandusky Register,* July 14, 1863; William H. Clough to Deborah Hayden, July 22, 1863, in *The Elyria Independent Democrat,* August 5, 1863; Thaddeus S. Potter, "The Battle of Gettysburg"; Stephen Strange military service records, National Archives.

84. Sawyer, *The Eighth Ohio at Gettysburg,* p. 6; Sawyer, *A Military History of the 8th Regiment Ohio Vol. Inf'y,* p. 130; *Cleveland Morning Leader,* July 14, 1863.

85. Galwey, p. 113-114; *Cleveland Morning Leader,* July 16, 1863.

86. Henry J. Hunt, "The Third Day at Gettysburg," *Battles and Leaders of the Civil War,* vol. III, p. 374; Sawyer, *The Eighth Ohio at Gettysburg,* p. 7.

87. Thaddeus S. Potter, "On Skirmish."

88. Coddington, p. 489-491.

89. William H. Clough to Deborah Hayden, July 22, 1863, in *The Elyria Independent Democrat,* August 5, 1863; Potter, "On Skirmish."

90. Coddington, p. 506; *Official Records,* vol. 27, pt. 1, p. 750.

91. Henry A. Brotts, "Repelling Pickett's Men"; Potter, "On Skirmish." Sawyer mentioned in a letter written to his congressman the next day that on July 3 the 8th Ohio was accompanied by "one or two fragments" of unnamed regiments.

92. Franklin Sawyer to Samuel T. Worcester, July 4, 1863, in the *Fremont Journal,* July 17, 1863; Sawyer, *The Eighth Ohio at Gettysburg,* p. 7; Wells W. Miller and Henry A. Brotts military service records, National Archives.

93. Sawyer to Worcester, July 4, 1863; *Official Records,* vol. 27, pt. 1, p. 462; Coddington, p. 507.

94. William H. Clough to Deborah Hayden, July 22, 1863, in *The Elyria Independent Democrat,* August 5, 1863; Sawyer, *The Eighth Ohio at Gettysburg,* p. 7.

95. *Official Records,* vol. 27, pt. 1, p. 462; Horace Judson to John B. Bachelder, October 17, 1887, in *The Bachelder Papers,* vol. III, p. 1516; *Cleveland Morning Leader,* July 16, 1863; Galwey, p. 118-119; Edward Jones military service records, National Archives. Corporal Silas Judson died of his wounds September 9, 1863.

96. Lucien Abbott to Horace R. Pond, July 4, 1863, in *The Elyria Independent Democrat,* July 15, 1863; Benson E. Beamon to his mother, July 4, 1863, in *The Elyria Independent Gazette,* July 15, 1863.

97. Coddington, p. 507-508.

98. Sawyer, *The Eighth Ohio at Gettysburg,* p. 7; Potter, "On Skirmish."

99. David Shultz, *"Double Canister at Ten Yards": The Federal Artillery and the Repulse of Pickett's Charge* (Redondo Beach, Calif.: Rank and File Publications, 1995), p. 18, 32, 48.

100. Kent M. Brown, *Cushing of Gettysburg: The Story of a Union Artillery Commander* (Lexington: The University Press of Kentucky, 1993), p. 134, 166-167; *Ohio Rosters,* vol. II, p. 89-120.

101. Shultz, p. 52, 55.

102. Sawyer, *The Eighth Ohio at Gettysburg,* p. 7, 8.

103. Galwey, p. 118; Galwey to his father, July 5, 1863, in the *Cleveland Plain Dealer,* date unknown; *Official Records,* vol. 27, pt. 1, p. 462; Arrington, p. 33, 34; *Ohio Rosters,* vol. II, p. 252, 253, 740; John Miller and James Richmond military service records, National Archives. Sawyer's after-action report incorrectly identified Corporal Miller as Sergeant Daniel Miller, also of Company G. In Lieutenant Galwey's July 5 letter home he claimed the third captured flag belonged to the 16th North Carolina. Sawyer never was able to identify it positively, as he reported July 5: "One captured by Private James Richmond ... was taken from him on the field by a staff officer of our army, but whose name is unknown."

104. *Official Records,* vol. 27, pt. 1, p. 462; Sawyer, *The Eighth Ohio at Gettysburg,* p. 8; William H. Clough to Deborah Hayden, July 22, 1863, in *The Elyria Independent Democrat,* August 5, 1863.

105. Busey, *These Honored Dead,* p. 220-222; Benson E. Beamon to his mother, July 4, 1863, in *The Elyria Independent Gazette,* July 15, 1863. The regiment's number of wounded was derived by subtracting the killed/mortally wounded and missing men from the 8th's total loss of 102.

106. Sawyer to Samuel T. Worcester, July 4, 1863, in the *Fremont Journal,* July 17, 1863; David S. Koons, "The 8th Ohio at Gettysburg," *The National Tribune,* November 5, 1908; Galwey, p. 119; John D. Madeira quoted in "Gettysburg Memorials: The Eighth and Seventy-Fifth Ohio on that Memorable Field," *The Ohio Soldier,* January 14, 1888.

107. Sawyer, *The Eighth Ohio at Gettysburg,* p. 8; Galwey, p. 119; Kepler, p. 131-132; Potter, "On Skirmish."

108. *Official Records,* vol. 27, pt. 1, p. 463, 459; Busey, *These Honored Dead,* p. 219. Craig reported only 102 prisoners were turned over to him on July 3. Originally buried in the Peter Frey orchard, Private Sheak was reinterred in the New Jersey plot, Gettysburg National Cemetery.

109. Azor H. Nickerson, "Personal Recollections of Two Visits to Gettysburg," p. 21.

110. Angelo D. Juarez, "The Tarnished Saber: Major Azor Howett Nickerson, USA, His Life and Times," unpublished manuscript; *Official Records,* vol. 25, pt. 1, p. 373; Sawyer, *The Eighth Ohio at Gettysburg,* p. 5.

111. Nickerson, "Personal Recollections of Two Visits to Gettysburg," p. 21.

112. Gillespie, p. 150; *Official Records,* vol. 27, pt. 1, p. 992.

113. *Ibid.,* p. 992; Gillespie, p. 151.

114. *Official Records,* vol. 27, pt. 1, p. 914-916, 958, 992-993; Gary Kross, "Action on the Eastern Flank," *Blue & Gray* (June 1997), p. 57.

115. Eric J. Wittenberg, *Gettysburg's Forgotten Cavalry Actions* (Gettysburg: Thomas Publications, 1998), p. 12; Gillespie, p. 149, 151. From the First Ohio Squadron an unknown number of troopers was detached at Gettysburg to serve as couriers and orderlies. One of these men, Private Jonas L. Thornton of Company A, 1st Ohio Cavalry, was assigned as an orderly to General Alexander Hays' division staff, 2nd Corps. His performance July 3 so impressed Hays that Thornton was recommended for and promoted to a second lieutenancy, though he never mustered at that rank.

116. Wittenberg, p. 15; Gillespie, p. 152; *Official Records,* vol. 27, pt. 1, p. 993.

117. Coddington, p. 524-525; Gillespie, p. 153; H. Chester Parsons, "Farnsworth's Charge and Death," *Battles and Leaders of the Civil War,* vol. III, p. 394.

118. *Ibid.,* p. 396; Gillespie, p. 154.

119. Huntington, "Notes of Service."

120. Gaul, "Fifth Ohio Volunteer Infantry at Gettysburg."

121. Hurst, p. 75; Samuel Fellers to William Millikin, July 12, 1863, in the *Fayette County Herald,* July 30, 1863; *Ohio Rosters,* vol. VI, p. 151.

122. George P. Metcalf memoir.

123. Howe, *Historical Collections of Ohio,* vol. I, p. 884.

124. Alfred E. Lee, "Reminiscences of the Gettysburg Battle," p. 60.

Aftermath

1. Andrew L. Harris to John B. Bachelder, March 14, 1881, in *The Bachelder Papers,* vol. II, p. 747.

2. *Ibid.,* p. 747; Andrew L. Harris, July 11, 1863, in the *Eaton Weekly Register,* July 23, 1863.

3. George B. Fox to his father, July 4, 1863.

4. Ladley, p. 144.

5. Andrew L. Harris, July 11, 1863, in the *Eaton Weekly Register*, July 23, 1863; Edward C. Culp, July 5, 1863, in the *Norwalk Reflector*, July 21, 1863. The "Mrs. Culp" referred to most likely was Elizabeth "Aunt Polly" Culp, who lived on the north side of the York Pike near its junction with the Hanover Road.

6. George B. Fox to his father, July 4, 1863; *The Bachelder Papers*, vol. II, p. 747, 1145; *Record of Service of Connecticut Men in the Army and Navy of the United States during the War of the Rebellion* (Hartford: Press of The Case, Lockwood & Brainard Company, 1889), p. 641.

7. Wilmont A. Mills to his father, July 9, 1863, in the *Tiffin Tribune*, July 31, 1863.

8. George P. Metcalf memoir.

9. William Ackerman military service records, National Archives. Originally buried in James Pierce's orchard, Ackerman was reinterred in Ohio Plot B-4, Gettysburg National Cemetery.

10. Martin L. Buchwalter diary.

11. Smith, p. 123-124.

12. Howe, *Historical Collections of Ohio*, vol. I, p. 884; James S. Robinson to Wladimir Krzyzanowski, May 30, 1863, J.S. Robinson Papers, Ohio Historical Society; Warner, p. 407; *The Democrat* [Kenton], January 21, 1892.

13. Alfred E. Lee, "Reminiscences of the Gettysburg Battle," p. 60.

14. *History of Hocking Valley, Ohio* (Chicago: Inter-State Publishing Co., 1883), p. 1261.

15. Benjamin Morgan diary.

16. Benjamin Morgan to relatives, July 31, 1863.

17. "Outis," July 4, 1863, in *The Marietta Register*, July 17, 1863; William Jenvey quoted in Andrews, p. 627.

18. Unidentified 55th Ohio correspondence, July 26, 1863, in the *Norwalk Reflector*, August 14, 1863.

19. Eugene Powell, "Rebellion's High Tide," pt. 2, *The National Tribune*, July 5, 1900.

20. William H.H. Tallman memoir.

21. Gaul, "Fifth Ohio Volunteer Infantry at Gettysburg."

22. Sherman R. Norris, "Ohio at Gettysburg." Norris' brigade commander, Charles Candy, reported that about "1,500 stand of arms, mostly Enfield rifles," were recovered from his brigade's front on Culp's Hill.

23. John H. Merrell diary; Huntington, "Notes of Service."

24. Lyman D. Ames to the *Conneaut Reporter*, July 5, 1863, reprinted July 18, 1863 in the *Cleveland Morning Leader*; David Lewis, July 5, 1863, in the *Bucyrus Weekly Journal*, July 17, 1863.

25. Charles H. Merrick military service records, National Archives; Marian J. Morton, *Women in Cleveland: An Illustrated History* (Bloomington: Indiana University Press, 1995), p. 54-55. Born in 1825 at Hinkley, Leicestershire, Myra King married Charles Merrick in 1848, the same year she was prompted to study medicine. Two years after the Civil War she helped establish the Cleveland Homeopathic College for Women, and in 1878 the Women's and Children's Free Medical and Surgical Dispensary. The Merricks divorced in 1881.

26. Charles H. Merrick to Myra Merrick, July 6, 7, 10, 12

and 13, 1863, Western Reserve Historical Society.

27. Azor H. Nickerson, "Personal Recollections of Two Visits to Gettysburg," p. 22. Philip Tracy eventually was buried in Ohio Plot B-22, Gettysburg National Cemetery.

28. Ibid., p. 22-23.

29. Ibid., p. 25.

30. Sawyer, *A Military History of the 8th Regiment Ohio Vol. Inf'y*, p. 179.

31. *Roster and Record of Iowa Soldiers in the War of the Rebellion*, vol. II (Des Moines: Emory H. English, State Printer, 1908), p. 8, 136.

32. George G. Washburn in *The Elyria Independent Democrat*, July 22, 1863.

33. *Ibid.*

34. *Ibid.*

35. *The Elyria Independent Democrat*, July 29, 1863.

36. *Ohio Rosters*, vol. II, p. 739, 740; *The Portage County Democrat*, August 5, 1863.

37. *Eaton Weekley Register*, July 30, 1863; Ladley, p. 147.

38. William H. Clough to Deborah Hayden, July 22, 1863, in *The Elyria Independent Democrat*, August 5, 1863.

39. Charles H. Merrick to Myra Merrick, July 15, 1863.

40. *The Elyria Independent Democrat*, July 29, 1863.

41. *The Summit County Beacon*, August 6, 1863.

42. 107th Ohio file, Gettysburg National Military Park library; *Ohio Rosters*, vol. VII, p. 648, 782.

43. *The Sandusky Register* clipping, circa May 1920, 107th Ohio file, GNMP library.

44. Fee, *Bringing the Sheaves*, p. 447-448.

45. Department of the Susquehanna General Order No. 2, published August 6, 1863, in *The Summit County Beacon*; Frassanito, *Early Photography at Gettysburg*, p. 366.

46. W.D. Siegfried, July 14, 1863, in the *Zanesville Daily Courier*, July 18, 1863.

47. Hurst, p. 77.

48. Galwey, p. 121-122.

49. Charles H. Merrick to Myra Merrick, July 15, 1863.

50. Busey & Martin, p. 280; Coddington, p. 537-539.

51. Wittenberg, p. 84; William H. Carter, *The Life of Lieutenant General Chaffee* (Chicago: University of Chicago Press, 1917), p. 31-32.

52. *Official Records*, vol. 27, pt. 1, p. 916; Thomas M. Covert to his wife, July 2, 1863, Western Reserve Historical Society.

53. *Official Records*, vol. 27, pt. 1, p. 166, 993; Wells A. Bushnell, "Historical Sketch of Companies A and E, Sixth Regiment Ohio Volunteer Cavalry," p. 195-196, 6th O.V.C. regimental papers, Western Reserve Historical Society; *Ohio Rosters*, vol. XI, p. 777, 778. The 6th Ohio troopers captured at Emmitsburg who perished during imprisonment were Corporal William Haycox, Private Robert J. Greer and Private Allen Miller, all of Company C.

54. Gillespie, p. 155.

55. Ibid., p. 155-156.

56. Ibid., p. 156, 157.

57. Ibid., p. 158; *Official Records*, vol. 27, pt. 2, p. 753.

58. *Ibid.*, p. 753; Gillespie, p. 158, 159.

59. Bushnell, p. 196-197; Norman A. Barret, July 13,

1863, in the *Western Reserve Chronicle,* July 22, 1863; Jacob A. Sager to his sister and brother, July 12, 1863, in the Alcinus W. Fenton Papers, Western Reserve Historical Society.

60. Harry M. Dean, July 5, 1863, in *The Portage County Democrat,* July 15, 1863.

61. Mathias Schwab Jr. to his parents, July 17, 1863, Cincinnati Historical Society. In October 1869, Schwab died of suffocation while fighting a fire at the Merchants' Exchange in Cincinnati.

62. William H.H. Tallman memoir.

63. Benjamin F. Stone Jr. to Olivia Allston, July 17, 1863; Ladley, p. 144; Jacob F. Mader to Mary L. Hartmeyer, July 12, 1863.

64. Unidentified 55th Ohio correspondence, July 26, 1863, in the *Norwalk Reflector,* August 14, 1863.

65. George P. Metcalf memoir.

66. Ibid.; Henry Henney diary.

67. Moses Pugh quoted in Osborn, p. 250.

68. John H. Merrell diary.

69. *Official Records,* vol. 27, pt. 1, p. 928, 995.

70. James Barnet, editor, *The Martyrs and Heroes of Illinois in the Great Rebellion* (Chicago: Press of J. Barnet, Book and Job Printer, 1866), p. 57.

71. *Ibid.,* p. 58, 60, 64-71, 72, 74-75.

72. John M. Waite to his father, July 7, 1863, in the *Chicago Tribune,* July 17, 1863, reprinted July 22 in *The Ohio Repository* [Canton].

73. Bushnell, p. 197; Gillespie, p. 161.

74. *Official Records,* vol. 27, pt. 1, p. 995; Thomas M. Covert to his wife, July 27, 1863; Delos R. Northway to friends, July 7, 1863, in "Extracts From the Diary of ...," p. 120.

75. Bushnell, p. 198; Gillespie, p. 162; *Ohio Rosters,* vol. XI, p. 327, 756.

76. Bushnell, p. 199; Delos R. Northway to friends, July 9, 1863, op. cit., p. 120; Ladley, p. 143.

77. Jacob A. Sager, July 12, 1863; Delos R. Northway to friends, July 9, 1863, op. cit., p. 120.

78. Gillespie, p. 163.

79. Bushnell, p. 199-200; Gillespie, p. 163; *Official Records,* vol. 27, pt. 1, p. 709, 996.

80. Samuel L. Gillespie, July 27, 1863, in the *Fayette County Herald,* August 13, 1863.

81. George B. Fox to his parents, July 13, 1863, Cincinnati Historical Society.

82. Ibid.

83. *Official Records,* vol. 27, pt. 2, p. 310; pt. 1, p. 91.

84. *Ibid.,* pt. 1, p. 92-93; Gillespie, July 27, 1863, in the *Fayette County Herald,* August 13, 1863.

85. Thomas M. Covert to his wife, July 27 and 30, 1863.

86. Henry J. Knapp, "Gettysburg by a Soldier in the Ranks." Knapp's arm wound occurred May 8, 1864 at Mill Creek Gap, Georgia.

87. William G. LeDuc, *Recollections of a Civil War Quartermaster* (St. Paul, Minn.: North Central Publishing Company, 1963), p. 99; Benjamin F. Stone Jr. to Olivia Allston, July 17, 1863.

88. Barnet, p. 76-77.

89. Ibid., p. 77; "Death of Major W.H. Medill," *The Ohio Repository,* July 22, 1863.

90. Sawyer, *A Military History of the 8th Regiment Ohio Vol. Inf'y,* p. 136-137; John H. Merrell diary.

91. David Thomson to Mary Thomson, July 16, 1863.

92. David Thomson to Mary Thomson, August 12, 1863.

93. Elizabeth Sykes diary and miscellaneous family records, Tony Lemut Collection; *Norwalk Reflector,* July 14, 1863; Andrew J. Sykes military service and pension records, National Archives.

94. *Official Records,* vol. 27, pt. 1, p. 187; Busey & Martin, p. 275.

95. Alfred Goodin to his father, July 22, 1863, in *The Hardin County Republican,* August 21, 1863.

96. Jeremiah Williams to Flora Williams, August 1, 1863, in *The Spirit of Democracy,* August 19, 1863; Jeremiah Williams military service records, National Archives. Presumably due to his newspaper background, Williams was appointed in September 1863 to a three-officer committee by fellow Libby inmates to examine prison conditions. The committee's full report and resolutions adopted by Libby's prisoners can be found in *Official Records,* series II, vol. 6, p. 301-303.

97. Joseph F. Potts to Benjamin Morgan, November 22, 1863, courtesy of Jacqueline Ann Lane.

98. Alphonso C. Davis to Josiah Davis, August 7, 1863, in the *Eaton Weekly Register,* August 27, 1863. Davis rejoined the 75th Ohio in October 1863. He was promoted to first lieutenant in February 1865.

99. *Eaton Weekly Register,* August 27, 1863; *Ohio Rosters,* vol. VI, p. 242.

100. *Official Records,* vol. 27, pt. 1, p. 182; *Ohio Memorials at Gettysburg,* p. 38, lists 86 missing in the 75th Ohio. Elias Clear military service records, National Archives; *The Democratic Press* [Eaton], July 23, 1863.

101. Reid, *Ohio in the War,* vol. I, p. 99, 101, 103, 107, 164; *The Record of Hon. C.L. Vallandigham on Abolition, the Union, and the Civil War* (Columbus: J. Walter & Co., 1863), p. 204-205, 252-256. Vallandigham (1820-1871) was a native of Columbiana County, Ohio, and lived in Dayton for a number of years.

102. *Eaton Weekly Register,* July 16 and 23, 1863.

103. *The Democratic Press,* July 16 and 23, 1863.

104. *Eaton Weekly Register,* July 30, 1863.

105. *Official Records,* vol. 29, pt. 1, p. 8; Sawyer, *A Military History of the 8th Regiment Ohio Vol. Inf'y,* p. 140; Kepler, p. 141; Galwey, p. 136.

106. When the 8th Ohio's term of service expired June 25, 1864 at Petersburg, Va., only 72 officers and enlisted men were present for duty. The regiment mustered out July 13, 1864. Its veteran enlistees and recruits, along with those from the 4th Ohio, were consolidated and designated the 4th Battalion Ohio Infantry. This organization served in the Army of the Potomac until its muster-out July 12, 1865. [Reid, *Ohio in the War,* vol. II, p. 69; *Ohio Rosters,* vol. II, p. 236].

107. George B. Fox to Benjamin Morgan, August 25, 1863, courtesy of Jacqueline Ann Lane; Reid, *Ohio in the War,* vol. II, p. 436; *Official Records,* vol. 28, pt. 2, p. 74, 76.

108. Andrew L. Harris to Benjamin Morgan, August 26, 1863, courtesy of Jacqueline Ann Lane.

Epilogue

1. Azor H. Nickerson, "Personal Recollections of Two Visits to Gettysburg," p. 26.

2. *Revised Report made to the Legislature of Pennsylvania relative to the Soldiers' National Cemetery, at Gettysburg* (Harrisburg: Singerly & Myers, 1867), p. 5-6. Hereafter referred to as *SNC Report;* Frank L. Klement, "Ohio and the Dedication of the Soldiers' Cemetery at Gettysburg," *Ohio History* (vol. 79, no. 2, Spring 1970), p. 79, 80.

3. Klement, p. 81-82; Busey, *These Honored Dead,* p. 356; Frassanito, *Early Photography at Gettysburg,* p. 167; *SNC Report,* p. 162.

4. *SNC Report,* p. 161-162; Klement, p. 80.

5. Klement, p. 82, 85.

6. Ibid., p. 86.

7. "The Ohio Delegation at Gettysburg," *Ohio State Journal,* November 23, 1863.

8. Nickerson, "Personal Recollections of Two Visits to Gettysburg," p. 26.

9. Ibid., p. 27; *The Springfield Republic,* November 27, 1863.

10. Klement, p. 87.

11. "Dedication Day at Gettysburg," *Ohio State Journal,* November 23, 1863; "The American Necropolis. Its Dedication at Gettysburg," *Cincinnati Daily Commercial,* November 23, 1863.

Cleveland newspaperman John S. Stephenson tramped the battlefield November 20, 1863 in company with Private Joseph Lloyd, Company B, 8th Ohio, and Private Charles H. Anderson, Company G, 29th Ohio. Both soldiers had been detached from their regiments and stationed at Gettysburg's Camp Letterman hospital. Stephenson, like thousands of other sightseers, could not resist collecting souvenirs of his visit. He brought back to Cleveland "a bloody handkerchief" found lying at the stone wall near where Alonzo Cushing's battery fought July 3; a cap with a bullet hole through the leather visor; "a rifle-cannon percussion shell, a handful of conical and round bullets — the latter from spherical case shells, and a *Rebel skull.* The latter we picked up near 'Round Top.' The wretch's body was nowhere to be found. Private Anderson said it must be a Rebel skull, from the fact that none of our men were killed in that portion of the field where it was found. The sight of that white skull, sans eyes, sans hair, sans flesh, sans skin, and sans almost every thing except ghostly hideousness, awakened sad and gloomy feelings in my mind. Perhaps this misguided defender of secession and States rights had a father, mother, brothers, sisters, and a sweetheart, away down in 'de land of cotton,' and there he was, with nothing but this poor apology for a head, kicking about upon the ground like a toad stool or a foot ball."

Gettysburg itself, Stephenson wrote, contained "a refined and intelligent society. [It] seems absolutely plethoric in pretty girls — fairly rivalling Cleveland in this respect. We never saw so many fine looking women in so small a place in our life before. Whether or not the beaux are equal to the supply of fair ones, we cannot say. If they are not, we advise young men of *means and leisure* to visit Gettysburgh [sic] and pick out a wife at once." [*Cleveland Plain Dealer,* November 23, 1863].

12. *Cincinnati Daily Commercial,* November 23, 1863.

13. *Ibid.*

14. *Ohio State Journal,* November 23, 1863; Klement, p. 89; Warner, p. 423.

15. *The Springfield Republic,* November 30, 1863.

16. Klement, p. 90, 82; *Cincinnati Daily Commercial,* November 23, 1863; Nickerson, "Personal Recollections of Two Visits to Gettysburg," p. 27.

17. Klement, p. 76, 91; Washington *Morning Chronicle,* November 21, 1863.

18. *Cincinnati Daily Commercial,* November 23, 1863.

19. Nickerson, "Personal Recollections of Two Visits to Gettysburg," p. 27.

20. Ibid., p. 27-28. Lincoln's words used here are from the "Hay Draft" of the Gettysburg Address at the Library of Congress.

21. Klement, p. 93; *Ohio State Journal,* November 23, 1863.

22. *SNC Report,* p. 106-111, 161; Klement, p. 98; *Ohio Memorials at Gettysburg,* p. 5, 6, 7, 9.

23. *Ibid.,* p. 9, 52; Dennis M. Keesee, *Too Young To Die: Boy Soldiers of the Union Army 1861-1865* (Huntington: Blue Acorn Press, 2001), p. 214; John T. Raper, "Gettysburg," *The Ohio Soldier,* September 24, 1887, p. 90.

24. *Ohio Memorials at Gettysburg,* p. 90; Charles E. Creager, *The Fourteenth Ohio National Guard – The Fourth Ohio Volunteer Infantry* (Columbus: Press of the Landon Printing & Publishing Co., 1899), p. 46-48; *Champion City Times* [Springfield], September 15 and 21, 1887.

25. *Ohio Memorials at Gettysburg,* p. 27-28, 90-91; *The Ohio Soldier,* September 24, 1887, p. 90.

26. *Columbus Sunday Dispatch,* June 29, 1913; *The Governors of Ohio,* p. 148. Nine veterans died during the 1913 Gettysburg reunion, including 73-year-old Frank D. Moran of Kinsman, Trumbull County. A sergeant in Company B, 6th Ohio Cavalry, at the time of the battle, Moran succumbed to heatstroke.

27. William E. Parmelee, "At Gettysburg."

28. John S. Stephenson, "From Gettysburg," *Cleveland Plain Dealer,* November 23, 1863; James S. Robinson quoted in *Ohio Memorials at Gettysburg,* p. 73.

Commemorative medal presented to Ohio soldiers at the time of the battle's 50th anniversary in 1913. A state seal shield surrounded by a laurel wreath was suspended from a pin-backed, state-shaped piece containing the raised words "Ohio Survivors of the Battle of Gettysburg July 1863." A silk ribbon mimicking the national flag also was suspended from the pin clasp. This example is reproduced at almost twice actual size.

Brad L. Pruden Collection

BIBLIOGRAPHY

Abbreviations

CHS — Cincinnati Historical Society.
GNMP — Gettysburg National Military Park library.
NA — National Archives, Washington, D.C.
OHS — Ohio Historical Society, Columbus.
USAMHI — United States Army Military History Institute, Carlisle Barracks, Pa.
WRHS — Western Reserve Historical Society, Cleveland.

Manuscript materials

107th Ohio descriptive book, Record Group 94, NA.
Ames, Lyman D. (29th Ohio), diary, *Civil War Times Illustrated* Collection, USAMHI.
Barlow, Francis C., letters, Massachusetts Historical Society, Boston.
Bope, Abraham (61st Ohio), letters, Tony Lemut Collection, Parma, Ohio.
Buchwalter, Martin L. (73rd Ohio), diary, Jeffrey J. Kowalis Collection, Orland Park, Ill.
Bushnell, Wells A. (6th Ohio Cavalry), memoir/unpublished history of Companies A and E, 6th Ohio Cavalry Regimental Papers, WRHS.
Covert, Thomas M. (6th Ohio Cavalry), letters, WRHS.
Cox, Samuel S., letter, Correspondence to the Governor and Adjutant General of Ohio, 1861-1866, OHS.
Creighton, William R. (7th Ohio), miscellaneous papers, WRHS.
Evans, Thomas (25th Ohio), journal/memoir, OHS.
Fox, George B. (75th Ohio), letters, CHS; letters, Jacqueline Ann Lane Collection, Lebanon, Ohio.
Gardner, Isaac W. (Battery I, 1st OVLA), letters, Harrisburg Civil War Round Table–Gregory A. Coco Collection, USAMHI.
Gildea, James (Battery L, 1st OVLA), memoir, WRHS.
Gillis, Joseph (82nd Ohio), letter, Joseph H. Gillis Collection, Youngstown, Ohio.

Haines, Elwood P. (29th Ohio), diary, Stephen Altic Collection, Columbus.
Harris, Andrew L. (75th Ohio), letters, Jacqueline Ann Lane Collection.
Hayden, Elijah (8th Ohio), letter, Donald Lingafelter Collection, Mentor, Ohio.
Henney, Henry C. (55th Ohio), diary, *Civil War Times Illustrated* Collection, USAMHI.
Hubler, Simon (143rd Pennsylvania), reminiscences, Civil War Miscellaneous Collection, USAMHI.
Irish, Edward H. (8th Ohio), court-martial transcript, Record Group 153, Records of the Office of the Judge Advocate General (Army), Court-Martial Case Files 1809-1894, NA.
Keeler, Alonzo (55th Ohio), diary, Civil War Miscellaneous Collection, USAMHI.
Kline, Valentine (61st Ohio), court-martial transcript, Record Group 153, NA.
Kratz, John (107th Ohio), letter, Ron Chojnacki Collection, Medina, Ohio.
Laird, George F. (4th Ohio), letters, Barry L. Cornell Collection, Rittman, Ohio.
Mader, Jacob F. (61st Ohio), letters, Mac Schumm Collection, Circleville, Ohio.
Merrell, John H. (Battery H, 1st OVLA), transcript of diary, Barbara Linderholm Collection, Davis, Calif.
Merrick, Charles H. (8th Ohio), letters, C.H. Merrick Papers, WRHS.
Mesnard, Luther B. (55th Ohio), memoir, Civil War Miscellaneous Collection, USAMHI.
Metcalf, George P. (136th New York), memoir, OHS.
Meyer, Seraphim (107th Ohio), letters, Record Group 94, and court-martial transcript, Record Group 153, NA.
Milledge, George (66th Ohio), letters, Robert L. Brake Collection, USAMHI.
Mitchell, William D.W. (82nd Ohio), letter, Stanley R. Burleson Collection, Yukon, Okla.
Morgan, Benjamin (75th Ohio), letters, diary and memoir, Jacqueline Ann Lane Collection.
Mouat, David (29th Pennsylvania), memoir, Historical Society of Pennsylvania, Philadelphia.
Parmater, Nathan L. (29th Ohio), diary, OHS.
Parmelee, William E. (Battery H, 1st OVLA), letter, Samuel P. Bates Collection, Pennsylvania Division of Public Rec-

ords, Harrisburg.

Potts, Joseph F. (75th Ohio), letter, Jacqueline Ann Lane Collection.

Robinson, James S. (82nd Ohio), letters, J.S. Robinson Papers, OHS.

Ross, Anthony W. (73rd Ohio), letter, A.W. Ross Papers, OHS.

Russell, Robert H. (66th Ohio), letter, L.M. Strayer Collection, Dayton, Ohio.

Sager, Jacob A. (6th Ohio Cavalry), letters, Alcinus W. Fenton Papers, WRHS.

Sayre, William M. (66th Ohio), letter, Civil War Miscellaneous Collection, USAMHI.

Schwab, Mathias Jr. (5th Ohio), letters, CHS.

Soden, Edward (6th Ohio Cavalry), letter, Ken Lawrence Collection, Orwell, Ohio.

Southerton, William B. (75th Ohio), reminiscences, OHS.

Steiner, Barnet T. (107th Ohio), letter, Brian Zimmerman Collection, Canton, Ohio.

Stone, Benjamin F. Jr. (73rd Ohio), letters, Ross County Historical Society, Chillicothe, Ohio.

Sykes, Andrew J. (55th Ohio), and Sykes, Elizabeth, diary and letter, Tony Lemut Collection.

Tallman, William H.H. (66th Ohio), typescript of memoir, 66th Ohio file, GNMP.

Thomson, David (82nd Ohio), letters, David G. Thomson Collection, Edina, Minn.

Wallace, William (4th Ohio), diary, OHS.

Wren, Daniel B. (75th Ohio), letter, Jacqueline Ann Lane Collection.

Zachman, Daniel (82nd Ohio), diary, Maureen Shepard Collection, Cardington, Ohio.

Published diaries, journals & correspondence

Ames, Blanche Butler, compiler, *Chronicles from the Nineteenth Century: Family Letters of Blanche Butler and Adelbert Ames,* 2 vols., n.p., 1957.

Angle, Paul M., editor, *Three Years in the Army of the Cumberland: The Letters and Diary of Major James A. Connolly,* Bloomington: Indiana University Press, 1959.

Hitz, Louise W., editor, *Letters of Frederick C. Winkler 1862-1865,* privately published, 1963.

Ladd, David L. & Audrey J., editors, *The Bachelder Papers: Gettysburg in Their Own Words,* 3 vols., Dayton: Morningside House, Inc., 1994-1995.

Ladley, Oscar D., *Hearth and Knapsack: The Ladley Letters, 1857-1880,* edited by Carl M. Becker & Ritchie Thomas, Athens: Ohio University Press, 1988.

Letters of William Wheeler of the Class of 1855, Yale College, Cambridge: H.O. Houghton & Co., 1875.

Marcus, Edward, editor, *A New Canaan Private in the Civil War: Letters of Justus M. Silliman, 17th Connecticut Volunteers,* New Canaan, Conn.: New Canaan Historical Society, 1984.

Northway, Delos R., "Extracts from the Diary of Major Delos R. Northway, Co. A, Sixth O.V.C.," *Souvenir Fiftieth Annual Reunion of the Sixth Ohio Veteran Volunteer Cavalry Association Held at Warren, Ohio, October 5th, 1915,* n.p.,

n.d.

Pennoyer, Robert T. & Omvig, Mark, editors, *Diaries of Pvt. John W. Houtz, 66th Ohio Volunteer Infantry 1863-1864,* Homer, N.Y.: privately published, 1994.

Quaife, Milo M., editor, *From the Cannon's Mouth: The Civil War Letters of General Alpheus S. Williams,* Detroit: Wayne State University Press, 1959.

Souder, Emily B.T., *Leaves from the Battle-Field of Gettysburg, A Series of Letters Written from a Field Hospital and National Poems,* Philadelphia: Caxton Press, 1864.

Published memoirs & reminiscences

Applegate, John S., *Reminiscences and Letters of George Arrowsmith of New Jersey,* Red Bank, N.J.: John H. Cook, 1893.

Dawes, Rufus R., "With the Sixth Wisconsin at Gettysburg," *Sketches of War History 1861-1865,* vol. 3, Cincinnati: Robert Clarke & Co., 1890.

——, *A Memoir: Rufus R. Dawes,* New York: Devinne Press, 1900.

Galwey, Thomas F., *The Valiant Hours,* edited by W.S. Nye, Harrisburg: The Stackpole Company, 1961.

Howard, Oliver O., *Autobiography of Oliver Otis Howard, Major General,* 2 vols., New York: Baker & Taylor Co., 1907.

Jewett, Leonidas M., "From Stafford Heights to Gettysburg in 1863," *Sketches of War History 1861-1865,* vol. 5, Cincinnati: The Robert Clarke Company, 1903.

Jones, Terry L., editor, *The Civil War Memoirs of Captain William J. Seymour: Reminiscences of a Louisiana Tiger,* Baton Rouge: Louisiana State University Press, 1991.

LeDuc, William G., *Recollections of a Civil War Quartermaster,* St. Paul, Minn.: North Central Publishing Company, 1963.

Rice, Ralsa C., *Yankee Tigers: Through the Civil War with the 125th Ohio,* edited by Richard A. Baumgartner & Larry M. Strayer, Huntington, W.Va.: Blue Acorn Press, 1992.

Sawyer, Franklin, *The Eighth Ohio at Gettysburg,* Washington: E.J. Gray Printer, 1889.

Schurz, Carl, *The Reminiscences of Carl Schurz,* 3 vols., New York: The McClure Company, 1908.

Scribner, Benjamin F., *How Soldiers Were Made,* Huntington, W.Va.: Blue Acorn Press, 1995.

Stiles, Albert W., "Reminiscences of the Charge of Company A, Sixth Ohio Volunteer Cavalry, at Upperville, Va., June 21, 1863," *Report of the Thirty-Fifth Annual Reunion Sixth Ohio Veteran Volunteer Cavalry Association Held at Warren, Ohio, October 2, 1900,* Ravenna, Ohio: G.R. Braden, Printer, n.d.

Official records & government publications

Bates, Samuel P., *History of Pennsylvania Volunteers, 1861-5,* vol. V, Harrisburg: B. Singerly, State Printer, 1871.

Connecticut. Adjutant General. *Record of Service of Connecticut Men in the Army and Navy of the United States during* the War of the Rebellion, Hartford: Press of The Case, Lockwood & Brainard Company, 1889.

Davis, George B., Perry, Leslie J. & Kirkley, Joseph W., Board of Publication. Cowles, Calvin D., compiler, *Atlas to Accompany the Official Records of the Union and Confederate Armies*, Washington: Government Printing Office, 1891-1895.

Iowa. Adjutant General. *Roster and Record of Iowa Soldiers in the War of the Rebellion*, vol. II, Des Moines: Emory H. English, State Printer, 1908.

New York Monuments Commission. *Final Report of the Battlefield of Gettysburg*, 3 vols., Albany: J.B. Lyon Company, 1900.

Ohio. Roster Commission. *Official Roster of the Soldiers of the State of Ohio in the War of the Rebellion, 1861-1866*, 12 vols., Akron, Cincinnati, Norwalk, 1886-1895.

Report of the Congressional Committee on the Conduct of the War, 1865 series, vol. 1.

Report of the Gettysburg Memorial Commission of Ohio, 2nd edition, Columbus: Press of Nitschke Bros., 1889.

Revised Report made to the Legislature of Pennsylvania relative to the Soldiers' National Cemetery, at Gettysburg, Harrisburg: Singerly & Myers, 1867.

Revised United States Army Regulations of 1861, Washington: Government Printing Office, 1868.

United States War Department. *The War of the Rebellion: A Compilation of the Official Records of the Union and Confederate Armies*, Washington: Government Printing Office, 1880-1901.

Newspapers & periodicals

* Denotes post-Civil War newspaper or edition.

Ashland Union
Ashtabula Sentinel
Ashtabula Weekly Telegraph
Belmont Chronicle [St. Clairsville]
Bucyrus Weekly Journal
Champion City Times * [Springfield]
Cincinnati Daily Commercial
Cincinnati Daily Times
Cincinnati Enquirer *
Cincinnati Gazette
The Circleville Democrat
Cleveland Herald
Cleveland Morning Leader
Cleveland Plain Dealer
Columbus Daily Express
Columbus Evening Dispatch *
Columbus Gazette
Conneaut Reporter
Delaware Gazette
The Democrat * [Kenton]
The Democratic Press [Eaton]
Eaton Weekly Register
The Elyria Independent Democrat
The Elyria Independent Gazette
Fayette County Herald [Washington Court House]
Fremont Journal

Hancock Jeffersonian [Findlay]
The Hardin County Republican [Kenton]
Mahoning Register [Youngstown]
Mansfield Daily Herald
The Marietta Register
Marietta Sunday Observer *
Morning Chronicle [Washington, D.C.]
The Mount Vernon Republican
Norwalk Reflector
The Ohio Democrat [New Philadelphia]
The Ohio Repository [Canton]
Ohio State Journal [Columbus]
The Portage County Democrat [Ravenna]
The Sandusky Register
The Spirit of Democracy [Woodsfield]
The Springfield Republic
The Summit County Beacon [Akron]
Tiffin Tribune
Toledo Blade
The Tuscarawas Advocate [New Philadelphia]
Urbana Citizen and Gazette
Urbana Union
Western Reserve Chronicle [Warren]
The Wyandot Pioneer [Upper Sandusky]
Zanesville Daily Courier

Bertholf, Gilbert D., "The Twelfth Corps. The Part They Took in the Big Battle of Gettysburg," *The National Tribune*, May 11, 1893.

Brotts, Henry A., "Repelling Pickett's Men," *The National Tribune*, September 1, 1910.

Carver, James, "At Gettysburg," *The National Tribune*, April 30, 1914.

"The Civil War Diary of Orin G. Dority (Part 1)," *Northwest Ohio Quarterly*, Winter 1964-1965.

Clements, George S., "The 25th Ohio at Gettysburg," *The National Tribune*, August 6, 1891.

Culp, Edward C., "From the 25th Ohio," *The National Tribune*, June 4, 1885.

——, "Gettysburg: Reminiscences of the Great Fight by a Participant," *The National Tribune*, March 19, 1885.

Dickelman, Joseph L., "Gen. Carroll's Gibraltar Brigade at Gettysburg," *The National Tribune*, December 10, 1908.

Gaul, Joseph L., "The Fifth Ohio Volunteer Infantry at Gettysburg," *The Ohio Soldier and National Picket Guard*, March 24, 1894.

"Gettysburg Memorials: The Eighth and Seventy-Fifth Ohio on that Memorable Field," *The Ohio Soldier*, January 14, 1888.

Hart, Samuel W., "At Gettysburg with the Twelfth Corps," *The National Tribune*, June 23, 1927.

——, "Meade at Gettysburg. Failure to Improve His Opportunity and Crush Lee's Army," *The National Tribune*, October 15, 1903.

Hartwig, D. Scott, "The 11th Army Corps on July 1, 1863," *The Gettysburg Magazine*, January 1990.

"Historical Sketches of the United States Army," *Journal of the Military Service Institution*, September 1890.

Hollis, David R., editor, "Hollis Correspondence," *Indiana*

Magazine of History, vol. 36, 1940.

Kepf, Kenneth M., "Dilger's Battery at Gettysburg," *The Gettysburg Magazine,* January 1991.

Klement, Frank L., "Ohio and the Dedication of the Soldiers' Cemetery at Gettysburg," *Ohio History,* Spring 1970.

Knapp, Henry J., "Gettysburg by a Soldier in the Ranks," *Jefferson Gazette,* February 8, 1912.

Koons, David S., "The 8th Ohio at Gettysburg," *The National Tribune,* November 5, 1908.

Kozlowski, L.J., "To Stand For All They Won: Rufus Dawes of the Iron Brigade," *Timeline,* March-April 1995.

Kross, Gary, "Gettysburg Vignettes: Action on the Eastern Flank," *Blue & Gray,* June 1997.

——, "The XI Corps at Gettysburg July 1, 1863," *Blue & Gray,* December 2001.

Lee, Alfred E., "Reminiscences of the Gettysburg Battle," *Lippincott's Magazine,* July 1883.

——, "The Eleventh Corps. The Disadvantages Under Which It Fought at Gettysburg," *Philadelphia Weekly Press,* January 26, 1887.

Lynn, Joseph R., "At Gettysburg. What the 29th Ohio did During the Three Days' Fighting," *The National Tribune,* October 7, 1897.

Mewborn, Horace, "The Operations of Mosby's Rangers," *Blue & Gray,* April 2000.

Morgan, John T., "Wounded at Gettysburg," *The National Tribune,* May 22, 1924.

Nickerson, Azor H., "Personal Recollections of Two Visits to Gettysburg," *Scribner's Magazine,* July 1893.

Norris, Sherman R., "Ohio at Gettysburg. The Regiments that Participated in the Great Battle," *The National Tribune,* June 9, 1887.

O'Brien, Kevin E., " 'A Perfect Roar of Musketry': Candy's Brigade in the Fight for Culp's Hill," *The Gettysburg Magazine,* July 1993.

Parmelee, William E., "At Gettysburg. The Experience of an Ohio Artilleryman," *The National Tribune,* September 2, 1886.

Parsons, William T. & Heimburger, Mary S., editors, "Shuler Family Correspondence," *Pennsylvania Folklife,* Spring 1980.

Peck, Albert W., "Gettysburg. The Part Taken by the Eleventh Corps," *The National Tribune,* December 12, 1889.

Potter, Thaddeus S., "The Battle of Gettysburg," *The National Tribune,* August 5, 1882.

——, "On Skirmish. Gallant Behavior of the 8th Ohio at Gettysburg," *The National Tribune,* January 24, 1895.

Powell, Eugene, "Rebellion's High Tide: Dashed Against the Immovable Rocks of Gettysburg," 2 parts, *The National Tribune,* June 28 and July 5, 1900.

Raper, John T., "Gettysburg," *The Ohio Soldier,* September 24, 1887.

Rosenberger, H.E., editor, "Ohiowa Soldier," *Annals of Iowa,* Fall 1961.

Silverman, Jason H., editor, " 'The Excitement Had Begun!' The Civil War Diary of Lemuel Jeffries, 1862-1863," *Manuscripts,* Fall 1978.

Sweetland, Andrew F., "The 55th Ohio at Gettysburg," *The National Tribune,* September 9, 1909.

Trimble, Tony L., " 'Agate': Whitelaw Reid Reports from Gettysburg," *The Gettysburg Magazine,* July 1992.

Wasson, Stanley P., editor, "Civil War Letters of Darwin Cody," *The Ohio Historical Quarterly,* October 1959.

Wittke, Carl, "Ohio's Germans, 1840-1875," *The Ohio Historical Quarterly,* October 1957.

Wright, George B., "Hon. David Tod. Biography and Personal Recollections," *Ohio Archaeological and Historical Publications,* October 1899.

Regimental & company histories

Barlow, Albert R., *Company G: A Record of the Services of One Company of the 157th N.Y. Vols. in the War of the Rebellion,* Syracuse: A.W. Hall, 1899.

Carroon, Robert G., *From Freeman's Ford to Bentonville: The 61st Ohio Volunteer Infantry,* Shippensburg, Pa.: Burd Street Press, 1998.

Creager, Charles E., *The Fourteenth Ohio National Guard – The Fourth Ohio Volunteer Infantry,* Columbus: Press of the Landon Printing & Publishing Co., 1899.

Culp, Edward C., *The 25th Ohio Vet. Vol. Infantry in the War for the Union,* Topeka: Geo. W. Crane & Co., 1885.

Curry, William L., *Four Years in the Saddle: History of the First Regiment Ohio Volunteer Cavalry, War of the Rebellion 1861-1865,* Columbus: Champlin Printing Co., 1898.

Gillespie, Samuel L., *A History of Company A, First Ohio Cavalry 1861-1865,* Washington Court House, Ohio: Press of Ohio State Register, 1898.

Grebner, Constantin, *We Were the Ninth: A History of the Ninth Regiment, Ohio Volunteer Infantry April 17, 1861, to June 7, 1864,* Kent, Ohio: Kent State University Press, 1987.

Hurst, Samuel H., *Journal-History of the Seventy-Third Ohio Volunteer Infantry,* Chillicothe: 1866.

Kepler, William, *History of the Three Months' and Three Years' Service of the Fourth Regiment Ohio Volunteer Infantry in the War for the Union,* Cleveland: Leader Printing Company, 1886. Reprinted as *4th Ohio Volunteers* in 1992 by Blue Acorn Press.

Osborn, Hartwell, *Trials and Triumphs: The Record of the Fifty-fifth Ohio Volunteer Infantry,* Chicago: A.C. McClurg & Co., 1904.

Sawyer, Franklin, *A Military History of the 8th Regiment Ohio Vol. Inf'y: Its Battles, Marches and Army Movements,* Cleveland: Fairbanks & Co. Printers, 1881. Reprinted as *8th Ohio Volunteer Infantry* in 1994 by Blue Acorn Press.

SeCheverell, J.H., *Journal History of the Twenty-Ninth Ohio Veteran Volunteers, 1861-1865. Its Victories and its Reverses,* Cleveland: 1883.

Smith, Jacob, *Camps and Campaigns of the 107th Regiment Ohio Volunteer Infantry from August, 1862, to July, 1865,* n.p., 1910.

Thackery, David T., *A Light and Uncertain Hold: A History of the Sixty-sixth Ohio Volunteer Infantry,* Kent, Ohio: Kent State University Press, 1999.

Underwood, Adin B., *The Three Years' Service of the Thirty-third Mass. Infantry Regiment 1862-1865,* Boston: A. Williams & Co., 1881. Reprinted as *33rd Massachusetts* in 1993 by Blue Acorn Press.

Wallace, Frederick S., *The Sixty-first Ohio Volunteers, 1861-1865,* Marysville, Ohio: Theodore Mullen, 1902.

Wilson, Lawrence, *Itinerary of the Seventh Ohio Volunteer Infantry,* New York: The Neale Publishing Company, 1907.

Wood, George L. *The Seventh Regiment: A Record,* New York: James Miller, 1865.

Military histories, biographies & reference works

Arrington, Benjamin T., *The Medal of Honor at Gettysburg,* Gettysburg: Thomas Publications, 1996.

Barnet, James, editor, *The Martyrs and Heroes of Illinois in the Great Rebellion,* Chicago: Press of J. Barnet, Book and Job Printer, 1866.

Bigelow, John Jr., *Chancellorsville,* New York: Konecky & Konecky, 1995.

Boatner, Mark M., *The Civil War Dictionary,* New York: David McKay Company, Inc., 1959.

Brennan, J. Fletcher, editor, *A Biographical Cyclopaedia and Portrait Gallery of Distinguished Men, with an Historical Sketch of the State of Ohio,* Cincinnati: John C. Yorston & Company, 1879.

Brown, Kent M., *Cushing of Gettysburg: The Story of a Union Artillery Commander,* Lexington: The University Press of Kentucky, 1993.

Browne, Edward C., "Captain James Freeman Huntington, 1st Regiment Ohio Light Artillery, Battery H," unpublished manuscript.

Busey, John W., *These Honored Dead: The Union Casualties at Gettysburg,* Hightstown, N.J.: Longstreet House, 1996.

Busey, John W. & Martin, David G., *Regimental Strengths and Losses at Gettysburg,* Hightstown, N.J.: Longstreet House, 1994.

Carter, William H., *The Life of Lieutenant General Chaffee,* Chicago: University of Chicago Press, 1917.

Christ, Elwood W., *"Over a Wide, Hot ... Crimson Plain": The Struggle for the Bliss Farm at Gettysburg July 2nd and 3rd, 1863,* Baltimore: Butternut and Blue, 1994.

Coco, Gregory A., *A Strange and Blighted Land, Gettysburg: The Aftermath of a Battle,* Gettysburg: Thomas Publications, 1995.

——, *A Vast Sea of Misery: A History and Guide to the Union and Confederate Field Hospitals at Gettysburg, July 1-November 20, 1863,* Gettysburg: Thomas Publications, 1988.

Coddington, Edwin B., *The Gettysburg Campaign: A Study in Command,* Dayton: Morningside Bookshop, 1979.

Colonel Richard Enderlin, Chillicothe: Scholl Printing Co., 1925.

Crumb, Herb S., editor, *The Eleventh Corps Artillery at Gettysburg,* Hamilton, N.Y.: Edmonston Publishing, 1991.

Cullum, George W., *Biographical Register of the Officers and Graduates of the U.S. Military Academy,* Boston: Houghton, Mifflin and Company, 1891.

Fox, William F., *Regimental Losses in the American Civil War 1861-1865,* Dayton: Press of Morningside Bookshop, 1985.

Frassanito, William A., *Early Photography at Gettysburg,* Gettysburg: Thomas Publications, 1995.

Gallagher, Gary W., editor, *The First Day at Gettysburg,* Kent, Ohio: Kent State University Press, 1992.

Governors of Ohio, The, Columbus: The Ohio Historical Society, 1969.

Hamlin, Augustus C., *The Battle of Chancellorsville,* Bangor: privately published, 1896.

Hunt, Roger D. & Brown, Jack R., *Brevet Brigadier Generals in Blue,* Gaithersburg, Md.: Olde Soldier Books, Inc., 1997.

Johnson, Robert U. & Buel, Clarence C., editors, *Battles and Leaders of the Civil War,* 3 vols., New York: The Century Company, 1888.

Jones, Terry L., *Lee's Tigers: The Louisiana Infantry in the Army of Northern Virginia,* Baton Rouge: Louisiana State University Press, 1987.

Juarez, Angelo D., "The Tarnished Saber: Major Azor Howett Nickerson, USA, His Life and Times," unpublished manuscript.

Kaufmann, Wilhelm, *Die Deutschen im Amerikanischen Bürgerkrieg,* München: R. Oldenburg, 1911.

Lane, Irene Morgan, "Lieutenant Colonel Ben Morgan 1823-1898," unpublished manuscript.

Lash, Gary G., *The Gibraltar Brigade on East Cemetery Hill,* Baltimore: Butternut and Blue, 1995.

Lindsey, David, *"Sunset" Cox: Irrepressible Democrat,* Detroit: Wayne State University Press, 1959.

Long, E.B., *The Civil War Day by Day: An Almanac 1861-1865,* Garden City, N.Y.: Doubleday & Company, Inc., 1971.

Martin, David G., *Gettysburg July 1,* Conshohocken, Pa.: Combined Books, Inc., 1996.

Military History of Ohio, The (Ross County edition), Toledo: H.H. Hardesty, 1887.

Otis, George A., *The Medical and Surgical History of the Civil War,* 15 vols., Wilmington, N.C.: Broadfoot Publishing Co., 1991.

Pfanz, Harry W., *Gettysburg: The Second Day,* Chapel Hill: The University of North Carolina Press, 1987.

——, *Gettysburg: Culp's Hill and Cemetery Hill,* Chapel Hill: The University of North Carolina Press, 1993.

——, *Gettysburg – The First Day,* Chapel Hill: The University of North Carolina Press, 2001.

Pula, James S., *For Liberty and Justice: The Life and Times of Wladimir Krzyzanowski,* Chicago: Polish American Congress Charitable Foundation, 1978.

Reid, Whitelaw, *Ohio in the War: Her Statesmen, Generals and Soldiers,* 2 vols., Cincinnati: The Robert Clarke Company, 1895.

Shultz, David, *"Double Canister at Ten Yards": The Federal Artillery and the Repulse of Pickett's Charge,* Redondo Beach, Calif.: Rank and File Publications, 1995.

Taylor, Eugene E., *Gouverneur Kemble Warren: The Life and Letters of an American Soldier*, Boston: Houghton-Mifflin Company, 1932.

Ward, Stephen H., *Buckeyes All: A Compendium and Bibliography of Ohio in the Civil War,* 3 vols., 2 supplements, Dayton: privately printed, 1999-2001.

Warner, Ezra J., *Generals in Blue,* Baton Rouge: Louisiana

State University Press, 1992.

——, *Generals in Gray,* Baton Rouge: Louisiana State University Press, 1959.

Wittenberg, Eric J., *Gettysburg's Forgotten Cavalry Actions,* Gettysburg: Thomas Publications, 1998.

Miscellaneous works

Andrews, Martin R., editor & compiler, *History of Marietta and Washington County, Ohio and Representative Citizens,* vol. III, Chicago: Biographical Publishing Company, 1902.

Bell, Raymond M., *The Ancestry of Richard Milhous Nixon,* Washington, Pa.: privately printed, 1970.

Blue, Herbert T.O., *History of Stark County, Ohio,* Chicago: The S.J. Clarke Publishing Company, 1928.

Brancaforte, Charlotte L., editor, *The German Forty Eighters in the United States,* New York: Peter Lang, 1989.

Burnham, Roderick H., *The Burnham Family; or Genealogical Records of the Descendants of the Four Emigrants of the Name, Who Were Among the Early Settlers in America,* Hartford, Conn.: Press of Case, Lockwood & Brainard, 1869.

Cleveland und sein Deutschthum, Cleveland: German-American Biographical Publishing Co., 1907.

Dunkelman, Mark H., *The Coster Avenue Mural in Gettysburg,* Providence, R.I.: 1989.

Fee, William I., *Bringing the Sheaves: Gleanings from Harvest Fields in Ohio, Kentucky and West Virginia,* Cincinnati: Cranston & Curts, 1896.

Ferris, Mary W., compiler, *Dawes-Gates Ancestral Lines: A Memorial Volume Containing the American Ancestry of Rufus R. Dawes,* vol. I, privately printed, 1943.

Graham, A.A., compiler, *History of Richland County, Ohio: Its Past and Present,* Mansfield: A.A. Graham & Co., Publishers, 1880.

History of Hocking Valley, Ohio, Chicago: Inter-State Publishing Co., 1883.

History of Preble County, Ohio, with Illustrations and Biographical Sketches, Cleveland: W.W. Williams, 1881.

Howe, Henry, *Historical Collections of Ohio,* 2 vols., Cincinnati: C.J. Krehbiel & Co., 1904.

Hubbert, Henry C., *Ohio Wesleyan's First Hundred Years,* Delaware: Ohio Wesleyan University, 1943.

Keesee, Dennis M., *Too Young To Die: Boy Soldiers of the Union Army 1861-1865,* Huntington, W.Va.: Blue Acorn Press, 2001.

Morton, Marian J., *Women in Cleveland: An Illustrated History,* Bloomington: Indiana University Press, 1995.

Perrin, William H., editor, *History of Stark County, with an Outline Sketch of Ohio,* Chicago: Baskin & Battey, 1881.

Record of Hon. C.L. Vallandigham on Abolition, the Union, and the Civil War, Columbus: J. Walter & Co., 1863.

Williams, William W., *History of the Firelands, comprising Huron and Erie Counties, Ohio,* Cleveland: Press of Leader Printing Company, 1879.

INDEX

Page numbers appearing in boldface indicate photographs or illustrations.

A

Abbott, Lucien, 144, 157
Ackerman, George, **59**
Ackerman, William, 170
Adams County, Pa., 35, 52, 182-183, 188
Adelphi, Ohio, 32
"Agate" (Whitelaw Reid), 75
Akron, Ohio, 10, 110, 136, 138
Albright, M.L. (photographer), 130
Aldie, Va., 22, 27, 29, 190
Alexandria, Va., 31
Allen, Isaac J., 208, 209, 211
Allison, John, 69
Almshouse, Adams County, 44, 53, 54, 60, 68, 172
Alter, Joseph B., **51**
Alvord, Aaron M., **154**
Ames, Adelbert, **21**, 44, 45, 46, 47, 49, 51, 52, 53, 54, 60, 64, 65, 68, 69, 78, 91, 92, 106, 107, 110, 114, 115, 167, 168, 169, 172, 193, 204
Ames, Lyman D., 34, 175
Amsberg, George von, 59
Anderson, Charles, 207, 210, 211
Anderson, Lorenzo D., **199**
Anderson, Richard H., 101
Anderson, Robert, 207
Andersonville National Cemetery, 201
Andersonville (Ga.) prison, 186, 192, 201
Antietam, battle of, 72, 88, 156, 160, 190
Antietam Creek, 193, 194
Antioch College, 113
Arlington National Cemetery, 159
Army corps (C.S.),
  First, 23
  Second, 23, 103
  Third, 23
Army corps (U.S.),

1st, 23, 30, 37, 38, 39, 42, 43, 59, 63, 66, 75, 77, 78, 90, 102, 103, 170
2nd, 9, 22, 24, 26, 30, 31, 34, 66, 75, 77, 83, 86, 102, 116, 120, 122, 153, 157, 175, 176, 177, 178, 179, 180, 204
3rd, 18, 25, 30, 72, 75, 86, 96, 100, 101, 102
5th, 9, 21, 22, 25, 33, 75, 96, 97, 99, 100, 102
6th, 100, 102, 169
11th, 9, 14, 15, 16, 17, 18, 20, 21, 24, 25, 30, 31, 32, 34, 35, 37, 38, 39, 40, 42, 43, 48, 49, 54, 58, 61, 63, 64, 65, 66, 67, 69, 71, 75, 76, 86, 90, 94, 106, 112, 114, 116, 120, 123, 150, 167, 170, 171, 172, 182, 188, 189, 193, 195, 199, 204
12th, 9, 25, 29, 34, 72, 73, 77, 91, 102, 103, 104, 105, 125, 127, 128, 130, 133, 134, 140, 146, 174, 204
20th, 60, 71, 171, 204
Army of Northern Virginia, 13, 23, 191
Army of the Cumberland, 10, 22, 71, 198, 204, 211
Army of the Potomac, 9, 13, 14, 15, 19, 20, 22, 23, 29, 30, 31, 33, 35, 40, 72, 76, 102, 124, 146, 148, 151, 162, 169, 176, 187, 192, 196, 199, 203, 204
Artillery Reserve, 9, 21, 22, 89, 124, 125, 146, 147, 149, 151
Ashby's Gap, Va., 27
Ashland County, Ohio, 63, 186
Ashtabula, Ohio, 100, 101
Ashtabula County, Ohio, 73, 134, 138, 185, 191
Ashtabula Weekly Telegraph, 100
Athens County, Ohio, 52, 68
Atlanta, Ga., 41, 187
Atlantis, 18
Austin, James S., 46
Avery, Isaac, 46, 61, 106, 114, 116

B

Bacon, Oscar E., 180
Baker, Mortimer, 29
Ball, Volney, 9
Baltimore, Md., 23, 35, 84, 180, 187, 207
Baltimore Pike, 67, 68, 69, 73, 74, 76, 77, 90, 102, 105, 106, 116, 120, 126, 131, 146, 151, 160, 161
Baltimore Street (Gettysburg), 44, 57, 65, 167, 208, 209
Bancroft, Eugene, 49
Barclay, John K., 123
Bare, Thomas G., 138
Barker's Chicago Dragoons, 190
Barlow, Francis C., **21**, 37, 38, 40, 44, 45, 46, 47, 48, 49, 53, 54, 61, 64
Barret, Norman A., **27,** 187
Barrett, Joseph, 84
Battel, B.F. Gallery of Art, 138
Baughman, Samuel P., 114
Bayou Teche, La., 17
Beamon, Benson, 144, 157
Beaver, Pa., 120
Beckett, David C., **41**
Bedford, Ohio, 180
Beiser, Friedrich, **44**
Bell, James H., **59,** 60
Belle Isle (Va.) prison, 63, 82, 200, 201
Bellevue, Ohio, 67, 79
Belmont County, Ohio, 51, 71, 192
Bending, Henry R., **60**
Benedict, George A., 207
Benham's (photographer), 145
Benner, Josiah, 45, 53, 69, 172
Benner's Hill, 90, 92, 93, 147, 174
Bentonville, N.C., battle of, 190
Berlin, Md., 196, 197
Berlin, Pa., 162
Bern, Switzerland, 45
Bertholf, Gilbert D., 141

Big Round Top, 75, 163
Biggerstaff, Elisha, 50
Biggs, John C., 180
Billau, George, 110, 111
Bishop's Photographic Gallery, 127
Blackford, Eugene, 43
Blair, Montgomery, 207, 210
Bliss, William, 86, 145
Bliss farm, 87, 144, 155
Blocher's Knoll, 44, 45, 46, 48, 52, 54, 200
Bloody Angle, 158
Blue Ridge Mountains, 23, 27
Boalt, Frederick H., 81, **82**
Bohm, Edward H., **139**
Bonnaughtown, Pa., 75
Boonsboro, Md., 188, 190, 192
Bope, Abraham, 89
Bourbach le Bas, Alsace, 19
Bowers, James, **111**
Bown, William H.H., 37, 41, 88
Braddock, Stephen J., 95
Brady, Allen G., 45, 106, 107, **112**
Brady, Mathew B., 157
Bragg, Braxton, 202
Braun, Samuel, 111
Brearly, Samuel L., **118**
Breck, George, 107
Brent, Edmund V., 60
Brenton, Joseph L., 24, 175
Brewster, Oscar, **137**
Brickyard Lane, 68, 92, 106, 112, 118
Briggs, Jasper C., 84
Briggs, Mahlon B., 69
Brinker, John H., 64, 68, 111, 112
Brinkman, Henry C., 132
Brockenbrough, J.M., 153, 154
Brockway, Green, 90
Bromley, Edward, **169**
Brooke's Station, Va., 19, 188
Brooklyn, N.Y., 203
Brooks, Norman, 120
Brotts, Henry A., 146, 154, 155, 180
Brough, John, 10, 207, **209**, 210
Brown, Daniel, 80
Brown, Daniel W., 205, 208, 211
Brown, John C., 143
Brown, John M., 47, 78
Brown, Moses, **80**
Brown, Philip P. Jr., **40**, 59
Brown, William, 156
Bruceville, Md., 34, 35
Brüggemeyer, Joseph, **44**
Bryan, Abraham, 122, 144, 157
Bryan house, **157**
Buchwalter, Luther M., **32**
Buchwalter, Martin L., 24, 120, 170
Buckley, Daniel, 143
Buell, Frank, 94

Buffalo, N.Y., 69
Buford, John, 35, 38, 190, 191, 192
Bull Run Mountain, 27, 29
Burk, John, 156
Burnham, Stowel L., 24, 36, 56, **70**, 197
Burns, John, 210
Bushnell, Wells A., 187, 192, 193
Butler County, Ohio, 22, 202
Butts, Charles E., **127**

C

Cadiz, Ohio, 162
Cadwallader, John (photographer), 30, 93
Cadwallader & Tappan (photographers), 104
Caldwell, David B., 115
Call, William R., 85
Cambridge, Ohio, 208
Camden, Ohio, 114
Camp Asylum, S.C., 51
Camp Chase, Ohio, 121
Camp Cleveland, Ohio, 20
Camp Dennison, Ohio, 178
Camp Letterman (Gettysburg), 127, 134, 180, 181, 205
Camp Parole, Md., 45, 200
Candy, Charles, **72**, 73, 74, 75, 77, 78, 105, 126, 130, 131, 134, 135, 136, 138
Canton, Ohio, 19, 35, 50, 118, 190, 196
Cantwell, Jacob Y., 70, **171**
Cantwell, James, 56, 171
Capron, E.P.H. & Bros. (photographers), 113
Carlisle, Pa., 35
Carlisle Road, 40, 43, 54, 59, 61, 70, 71
Carlisle Street (Gettysburg), 209
Carpenter, Leonard W., **117**, 119
Carroll, Charles, 139
Carroll, Samuel S., **26**, 34, 77, 86, 87, 88, 116, 117, 118, 120, 123, 146, 160, 212
Carroll, Vincent, 50
Carver, James, 79
Case, George, 134
Cashtown, Pa., 184
Catlett's Station, Va., 25
Catoctin Mountain, 31, 32, 34, 187
Cavalry Corps (U.S.), 9, 21, 22, 27, 34, 162, 185, 192
Cedar Mountain, Va., battle of, 56, 72
Cemetery Hill, 39, 40, 43, 48, 61, 62, 63, 64, 65, 66, 67, 76, 77, 78, 86, 87, 88, 89, 90, 92, 93, 94, 96, 101, 102, 103, 106, 107, 122, 124, 142, 145, 146, 149, 150, 151, 152, 154, 159, 164, 170, 172, 208
Cemetery Ridge, 74, 76, 86, 146, 157,

158, 208
Centerville, Va., 13, 25, 26
Centerton, Ohio, 197
Chadwick, Joseph, **63**
Chaffee, Adna R., **185**
Chaffee, Orestes P., 185
Chaffee, Sheburn H., 185
Chaffee, Truman E., 185
Chambersburg, Pa., 30, 35
Chambersburg Street (Gettysburg), 209
Champaign County, Ohio, 72, 128, 130
Chancellorsville, Va., battle of, 13, 14, 15, 16, 17, 18, 19, 20, 21, 22, 33, 38, 45, 52, 53, 60, 66, 69, 72, 73, 86, 88, 91, 94, 95, 100, 106, 127, 135, 147, 148, 151, 156, 160, 169, 170, 180, 181, 190, 197, 201
Chapel Road, 38
Charleston, S.C., 204
Chase, Salmon P., 207
Chattanooga, Tenn., 169, 198
Chester, Albert E., 186
Chicago, Ill., 190, 191, 196
Chicago Tribune, 190
Chickamauga, battle of, 204
Chillicothe, Ohio, 21, 66, 68, 85, 92, 142, 160
Christian Commission, 177, 182
Cincinnati, Ohio, 13, 17, 18, 40, 41, 44, 51, 62, 72, 75, 99, 113, 131, 132, 133, 134, 151, 178, 187, 201, 209, 210
Cincinnati Daily Commercial, 206, 208
Cincinnati Daily Times, 132
Cincinnati Enquirer, 209
Cincinnati Gazette, 75
Cincinnati Law School, 53
Circleville, Ohio, 60, 188
Circleville Democrat, 83
Clark, Horace S., 84
Clark, Mervin, 141
Clark County, Ohio, 72, 130
Clear, Elias, 200, 201, 202, 203
Clements, George S., 109
Clermont County, Ohio, 151
Cleveland, Grover, 212
Cleveland, Ohio, 10, 17, 18, 24, 25, 26, 61, 62, 68, 73, 90, 100, 110, 111, 138, 139, 144, 176, 180, 190, 208, 212
Cleveland Herald, 105, 111, 207
Cleveland Light Guard Zouaves, 105
Cleveland Medical College, 120
Cleveland Plain Dealer, 105
Clough, William H., 152, 154, 159, 180
Clyde, Ohio, 145
Cobbledick, William H., 62
Coddington, Edwin B., 14, 15, 30
Cody, Darwin, 90
Coggeshall, William, 208
Cold Harbor, Va., 94

Cole, W.C., 178
Columbiana, Ohio 59
Columbiana County, Ohio, 19, 202
Columbus, Ohio, 16, 18, 60, 65, 121, 129, 171, 181, 205, 207
Comfort, Henry, 57
Conlan, James, 156
Conneaut, Ohio, 29, 34
Conneaut Reporter, 175
Connecticut troops,
    Infantry:
    14th Connecticut, 145
    17th Connecticut, 18, 44, 45, 49, 51, 53, 64, 68, 106, 107, 112, 114, 168
Constitution, Ohio, 104
Coolidge, Calvin, 104
Coons, John, 26
Copse of Trees, 153, 158
Corbin, James H., 130
Corman, John, 111
Coshocton, Ohio, 190
Coster, Charles R., 61, 66, 106
Costin, John, 70
Covert, Charles T., **94**
Covert, Thomas M., 185, 191, 195
Cox, Samuel S., 22
Cozine, Peter A., 132
Craig, Alfred T., 160
Crall, James S., **56**
Crane, Orrin, 139
Crawford, J.S., 166, 171
Crawford County, Ohio, 19, 80, 87
Creighton, William R., 73, **105,** 106, 138, 139, 140, 141
Cross, Marion G., **61**
Cross Keys, Va., battle of, 56, 171, 201
Crubaugh, Jeremiah, 114
Crubaugh, Joseph, 114
Culp, Edward C., 46, **64,** 65, 78, 91, 109, 168
Culp, Elizabeth, 168
Culp's Hill, 77, 90, 102, 103, 104, 105, 106, 119, 123, 125, 126, 127, 129, 130, 131, 132, 135, 137, 139, 140, 141, 142, 146, 149, 151, 164, 165, 167, 173, 174, 187, 212
Cumberland Valley, 23
Curtin, Andrew G., 205, 207
Curtiss, Edward T., 138, **174**
Curtner, Ira, 114
Cushing, Alonzo H., 158
Custer, George A., 9, 34, **162,** 185, 186, 187, 193
Cuyahoga County, Ohio, 17, 19, 59, 73
Cuyahoga Falls, Ohio, 135

D

Dafford, Robert, 98
Dailey, Zachariah, **51**

Dammert, William, 44
Daniel, Junius, 132
Daniels, Oramel G., **156**
Danville, Va., 60
Davis, Alphonso C., 52, 200
Davis, Asa O., 207
Davis, Edward I., 101
Davis, Jefferson P., **16**
Davis, John, 69
Davis, Joseph R., 153, 155
Davis, Lewis, 207
Davis, Llewellyn R., **140**
Davis, William B., **83**
Dawes, Charles G., 104
Dawes, Henry, 104
Dawes, Rufus R., 9, **104,** 105
Dayton, Ohio, 201
Dean, Harry M., 138, 187
DeBeck, William L., 22
Debolt, John, 117
Defiance County, Ohio, 19
Delameter, John N., **199**
Delaware, Ohio, 10, 42, 70, 71, 73, 116, 194, 199
Delaware County, Ohio, 31, 37, 42, 63, 72, 117, 126, 127
Delaware Gazette, 70
Dennison, William, 87, 120, 207, **209,** 210
Department of Florida, 100
Department of Washington, 22
Department of the South, 204
Department of the Susquehanna, 182
DePuy, John W., 154
Deshler, Charles H., 52
Detty, Enoch M., 205
Deubel, Conrad, **111**
Devil's Den, 96, 103
Dickelman, Joseph L., 117, 118
Dickson, William J., **70**
Die Deutschen Organisation, 17
Dilger, Hubert, 16, **38,** 39, 40, 41, 42, 43, 44, 45, 46, 58, 59, 60, 67, 69, 89, 90, 91
Dobbin house, 67, 78
Dolbear, Byron, **116,** 117
Doles, George, 42, 45, 46, 49, 50, 54, 57, 58, 70
Dority, Orin G., 90, 91, 94, 148
Dorr, David, 96
Dorries, Frederick, 22
Doubleday, Abner, 66
Dover, Ohio, 114
Duane (U.S. cutter), 53
Dumfries, Va., 24, 25
Dunn, Thomas, 206, 207
Dunne, John, 20

E

Early, Jubal A., 45, 46, **49,** 61, 70, 72, 106, 120, 125, 167
East Cemetery Hill, 68, 69, 92, 106, 107, 109, 115-116, 117, 120, 123, 141, 142, 167, 206, 212
Eaton, Ohio, 180, 201, 202, 203
Eby, Isaac, **114**
Eckerly, Louis, 200
Edelblute, Jacob, 63
Edelblute, Lewis, 63
Edgar, Addison H., 87
Edgell, Frederick, 90, 149
Edinburgh, Scotland, 72
Edmonds, John N., 94
Edwards' Ferry, Va., 30, 31
Eichsteten, Baden, 85
Elliott, Gilbert M., 139
Elliott, Silas G., **137**
Elliott, Walter, **133**
Elyria, Ohio, 13, 152, 159, 160, 175, 178, 179, 180, 181
Elyria Independent Democrat, 178
Emmitsburg, Md., 34, 35, 37, 45, 68, 162, 185, 186, 189
Emmitsburg Road, 37, 44, 67, 69, 75, 78, 82, 85, 86, 87, 88, 96, 100, 120, 122, 123, 142, 144, 145, 152, 154, 157, 158, 159, 163, 180, 209
Enderlin, Richard, **85,** 86
Enfield rifle muskets, 41, 47, 55, 88, 112, 136
England, George, 85
Erie County, Ohio, 68, 73, 143, 146
Esselen, Christian, 18
Evans, Joseph, 159
Evans, Thomas, 15
Everett, Edward, 208, 210
Evergreen Cemetery, 66, 67, 76, 90, 94, 107, 112, 116, 125, 160, 180, 205
Ewell, Richard S., 23, 40, 45, 90, 103, 125, 126, 139, 141, 146, 147, 166, 186, 194
Ewing, William A., **93,** 94, 147, 148, 149, **152,** 174

F

Fair Oaks, Va., battle of, 14
Fairchild, John G., 156, 180
Fairfax Court House, Va., 25, 26, 29
Fairfield, Ohio, 14
Fairfield, Pa., 52, 185
Falling Waters, W.Va., 194, 195
Falmouth, Va., 13, 24, 152
Farnsworth, Elon J., 34, 162, 163, 164
Farr, Edward W., **136**
Fayette County, Ohio, 22, 68
Fee, John, 182

Fee, William, 150, 182
Felicity, Ohio, 182
Fellers, Samuel, 24, 84, 165
Field, Theodore G., 95
Firelands, 87
First Bull Run, battle of, 21
Fisher, Joseph W., 99, 100
Foraker, Joseph B., 211, 212
Forbes, Edwin, 67
Ford, Alonzo, 52
Forrest, Nathan Bedford, 18
Fort Pickens, Fla., 100
Fort Sumter, S.C., 190, 207, 208
Fort Washington, Md., 101
Forty-Eighters, 17, 18
Foster, Romeo W., 156
Fostoria, Ohio, 193
Fourgeres, Louis, 95
Fowler, Douglas, 51
Fowler, Lorenzo, 113
Fox, George Benson, 37, 68, 69, 78, 113, **115,** 120, 167, 168, 193, 194
Frankfurt-am-Main, Germany, 71
Franklin, Ohio, 53, 209
Franklin County, Ohio, 17
Franklin Grays, 53
Franklin Mills, Ohio, 180
Frederick, Md., 33, 34, 188, 190, 191, 195
Fredericksburg, battle of, 21, 86, 100, 122, 148, 160, 181
Fredericksburg, Va., 23
Fremont, Ohio, 145
Friend, Charles W., 22
Fulton County, Ohio, 14, 148
Funkstown, Md., 192, 193
Furbish, W.H. (photographer), 199

G

Gainesville, Fla., 51, 114
Gainesville, Va., 26, 29, 31
Gale, C.A. (photographer), 91
Gallagher, Charles, 153
Galwey, Thomas, 24, 26, 29, 33, 34, 75, 86, 123, 144, 145, 153, 156, 159, 160, 184
Gambee, Charles B., 21, 67, **79,** 81, 82, 189, 190
Gambier, Ohio, 97, 195
Ganson, B.F., **130**
Gardner, Isaac W., 16, 46
Garlic, T.T. (photographer), 97
Garrett, John, **89**
Gaul, Joseph L., 78, 131, **132,** 134, 151, 165, 174
Geary, John W., 25, 72, 74, 77, 78, **102,** 105, 125, 126, 131, 139, 140, 141
Geauga County, Ohio, 73, 141
Geist, Philip, **25**

Georgetown, Ohio, 151
Georgia troops,
 Infantry:
 4th Georgia, 57
 44th Georgia, 57
Gephart, George W., 68, 83, 84
German Reformed Church, 142
Gettysburg, battle of, 9, 10, 13, 19, 20, 22, 41, 47, 53, 56, 61, 62, 64, 69, 70, 80, 88, 100, 101, 105, 118, 133, 139, 147, 164, 169, 173, 175, 177, 184, 190, 191, 192, 195, 196, 197, 199, 202, 205, 206, 212
Gettysburg, Pa., 13, 24, 35, 37, 38, 39, 40, 41, 43, 44, 45, 54, 55, 57, 58, 60, 61, 63, 64, 66, 68, 72, 73, 75, 78, 88, 89, 99, 106, 111, 127, 134, 142, 143, 147, 153, 162, 166, 167, 168, 169, 170, 171, 172, 173, 178, 179, 180, 181, 182, 187, 189, 193, 198, 200, 204, 205, 207, 208, 209, 210, 212
Gettysburg Address, 210
Gettysburg Battlefield Memorial Association, 211
Gettysburg National Cemetery, 85, 205, 206, 211
Gibbon, John, 116
Gibbs, Frank C., 22, **97,** 98, 99, 100
Gibraltar Brigade, 116, 160
Gildea, James, 22, 75, 97, 98, 99, 100
Gillespie, Samuel L., 26-27, 34, 161, 162, 163, 164, 185, 186, 191, 192, 193, 195
Gillis, Charles J., 46
Gillis, Joseph, 41, **42,** 63
Gilsa, Leopold von, 44, 45, 46, 48, 49, 51, 106, 107, 114
Ginn, John, 114
Goddard, John H., **46**
Goodin, Alfred, 200
Goose Creek, 24, 29, 45
Gordon, George H., 204
Gordon, John B., 46, 48, **49,** 50, 54, 60, 61
Graceland Cemetery (Chicago), 196
Granite School House, 95
Granite School House Road, 76, 89, 120
Granville, Ohio, 21, 23
Grant, Ulysses S., 10, 14
Gray, Stephen, 128, 129
Greencastle, Pa., 37, 68
Greene, George S., 74, 75, 77, **102,** 103, 104, 106, 125, 126, 128, 129, 134, 135, 136, 138, 140, 141
Greenfield, Ohio, 143
Greenwood, Pa., 184
Gregg, David M., 27, 162, 185
Gregg, James, 146, 152, 153, 155
Greiner, George B., 84

Gridley, William Jr., 180
Griffin, Charles, 21
Grisso, Orris, 212
Griswold & Howard's Gallery, 65
Grodzicki, Anthony, 88, 89
Groveton, Va., battle of, 56
Grubb, Peter, 86, **87,** 88, 120
Guinn, Catherine, 120, 180
Gum Springs, Va., 31
Gunn, Orlando, 135, 138
Gustin, Joseph I., 53
Guthrie, Herbert F., 22, 98, **99,** 100
Guy, William, 128, 129

H

Hagerstown, Md., 32, 184, 185, 190, 191, 193, 194, 195
Hagy farm, 40, 42
Hall, John W., 111
Halleck, Henry W., 33
Hamilton, Ohio, 17
Hamilton County, Ohio, 17, 22, 51, 69
Hamlin, Augustus C., 16
Hammel, John M., **103**
Hampshire, England, 95
Hancock, Cornelia, 176
Hancock, Winfield S., 22, 66, 74, 75, 116
Hanover, Pa., 34, 35, 75, 97, 141, 162, 163
Hanover Junction, Pa., 207
Hanover Road, 90
Hardin County, Ohio, 15, 58, 87, 199, 200
Hardin County Republican, 56
Hardy, Alpheus W., 136
Harl, James W., 117
Harmon, J.M., **58**
Harnit, Joseph M., **31**
Harpers Ferry, W.Va., 33
Harris, Andrew L., 22, 45, 49, 51, 52, 53, 54, 63, 64, 68, 69, 78, 92, 106, 107, 109, 114, 120, 141, 167, **168,** 169, 170, 193, 204, 212
Harrisburg, Pa., 23, 24, 121, 207
Harrisburg Road, 44, 54, 61, 166, 171
Harrison, Charles, 49
Harrison County, Ohio, 34, 162
Harrisonburg, Va., 200
Hart, Samuel W., 73, 151
Hartley, Benjamin, 69
Hartwood Church, Va., 25
Harvard University, 21
Hatfield, Samuel M., 85
Haughton, Nathaniel, **53,** 54
Hawkins, Isaac N., **164**
Haw's Shop, Va., battle of, 191, 194
Hayden, Deborah, 180, 181
Hayden, Elijah, 13, 26, 145, 154, 159, 180, 181
Hayden, Ella, 13, 159

Hayes, Edward, 134, 135, 136, 137, 138
Haynes, William E., 85
Hays, Alexander, 87, 145, 153, 159
Hays, Harry T., 46, 61, **106,** 107, 109, 115, 116, 118, 123, 142, 206
Hayward, George, 135, 136
Hazel Grove, Va., 22
Hazlett, Charles E., **96,** 97
Heckman, Lewis, 22, 61, 62
Heidlersburg, Pa., 45
Helmich, George, 181, 182
Henney, Henry C., 24, 31, 32, 34, 35, 67, 76, 150, 189
Hershey, Oliver, **109**
Hess, Joseph O., **193**
Higgins, Thomas, 84, 85, 86
High Street (Gettysburg), 142
Highland County, Ohio, 68, 165
Hill, Ambrose P., 23, 38, 82, 90, 101, 122, 142, 146, 194
Hill, Harlan, 181
Hill, Hiram C., 181
Hill, John, 181
Hill, Wallace, 90, 94, **95,** 96, 147, 148, 149, 172
Hissey, Absalom, 85
Hitchcock, George, 146
Hitt, Joseph W., 136
Hively, Augustus, **103**
Hoag & Quick's studio, 99
Hocking County, Ohio, 68
Hollis, Joseph H., 19
Homer, Ohio, 180
Hood, John B., 163
Hooker, Joseph, **12,** 13, 14, 17, 20, 22, 23, 24, 29, 30, 33, 89, 148, 196
Hopkins, Edwin P., **152**
Horner's Mills, Pa., 38
Hornung, Conrad F., 65
Horse Artillery, 9, 192
Hotchkiss shells, 147
Houtz, John W., 128
Howard, Charles H., 65
Howard, Oliver O., **14,** 15, 16, 17, 19, 30, 37, 38, 39, 43, 46, 48, 61, 63, 64, 66, 86, 103, 115, 116, 193
Howe, Henry, 42
Hubbell, William L., 53
Hubler, Simon, 78, 79
Huey, Pennock, 185, 190
Humphrey, George C., 113
Humphreys, Andrew A., 100, 101
Hunt, Henry J., 14, 92, 100, 148, 149, 153
Hunt, Lester T., 70
Hunterstown, Pa., 162
Huntington, James F., 22, 25, 33, 89, 90, 94, 102, 116, 124, 125, 146, **147,** 149, 151, 164, 174

Huron County, Ohio, 19, 68, 81, 82, 87, 123, 144, 197, 198, 199
Hurst, Samuel H., 20, 32, 66, 83, 93, **142,** 165, 183, 212

I

Illinois troops,
    Cavalry:
        8th Illinois, 190
Indiana troops,
    Infantry:
        14th Indiana, 26, 116, 117, 160, 177
Iowa troops,
    Infantry:
        9th Iowa, 178
Ireland, David, 135
Irish, Edward H., 144, 177
Ironton, Ohio, 99
Iron Brigade, 9, 103

J

Jack, Jason J., **145**
Jack, John H., 144, 152
Jackson, Andrew, 92, 115, 118, 119
Jackson, Thomas J. (Stonewall), 14, 15, 140, 166
Jackson County, Ohio, 68, 84
Jacoby, Henry, 70
James, Robert, 101
James Island, S.C., 204
James River, 200
James shells, 147
Jefferson, Md., 31
Jeffries, Lemuel, 26, 86, 101, 117, 119
Jenvey, William, 94, 95, 102, 148, 172
Jewett, Leonidas M., 31, 33, 35, 36, 60, 63
Johnson, Andrew, 209
Johnson, Edward, 103, 106, 125, 132, 133, **140,** 141, 142
Johnson, Isaac, 62
Johnson, Josiah D., 136
Jones, Edward, 156, **178**
Jones, Hilary, 45, 46, 49
Jones, J.M., 127
Jones, John P., 82
Jones, Noah, 22, 162, 186
Jones, William, 180
Jones, William E., 186
Jones' Crossroads, Md., 194
Judson, Horace, 156
Judson, Silas, 156

K

Kane, Thomas L., 126, 131, 132
Keeler, Alonzo, 143
Keirsh, Jacob, 94
Kellogg, Charles W., **134**
Kelly, James, 156, 176

Kennedy, Michael, 85
Kennesaw Mountain, Ga., 41, 43, 44
Kenney, William, 156, 176
Kenton, Ohio, 56, 70, 86, 201
Kenyon College, 97, 195
Kepler, William, 30, 31, 75, 86, 116, 117, 120, 203
Kernstown, Va., battle of, 72
Kilpatrick, H. Judson, 33, 34, 161, 162, **163,** 164, 185, 186, 187, 190, 191, 192, 193, 194
King, Charles H., 172
Kinkler, Henry, 20
Kline, Asa, 99
Klingle, Daniel, 100, 101
Knapp, Henry J., 74, 76, 105, 135, 137, 138, 195
Knox County, Ohio, 117
Knoxville Register, 18
Koblenz, Germany, 110
Kolb's Farm, Ga., battle of, 43
Koogle, Henry C., **184**
Koons, David S., 159
Kratz, John, 20, **50**
Krzyzanowski, Wladimir, 21, 40, 41, 44, 48, **54,** 55, 62, 115

L

Lacey, Charles, 148
Ladd, Charles, 50
Ladley, Oscar D., 17, 18, 24, 26, **113,** 114, 115, 167, 168, 180, 188, 192
Lahmiller, Andrew, 111
Laird, George F., 26, 34, **35**
Lake County, Ohio, 73, 139
Lamon, Ward H., 208, 209, 210
Lancaster, Ohio, 195
Lander, Frederick W., 72
Laraba, Jonathan, 69
Laughlin, Hiram, **25**
Law, Evander M., 161
Lawson, Henry M., 85
Layton, William C., 55
Leake, Elisha L., 84
Ledig, August, 56, 57
LeDuc, William G., **195**
Lee, Alfred E., **11,** 37, 38, 39, 41, 42, 54, 55, 57, 70, **71,** 166, 171, 172, 211
Lee, John C., 21
Lee, Robert E., 13, 14, 22, 23, 27, 29, 30, 33, 35, 37, 75, 146, 160, 169, 184, 185, 187, 188, 190, 191, 193, 194, 195, 196, 199, 203
Leesburg, Va., 29
Lehnhard, John, 96
Leigh, Benjamin W., 141
Leister house, 124, 151, 160
Lewis, David, 123, 144, 156, 175
Libby prison, 19, 29, 45, 47, 61, 64, 200

Licking County, Ohio, 22, 123
Lincoln, Abraham, 10, 19, 23, 33, 201, 202, 207, 209, 210
Little Round Top, 74, 77, 86, 96, 97, 98, 103
Littlestown, Pa., 34, 73, 187
Liverpool, Ohio, 165
Lloyd, Joseph, 153
Lofland, Gordon, 208, 209
Logan County, Ohio, 72, 129, 130, 151
Long, Richard, **68**, 82
Long Lane (Gettysburg), 142, 154
Longstreet, James, 23, 96, 99, 103, 146, 161, 163, 194
Longworth, Martin, 87
Loomis, Finney R., **156**
Lorain County, Ohio, 19, 73, 165, 178, 181
Loudoun Valley, 27, 29
Loufman, James, 148
Louisiana Tigers, 106, 110-111, 114, 115, 119
Louisiana troops,
    Infantry:
    1st Louisiana, 138
    8th Louisiana, 111, 112
Louisville, Ohio, 49
Lowe, John R., **81**
Lucas County, Ohio, 90, 94
Ludlum, B.F., 151
Lutheran Theological Seminary, 168
Lutz, John M., 47, 112
Lynchburg, Va., 72
Lynn, Joseph R., 105, 138

M

Macon, Ga., 60
Madeira, John D., 66, 159, **160**
Mader, Jacob F., 89, 91, **188**
Mahan, Isaiah, 42
Mahler, Francis, 55, 56
Mahoning County, Ohio, 73
Maine troops,
    Artillery:
    5th Maine Battery, 107, 117
    Infantry:
    20th Maine, 21, 47
Maloney, William, 51, 110
Malta, Ohio, 104
Manassas, plains of, 26, 204
Manassas Junction, Va., 25
Manchester, Md., 185
Manning, Nathaniel J., 18, 51, 64
Mansfield, Ohio, 42
Marietta, Ohio, 22, 94, 95, 104, 147, 148, 149, 151, 207
Marietta College, 104
Marietta Register, 172
Marietta & Cincinnati Railroad, 66

Marion, Ohio, 31, 58, 65, 119, 158
Marion County, Ohio, 72, 129
Marks, James O., 72
Marsh, John G., 136
Marsh Creek, 37, 38
Marshall, James, 84
Marshall, M.K. (photographer), 60
Marshall's Ambrotype & Photograph Gallery, 188
Martin, Augustus P., 97, 100
Martinsburg, W.Va., 200
Marysville, Ohio, 57
Mason, John S., 207
Massachusetts troops,
    Infantry:
    9th Massachusetts, 99
    33rd Massachusetts, 66, 67, 106
Massie, Harrison, 99
Massillon, Ohio, 110, 190
Maumee, Ohio, 94
Maurer, Samuel, 110, 111
Mayo, Robert M., 153, 154, 155
McAbee, Harry M., 120, 121, 161, **175**
McAdams, Lyman H., **73**
McAdams (photography) studio, 31
McArthur, Ohio, 85, 172
McCarran, Joseph, 140
McCillips, John, 123
McClellan, George B., 72, 196
McClelland, Samuel M., **78**
McCommon, James S., **164**
McCormick, Jacob, 111
McCully, David, 115
McDowell, Va., battle of, 56, 78, 201
McDowell, Lieutenant, 207
McGehee, George W., 85
McGregor, John, 202
McGroarty, Stephen J., **41**, 59, 89, 103
McGroarty, William H., 41
McGuire, Bernard, 156
McIntire's Gallery, 118
McKay, George, 105
McKell, James C., **143**
McKesson, Lester V., 122
McKnight's Hill, 107
McLaws, Lafayette, 99, 101
McLean, Nathaniel C., 18, 19, 21
McLuen, William, 85
McMasters, William, 186
McMillan's Woods, 148
McPherson, Edward, 62
McSherrystown, Pa., 75
Mead, Sherman H., **186**
Meade, George G., **33**, 34, 35, 37, 66, 75, 76, 89, 96, 102, 103, 105, 124, 146, 151, 153, 159, 160, 166, 169, 185, 187, 193, 194, 195, 196, 203
Mechanicsburg, Ohio, 128
Mechanicstown, Md., 37, 88, 89

Medal of Honor, 16, 21, 38, 82, 85, **86,** 151, 159
Medill, Joseph, 190, 191, 195
Medill, William H., **190**, 191, 195
Medina County, Ohio, 32, 66, 121, 150, 156, 160, 165
Mell, Joseph R., **60**
Melton, James J., 140
Menchey's Spring, 141
Mendenhall, John A., 115
Meredith, Philander C., 70
Merrell, James H., 139
Merrell, John H., 35, 89, **148,** 149, 175, 190, 197
Merrick, Charles H., 34, 175, 176, 177, 178, 181, 184
Merrick, Myra, 175
Merritt, Wesley, 163
Mesnard, Luther B., 14, 34, 81, 82, 150
Metcalf, George P., 9, 32, 39, 66, 150, **165,** 169, 170, 189
Meyer, Edward S., 19, 47
Meyer, Seraphim, 19, 20, 45, **47,** 49, 54, 64, 65
Meyers, Jonathan E., 180
Meysenburg, Theodore A., 64, 65
Miami County, Ohio, 91
Miami River, 53
Miami University, 22, 168, 209
Michigan troops,
    Cavalry:
    5th Michigan, 185
Middleburg, Va., 27
Middletown, Md., 31, 32, 33, 45, 189
Milan, Ohio, 143
Milledge, George, 130
Miller, Andrew, **143**
Miller, Henry, 143
Miller, Jacob, 195
Miller, John, 159
Miller, Mathew G., **58**
Miller, Samuel, **65**
Miller, Warren, 85
Miller, Wells W., 86, 88, 146, 153, 154, 155, 159
Mills, Wilmont A., 169
Milroy, Robert H., 23
Milton, Ohio, 60
Miraben, Leonidas, **95**
Mississippi River, 53
Mitchell, William D.W., 16, **57**
Mogadore, Ohio, 181
Monocacy Bridge, Md., 34
Monroe County, Ohio, 19, 51, 94
Monterey, Pa., 68, 185, 187, 191, 192
Montgomery County, Ohio, 103, 201
Moon, Thomas, 158
Moore, Kate, **182**
Moore, Lewis R., 96

Moore, Sarah, 151, 182
Moore, W.H. (photographer), 119, 158
Moore, William S., **150,** 151, 182, 183
Morey, Elias W., **141**
Morgan, Benjamin, 17, 19, 22, 25, **52,**
    53, 69, 172, **173,** 200
Morgan, John Hunt, 10
Morgan, John T., **128**
Morgan, Sarah X., **173**
Morgan County, Ohio, 94, 95, 104, 121
Morris Island, S.C., 204
Morton, Oliver P., 207
Mosby, John S., 29
Moses, L.T., 91
Mouat, David, 139
Mount Vernon, Ohio, 60
Mueller, Charles, 20, 45, 50
Mulharen, James C., 113, 180, 202
Mulharen, Thomas, 180
Mummasburg Road, 40, 43, 59
Munroe, Charles R., 46
Murfreesboro, Tenn., 127
Murray, Michael, **51**
Muskingum County, Ohio, 96
Muskingum River, 104
Myer, John R., 143

N

Napoleon guns, 40, **43,** 46, 61, 62, 67,
    97, 99, 101, 106, 107
Nelson, Joseph, 85
Newark, Ohio, 201
New Bloomington, Ohio, 58
New Hampshire troops,
    Artillery:
    1st New Hampshire Battery, 90, 149
New Haven, Ohio, 197
New Hope Church, Ga., battle of, 74,
    86, 106
New Philadelphia, Ohio, 20
New Rumley, Ohio, 34, 162
New York, N.Y., 178, 203
New York *Tribune,* 75
New York troops,
    Artillery:
    Battery I, 1st New York Light, 69,
      115
    13th New York Battery, 43
    Cavalry:
    2nd New York (Harris Light), 27, 192
    Infantry:
    14th Brooklyn, 105
    45th New York, 40, 41, 43
    58th New York, 55
    60th New York, 138, 139
    119th New York, 55, 115
    134th New York, 21
    136th New York, 9, 32, 66, 67, 68, 84,
      150, 165

137th New York, 135
157th New York, 40, 59, 103
Nicholls, Francis T., 138
Nickerson, Azor H., 77, 88, 123, 144,
    145, 160, 161, 176, **177,** 178, 179,
    205, 207, 210
Nickerson, Franklin B., 120, 121
Nixon, George III, **85,** 86
Nixon, Richard M., 85, 86
Nobel Peace Prize, 104
Noble, William H., **168,** 169
Norris, Sherman R., 138, 139, 174
North, John, 113
North Carolina troops,
    Infantry:
    6th North Carolina, 61
    34th North Carolina, 159
North Fairfield, Ohio, 82
Northway, Delos R., 27, 29, **191,** 192
Northwest Territory, 9
Norton, George W., 22, **90,** 94, 147, 148,
    149
Norton, Ohio, 135
Norwalk, Ohio, 82, 87, 123, 154, 172
Norwalk Light Guard, 88
Norwalk Reflector, 53
Nussbaum, Frederick, 66, 68, 111, 112,
    141

O

Oakland Cemetery (Sandusky), 181
Oak Hill, 39, 40, 42, 43, 44, 45, 46, 146
Oak Ridge, 59
Oberlin College, 82, 140
O'Garra, Thomas, 69
Ogden, James, 212
Ohio Brigade, 18, 21
Ohio General Assembly, 211
Ohio Penitentiary, 205
Ohio River, 53, 98
Ohio State Journal, 71, 208
Ohio troops,
    Artillery:
    Battery E, 1st Light O.N.G., 212
    Battery H, 1st Ohio Light, 14, 21, 22,
      25, 29, 30, 35, 89, 90, 91, 93, 94,
      146, 147, 148, 149, 151, 152, 175,
      190, 204
    Battery I, 1st Ohio Light, 16, 21, 38,
      39, 40, 43, 44, 46, 59, 90
    Battery K, 1st Ohio Light, 21, 22, 61,
      62, 106
    Battery L, 1st Ohio Light, 21, 22, 75,
      97, 98, 99, 100, 204
    14th Ohio Battery, 185
    Cavalry:
    First Ohio Squadron, 22, 33, 162,
      163, 185, 186, 187, 191, 195
    1st Ohio, 22, 26, 187, 194

6th Ohio, 22, 23, 27, 29, 136, 185,
    186, 187, 191, 192, 194, 195, 204
Infantry:
4th Ohio, 26, 27, 30, 31, 34, 35, 56,
    75, 77, 86, 87, 88, 101, 116, 117,
    118, 119, 120, 126, 158, 160, 175,
    203, 207, 212
5th Ohio, 72, 74, 78, 126, 131, 132,
    133, 134, 151, 165, 174, 184, 187,
    212
7th Ohio, 25, 29, 72, 73, 78, 105, 106,
    126, 134, 138, 139, 140, 141, 174,
    187
8th Ohio, 24, 26, 27, 29, 33, 34, 75,
    77, 86, 87, 88, 120, 122, 123, 143,
    144, 145, 146, 151, 153, 154, 155,
    156, 157, 158, 159, 160, 161, 175,
    176, 177, 178, 179, 180, 184, 196,
    203, 205
13th Ohio, 57
14th Regiment O.N.G., 212
16th Ohio, 113
18th Ohio, 94
25th Ohio, 15, 18, 19, 21, 44, 45, 46,
    47, 49, 50, 51, 53, 64, 68, 91, 106,
    107, 109, 110, 112, 167, 168, 172,
    193, 200, 204, 207
29th Ohio, 25, 29, 34, 72, 73, 74, 76,
    105, 126, 134, 135, 136, 137, 138,
    139, 141, 151, 174, 175, 181, 195,
    212
55th Ohio, 14, 18, 21, 24, 32, 33, 34,
    53, 61, 66, 67, 78, 79, 80, 81, 82, 93,
    142, 143, 144, 150, 151, 169, 170,
    172, 181, 188, 189, 197, 198
61st Ohio, 16, 31, 33, 35, 37, 41, 43,
    59, 60, 63, 88, 89, 91, 103, 150, 151,
    182, 188
66th Ohio, 72, 73, 78, 126, 127, 128,
    129, 130, 136, 151, 173, 188
73rd Ohio, 20, 21, 24, 32, 66, 67, 68,
    76, 82, 83, 84, 85, 86, 92, 93, 120,
    142, 143, 159, 160, 164, 165, 170,
    183, 195, 205
75th Ohio, 16, 17, 18, 19, 22, 24, 25,
    31, 35, 37, 44, 45, 49, 51, 52, 53, 63,
    64, 68, 69, 92, 106, 107, 112, 113,
    114, 115, 118, 120, 121, 167, 168,
    169, 171, 172, 173, 180, 188, 192,
    200, 202, 203, 204, 207
82nd Ohio, 15, 16, 18, 21, 24, 36, 37,
    41, 42, 54, 55, 56, 57, 58, 62, 63, 65,
    69, 70, 71, 86, 166, 171, 180, 197,
    199, 200, 201, 211
89th Ohio, 211
93rd Ohio, 207
107th Ohio, 18, 19, 20, 25, 34, 35, 44,
    45, 47, 49, 50, 51, 54, 63, 64, 65, 66,
    68, 76, 106, 107, 109, 110, 111, 112,

115, 120, 141, 170, 181, 204, 212
123rd Ohio, 198
Ohio Wesleyan University, 42, 71, 126
"Old Bricktop," 26, 77, 116
Oliver, Fidelia, 127
O'Neal, Edward A., 42
O'Neil, Owen, 148
Opert, Lewis, 62
Orange & Alexandria Railroad, 25
Ordnance rifles, 3-inch, 29, **30,** 43, 69, 107, 149, 152, 185
O'Reilly, James K., **24**
Orwell, Ohio, 185, 191
Osborn, Thomas W., 43, 61, 62, 90, 154

P

Page, R.C.M., 40
Painesville, Ohio, 175
Palmer, Joshua G., **128**
Pancoast, William, **109**
Pardee, Ario, 131, 132
Pardee Field, 134, 151
Parent, Caleb, 120
Parma, N.Y., 128
Parmater, Nathan L., 25, 29, 30, 34, 135, 137, 141
Parmelee, William E., 14, 89, 146, 147, **148,** 151, **152,** 212
Parmely, Charles, 181
Parrott rifles, 90, 93, 94, 97, 147, 148, 149
Patrick, John H., 72, **74,** 132, 134
Patterson, James H., 158
Patterson, Ohio, 54
Peace Democrats, 201
Peach Orchard, 103, 146
Peachtree Creek, Ga., battle of, 41, 59
Peck, Albert W., 112
Pein & Co. Photograph Gallery, 184
Pemberton, Alexander, 50
Pender, W. Dorsey, 82
Penfield, William C., **82**
Peninsula campaign, 190
Pennington, Alexander C.M. Jr., 186
Pennsylvania College, 41, 60
Pennsylvania troops,
  Artillery:
  Battery F & G, 1st Pennsylvania Light, 90
  Infantry:
  Pennsylvania Reserves, 99
  28th Pennsylvania, 73, 126, 136
  29th Pennsylvania, 139
  62nd Pennsylvania, 9
  74th Pennsylvania, 41
  75th Pennsylvania, 55, 56, 57
  111th Pennsylvania, 133
  143rd Pennsylvania, 78

147th Pennsylvania, 73, 74, 126, 131, 132, 133
Perigo, William H. **152**
Perrin, Wilkinson D., **94**
Peters, D.C., 180
Peters, John G., 144
Peterson, Anton, 50
Pettibone, Channing L., **119**
Pettigrew, James J., **153,** 157
Philadelphia, Pa., 23, 110, 127, 144, 171, 212
Pickaway County, Ohio, 68, 83
Pickett, George E., 146, **153,** 157, 210
Pickett's Charge, 10, 158, 160, 162
Pierce, John W., 207
Pierce, Ohio, 50
Pierce, Wilbur F., 88, 146, 156
Pierpont, Francis H., 94
Pierpont Battery, 94, 147, 148, 172
Pike County, Ohio, 68
Pipe Creek, 35
Piqua, Ohio, 91
Pittsburgh, Pa., 94, 105, 148, 207
Pleasanton, Alfred, 22, 29, 34, 162
Plum Run, 97, 98, 163
Plum Run Valley, 97
Pollock, John, 141
Pollock, William, 150
Pontious, Benjamin F., 136
Portage County, Ohio, 23, 46, 73, 106
Port Hudson, La., 196
Port Republic, Va., battle of, 72, 127, 132
Portsmouth, Ohio, 97, 98
Potomac River, 23, 30, 31, 34, 184, 187, 190, 191, 193, 194, **196,** 197, 199
Pottenger, Thomas, 114
Potter, Martin D., 208, 209, 210
Potter, Thaddeus S., 77, 124, 146, 152, 154, 157
Potts, Joseph F., 115, 200
Powell, Eugene, 72, **126,** 127, 128, 129, 130, 131, 173
Powell, Robert M., 161
Powers Hill, 76, 89
Preble County, Ohio, 52, 114, 168, 180, 200, 201, 202, 203
Price, J.G. (photographer), 20
Prior, Johnston, 84
Pritchard, John R., **119**
Pugh, Moses, **189,** 190
Pyles, Leonidas, 99

R

Raikes, Wesley, 113, 114
Rannells, C.S., 172
Rannells, William J., 171, **172**
Rappahannock River, 13, 22, 23, 203

Ravenna, Ohio, 23, 40, 91, 138
Ray, James, 84
Reckard, Frank B., 94
Reed, Amos T., 85
Reed, Benjamin F., 99
Reed, Cecil C., 61, 62
Reed, Joseph, 85
Reese, John L., 191
Regnier, Frederick A., **149**
Reichard, Philip, 202
Reid, John, 123
Reid, Whitelaw, **75,** 201
Reily, James, 17
Reily, Robert, **17,** 22
Republic, Ohio, 169
Resaca, Ga., battle of, 58, 70, 79, 190, 198
Reynolds, Gilbert H., 107
Reynolds, James M., 91
Reynolds, John F., 23, 30, 37, 38, 39, 41, 66, 75, 89
Rhine River, 110
Rice, Thomas H., 84
Richardson, William P., **19,** 22
Richey, James, **133**
Richland County, Ohio, 19, 56, 70, 171
Richmond, James, 159
Richmond, Va., 19, 22, 23, 60, 63, 82, 114, 186, 194, 199, 200, 201
Richmond rifle musket, 189
Ricketts, R. Bruce, 90, 107, 116, 124
Ridgelawn Cemetery (Elyria), 181
Ringgold, Ga., battle of, 105, 106, 141
Robinson, James S., 15, 16, 37, **42,** 55, 56, 57, 62, 63, 69, 86, 166, 171, 211, 212
Rock Creek, 44, 45, 46, 48, 51, 53, 54, 77, 78, 90, 103, 105, 112, 125, 172, 173, 176, 177
Rodamour, Columbus, 61, 62
Rodes, Robert E., 40, 42, 70, 125, 132, 142
Rodgers, Samuel, **187**
Roloson, Wesley H., **31**
Roosters (7th Ohio), 73, 138, 139, 140
Rootstown, Ohio, 46
Rosecrans, William S., 10, 18
Ross, Anthony W., 24
Ross County, Ohio, 32, 66, 68, 85, 92, 142
Running Half-Moons, 69, 115
Russell, George A., 52
Russell, Robert H., 130

S

Sager, Jacob A., 187, 192, **194**
Sandusky, Ohio, 122, 146, 181
Sandusky County, Ohio, 50, 159
Sandusky Register, 122, 181

Satterlee General Hospital, 144
Savannah, Ga., 138
Sawyer, Franklin, 33, 34, 86, 87, 88, 122, **123,** 124, 144, 145, 146, 152, 153, 154, 155, 156, 157, 158, 159, 160, 161, 178, 196, 203
Sayre, William M., 130
Schenck, Robert C., 209, 210
Schenkl shells, 147
Scherhag, Philip, **110**
Schiely, Charles M., 61, **62**
Schild, Caspar, 111
Schimmelfennig, Alexander, 39, 40, 44, 45, 48, 54, 58, 59, 60
Schram, Henry, 94
Schurz, Carl, 21, 37, **38,** 39, 42, 43, 44, 45, 48, 54, 61, 66, 115
Schwab, Mathias Jr., 187, 188
Scioto County, Ohio, 97
Scofield, William E., **65**
Scott, William, 129
Scripture, Z. Clark, 40, 44, 90, 91
Seaman, Elisha B., 151
Seas, Henry, **58**
Second Bull Run, battle of, 53, 95, 165, 171, 189, 197, 201, 209
Sedgwick, John, 100
Seeley, Francis W., 100, 101
Seminary Ridge, 59, 86, 93, 95, 146, 153, 169, 171
Seneca County, Ohio, 19, 61, 68, 178, 181, 189
Senter, George B., 208, 209
Seven Days, battles of, 100
Seville, Ohio, 180
Sewald, Charles C., 179
Seward, William H., 207, 210
Seymour, Horatio, 207
Sharps carbines, 163, 187, 191
Shattuck, Benjamin, 84
Shattuck, Samuel A., 85
Sheak, Jacob, 160
Shearer, George W., **116**
Shellenberger, Ephraim, **59**
Sheller, Solomon, 80
Shenandoah Valley, 23, 53, 95, 200, 204
Shenandoah River, 132
Shenkel, Jacob, 9
Sherfy, John, 96, 146
Sherman, Eldridge, **181**
Sherman, William T., 187, 198, 204
Shiloh, battle of, 75
Shiplin, Philip, 69
Shoub, Samuel J., 87
Shuler, Silas, 111
Shultz, Emanuel M., 52
Sickles, Daniel E., 72, 75, 96, **102,** 148
Siegfried, W.D., 182
Sigel, Franz, 14, 18, 38

Silsby, Alonzo, 90
Simmons, Philip N., **30**
Simonds, F.A. (photographer), 66, 68, 85, 160
Skinner, Sidney, 63
Slocum, Henry W., 72
Slyder, John, 163
Smith, Alfred, 159
Smith, Elnathan M., 159
Smith, Horace B., **201**
Smith, J.B. (photographer), 148
Smith, Jacob, 34, 35, 63, 64, 76, 120, 170
Smith, Orland, 21, **66,** 67, 78, 82, 83, 85, 86, 87, 92, 106, 142, 159, 160, 165, 169, 188
Snickers' Gap, Va., 27
Snover, Lemuel, **178**
Snow, Jasper S., 37, 54
Soden, Edward, 136
Soden, Matthias, 136
South Mountain, 31, 32, 33, 184, 185, 187, 193
Southerton, William B., 31, 35, 44, 52, 64, 69, 92, 112, 113, 115, 120
Spangler, George, 76, 120, 151
Spangler, Henry, 106, 126, 131
Spangler's Spring, 151
Spears, William B., 114
Speier, William, 111
Spencer, Harlow N., **141**
Spencer repeating rifles, 162
Sperry, Isaac J., 84
Spidel, Ezra, 138
Spooner, Henry K., 34, 181
Spotsylvania, Va., battle of, 116, 119, 123, 159
Springdale, Ohio, 51
Springfield, Ohio, 113, 127, 212
Springfield Republic, 208
Springfield rifle muskets, 119
Stacey, Charles, **81,** 82
Stafford County, Va., 20
Stafford Court House, Va., 24
Stahel, Julius, 22, 30, 33
Stanhope, Benjamin C., 22, 27
Stanton, Edwin M., 207
Stark County, Ohio, 17, 19, 49, 50, 58, 190
Stark County Republican, 190
Starrett, John A., 114
Staunton, Va., 200
Stedman, William, 22, **23**
Steiner, Barnet T., **50**
Stein's Photographic Gallery, 23
Steinwehr, Adolph von, 21, 37, 39, 40, 61, 66, 115, 168
Steinwehr Avenue (Gettysburg), 209
Stephenson, John S., 212

Stephenson's Depot, Va., 23
Sterling, William R., 29
Steuart, George H., 103, 106, 131, 132
Steubenville, Ohio, 133, 207
Stevens, Greenleaf T., 117
Stevens, Wilbur F., 73, 134, 138
Stevens' Knoll, 107
Stevens' Run, 60, 146
Stewart, Gordon A., 86, 87
Stiles, Albert W., **29**
Stone, Benjamin F. Jr., **92,** 188, 195
Stones River, battle of, 207
Stonewall Brigade, 125, 140
Strange, Stephen, 152
Strasburg, Va., battle of, 201
Stratton, Isaac, 106
Stratton Street (Gettysburg), 61, 142
Strobel, Lucas, 111
Strode, William H., **158**
Stuart, J.E.B., 27, 29, 34, 35, 162, 185, 190, 193
Styer, William H., 151, **152**
Suhrer, Fernando C., 112
Summersville, Ohio, 57
Summit County, Ohio, 19, 73, 111
Summit County Beacon, 135
Surles, Henry, **133**
Sussex, England, 52
Sutliff, James P., 46
Sweet, Mark, **129**
Sweetland, Andrew F., 66, 80-81
Sweetland, Daniel, 81
Sykes, Andrew J., **197,** 198, 199
Sykes, Elizabeth, 197, **198,** 199
Sykes, Flora, 197, **198**
Sykes, George, 25, 75, 96, 97, 100
Sykes, Libbie, 198
Sykes, Otis, 198
Sykes, William, 197, **198,** 199
Symmes, Henry E., 134

T

Taifel, Christian, 110
Tallcott, Charles G., **73**
Tallmadge Cemetery, 181
Tallman, William H.H., 73, 74, 78, 151, 173, 188
Taneytown, Md., 34, 75, 76, 89, 136
Taneytown Road, 38, 39, 67, 75, 78, 80, 86, 116, 120, 124, 150, 160, 163, 209
Taylor, C.C. (photographer), 59
Taylor, Perry, 69
Temple, Francis M., **98**
Temple, Joel T., 98
Terry, John, 85
Tescher, John F., **45**
Texas troops,
    Cavalry:
        4th Texas, 17

Infantry:
5th Texas, 161
Theis, John G., **95**
Third Volunteer Brigade (Artillery Reserve), 21, 22, 89, 146, 147
Thomas & Shell (photographers), 193
Thomas, David, **137**
Thomas, Edward L., 122, 154
Thomas, L. Campbell, 186
Thomson, David, 18, 36, 54, **56**, 57, 62, 70, 197
Thornburg, Thomas H., 124, 144
Thoroughfare Gap, Va., 29
Thurmont, Md., 37
Tidball, John C., 9, **192**
Tiffin, Ohio, 111, 179
Tillett, Ignatius, **109**
Tobin, Morris, 191
Tod, David, 22, 128, 205, 207, **208**, 209, 210, 211
Toledo, Ohio, 10, 22, 30, 53, 93, 148, 152, 159
Toledo Blade, 93
Townsend, E.P., 127
Trachsel, Frederick, 111
Tracy, Philip, 144, 177
Trimble, Isaac R., 153, 155, 157
Trostle, Emanuel, 87
Trumbull County, Ohio, 73, 141, 202
Tucker, Patrick, 9, **100**
Tullahoma, Tenn., 10
Turner, Samuel, 85
Tuscarawas County, Ohio, 17, 19, 111
Tweedale, Robert, 191, 192
Two Taverns, Pa., 73, 74, 162
Tyler, E.B., 207
Tyler, Robert O., 124, 151

U

Union County, Ohio, 57, 72, 128
Union Mills, Md., 75
Uniontown, Md., 34, 35, 75
Upperville, Va., 27, 29, 190
Upright, George T., 156
Urbana, Ohio, 127, 128, 130
Usher, John P., 207, 210
U.S. Military Academy, 21, 162
U.S. troops,
    Artillery:
    Battery M, 2nd U.S., 186
    Battery A, 4th U.S., 158
    Battery G, 4th U.S., 46
    Battery K, 4th U.S., 100, 101
    Battery D, 5th U.S., 96
    Cavalry:
    1st Dragoons, 72
    6th U.S., 185
    Infantry:
    1st U.S., 72

5th U.S., 82
9th U.S. Colored Troops, 141
11th U.S., 9, 100
Utica, N.Y., 148

V

Vallandigham, Clement L., 10, 201, **202,** 207, 209
Van Guntian, Christian, **110**
Van Loo, Leon (photographer), 75
Veteran Reserve Corps, 121
Vicksburg, Miss., 10, 23, 24, 178, 189, 196, 198
Vignos, Augustus, **49,** 50
Vincent, Strong, 96, 97
Vinton County, Ohio, 68, 85
Virginia troops,
    Infantry:
    4th Virginia, 141
    38th Virginia, 159

W

Wadsworth, James S., 103, 126
Wadsworth, Ohio, 138
Wainwright, Charles S., 90
Wainwright Avenue (Gettysburg), 68
Waite, John M., 191
Waldo, Ohio, 129
Walker, Aaron, 150
Walker, E.S. (photographer), 16
Walker, James A., 140
Wallace, William, 77, **118**
Waller, George M., **84**
Walworth, William, 98, 99
War of 1812, 208
Ward, Samuel, 85
Warren, Gouverneur K., 96, 97, 102
Warren, Henry B., **144**
Warren County, Ohio, 53, 172
Warren, Ohio, 27, 59
Warrenton, Va., 26, 27
Washburn, Frederick S., 178
Washburn, George G., 178, 179, 180, 181, 184
Washington, D.C., 23, 26, 33, 34, 35, 149, 184, 187, 194, 205, 207
Washington County, Ohio, 94
Washington Court House, Ohio, 10, 162
Washington Street (Gettysburg), 40, 60, 67, 79-80, 142
Wauhatchie, Tenn., 32
Waverly, Ohio, 85
Wayne County, Ohio, 19
Wayne County *Democrat,* 26
Weaver, Peter S., 141
Weaver, Samuel, 205, 207
Weber, Otto, 65
Weed, Stephen H., 97
Weidman, Christian, 43

Weisensa, George, 84
Welch, Girard, **116**
Welch, William, 156, 176
Wells, William W., 122, 123
Wendelkin, Martin, 96
Western Reserve Chronicle, 27
Westfall, Levi, 200
Westminster, Md., 34, 89, 185
West Alexandria, Ohio, 52, 200
West Point (also see U.S. Military Academy), 26, 97, 163, 192
West Virginia troops,
    Artillery:
    Battery C, 1st West Virginia Light, 90, 94, 95
    Cavalry:
    1st West Virginia, 186
    Infantry:
    7th West Virginia, 116, 117
Wheatfield, The, 100, 103
Wheatfield Road, 97, 98
Wheeler, Thomas, 69
Wheeler, William, **43,** 44, 45, 58, 60, 94
White, Israel, 110
Whitworth shells, 147
Wickham, Charles P., **53**
Wiedrich, Michael, 69, 94, 107, 110, 111, 112, 115, 116, 120, 141
Wilkeson, Bayard, 46, 49
Wilkesville, Ohio, 195
Williams, Alpheus S., 125, 131
Williams, Aristarches H., 59
Williams, Daniel W., **91**
Williams, Flora, 200
Williams, Jeremiah, 21, 45, 46, 50, 200
Williams, John, 136
Williams, William M.N., 123
Williamsport, Md., 23, 184, 190, 191, 192, 194, 195, 196
Williamsport, Ohio, 83
Willis, Isaac, 84
Wills, David, 205, 207, 210
Wilson, Charles L., 61, 172
Wilson, Eli, 49
Wilson, George R., 156
Wilson, Lawrence, 25
Winchester, Va., 23
Winder's Sky-Light Gallery, 51
Windsor, Ohio, 138
Winebrenner's Run, 106, 118
Winslow, Philip, 58
Wisconsin troops,
    Infantry:
    6th Wisconsin, 9, 103, 104
    26th Wisconsin, 55
Wood, John T., 46, 53, 168
Woodruff, George A., 86
Woodsfield, Ohio, 19, 21
Wooster, Ohio, 26, 45, 50

Wren, Daniel B., 61, 200
Wright, Charles M., **121**
Wright, Myron T., 135, 137, **138**
Wyandot County, Ohio, 31, 68

X

Xenia, Ohio, 75, 150, 182

Y

Yellow Springs, Ohio, 113, 114
York, Pa., 35
York Street (Gettysburg), 168, 209
Yorktown, Va., 100
Young, Peter F., 50, 54, 68, 110, 111, 112
Young, Sylvanus, 63
Youngstown, Ohio, 208

Z

Zachman, Daniel, 55
Zanesville, Ohio, 97, 182
Zanesville Daily Courier, 182
Zeische, Charles, 62
Ziegler, John, 78
Ziegler's Grove, 86, 88, 116, 159

About the author

Richard A. Baumgartner is a former award-winning journalist who worked between 1975 and 1991 for Gannett and Knight-Ridder newspapers in West Virginia and California as a feature writer, artist, designer and graphics editor. A Wisconsin native, he is a graduate of the University of Missouri School of Journalism. Among his published works are the books *Yankee Tigers: Through the Civil War with the 125th Ohio*; *Blood & Sacrifice: The Civil War Journal of a Confederate Soldier*; *Fritz: The World War I Memoir of a German Lieutenant,* and a number of articles for *Military History* magazine. He is a recipient of the Richard B. Harwell and Alexander C. McClurg awards, and was a consultant for the Time-Life Books series *Voices of the Civil War.* A full-time researcher and writer, Baumgartner lives in the Ohio River city of Huntington, West Virginia.

To bring additional information and photographs related to Ohio at Gettysburg to the author's attention, contact him in care of Blue Acorn Press, P.O. Box 2684, Huntington, WV 25726.

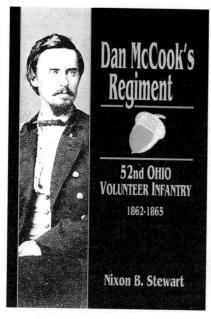
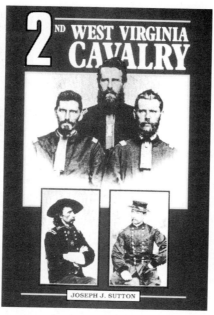